C For Dummies, Volume II

Cheat Sheet

Pointer pointers

A pointer must always be of the same type as the variable it's pointing at.

Declaring a pointer variable does not *create* the type of variable it points at. It creates a pointer variable.

Though pointers are declared with an asterisk, they are not always used with an asterisk.

Pointers must be initialized before they can be used.

Initialize a pointer by assigning it to a variable (of the same type).

To assign a pointer to a variable, use an ampersand with the variable's name:

```
m_address = &memory;
```

To assign a pointer to an array, do not use the ampersand:

```
s_address = string;
```

To assign a pointer to an array element, use the ampersand:

```
element = &string[2];
```

Without an asterisk, an initialized pointer holds a memory address.

With an asterisk, an initialized pointer holds a value (the value of the variable the pointer points at).

The `printf` Conversion Characters

Conversion Character	Displays Argument (Variable's Contents) As
%c	Single character
%d	Signed decimal integer (`int`)
%e	Signed floating-point value in E notation
%f	Signed floating-point value (`float`)
%g	Signed value in %e or %f format, whichever is shortest
%i	Signed decimal integer (`int`)
%o	Unsigned octal (base 8) integer (`int`)
%s	String of text
%u	Unsigned decimal integer (`int`)
%x	Unsigned hexadecimal (base 16) integer (`int`)

Access Modes for the `fopen` Function

Mode	Opens File For	File Created?	Existing File?
"r"	Reading only	No	If not found, `fopen` returns an error
"w"	Writing	Yes	Overwritten
"a"	Appending	Yes	Appended to
"r+"	Reading and writing	No	If not found, `fopen` returns an error
"w+"	Reading and writing	Yes	Overwritten
"a+"	Reading and appending	Yes	Appended to

Pointers and Array Brackets

Array Notation	Pointer Equivalent
array[0]	*a
array[1]	*(a+1)
array[2]	*(a+2)
array[3]	*(a+3)
array[x]	*(a+x)

IDG
BOOKS
WORLDWIDE

...For Dummies: #1 Computer Book Series for Beginners

C For Dummies® Volume II

Cheat Sheet

The `printf` Escape Sequences

Sequence	Represents
\a	The speaker beeping
\b	Backspace (move the cursor back, no erase)
\f	Form feed (eject printer page; ankh character on the screen)
\n	Newline, like pressing the Enter key
\r	Carriage return (moves the cursor to the beginning of the line)
\t	Tab
\v	Vertical tab (moves the cursor down a line)
\\	The backslash character
\'	The apostrophe
\"	The double quote character
\?	The question mark
\0	The "null" byte (backslash-zero)
\0	A character value in octal (base 8)
\xH	A character value in hexadecimal (base 16)
\XH	A character value in hexadecimal (base 16)

Typical pointer setup and use

First, create a pointer of the proper type:

```
float *f;
```

Second, assign it to a variable's memory location:

```
f = &boat;
```

Finally, use the pointer:

```
printf("%.0f",*f);
```

Without its asterisk, the pointer is a memory location.

With its asterisk, the pointer equals the value at the memory location.

Always use the same type of pointer as the variables it examines: `float`s for `float`s, `int`s for `int`s, and so on.

Always *initialize* a pointer before you use it! Set the pointer equal to the address of some variable in memory.

Pointers, Parentheses, and Math

Pointer Thing	Memory Address	Memory Contents
p	Yup	Nope
*p	Nope	Yup
*p++	Incremented after value is read	Unchanged
*(p++)	Incremented after value is read	Unchanged
(*p)++	Unchanged	Incremented after it's used
*++p	Incremented before value is read	Unchanged
*(++p)	Incremented before value is read	Unchanged
++*p	Unchanged	Incremented before it's used
++(*p)	Unchanged	Incremented before it's used
p*++	Not a pointer	Not a pointer
p++*	Not a pointer	Not a pointer

The ++ operator is used in this table, though you can substitute any math operation. **Tip:** Use parentheses to isolate part of the pointer problem, and the answer will always work out the way you want.

...For Dummies: #1 Computer Book Series for Beginners

C
FOR
DUMMIES®
VOLUME II

C
FOR
DUMMIES®
VOLUME II

by Dan Gookin

IDG Books Worldwide, Inc.
An International Data Group Company

Foster City, CA ♦ Chicago, IL ♦ Indianapolis, IN ♦ Southlake, TX

C For Dummies, Volume II

Published by
IDG Books Worldwide, Inc.
An International Data Group Company
919 E. Hillsdale Blvd.
Suite 400
Foster City, CA 94404
http://www.idgbooks.com (IDG Books Worldwide Web site)
http://www.dummies.com (Dummies Press Web site)

Library of Congress Catalog Card No.: 94-77739

ISBN: 1-56884-915-X

Printed in the United States of America

10 9 8 7 6 5 4 3 2 1

1E/RV/QU/ZX/IN

Distributed in the United States by IDG Books Worldwide, Inc.

Distributed by Macmillan Canada for Canada; by Transworld Publishers Limited in the United Kingdom and Europe; by WoodsLane Pty. Ltd. for Australia; by WoodsLane Enterprises Ltd. for New Zealand; by Longman Singapore Publishers Ltd. for Singapore, Malaysia, Thailand, and Indonesia; by Simron Pty. Ltd. for South Africa; by Toppan Company Ltd. for Japan; by Distribuidora Cuspide for Argentina; by Livraria Cultura for Brazil; by Ediciencia S.A. for Ecuador; by Addison-Wesley Publishing Company for Korea; by Ediciones ZETA S.C.R. Ltda. for Peru; by WS Computer Publishing Company, Inc., for the Philippines; by Unalis Corporation for Taiwan; by Contemporanea de Ediciones for Venezuela. Authorized Sales Agent: Anthony Rudkin Associates for the Middle East and North Africa.

For general information on IDG Books Worldwide's books in the U.S., please call our Consumer Customer Service department at 800-762-2974. For reseller information, including discounts and premium sales, please call our Reseller Customer Service department at 800-434-3422.

For information on where to purchase IDG Books Worldwide's books outside the U.S., please contact our International Sales department at 415-655-3023 or fax 415-655-3299.

For information on foreign language translations, please contact our Foreign & Subsidiary Rights department at 415-655-3021 or fax 415-655-3281.

For sales inquiries and special prices for bulk quantities, please contact our Sales department at 415-655-3200 or write to the address above.

For information on using IDG Books Worldwide's books in the classroom or for ordering examination copies, please contact our Educational Sales department at 800-434-2086 or fax 817-251-8174.

For press review copies, author interviews, or other publicity information, please contact our Public Relations department at 415-655-3000 or fax 415-655-3299.

For authorization to photocopy items for corporate, personal, or educational use, please contact Copyright Clearance Center, 222 Rosewood Drive, Danvers, MA 01923, or fax 508-750-4470.

 is a trademark under exclusive license to IDG Books Worldwide, Inc., from International Data Group, Inc.

About the Author

Dan Gookin got started with computers back in the post-slide-rule age of computing: 1982. His first intention was to buy a computer to replace his aged and constantly breaking typewriter. Working as slave laborer in a restaurant, however, he was unable to afford the full "word processor" setup and settled on a computer that had a monitor, keyboard, and little else. Soon his writing career was under way with several submissions to fiction magazines and lots of rejections.

His big break came in 1984, when he began writing about computers. Applying his flair for fiction with a self-taught knowledge of computers, Gookin was able to demystify the subject and explain technology in a relaxed and understandable voice. He even dared to add humor, which eventually won him a column in a local computer magazine.

Eventually Gookin's talents came to roost as a ghost writer at a computer book publishing house. That was followed by an editing position at a San Diego computer magazine. During this time, he also regularly participated in a radio talk show about computers. In addition, he kept writing books about computers, some of which became minor best-sellers.

In 1990, Gookin came to IDG Books Worldwide with a book proposal. From that initial meeting unfolded an idea for an outrageous book: a long overdue and original idea for the computer book for the rest of us. What became *DOS For Dummies* blossomed into an international best-seller with hundreds of thousands of copies in print and many translations.

Today Gookin still considers himself a writer and computer "guru" whose job it is to remind everyone that computers are not to be taken too seriously. His approach to computers is light and humorous, yet very informative. He knows that the complex beasts are important and can help people become productive and successful. Gookin mixes his knowledge of computers with a unique, dry sense of humor that keeps everyone informed — and awake. His favorite quote is, "Computers are a notoriously dull subject, but that doesn't mean I have to write about them that way."

Gookin's titles for IDG Books Worldwide include the best-selling *DOS For Dummies* and *WordPerfect For Dummies, WordPerfect 6 For Dummies, PCs For Dummies, Word For Windows For Dummies,* and the *Illustrated Computer Dictionary For Dummies*. All told, he has written more than 30 books about computers and contributes regularly to *DOS Resource Guide, InfoWorld,* and *PC Computing.* Gookin holds a degree in communications from the University of California–San Diego and lives with his wife and boys in the as-yet-untamed state of Idaho.

ABOUT IDG BOOKS WORLDWIDE

Welcome to the world of IDG Books Worldwide.

IDG Books Worldwide, Inc., is a subsidiary of International Data Group, the world's largest publisher of computer-related information and the leading global provider of information services on information technology. IDG was founded more than 25 years ago and now employs more than 8,500 people worldwide. IDG publishes more than 275 computer publications in over 75 countries (see listing below). More than 60 million people read one or more IDG publications each month.

Launched in 1990, IDG Books Worldwide is today the #1 publisher of best-selling computer books in the United States. We are proud to have received eight awards from the Computer Press Association in recognition of editorial excellence and three from *Computer Currents'* First Annual Readers' Choice Awards. Our best-selling *...For Dummies®* series has more than 30 million copies in print with translations in 30 languages. IDG Books Worldwide, through a joint venture with IDG's Hi-Tech Beijing, became the first U.S. publisher to publish a computer book in the People's Republic of China. In record time, IDG Books Worldwide has become the first choice for millions of readers around the world who want to learn how to better manage their businesses.

Our mission is simple: Every one of our books is designed to bring extra value and skill-building instructions to the reader. Our books are written by experts who understand and care about our readers. The knowledge base of our editorial staff comes from years of experience in publishing, education, and journalism — experience we use to produce books for the '90s. In short, we care about books, so we attract the best people. We devote special attention to details such as audience, interior design, use of icons, and illustrations. And because we use an efficient process of authoring, editing, and desktop publishing our books electronically, we can spend more time ensuring superior content and spend less time on the technicalities of making books.

You can count on our commitment to deliver high-quality books at competitive prices on topics you want to read about. At IDG Books Worldwide, we continue in the IDG tradition of delivering quality for more than 25 years. You'll find no better book on a subject than one from IDG Books Worldwide.

John Kilcullen
CEO
IDG Books Worldwide, Inc.

Steven Berkowitz
President and Publisher
IDG Books Worldwide, Inc.

Eighth Annual
Computer Press
Awards ≥1992

Ninth Annual
Computer Press
Awards ≥1993

Tenth Annual
Computer Press
Awards ≥1994

Eleventh Annual
Computer Press
Awards ≥1995

IDG Books Worldwide, Inc., is a subsidiary of International Data Group, the world's largest publisher of computer-related information and the leading global provider of information services on information technology. International Data Group publishes over 275 computer publications in over 75 countries. Sixty million people read one or more International Data Group publications each month. International Data Group's publications include: **ARGENTINA:** Buyer's Guide, Computerworld Argentina, PC World Argentina; **AUSTRALIA:** Australian Macworld, Australian PC World, Australian Reseller News, Computerworld, IT Casebook, Network World, Publish, Webmaster; **AUSTRIA:** Computerwelt Osterreich, Networks Austria, PC Tip Austria; **BANGLADESH:** PC World Bangladesh; **BELARUS:** PC World Belarus; **BELGIUM:** Data News; **BRAZIL:** Annuário de Informática, Computerworld, Connections, Macworld, PC Player, PC World, Publish, Reseller News, Supergamepower; **BULGARIA:** Computerworld Bulgaria, Network World Bulgaria, PC & MacWorld Bulgaria; **CANADA:** CIO Canada, Client/Server World, ComputerWorld Canada, InfoWorld Canada, NetworkWorld Canada, WebWorld; **CHILE:** Computerworld Chile, PC World Chile; **COLOMBIA:** Computerworld Colombia, PC World Colombia; **COSTA RICA:** PC World Centro America; **THE CZECH AND SLOVAK REPUBLICS:** Computerworld Czechoslovakia, Macworld Czech Republic, PC World Czechoslovakia; **DENMARK:** Communications World Danmark, Computerworld Danmark, Macworld Danmark, PC World Danmark, Techworld Denmark; **DOMINICAN REPUBLIC:** PC World Republica Dominicana; **ECUADOR:** PC World Ecuador; **EGYPT:** Computerworld Middle East, PC World Middle East; **EL SALVADOR:** PC World Centro America; **FINLAND:** MikroPC, Tietoverkko, Tietoviikko; **FRANCE:** Distributique, Hebdo, Info PC, Le Monde Informatique, Macworld, Reseaux & Telecoms, WebMaster France; **GERMANY:** Computer Partner, Computerwoche, Computerwoche Extra, Computerwoche FOCUS, Global Online, Macwelt, PC Welt; **GREECE:** Amiga Computing, GamePro Greece, Multimedia World; **GUATEMALA:** PC World Centro America; **HONDURAS:** PC World Centro America; **HONG KONG:** Computerworld Hong Kong, PC World Hong Kong, Publish in Asia; **HUNGARY:** ABCD CD-ROM, Computerworld Szamitastechnika, Internetto online Magazine, PC World Hungary, PC-X Magazin Hungary; **ICELAND:** Tolvuheimur PC World Island; **INDIA:** Information Communications World, Information Systems Computerworld, PC World India, Publish in Asia; **INDONESIA:** InfoKomputer PC World, Komputek Computerworld, Publish in Asia; **IRELAND:** ComputerScope, PC Live!; **ISRAEL:** Macworld Israel, People & Computers/Computerworld; **ITALY:** Computerworld Italia, Macworld Italia, Networking Italia, PC World Italia; **JAPAN:** DTP World, Macworld Japan, Nikkei Personal Computing, OS/2 World Japan, SunWorld Japan, Windows NT World, Windows World Japan; **KENYA:** PC World East African; **KOREA:** Hi-Tech Information, Macworld Korea, PC World Korea; **MACEDONIA:** PC World Macedonia; **MALAYSIA:** Computerworld Malaysia, PC World Malaysia, Publish in Asia; **MALTA:** PC World Malta; **MEXICO:** Computerworld Mexico, PC World Mexico; **MYANMAR:** PC World Myanmar; **NETHERLANDS:** Computer! Totaal, LAN Internetworking Magazine, LAN World Buyers Guide, Macworld Netherlands, Net, WebWereld; **NEW ZEALAND:** Absolute Beginners Guide and Plain & Simple Series, Computer Buyer, Computer Industry Directory, Computerworld New Zealand, MTB, Network World, PC World New Zealand; **NICARAGUA:** PC World Centro America; **NORWAY:** Computerworld Norge, CW Rapport, Datamagasinet, Financial Rapport, Kursguide Norge, Macworld Norge, Multimediaworld Norge, PC World Ekspress Norge, PC World Nettverk, PC World Norge, PC World ProduktGuide Norge; **PAKISTAN:** Computerworld Pakistan; **PANAMA:** PC World Panama; **PEOPLE'S REPUBLIC OF CHINA:** China Computer Users, China Computerworld, China InfoWorld, China Telecom World Weekly, Computer & Communication, Electronic Design China, Electronics Today, Electronics Weekly, Game Software, PC World China, Popular Computer Week, Software Weekly, Software World, Telecom World; **PERU:** Computerworld Peru, PC World Profesional Peru, PC World SoHo Peru; **PHILIPPINES:** Click!, Computerworld Philippines, PC World Philippines, Publish in Asia; **POLAND:** Computerworld Poland, Computerworld Special Report Poland, Cyber, Macworld Poland, Networld Poland, PC World Komputer; **PORTUGAL:** Cerebro/PC World, Computerworld/Correio Informático, Dealer World Portugal, Mac*In/PC*In Portugal, Multimedia World; **PUERTO RICO:** PC World Puerto Rico; **ROMANIA:** Computerworld Romania, PC World Romania, Telecom Romania; **RUSSIA:** Computerworld Russia, Mir PK, Publish, Seti; **SINGAPORE:** Computerworld Singapore, PC World Singapore, Publish in Asia; **SLOVENIA:** Monitor; **SOUTH AFRICA:** Computing SA, Network World SA, Software World SA; **SPAIN:** Communicaciones World España, Computerworld España, Dealer World España, Macworld España, PC World España; **SRI LANKA:** Infolink PC World; **SWEDEN:** CAP&Design, Computer Sweden, Corporate Computing Sweden, Internetworld Sweden, it.branschen, Macworld Sweden, MaxiData Sweden, MikroDatorn, Natverk & Kommunikation, PC World Sweden, PCaktiv, Windows World Sweden; **SWITZERLAND:** Computerworld Schweiz, Macworld Schweiz, PCtip; **TAIWAN:** Computerworld Taiwan, Macworld Taiwan, NEW ViSiON/Publish, PC World Taiwan, Windows World Taiwan; **THAILAND:** Publish in Asia, Thai Computerworld; **TURKEY:** Computerworld Turkiye, Macworld Turkiye, Network World Turkiye, PC World Turkiye; **UKRAINE:** Computerworld Kiev, Multimedia World Ukraine, PC World Ukraine; **UNITED KINGDOM:** Acorn User UK, Amiga Action UK, Amiga Computing UK, Apple Talk UK, Computing, Macworld, Parents and Computers UK, PC Advisor, PC Home, PSX Pro, The WEB; **UNITED STATES:** Cable in the Classroom, CIO Magazine, Computerworld, DOS World, Federal Computer Week, GamePro Magazine, InfoWorld, I-Way, Macworld, Network World, PC Games, PC World, Publish, Video Event, THE WEB Magazine, and WebMaster; online webzines: JavaWorld, NetscapeWorld, and SunWorld Online; **URUGUAY:** InfoWorld Uruguay; **VENEZUELA:** Computerworld Venezuela, PC World Venezuela; and **VIETNAM:** PC World Vietnam.   3/24/97

Author's Acknowledgments

Thanks to Nan Borreson, of Borland, and Tracy Van Hoof, of Microsoft, for their assistance in obtaining up-to-date compilers for this book. Thanks to John Rodman, of Microsoft, for returning my phone call! Gracious thanks go to Sandy "Pointers Aren't That Hard" Gookin, for previewing my text, and to Scott Brown, of South Dakota, for his suggestions and input; thanks also to Craig Arnush, Joseph McCloskey, and Mitchell Waite, for minor assistance here and there.

No animals were harmed during the writing, editing, or production of this book.

The author has striven to include as much inoffensive humor as possible, though some Elvis fans may be upset. Too bad!

Publisher's Acknowledgments

We're proud of this book; please send us your comments about it by using the IDG Books Worldwide Registration Card at the back of the book or by e-mailing us at feedback/dummies@idgbooks.com. Some of the people who helped bring this book to market include the following:

Acquisitions, Development, and Editorial

Project Editor: Rebecca Whitney

Acquisitions Editor: Gareth Hancock

Technical Editor: Greg Guntle

Editorial Manager: Mary C. Corder

Editorial Assistant: Chris H. Collins

Production

Project Coordinator: Valery Bourke

Layout and Graphics: Brett Black, J. Tyler Connor, Maridee V. Ennis, Angela F. Hunckler, Yvette Lillge, Drew R. Moore, Brent Savage, Kathie Schutte, Michael A. Sullivan

Proofreaders: Carol Burbo, Laural L. Bowman, Rachel Garvey, Nancy Price, Ethel Winslow, Karen York

Indexer: Sharon Duffy

Special Help

Suzanne Packer, Lead Copy Editor

General and Administrative

IDG Books Worldwide, Inc.: John Kilcullen, CEO; Steven Berkowitz, President and Publisher

IDG Books Technology Publishing: Brenda McLaughlin, Senior Vice President and Group Publisher

Dummies Technology Press and Dummies Editorial: Diane Graves Steele, Vice President and Associate Publisher; Judith A. Taylor, Brand Manager; Kristin A. Cocks, Editorial Director

Dummies Trade Press: Kathleen A. Welton, Vice President and Publisher; Stacy S. Collins, Brand Manager

IDG Books Production for Dummies Press: Beth Jenkins, Production Director; Cindy L. Phipps, Supervisor of Project Coordination, Production Proofreading, and Indexing; Kathie S. Schutte, Supervisor of Page Layout; Shelley Lea, Supervisor of Graphics and Design; Debbie J. Gates, Production Systems Specialist; Tony Augsburger, Supervisor of Reprints and Bluelines; Leslie Popplewell, Media Archive Coordinator

Dummies Packaging and Book Design: Patti Sandez, Packaging Specialist; Lance Kayser, Packaging Assistant; Kavish + Kavish, Cover Design

◆

The publisher would like to give special thanks to Patrick J. McGovern, without whom this book would not have been possible.

◆

Contents at a Glance

Cartoons at a Glance

By Rich Tennant • Fax: 508-546-7747 • E-mail: the5wave@tiac.net

page 912

page 726

page 1032

page 972

page 850

Table of Contents

Introduction

· ·

*W*elcome to *C For Dummies,* Volume II, perhaps the most eagerly awaited computer book of all time.

This book and *C For Dummies,* Volume I, are really one book. This half of the book just picks up where the first volume left off, which is why the chapter and page numbers may look odd to you.

Why was this done?

Trust me, I was not out to annoy you or let you down. This was all meant to be one book, but the original book was so fat that the publisher, in his Solomon-like wisdom, decided to split the thing in two. What you have here is the latter part. The meaty stuff. Things that other C language books may not even touch on.

Between Volume I and Volume II of this book, the publisher and the author had numerous other commitments (primarily something called Windows 95) that unfortunately delayed the release of this book. But that's all behind us now!

If you're just picking this book up off the shelf, scurry around for Volume I, which covers much of the basic material you need in order to work this here volume.

Is This Book for You?

If you're just starting out with computer programming or if you're new to the C language, you should first pick up *C For Dummies,* Volume I. Go ahead and buy this book too because you will need it in about 48 hours.

Otherwise, this book is for anyone who has been working with the C programming language and finds the following concepts befuddling:

- ✔ Strings
- ✔ Arrays
- ✔ Pointers
- ✔ Structures

- ✔ Disk access
- ✔ Multiple modules

This volume of the book covers all that stuff in a calm, informative, and entertaining manner. In fact, I'll go out on a limb and say that no other C programming book in history describes the concept of pointers as eloquently as what you find here.

Even if you're a C language pro who has been coding for years, you will see that the approach to these technical concepts is refreshing and educational. Don't let the word *Dummies* in the book's title fool you; this is advanced stuff for technical people, explained in a non-intimidating way.

About This Here Dummy Approach

This book is a tutorial. I know that it says *Reference* on the cover, and you can use the book as a reference. At its heart, though, this book is a lesson-by-lesson tutorial for learning some advanced and complex programming puzzles in C.

Each chapter in this book covers a broad topic in C: structures, pointers, arrays, and so on.

Each chapter is divided into several lessons. Each lesson covers a specific topic of the C language.

This books has lots of programs in it — more than 100. I've kept them short and to the point, which makes them easier to type and understand.

Quizzes end each lesson, and a final exam is at the end of each chapter. I put them in here mostly because every other C book does the same thing, and, golly, if they can get away with it, so can I!

Foolish Assumptions

I assume that you have a basic grasp of the C language, acquired either on your own or from *C For Dummies,* Volume I, or another book, probably one of the many horrid C books that litter the shelves.

Furthermore, I assume that you have a C language compiler, most likely one from Borland or Microsoft, though a generic C compiler should also work just fine.

You should also be familiar with your operating system and how to copy, move, rename, and delete files. (An organizational strategy for C programs on your hard disk is presented in Volume I.)

You should know how to work your text editor, compiler, and linker. This volume of the book merely commands you to save your source code and then compile and run. If you need to know more than that, read or reread Chapter 1 in Volume I.

All the programs in this book were compiled using Borland C++ Version 5. Almost all of them were also compiled and tested using Microsoft Visual C++ Version 1.5. Everything should run as listed, though you may find notes and exceptions in the text where necessary.

The programs created in this book are command-line (DOS) programs. You must configure your compiler to produce DOS programs (see your compiler's reference). I prefer using the compilers at the DOS prompt (in a DOS window in Windows 95, actually). You can, however, use your compiler's integrated environment to create the programs. Just make sure that you're creating DOS programs, and you'll be fine.

This book does not go into how to create Windows programs. The purpose here is to understand C, not to program Windows.

This book covers the C language specifically. It does not cover C++. Honestly, you can get *all* your programming chores done in C. You do not need C++ to be able to write Windows programs or games.

The Way Things Are Done Here

Stuff displayed on-screen (program output) looks like this:

```
Here I go, typing some stuff. La, la, la.
```

This special font is also used for function and variable names.

When you need to type something as a response to a program or question, it's presented in **bold text**.

Program names and the names of files LOOK LIKE THIS.

The programs you type appear in shaded text preceded by the program's name:

Name: SAMPLE.C

```
#include <stdio.h>

void main()
{
   puts("You are unique, just like everyone else.");
}
```

A long line of text may occasionally "wrap" in the program listing. The second line appears indented below the first one:

```
This line is so long and this book so narrow that cruel
            typesetters had to split it between two lines.
```

When you see something like this, *don't* type two separate lines. Just keep typing, and everything will fit on one line on your screen.

Icons Used in This Book

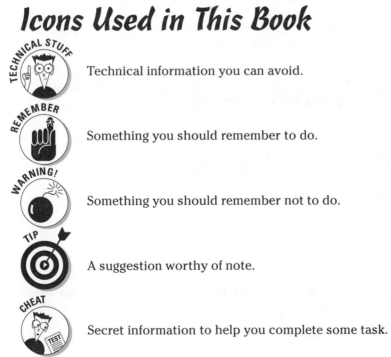

Technical information you can avoid.

Something you should remember to do.

Something you should remember not to do.

A suggestion worthy of note.

Secret information to help you complete some task.

 A blow-by-blow description of how a program works.

Something fishy with the Microsoft Visual C++ compiler.

 Something fishy with the Borland C++ compiler.

 Generic compiler fishy stuff.

Time to get up and get something to eat.

You've been programming so long that you've probably lost all blood flow to your legs. Go outside. Take a walk. Take a nap. Talk to a human. Give it a rest!

Final Thots

I humbly beg your forgiveness if you've waited too long for this book to show up. Put those grumblings aside — you have in your hands the long-awaited conclusion to *C For Dummies*, Volume I. Be prepared to finish your C language quest and continue your journey to programming guruhood.

Enjoy!

Chapter 8

Picking Up the C Pieces (Leftovers from Volume I)

• •

Lessons in This Chapter

▶ Knowing your place in this here Hello World

▶ More on math

▶ Avoiding the ugly goto command

▶ Printing for reals

▶ I'm bailing outta here!

Programs in This Chapter

HELLO.C	HELLO2.C	HELLO3.C	HELLO4.C
LIGHTS1.C	LIGHTS2.C	INCODD.C	DECODD.C
DROPNUKE.C	PRINTME1.C	PRINTME2.C	PRINTME3.C

Vocabulary Introduced in This Chapter

▶ kbhit

▶ pow

▶ sqrt

▶ goto

• •

*W*elcome back. If you can recall from our last episode, the fiendish Dr. Modulus was about to write a program that contained a loop to make the world spin backward!

Seriously, this chapter contains a few lessons designed to refresh fond memories of feats accomplished in *C For Dummies*, Volume I. This chapter has some review, some new stuff, and some strange stuff, all designed to get you merrily back in the mood for completing your C language learning journey.

Lesson 8-1: Knowing Your Place in This Here Hello World

Brush up your Shakespeare,
Start quoting him now.
Brush up your Shakespeare,
And the women you will wow!

— Cole Porter, *Kiss Me Kate*

Nothing impresses the ladies more than knowing some classical verse. Alas, nothing shall make them run screaming for cover like quoting a classical C program.

Take the beauty of the simple Hello World program, the appetizer in most C language books. It's carefully illustrated in Figure 8-1, but please don't type it.

Figure 8-1: HELLO.C, the classic C program that has started many a pro-gramming career.

```
#include <stdio.h>

void main()
{
    printf("Hello, World!\n");
}
```

HELLO.C is a classic the world over, taught to almost every human who yearns to study the C programming language. Alas, I left it out of the first volume of this book. Still, the program merits some discussion because it's more or less a classic. In a break with tradition, and to ensure that you're up to speed, I have chosen the Hello World program as your introduction to this second volume.

Getting over the bane of Hello World

From the primordial ooze of the slide-rule era arises the proto-computer programmer. From its mouth croaks some primitive program, the core of which contains one statement:

```
printf("Hello World!");
```

Or, if the tutorial's author is daring enough to introduce the \n concept, the statement can look like this:

```
printf("Hello World!\n");
```

Either of these statements is nestled in your typical C language program, belching forth the following line on the screen (providing that it all works):

```
Hello World!
```

That's the way it starts everywhere else, but not here.

✔ Life gets rough from Hello World on. In the classic Kernighan and Ritchie book, *The C Programming Language* (from whence the HELLO.C program originated), the very next program is one of those convert-Celsius-to-Fahrenheit programs. Yech!

✔ If you find any of these program samples baffling, you really should consider going through Volume I of this book to brush up on some basic C concepts.

✔ This volume of the book doesn't offer many soothing words of advice and the encouragement found in Volume I — that's where I tell you about typing programs and compiling and fixing pesky errors. This volume of the book merely commands you to "compile and run."

Finally, this book gets around to a silly Hello World program

A timid "Hello World" just won't do. You want to make sure that the populace knows you're there. To drive that point home, why not scream "Hello World" over and over until everyone must pound on the keyboard to shut you up? Type the following program, HELLO.C, into your editor:

A few things you should already know about HELLO.C

The program's basic skeleton consists of the `include` directive, bringing in the STDIO.H header file in all its glory (refer to Lesson 6-1 in Volume 1 of this book). Then comes the `void main()` thing and the curly brackets that enclose the entire program.

The core of the program is a `for` statement (refer to Lesson 4-5 in Volume I). Inside its parentheses are only the two required semicolons. There is no beginning, ending, or while-doing condition for the loop; it just repeats forever, as explained in Lesson 4-6 in Volume I:

```
for(;;)
```

What's repeated is a `printf` statement that spews out the phrase "Hello World!" The `%c` placeholder, or *conversion character*, reserves room for one character, which is specified after the comma in the `printf` statement, as explained in Lesson 2-5 in Volume I. The character is enclosed in single quotes, and the `\x` escape sequence flags the character as a hexadecimal value, also explained in Lesson 2-5. What `'\x20'` translates into is the space character, which sticks a space after the exclamation point in the `printf` output. Kind of a wacky way to do it, but this is review:

```
printf("Hello World!%c",'\x20');
```

Name: HELLO.C

```c
#include <stdio.h>

void main()
{
    for(;;)
    {
        printf("Hello World!%c",'\x20');
    }
}
```

Start over in your editor with a clean slate. Type the preceding source code exactly as written. This process should be review for you, and you can probably guess how the program turns out. In any event, double-check your work, save the file to disk as HELLO.C, and then compile and run.

Here is what the output should look like:

```
Hello World! Hello World! Hello World! Hello
World! Hello World! Hello World! Hello World!
Hello World! Hello World! Hello World! Hello
```

```
World! Hello World! Hello World! Hello World!
Hello World! Hello World! Hello World! Hello
World! Hello World! Hello World! Hello World!
Hello World!
```

And so on.

Press Ctrl+Break when the mood hits you.

- ✔ This program contains a basic for loop that repeats "Hello World!" (plus a space) forever, on and on, down the screen, until users get so sick that they decide to press Ctrl+Break or just switch off their computer. More details are offered in the preceding sidebar, "A few things you should already know about HELLO.C."

- ✔ The deal with %c and the '\x20' character is primarily review; you should remember what the % and \x things mean. However, using them is also a good way to specify a space in a string of text. Otherwise, you would see the following line and possibly forget to put a space after the exclamation point:

```
printf("Hello World! ");
```

- ✔ How could anyone know that 20 hex is the code for the space character? Easy: Appendix B in *C For Dummies,* Volume I, lists the ASCII codes for most of the characters you see on-screen.

- ✔ Alas, they don't have an escape sequence for a space. Oh, well.

- ✔ Because you went through Volume I and you thoroughly enjoyed Lesson 4-4, you know that you can also format the for statement in this program as follows:

```
for(;;)
  printf("Hello World!%c",'\x20');
```

The curly brackets are optional when you have only one statement in a for loop, but don't change your source code! You aren't finished with HELLO.C just yet.

- ✔ So I said "Hello, World!" and the world didn't say "Hello" back. . . .

Make it stop! Oh, please, make it stop!

It's tacky for a program to make users resort to whacking the Ctrl+Break keys to stop it. Tacky, tacky, tacky. A better solution is to have a program occasionally check the keyboard and find out whether a key has been pressed. If so, the program can sense impatience on behalf of the user and quit by itself. All you need is a function that senses impatience, and you're all set.

Function kbhit

The kbhit function is used to take a quick peek at the keyboard to see whether any keys have been pressed. Here is the format:

```
kbhit();
```

This function can be used by itself, where it returns a TRUE (nonzero) value or a FALSE (zero value). It's found most often in an if statement. The following header file is also required in order for khhit to work:

```
#include <conio.h>
```

This line should appear near the beginning of your source code.

kbhit checks only for keys that have been pressed; it doesn't read them like getch does or any other function that actually coughs up what has been typed.

Although the kbhit function returns a value, it's really more of a TRUE-FALSE type of thing. For example, if Hobart Homely has his elbow on the spacebar, kbhit returns a TRUE value (something other than zero). If Hobart hasn't touched the keyboard, kbhit returns FALSE (zero).

Programmers usually employ the kbhit function to merely check the keyboard, such as in a "press any key to stop" type of deal. If the character needs to be read, a proper keyboard-reading function (getch, for example) must be used.

Dreadful ruminations on your PC's keyboard buffer

The HELLO2.C program works because your PC's keyboard has a "type-ahead" buffer. In this small area of memory, the computer stores whatever you type, but only 16 characters. This buffer enables you to keep typing while the computer is doing something else, though you can type only as many as 16 characters. The idea was, I suppose, that the computer would never be so busy as to make you feel that you were typing too fast.

To prove it, stick a disk in drive A and type the following line at a DOS prompt:

```
DIR A:
```

While the computer is rooting around on drive A, type

```
CLS
```

Press Enter.

By the time the computer gets back from displaying the drive A directory, you see your CLS command displayed quickly, and then the screen clears. The reason is that the letters *C*, *L*, and *S* plus the Enter key were stored in the computer's keyboard buffer, waiting until they could be used. Until then, the value of the kbhit function is TRUE.

Alas, the C language and your compiler's C function library lack this type of impatience function. Perhaps you can write one on your own. Or maybe you can use the cuddly kbhit function, which returns a TRUE condition whenever a user has (impatiently or not) pressed a key on the keyboard.

You can use kbhit to break out of any loop. Just stick the following chunk of code somewhere inside the loop:

```
if(kbhit())
{
  break;
}
```

The condition that if tests for depends on the results of the kbhit function. If a key has been pressed, the condition is TRUE and if's statements are executed. In this case, the statement is break, which cancels the loop. You can read the whole thing like this: "If a key has been pressed, break outta this here loop."

The following program, HELLO2.C, demonstrates how this function can be used.

Name: HELLO2.C

```
#include <stdio.h>
#include <conio.h>

void main()
{
  for(;;)
  {
      printf("Hello World!%c",'\x20');
      if(kbhit())
      {
          break;
      }
  }
}
```

Using the HELLO.C program that's already in your editor, make the changes necessary to turn it into the source code illustrated here. The only true change is the addition of the if statement brake pedal. Save the file to disk as HELLO2.C.

Compile and run.

Again, you see

```
Hello World! Hello World! Hello World! Hello
World! Hello World! Hello World! Hello World!
Hello World!
```

And on and on.

This time, just tap the Enter key when you want it to stop. Slam! It comes screeching to a halt.

✔ The kbhit function requires the CONIO.H header file. Don't forget it! Refer to Lesson 6-1 in *C For Dummies,* Volume I, for more information about header files.

✔ I pronounce kbhit as "keyboard hit" or maybe even "kay-bee hit" if I'm in a hurry.

✔ There ain't no kbhit function in UNIX or ANSI C compilers, at least not since I last checked. Oh, well.

✔ Using your vast knowledge of C, you should know that the if statement used to break out of the endless loop can also be written as

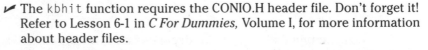
```
if(kbhit()) break;
```

This example is kosher because if has only one statement (refer to Lesson 4-1 in Volume I).

✔ A break command, not the if statement, breaks out of a loop (refer to Lesson 4-6 in Volume I).

✔ The kbhit function is like the "any key." It reads only characters that *can* be read on the keyboard, including all the symbol keys and function keys but not the Shift keys, Alt, Ctrl, the 5 on the numeric keypad, and a few other keys. If you plan to use kbhit as a "Press any key" function in your program, remember that PC users are timid. Tell them to "Press the Enter key" rather than "Press any key," and they will thank you for it.

Dealing with the leftovers of kbhit

The kbhit function doesn't read any characters from the keyboard. No, it just sits there and tells you whether any characters are "waiting" in the keyboard's type-ahead buffer — kind of like a dopey butler in a '40s screwball comedy who walks into the room and says "Da governor's at da door" and they scream back, "Well, let him in!" (Check out the preceding techy sidebar, "Dreadful ruminations on your PC's keyboard buffer.")

Although kbhit tells you that some keyboard typing has occurred, it never reads the characters. They sit in the type-ahead buffer and wait for the next function — or program — that reads them. In the case of the HELLO2.C program, it happens at the next DOS prompt. To prove it, run HELLO2.C again. Type

```
HELLO2
```

and press Enter. The screen goes berserk with "Hello World!"s.

Press the Z key.

The program stops, and at the next DOS prompt you see the letter *z:*

```
C:\PROJECTS> z
```

That happens because kbhit saw a key waiting in the keyboard buffer and the key was never read; no getch or other function bothered to pick up the waiting key — like a lonely little boy standing in front of the school at 4 p.m. because his mom forgot to pick him up. The next program (DOS, in this case) did read the key.

To repair the damage, a function should read that key before your program quits. You can do this by inserting a key-reading function just after the loop kbhit helped you break out of. The program HELLO3.C shows how it's done.

Name: HELLO3.C

```c
#include <stdio.h>
#include <conio.h>

void main()
{
  for(;;)
  {
      printf("Hello World!%c",'\x20');
      if(kbhit())
      {
            break;
      }
  }
  getch();
}
```

Modify the HELLO2.C source code in your editor. Add the new Line 15, which consists of the getch function all by its lonesome. Save the source code to disk as HELLO3.C.

Compile and run.

This time, as the program is running amok, press the Z key to stop it. It stops, all right — and you don't see the Z (or whatever key you pressed) displayed at the next DOS prompt.

- The advantage of kbhit is that it can tell whether a key has been pressed without the program stopping to wait for a key to be pressed. The disadvantage is that you must remember to read the key before the program is done.

- Refer to Lesson 3-6 in *C For Dummies,* Volume I, for more information about the getch function.

- You could declare a single character variable for getch to store whatever key was pressed, but it's not necessary here. getch by itself is the "press any key" function; a variable for getch to store what was typed isn't required.

There's also a while *loop solution*

One of the curses and blessings of C is that there's no single absolutely correct way to write any program. Some methods are more deliberate, and some are more elegant.

As stated in Volume I, whenever you see a for(;;) type of loop, you can invariably replace it with a while loop. This technique works marvelously for the HELLO programs because a while loop requires a condition for it to stop and kbhit just happens to be such a condition.

Name: HELLO4.C

```
#include <stdio.h>
#include <conio.h>

void main()
{
  while(!kbhit())
  {
      printf("Hello World!%c",'\x20');
  }
  getch();
}
```

Fire up a new screen in your editor and type this source code, the final variation of the Hello World program. Save the final result to disk as HELLO4.C.

Compile and run.

The output is the same, but the program looks cleaner, sleeker.

- ✔ Refer to Lesson 7-1 in *C For Dummies,* Volume I, for more information about `while` loops.

- ✔ You could even reduce the loop to the following:

```
while(!kbhit())
  printf("Hello World!%c",'\x20');
```

  This example works because only one statement is included in the `while` loop.

- ✔ The condition `while` evaluates is `!kbhit()`. The exclamation point, pronounced "not," means to reverse the condition of whatever happens to come next. When `kbhit` returns FALSE (meaning that no keys have been pressed), the `!` turns it into a TRUE and the loop keeps repeating. Only when a key is pressed and `kbhit` returns TRUE does the `!` turn it into a FALSE and the `while` loop stops repeating.

- ✔ Lesson 4-1 in Volume I of this book tells you that `!` means "not" in C. What is !TRUE is FALSE and vice versa.

- ✔ *Bunting* refers to festive decorations, typically banners, flags, or drapery. You see bunting mostly during political celebrations, colored red, white, and blue in the United States.

- ✔ One place where you want to use a `for` loop rather than `while` is when you want to repeat something a maximum number of times. Suppose that you want the computer to spew out "Hello World!" 10,000 times. If so, you should use a program such as HELLO3.C to get the job done, and you also have to declare an integer variable, such as `i`, and use the following `for` statement in Line 6:

```
for(i=0;i<10000;i++)
```

  This line tells the computer to loop through the following statements 10,000 times. However, your `kbhit` function also enables users to bail out if they get impatient. True, you could do this with a `while` loop, but it would be cumbersome.

Lesson 8-1 Quiz

1. What type of loop is used in the program HELLO.C?

    A. A `for` loop.

    B. An endless loop.

    C. A loop-de-loop.

    D. All of the above.

2. What does the `kbhit` function do?

    A. It checks to see how hard someone hit the keyboard.

    B. It checks to see whether any characters have been typed.

    C. It reads characters from the keyboard but doesn't store them.

    D. It returns TRUE while keys are being pressed on the keyboard.

3. Why is the `getch` function necessary in HELLO3.C?

    A. `getch`, the "press any key function," enables a user to pause the screen before returning to DOS.

    B. `getch` reads the character that `kbhit` found.

    C. `getch` is not necessary because it doesn't save the character in a variable.

    D. I just said `getch` to my wife, and she slapped me.

4. Suppose that the `kbhit` function is returning the value TRUE right now. What happens in the following loop:

```
while(!kbhit())
```

    A. The loop no longer repeats.

    B. The loop continues to repeat.

    C. The value of `kbhit` does not affect the loop.

    D. What loop?

5. What is the traditional gift for a couple's third wedding anniversary?

    A. Naugahyde.

    B. Copper or lead.

    C. Leather.

    D. Dueling pistols.

Lesson 8-2: More on Math

Most people think that computer programming is all math. Boy, are they wrong. It involves math, to be sure, but the hard part — figuring out the answer — is done by the computer. So what's the beef?

The main deal with math in a programming language is discovering what special symbols, spells, and dance steps are used to juggle the numbers.

The basic four computer math symbols should be very familiar to you by now:

- ✔ Addition symbol: +
- ✔ Subtraction symbol: –
- ✔ Multiplication symbol: *
- ✔ Division symbol: /

These doojabbies are common throughout computerdom. If you use a spreadsheet, they're the symbols you use to do math. All these symbols are clustered about your keyboard's numeric keypad. The most cryptic one is the asterisk (*) for multiplication.

Other than the symbols, the only other thing worth keeping in mind about math in C is that the calculation always goes on the *right* side of the equal sign. Therefore

```
meals=breakfast+lunch+dinner;
```

This equation, assuming that everything is a numeric variable, is correct. The following statement, however, is a boo-boo:

```
breakfast+lunch+dinner=meals;
```

The math goes on the right of the equal sign. Always.

- ✔ Goofing up a math equation is where you get those horrid Lvalue errors.
- ✔ Lesson 3-2 in Volume I of this book is where these mathematical concepts are introduced. Go there for a brush-up, if you need one.
- ✔ Looky at Table 3-3 in Volume I for another peek at C's basic mathematical symbols.

✔ You can always remember the cryptic mathematical symbols in the C language by looking at your keyboard's numeric keypad; each of the symbols is right there.

✔ Math problems in C work from left to right, the way you read. Some operations, however, have priority over others. If you forget, remember My Dear Aunt Sally from Lesson 3-8 in Volume I.

✔ Another mathematical symbol introduced in Volume I is the %, which means *modulus*. This dreadful topic can be reviewed by skimming over Lesson 5-7.

✔ It can be said that a C language operator exists for every odd symbol, shape, jot, and tittle on your keyboard. This statement is *almost* true. Pray that you never have to memorize them all.

Taking your math problems to a higher power

Two mathematical operations that seem to be lacking in C's almond cluster of symbols are the power-of symbol and the square root symbol. Of course, I'm assuming that you give a hoot about either of them, but you never know when they may crop up.

The power-of thing deals with problems that contain the words *squared* and *cubed* in addition to *power of.* For example:

"Four squared" means 4×4, or 4^2. The latter reads "Four to the second power."

"Four cubed" means $4 \times 4 \times 4$, or 4^3. This one reads "Four to the third power."

Higher than three, you just say the number, so $4 \times 4 \times 4 \times 4 \times 4$ is 4^5, or "four to the fifth power." (Don't even bother trying to figure out the answer; the computer does it for you!)

Alas, there just isn't any handy way to express 4^5 in C. There is no cool symbol. For example, you cannot write

```
answer=4▲5;
```

This line just doesn't work. It would be nice, but it just isn't so.

Function pow

The pow function is used to calculate one value taken to a certain power, such as 4 taken to the second power (4^2). Here's the format:

value = pow(n,p)

In this line, value, n, and p all must be double-precision variables (defined using the double declaration). The pow function calculates n to the p power. The answer is stored in the value variable.

To prevent your compiler from going mad, you must include the MATH.H header file at the beginning of your source code. Stick the following line up there somewhere:

#include <math.h>

This line is required for the pow function as well as for other math functions you may dare to use.

What you need is to draw on the C language's vast library of supplemental math functions. A few dozen functions compute such things as power-of, square root, terrifying trigonometric functions, and so on (see Table 8-1, later in this chapter). To take a number to a higher power, you use the pow function, described in the previous " Function pow" sidebar.

Using the pow function is easy — it's just like using any other function. Just declare your variables as doubles, include the MATH.H thing, and you're all set. So why not put it forth in one of those endearing math-sentence problems? To wit:

Suppose that you have tasked Milton, your brilliant, Mensa-club-leader son, with decorating the house for Christmas. Because he's too smart to drive, he directs you to go to the store and pick up 2^8 ("two to the eighth power") twinkly lights. You quickly dash off to your computer and use the C language to decipher what he means:

Name: LIGHTS1.C

```c
#include <stdio.h>
#include <math.h>

void main()
{
  double lights;

  lights=pow(2,8);     //figure 2 to the eighth power
  printf("Milton, we need %0.f lights.\n",lights);
}
```

Type this silly program on a new screen in your editor. Save the contraption to disk as LIGHTS1.C.

Compile and run. Hurry up — can't keep Milton waiting:

```
Milton, we need 256 lights.
```

There. Now you both know how many lights are needed. The computer successfully concluded that 2^8 is equal to 256.

- Two to the eighth power is written out longways, thus

```
2 x 2 x 2 x 2 x 2 x 2 x 2 x 2
```

- Refer to Table 2-2 in Volume I of this book for a list of `printf` conversion characters, such as the `%f` used in LIGHTS1.C. (Also refer to the nearby sidebar, "The more cryptic aspects of LIGHTS1.C.")

- The `pow` function expects to deal with `double` variables. In fact, many of the math functions deal with anything but integers.

- Constant values, such as 2 and 8 inside LIGHTS1.C, don't have to be `doubles` (or even typecast as `doubles`). Thankfully, the compiler is pretty smart about that stuff.

- Some languages and spreadsheets use the caret symbol (^) for *power,* as in 2^8 for 2^8 power. This technique doesn't work in C. (The ^ in C is a bitwise exclusive OR logical operation, whatever that means.)

- For more information about declaring a variable as a `double`, refer to Lesson 3-5 and Table 3-1 in Volume I of this book.

- You don't have to declare all your variables as `doubles` just to use the `pow` function. For example, you can type cast the variables inside the function:

```
v = pow((double)x,(double)n);
```

Even so, I recommend keeping the answer in a double-precision number because it may contain a large number of tiny values. Refer to Lessons 5-4 and 6-5 in Volume I of this book for more information about typecasting.

- If you're reading values for the `pow` function from the keyboard, beware that some bozo may type a negative number or zero for one of the values. According to the math geniuses, these types of calculations are in the realm of laughability, and your computer may respond accordingly. Check your compiler's reference documentation to see how the compiler handles oddball values in the `pow` function. Better still, use an `if` structure to weed out weirdo values after they're entered so as not to offend the `pow` statement's sensibilities.

The more cryptic aspects of LIGHTS1.C.

There's nothing truly cryptic about LIGHTS1.C, considering that you already have a good grasp on the C language. The only thing that may toss you for a loop is the `printf` formatting for printing the double-precision number. The following placeholder is used:

`%0.f`

The `printf` placeholder used for printing a floating-point number is `%f`. It works for both `floats` and `doubles`. If `%f` were specified in LIGHTS1.C, the output would look like this:

`Milton, we need 256.000000 lights.`

Therefore, you have to tell the compiler to lop off the decimal point and any "change" that happens to come after it. You do this with a `0.` (zero, period) sandwiched inside the `%f`. The zero means "whatever," and it doesn't limit the number of digits displayed to the left of the decimal point. Having nothing to the right of the decimal point tells the compiler not to display anything there, so `%0.f` displays the floating-point result but without any decimal part.

Rooting out the root

Another math problem you may have to work out is the square root. For the life of me, I can't cite a practical example because, honestly, I find all math stupid. In any event, no keyboard symbol in C is used to calculate the square root of a number. As with the power-of deal, you use a special function, `sqrt`.

Function `sqrt` (square root)

The `sqrt` function is used to divine the square root of a number — to find out which number, when multiplied by itself, equals the number you want the square root of. Something like that. In any event, it's not the "squirt" function. Here's the format:

`value = sqrt(n)`

The double variable `value` is equal to the square root of the double variable n in the preceding equation. Yes, everything must be

`double` here. You also need the following `include` at the beginning of your source code:

`#include <math.h>`

The only limitation on the `sqrt` function is that n, the number you're finding the root of, cannot be negative. According to the folks at Math, Inc., no such thing as the square root of a negative number exists — no, not in this here universe. When you try to figure a negative square root, strange things happen.

Since you and Milton have this thing going, you're going to surprise him by telling him the square root of the number of lights you bought for Christmas. To make that process easier, you devise the LIGHTS2.C program.

Type this program into your editor. Be careful when you're typing because that long `printf` line was split to fit into this book's format. Just type the whole thing and press Enter only after the semicolon on that line. Save this puppy to disk as LIGHTS2.C:

Name: LIGHTS2.C

```
#include <stdio.h>
#include <math.h>
#define TOOTH 253      //the squared (second power) symbol

void main()
{
  double lights;

  lights=sqrt(256);    //calculate the square root of 256
  printf("Milton, I got your %0.f%c
          lights.\n",lights,TOOTH);
}
```

Compile and run

```
Milton, I got your 162 lights.
```

The `sqrt` function boasts that the square root of 256 is 16. Or, to put it another way, 162 (or 16×16) is equal to 256. Milton would be pleased.

- ✔ The square root of 256 is 16, and 16 squared (16^2) is 256. Is math great or what?

- ✔ Character code 253 is equal to the tiny 2 — the squared number. Refer to Appendix B in *C For Dummies,* Volume I.

- ✔ Character code 251 is equal to the traditional square root symbol. Even if you can manage to get that symbol into your text editor, you still need the `sqrt` function to wrangle up a square root.

- ✔ The `%c` in the `printf` formatting string is used to bring in the special character, 253, defined as `TOOTH` earlier in the source code.

- ✔ Refer to Lesson 3-4 in Volume I of this book for more information about `#define`.

- ✔ No, `sqrt` is not pronounced "squirt."

- ✔ And no, `sqrt` is not what the Roman legions paraded on their standards. (That was `spqr`, which stands for *senatus populus que Romanus,* the senate, and people of Rome.)

Strange math? We got it!

Most C language libraries are just bursting with math functions. Lots of them. I've listed some of the more common ones in Table 8-1, along with their formats. Pretty much all of them want a double or float value, which makes sense when you figure that if math had no decimals, more of us would enjoy it.

Table 8-1	Weirdo Math Functions You'll Never Use		
Function	**What It Computes**	**Format**	**Include**
abs	The absolute value of an integer (the value without a minus sign)	a=abs(b)	STDLIB.H
acos	Arc cosine	x=acos(y)	MATH.H
asin	Arc sine	x=asin(y)	MATH.H
atan	Arc tangent	x=atan(y)	MATH.H
cos	Cosine	x=cos(y)	MATH.H
exp	Exponential	x=exp(y)	MATH.H
log	Natural logarithm	x=log(y)	MATH.H
log10	Base 10 logarithm	x=log10(y)	MATH.H
sin	Sine	x=sin(y)	MATH.H
tan	Tangent	x=tan(y)	MATH.H

✔ In Table 8-1, variables a, b, and c denote integer values. Variables x, y, and z are doubles.

✔ Even more complex functions than this one exist. Wise men truly run from them.

✔ The best source for discovering what these commands do and how they work is to look in your C language library reference that came with your compiler. If you're lucky, it's in a book; otherwise, it's in your compiler's online help feature. (You can always buy a good book as a reference; the Waite Group Press has some excellent C language "Bibles" available.)

✔ Most of the time, you can replace the variables in a math function's parentheses with constant values. For example:

```
x=sqrt(1024);
```

Something really odd to end the lesson

It's your old pal ++ again, and his sister, -- — the increment and decrement operators from days gone by. Favorites, to be sure, but they're kind of puzzling in a way. For example, consider the following snippet of code you may find lurking in someone else's program:

```
b=a++;
```

So the variable b equals the contents of variable a plus one. Or does it?

Remember that a++ can be a statement by itself. As such, doesn't it work out first? If so, does b equal a+1, or does b equal a and then a is incremented after it all? And will Jim realize that Barbara is cheating on him so that he'll be free to marry Jessica? Hmmm. . . .

It is a puzzle that has an answer — an important answer you have to know if you don't want your programs getting all goofy on you.

Refer to Lesson 4-7 in *C For Dummies,* Volume I, for more information about incrementing and decrementing with ++ and --.

The perils of using a++

Here's the rule about using ++ to increment a variable so that you know what happens before running the sample program:

> The variable is incremented last when ++ appears after it.

So

```
b=a++;
```

The compiler instantly slides the value of variable a into variable b when it sees this statement. Then the value of a is incremented. To drive this point home, test out the INCODD.C program.

Type this program into your editor. Save it to disk as INCODD.C:

Name: INCODD.C

```
#include <stdio.h>

void main()
{
```

```
int a,b;

a=10;
b=0;
printf("A=%i and B=%i before incrementing.\n",a,b);
b=a++;
printf("A=%i and B=%i after incrementing.\n",a,b);
}
```

Compile and run! Here's what the output looks like:

```
A=10 and B=0 before incrementing.
A=11 and B=10 after incrementing.
```

The first line makes sense; the a and b variables were given those values right up front. The second line proves the ++ conundrum. First, b is assigned the value of a, which is 10. Then a is incremented to 11.

✔ Whenever you see a variable followed by ++ in a C statement, know that the variable's value is incremented *last,* after any other math or assignments (equal-sign things) elsewhere on that line.

✔ A good way to remember this rule is that the ++ comes after the variable. It's as though C sees the variable first, raids its contents, and then — oh, by the way — it increments its value.

✔ This rule screws you up if you ever combine the ++ with something else inside an if comparison:

```
if(a=b++)
```

This technique is common — sticking the b++ inside the comparison rather than on a line before or afterward. You have to keep in mind, however, that b is incremented after the if command compares them. If the comparison is true, b is still incremented. Remember that when you notice that your program is acting funny.

Oh, and the same thing applies to a - -

The decrementing operator, - -, also affects a variable's value after any other math or equal-sign stuff is done in the program. To witness this effect, edit the INCODD.C program as follows:

1. Change incrementing in Line 9 to read decrementing.

2. Change the ++ in Line 10 to a - - operator.

3. Change `incrementing` in Line 11 to read `decrementing`.

Here's what the finished result should look like:

Name: DECODD.C

```c
#include <stdio.h>

void main()
{
    int a,b;

    a=10;
    b=0;
    printf("A=%i and B=%i before decrementing.\n",a,b);
    b=a--;
    printf("A=%i and B=%i after decrementing.\n",a,b);
}
```

Save the file to disk as DECODD.C. Compile and run. Here's the output, proving that decrementing happens after any math or assignments:

```
A=10 and B=0 before decrementing.
A=9 and B=10 after decrementing.
```

The value of b is equal to 10, which means that the a variable was decremented last.

All this makes sense, and you should understand it by now — or at least be aware of what's happening. If you can't remember the rule, just keep your incrementing or decrementing on a line by itself, as shown in this example:

```c
a++;
b=a;
```

Replacing Line 10 in either of the sample programs (INCODD.C or DECODD.C) with the preceding two lines means that variable a is incremented first — no matter what — and then b equals that new value. Even given this exception, C has a way to increment a variable first. It's strange. It's kooky. It's covered next.

Reflections on the strange ++a *phenomenon*

Load the program INCODD.C back into your editor.

Change Line 10 to read

```
b=++a;
```

This line looks stranger than it is. You can type it like this to avoid thinking that =++ is some weird C command:

```
b = ++a;
```

The ++ is still the incrementing operator. It still increases the value of the a variable. Because it comes before the variable, however, it means that the incrementing happens first. It reads, "Increase me first, and then do whatever else comes next."

Save the source code for INCODD.C to disk. Compile and run it. Here's what you see:

```
A=10 and B=0 before incrementing.
A=11 and B=11 after incrementing.
```

It worked! The ++a operation came first.

Again, this is just something strange you should know about. Rarely have I seen the ++ operator appear before a variable, but it can be done. It may help iron out some screwy things if you notice trouble when you're putting ++ after a variable name.

- You can use ++ before or after a variable when it appears on a line by itself. There is no difference between this:

  ```
  a++;
  ```

  and this:

  ```
  ++a;
  ```

- Yes, this process also works with decrementing. You can change Line 10 in DECODD.C to the following:

  ```
  b=--a;
  ```

  Save, compile, and run the program. Variable a is decremented first, and then its new value is given to variable b.

- Most people use the word *anxious* when they really mean *eager*.

✔ Don't even bother with the following:

```
++a++;
```

Your logical mind may ponder that this statement first increments the a variable and then increments it again. Wrong! The compiler thinks that you forgot something when you try to compile such a statement; you get one of the dreadful Lvalue required errors. That message means that the compiler was expecting another variable or number in there somewhere. Sorry, but the "fortress effect" of the incrementing or decrementing operators just doesn't work.

Lesson 8-2 Quiz

1. How is the problem "four to the seventh power," or 4^7, written in C?

   A. x = 4^7;

   B. x = 4**7;

   C. x = power(4,7);

   D. x = power(7,4);

2. How do you figure out the square root of 42 in C?

   A. x = $\sqrt{42}$;

   B. x = //42;

   C. x = sqrt(42);

   D. x = squirt(42);

3. Suppose that the value of gross is 15. What is the value of net after the following statement?

```
net=gross--;
```

   A. The value of net is 16.

   B. The value of net is 15.

   C. The value of net is 14.

   D. The value of net equals 15, but it then decrements to 14.

4. When is the following if comparison true?

```
if(++x==15)
```

A. When x is equal to 14.

B. When x is equal to 15.

C. When ++x is equal to 15.

D. When 15 is equal to 15.

5. How much do penny nails cost?

A. A penny each.

B. A penny for a bag.

C. Two for a penny.

D. One penny for two.

Bonus question! Worth a blue triangle!

You're visiting an aquatic park when your date accidentally falls into the walrus pen. It's mating season. What soothing words of encouragement do you offer while waiting for help to arrive?

A. "So . . . is the water cold?"

B. "No, I'm sure that dumb corn pones fall into this pen every day."

C. "If you see any fish floating around down there, don't rub yourself with them. It's close to feeding time."

D. "Ignore the tusks — just assert that you're not unfriendly."

Time to go to the fridge and get a beverage.

Lesson 8-3: Avoiding the Ugly GOTO Command

One of the smattering of true C language keywords is goto, which is pronounced "go to" and not "gotto." (It doesn't rhyme with grotto or Toto.) It's perhaps the most scorned word in the whole C language. Everyone — *everyone* — advises against its use primarily because there are better ways to do things.

- Most C language books don't teach anything about `goto`, other than a passing mention. One programmer, however, set out to find virtue for the vilified `goto`. He concocted a program that used a `goto` and could not be written any other way. Keep in mind that this guy was a top-notch C programmer and he had to *work* at it to get a justifiable `goto` program. For us mere mortals, this isn't an option.

- Alas, I don't have that program.

- Table 1-1 in *C For Dummies,* Volume I, lists all the C language keywords.

- If it's not a C language keyword, it's a function. `printf`, `atoi`, and `getch` are all functions. They aren't C language keywords.

- *Go to* — *Othello,* Act III, Scene 4.

"So what's this goto all about?"

The `goto` keyword is one of the C language's looping commands. `goto` causes the program to jump — go to — another spot. This spot is identified by a label, which is a short word followed by a colon on a line by itself (see the following sidebar, "Keyword `goto`").

- About the only time you can justifiably use a `goto` command is when your program detects an error and has no other way to bail out of a complex nested loop. For example, if your program can't open a file in the middle of a `for` loop in the middle of two other `for` loops, `goto` is just about the only way to get out of there sanely; a `break` statement just doesn't cut it.

- Try to keep your label names short and sweet — like variable names. Don't stick any spaces in there, or else the compiler will gag.

- Labels can come before or after the `goto` in your program. Wherever they are, the program picks up execution on the line that follows the label.

- Both `goto` and its label must be inside the same function. You cannot use `goto` to branch to a label in another function, no matter how hard you try. (If you could, well, it would be just horrible.)

An example of how not to use goto

Because you're going to waste an entire lesson reading about a C language keyword you will never use, I may as well make it fun. To do so, dust off those old plans you have for dropping a nuclear weapon on Redmond, Washington. Rather than risk disappointment and lose your deposit on the small plane rental, why not run the following program as a test simulation?

Keyword goto

The goto keyword controls how your program flows. Most C programs work from top to bottom. What goto does is cause the program to jump from one particular spot to another, skipping over a chunk of code. Here's the format:

goto *label*;

The goto keyword is used on a line by itself because it's a complete statement. It's followed by the name of a label that appears elsewhere in your source code. The line ends with a semicolon.

The label is a single word at the beginning of a line, followed by a semicolon:

label:

This word identifies the spot where the program continues after the goto statement.

There's nothing evil about goto, and there shouldn't be because the C language creator, St. Ritchie, would not have included it had that been so. The problem is that using goto encourages sloppy programming. Honestly, there are just better ways to loop in C — or to get out of a loop — than to use a goto.

This program, DROPNUKE.C, contains a loop that drops a bomblike character on Redmond. A kbhit function in the middle of that loop enables you to chicken out and change your mind by pressing a key to cancel the bomb drop. This is where the goto was stuck into the loop. Note the two endings — one where you blow up Redmond and the other where you save the town.

Name: DROPNUKE.C

```
#include <stdio.h>
#include <stdlib.h>
#include <dos.h>
#include <conio.h>

#define VIDEO 0x10      //Video interrupt
#define COLS 80         //Screen width
#define ROWS 25         //Screen rows
#define BOTTOM_ROW 24   //Bottom row
#define CENTER_COL 39   //Center column
#define BOMB 162        //bomb character

void pause(int seconds);
void cls(void);
void locate(int col,int row);

void main()
```

(continued)

(continued)

```
{
  int drop;

  cls();
  locate(CENTER_COL-3,BOTTOM_ROW);
  printf("REDMOND");
  locate(0,0);
  printf("Press Enter to drop nuclear weapon:");
  getch();

//This loop drops the bomb down to the city, slowly

  for(drop=0;drop<BOTTOM_ROW;drop++)
  {
      locate(CENTER_COL,drop);
      printf("%c",BOMB);
      pause(1); //pause one second
      if(kbhit())
      {
          goto cancel;
      }
  }
  locate(CENTER_COL-3,BOTTOM_ROW);
  printf("BOOM!!!\n");
  exit(0);                //quit here

cancel:
  locate(0,24);
  printf("You saved the town!\n");
  getch();                //read in kbhit char.
}

void pause(int seconds)
{
  delay(seconds*1000);      //Borland compilers
}

void cls(void)
{
  union REGS regs;

  regs.h.ah=0x06;      //call function 6, scroll window
  regs.h.al=0x00;      //clear screen
```

```
    regs.h.bh=0x07;      //make screen "blank" color
    regs.h.ch=0x00;      //Upper left row
    regs.h.cl=0x00;      //Upper left column
    regs.h.dh=ROWS-1;    //Lower right row
    regs.h.dl=COLS-1;    //Lower right column
    int86(VIDEO,&regs,&regs);

    locate(0,0);         //"Home" the cursor
}

void locate(int col,int row)
{
  union REGS regs;

  regs.h.ah=0x02;      //video function 2, move cursor
  regs.h.bh=0x00;      //video screen (always 0)
  regs.h.dh=row;       //cursor's row position
  regs.h.dl=col;       //cursor's col position
  int86(VIDEO,&regs,&regs);
}
```

Type the source code for DROPNUKE.C into your editor. Be careful, and double-check everything. Most of the functions in this program can be copied and pasted from other programs you should have from Volume I of this book: ZAPSCRN2.C and COUNTDWN.C. When you're done, save the file to disk as DROPNUKE.C.

Compile. Fix any errors or typos that may have crept in there. When it compiles fine, run it:

```
Press Enter to drop nuclear weapon:
```

See REDMOND at the bottom of the screen? Nuke it! Press Enter.

You should see a "bomb" fall from the top of the screen to the bottom. You can press the spacebar to cancel and save the town or just keep watching and then . . . BOOM!

I have no particular reason — none at all — for choosing Redmond, Washington, as the city to blast in this program. It may be the way the Redmond police doggedly nab speeders on West Lake Sammamish Parkway, but I've never gotten a ticket there. Supposedly, it's the Bellevue police who are the real snoots about it.

✔ The exit command (Line 44) is introduced in Lesson 8-4.

✔ The cls and locate functions in DROPNUKE.C were culled from the ZAPSCRN2.C program, found in Lesson 5-6 in Volume I of this book. Refer to that lesson to divine what they do and how they work.

✔ The pause delay loop in DROPNUKE.C was stolen from COUNTDWN.C in Lesson 7-2, also from Volume I.

✔ Because Microsoft C lacks the delay function, you have to write your own. Start by including the time.h header at the beginning of the DROPNUKE.C source code:

```
#include <time.h>
```

Next, prototype the delay function:

```
void delay(int duration);
```

Finally, add the delay function at the end of the source code:

```
void delay(int duration)
{
    clock_t done;

    done = duration + clock();
    while(done > clock())
        ;
}
```

This code is a direct substitute for the Borland C delay function.

✔ If you don't have a Borland or Microsoft compiler, you can't use the pause function in the DROPNUKE.C program. (Only Borland compilers have the delay function.) Instead, you should use the following for your pause function:

```
void pause(int seconds)
{
    int x;
    long d;

    for(x=0;x<seconds;x++)
        for(d=0;d<600000;d++);
}
```

This loop pauses the computer for about a second, more or less depending on how swift your computer is. To make the time longer, increase the value higher than 600,000 in the last line; decreasing that value makes the loop spin for a shorter duration.

✔ A knothole is not a hole at all!

Getting rid of the darn goto

Removing a goto from a program is easy when you put one in deliberately. When you just sit around all sloppy with your shirt buttoned up wrong and smelling like a goat, it's harder to remove a goto. Since I just bathed and double-checked my shirt buttons, here's what I would do to rewrite DROPNUKE.C without an ugly goto in it:

First, change the if-kbhit statement to the following:

```
if(kbhit())
{
  break;
}
```

This example should easily break you out of the for loop without incurring the wrath of goto. Make the preceding change in your source code, but don't compile yet!

The DROPNUKE.C program has two ending conditions. One is used when the town blows up and the second when a key is pressed and the town saved. An if-else is obviously needed to handle the two conditions, but what can be used to determine whether the town was saved? And what about the character sitting in the keyboard buffer and detected by the kbhit function? Riddles and riddles!

I'll let you think this over for a few seconds.

(Hum the theme from *Jeopardy!* here.)

Got it? I thought of two ways. The first uses the value of the drop variable. If drop is still less than BOTTOM_ROW, they must have broken out of the loop. If drop equals BOTTOM_ROW, however, the town was destroyed. Based on that, you can concoct the following if-else structure and tack it on the end of the program:

```
if(drop==BOTTOM_ROW)
{
  locate(CENTER_COL-3,BOTTOM_ROW);
  printf("BOOM!!!\n");
  exit(0);              //quit here
}
else
{
  locate(0,24);
  printf("You saved the town!\n");
```

(continued)

(continued)

```
  getch();              //read in kbhit char.
}
```

Make the preceding changes to the program and run the program again.

Hey! It works the same and without the `goto`.

- ✔ You can concoct this program in even more ways. The point is that `goto` is almost always not necessary. It's easier to think of a program without a `goto` in it than to unwrite a bad program that includes it.

- ✔ Lesson 8-1 has more information about the `kbhit` function.

Improving the program with a wee bit of animation

Now that `goto` has been excised, only one problem remains with DROPNUKE.C: The bomb doesn't really "drop." Instead, it looks more like 24 bombs are dropped, each of which goes down one line further than the one before it. This program is obviously in need of some animation.

You don't need graphics to do animation. All you need is an image that changes subtly. The human eye uses this phenomenon, called "persistence of vision," that keeps men looking at young ladies in bikinis even in the presence of their wives. Persistence of vision creates the illusion in your brain that the subtly changing image is really "moving." Actually, there's no movement.

To make the bomb appear to move is simple: Before drawing the bomb in a new position, you have to erase the bomb in its old position. It works like this:

1. Draw the bomb.

2. Wait a bit.

3. Erase the bomb.

4. Repeat.

The loop is already set up in DROPNUKE.C. All you have to add is a statement that erases the bomb:

```
printf("\b ");
```

The printf function displays the backspace character, shown with the \b escape sequence. It then displays a space. Insert this line in your DROPNUKE.C source code just after the if statement's right curly bracket at Line 40; make it so that this printf statement is the last thing in the for loop. The backspace moves the cursor under the bomb character displayed in Line 35, and the space character erases the bomb.

Save the change to disk. Compile and run the program. It appears as though the bomb gently floats to earth. This program should be much more satisfying.

Lesson 8-3 Quiz

1. Why shouldn't you use the goto keyword?

   A. Because there are just better ways to do things in C.

   B. Because I keep pronouncing it "gotto" in my head.

   C. Because the C language propriety meisters would be angered.

   D. Because it says in *The C Programming Language*, "Although we are not dogmatic on the matter, it does seem that goto statements should be used sparingly, if at all."

2. Okay, so if you do use a goto keyword, what does it do?

   A. It induces wrath, plain and simple.

   B. It causes the program to go to another place inside the computer's memory.

   C. It causes the program to go to a label and then keep reading instructions there.

   D. It causes pretty and scantily clad girls to come out and dance lasciviously for you. Oh. Wait. I thought that was the gogo keyword. Never mind.

3. Rewrite the following code snippet without the goto:

```
start:
printf("Hello Moon!\n");
goto start;
```

4. What does the following sign mean?

A. The idiot in front of you is drunk.

B. Musta been a big squirrel.

C. Slippery road.

D. Foreigner.

Lesson 8-4: Printing for Reals

Don't you find it rather odd that the printf statement doesn't send anything to your printer? In the olden days, it did. Older (I mean *much* older) computers lacked display screens, so printf really did print; all the computer's output went to a teletype machine. You would think that they would have dreamt up a displayf function when computers started coming with display screens, but no. And what about printing to a real-life printer? What's that statement called? Printprinterf?

The truth is that printing is a personal thing. It's up to you to concoct your own method of printing something on your PC's printer. The computer handles the details because that's what the computer's hardware (the BIOS) is for. But you have to write your own printing functions if you ever want your C programs to make any hard copy.

✔ The programs in this lesson assume that you have mulled over Lesson 5-6 in *C For Dummies,* Volume I. That's where you find out how to create BIOS function calls in C.

✔ It's a good idea to review all of Chapter 5 in Volume I because that's where the make-up-your-own-C-language-function stuff is.

✔ Windows uses its own printing functions, which are beyond the scope of this book. Yes, the programs you create in this lesson work if you have Windows and run the programs in a DOS window. If you're writing Windows programs, you probably will use one of the Windows printing functions rather than the prnchar function introduced here.

✔ I pronounce `prnchar` as "print character."

✔ If you're serious about printing in Windows, pick up one of those Windows C programming books to glean more information. I recommend anything written by Charles Petzold.

The exciting "Spew a page from the printer" program

Back in the old, pre-Industrial Revolution days of computing, the printer was this monstrous beast, often located in some other room. As a prank, young hackers wrote programs that automatically spit page after page from the printer, creating this massive mess (but not wasting paper, because nothing was printed). For extra, thigh-slapping delight, they made the printer beep after sending each page.

(Oh, those were the days.)

Ejecting a page from your printer is, of course, a handy thing to do. Laser printers don't print a page until you either fill it up with text or the printer's eject-page command is used. For any printer, ejecting a page is handy. I had a friend who ejected a page from his printer whenever he needed a clean sheet of paper.

The great thing about spitting paper from your printer is that one command does it. One command causes paper to jump out of just about every printer — from a 1979 Epson MX-80 to today's bazillion-dollar color laser printers. That command is the lowly ASCII character 12, hexadecimal value C. A powerful little booger.

The following program sends the eject-page command, character 12, to your printer. Type this program into your editor. Although that one long `printf` statement is split between two lines in this book, you don't have to do that in your editor. If you don't understand something in there, refer to the nearby "Evil secrets" sidebar for help.

Name: PRINTME1.C

```
#include <stdio.h>
#include <conio.h>
#include <dos.h>
#define PRINTER 0x17        //BIOS printer interrupt
#define LPT1 0x00           //LPT1, your first printer
#define EJECT 0x0c          //Eject page printer command
```

(continued)

(continued)

```
void eject();
void prnchar(char c);

void main()
{
  printf("Please ensure that your printer is on and ready
          to print.\n");
  printf("Press Enter:");
  getch();

/* Now eject a page from the printer */

  eject();

}

void eject(void)
{
  prnchar(EJECT);
}

void prnchar(char c)
{
  union REGS regs;

  regs.h.ah=0x00;        //print character function
  regs.h.al=c;           //character to print
  regs.x.dx=LPT1;        //printer port to print to
  int86(PRINTER,&regs,&regs);
}
```

Save the file to disk, naming it PRINTME1.C. Compile and run.

```
Please ensure that your printer is on and ready to print.
Press Enter:
```

Please, O, please, make sure that your printer is on before you press the Enter key.

Fzzzzztt!

A page slips smoothly from your printer.

✔ You could rename the PRINTME1.EXE file to EJECT.EXE and then use the EJECT command at the DOS prompt to always eject a page from your printer. Hey! A useful program in this book? No way!

REMEMBER

✔ Refer to Lesson 3-4 for more information about the #define directive.

✔ Functions must be declared before you can use them (refer to Lesson 5-1 in Volume I of this book).

✔ Refer to Lesson 2-5, also in Volume I, for more information about the getch function as used in PRINTME1.C.

WARNING!

✔ If your printer isn't on, DOS waits for it. Eventually, you see a printer time-out error. Some versions of DOS may wait forever if you don't turn on your printer. If you absolutely can't get your printer turned on, you can try pressing Ctrl+Break to stop the waiting, close the DOS window (in Windows 95), or just reset the computer if your hope dries up.

BLOW BY BLOW

Evil secrets inside PRINTME1.C

The first #define is for 17 hex, which is the interrupt number for the BIOS printer functions (just like 10 hex is the BIOS video interrupt, from Lesson 5-6 in *C For Dummies*, Volume I). The second #define tells the program that you're working with printer port 1, LPT1. (For some strange reason, LPT2 is 0x01.) The final #define sets the eject character code to 0C hex (12).

The eject function merely uses the prnchar function to send the eject-character code to the printer. Why? Because it's easier in C to call a function to eject a page than to remember what the eject code is all the time and then rewrite that code elsewhere in your program. To illustrate:

```
eject();
```

The preceding line is more descriptive and handier than this one:

```
prnchar(EJECT);
```

Or:

```
prnchar(0x0c);
```

Finally, the prnchar function, the core of this program, is what sends a single character to the PC's printer. It has the same construction as the video call used in ZAPSCRN1.C from Volume I. Refer to Lesson 5-6 for more information about the union REGS regs nonsense. The character to print, held in the c variable, is stuffed into a register variable, as is the printer port number (LPT1), and then the whole ugly mess is passed into the PC's BIOS for processing.

Incidentally, *all* printing on your PC is handled in this way. Even mighty Windows uses this BIOS function to talk with the printer. Of course, Windows has many "high level" functions of its own for printing. But somewhere down in the bowels of Windows lives something like the prnchar function in the PRINTME1.C program you just wrote.

For extra, thigh-slapping delight

The hackers who wrote the infinite eject-pages-from-the-printer programs also had the printer beep every time it ejected a page. You can do this too, with the PRINTME1.C program; it's purely optional, however.

Insert the following line in the `main` function, just before the call to the `eject` function:

```
prnchar(0x07);              //ring the bell!
```

Save. Compile. Run.

Beep!

Fzzzzztt!

Yes, the printer can beep. And yes, you can try this stunt on a network printer. The PC I have in my office, in fact, is printing to a network printer right now. Oh, such jocularity. . . .

Not every printer beeps when it sees character code `0x07`. Some do. Some don't.

✔ If you want to get really nerdy, you can include the following line at the top of your revamped source code:

```
#define BELL 0x07      //ring the bell
```

✔ Then you can change the new line to read

```
prnchar(BELL);          //ring the bell!
```

✔ Or you can just write a function called `prnbeep`:

```
void prnbeep(void)
{
    prnchar(BELL);
}
```

Printing some text

Printing text on the printer is cinchy, now that you have a `prnchar` function. Heck, you're just moments away from creating that PC "typewriter" program you've always dreamed of. . . .

The following modification to the PRINTME1.C program sends several characters to the printer, one after the other. Granted, this is a cruddy way to do things, inelegant and all that. A better solution is forthcoming, but for now, gander at the following source code example:

Name: PRINTME2.C

```c
#include <stdio.h>
#include <conio.h>
#include <dos.h>
#define PRINTER 0x17        //BIOS printer interrupt
#define LPT1 0x00           //LPT1, your first printer
#define EJECT 0x0c          //Eject page printer command

void eject(void);
void prnchar(char c);

void main()
{
  printf("Please ensure that your printer is on and ready
          to print.\n");
  printf("Press Enter:");
  getch();

  prnchar('T');             //print "Testing" on the printer
  prnchar('e');
  prnchar('s');
  prnchar('t');
  prnchar('i');
  prnchar('n');
  prnchar('g');
  eject();                  //spew out the page

}

void eject(void)
{
  prnchar(EJECT);
}

void prnchar(char c)
{
  union REGS regs;
```

(continued)

(continued)

```
   regs.h.ah=0x00;      //print character function
   regs.h.al=c;         //character to print
   regs.x.dx=LPT1;      //printer port to print to
   int86(PRINTER,&regs,&regs);
}
```

Nothing much changes between the preceding source code and what you see already on your screen. Just add the following lines to the PRINTME1.C text in your editor, just below the getch function and before the call to eject, as just shown:

```
prnchar('T');      //print "Testing" on the printer
prnchar('e');
prnchar('s');
prnchar('t');
prnchar('i');
prnchar('n');
prnchar('g');
```

Each character in the string Testing is sent to the printer via the prnchar function, one after the other. Note that those are single quotes, just as you would use in the putchar function, which, of course, this book hasn't introduced to you and probably never will.

Make your edits. Save the changes using the Save As command and name the new file PRINTME2.C. Compile and run.

Fzzzzztt!

Maybe the printer really isn't yours to command

Honestly, most of the fancy stuff is done on your printer via its own command set. For example, your printer may have several fonts installed. To activate one of them, you must send the proper string of characters to the printer, telling it not to print but to change fonts. This process is how word processors and Windows communicate with your printer.

It's possible to obtain for your printer a manual that lists the various commands and whatnot. If so, you can organize the various commands into strings and then send them to your printer by writing a program with the prnchar function. Graphics on the printer are also done this way, simply by sending the proper commands that tell the thing to draw a circle or whatever.

When it's not accepting commands, your printer otherwise just prints text, as you saw with the PRINTME2.C program. Also, the eject character, 0x0C, is a fairly common printer command. Just about every other command is fairly long and detailed. So don't get cocky.

Somewhere on the printed page, near the top, you should see the text
Testing printed.

✔ The printer is yours to command!

✔ You have to make the eject function the last thing you print because
all laser printers refuse to print a dot of ink until a whole page has been
sent to the printer. In this case, you fool the printer into thinking that a
whole page has been sent by forcing it to eject the page anyway.

✔ The putchar function is (finally) introduced in Lesson 9-2 in this book.

✔ Whoops! Did you forget to edit out the beep command? Better remove
that line from your source code if you don't want the computer to beep
just before it ejects a page. (Oh, har-har.)

A better, though more complex, way to print a line o' text

Printing a string of text one character at a time is really dumb. Yes, there's a
more efficient way to do it. The problem is that the technique involves
pointers, which is the subject of Chapter 10. You have to wade through all of
Chapter 9, on strings, before you even touch this weird and different aspect
of C. Until then, you can peruse the following source code:

Name: PRINTME3.C

```c
#include <stdio.h>
#include <conio.h>
#include <dos.h>
#define PRINTER 0x17        //BIOS printer interrupt
#define LPT1 0x00           //LPT1, your first printer
#define EJECT 0x0c          //Eject page printer command

void prnstring(char *string);
void eject(void);
void prnchar(char c);

void main()
{
  printf("Please ensure that your printer is on and ready
            to print.\n");
  printf("Press Enter:");
  getch();
```

(continued)

(continued)

```
  prnstring("Testing.\r\n");
  prnstring("Hey! It works!");
  eject();
}

void prnstring(char *string)
{
  while(*string)          //while there's a char to print
    prnchar(*string++);   //print it and increment
}

void eject(void)
{
  prnchar(EJECT);
}

void prnchar(char c)
{
  union REGS regs;

  regs.h.ah=0x00;        //print character function
  regs.h.al=c;           //character to print
  regs.x.dx=LPT1;        //printer port to print to
  int86(PRINTER,&regs,&regs);
}
```

Using the PRINTME2.C file already in your editor, make the appropriate changes to convert it into the preceding source code. Double-check to ensure that you got all the changes, and then save the file to disk as PRINTME3.C.

Compile and run that guy.

Fzzzzztt!

You should see essentially the same output as the PRINTME2.C program; the word *Testing* appears at the top of the page. No biggie, but the way it was done, with the prnstring function, is what's new. Unfortunately, you have to wait a few chapters to know how it works. Until then, gander at the nearby sidebar, "Ruminations on the prnstring function," for some hints.

The carriage-return escape sequence \r is needed in Line 17 because, unlike the display, your printer doesn't return to the first column when the \n escape sequence is used. You need *both* \r and \n.

In fact, if you're printing anything on your printer and want it printed in the first column, you should start that string with a \r escape sequence.

✔ Refer to Table 2-1 in Volume I of this book for more exciting escape characters.

✔ You may also want to start printing by sending initialization commands to your printer. This sequence of characters is different for each printer. You have to shell out the beaucoup bucks for your printer's "language" manual to discover what the codes are.

✔ Refer to Lesson 5-3 in Volume I of this book for more information about how strings are sent to a function.

✔ Strings themselves are discussed throughout Chapter 9.

✔ The weird * thing before a string variable name identifies that variable as a *pointer,* which you agonize over in Chapter 10.

Ruminations on the prnstring function

The prnstring function slides a string of text out to the printer, printing each character one after the other like magic (it isn't really magic — it's just more of the nature of how strings are stored in the C language, which you read about in the next chapter):

```
void prnstring(char *string)
```

The function requires a string variable, which is defined as *string (this is how string variables are passed to functions, as discussed in Lesson 5-3 in Volume I of this book):

```
while(*string)
```

The while loop inside the prnstring function uses a weird aspect of strings in C for its true-false condition. Essentially, it tests to see whether a character is in the string; if so, the condition is TRUE and the while loop prints that character. If no characters are in the string, the while loop condition is FALSE, and,

because it's the only statement in this function, the string is done printing.

Weirder than the while test condition is what's being sent to the printer in the prnchar function:

```
prnchar(*string++);
```

Without boggling you too much, the *string variable secretly points to where the string is stored in memory. The prnchar function prints the character the *string variable points to, and then the *string variable is incremented, pointing to the next character in the string. In a way, this works just like you read: one character after another. In the string ABCD, you read A, then increment to B, then to C, and finally to D.

It's thought-provoking how this contraption works, and — trust me — you will appreciate it all the more after reading the next two chapters. Sorry if the peek ahead frustrates you.

Lesson 8-4 Quiz

1. What is the printing function in the C language?

   A. printf

   B. displayf

   C. prnchar

   D. The C language has no printing function.

2. Even though the printf function doesn't use your printer, it's still called printf because

   A. Just a second; I need to go back and change my answer to the first question.

   B. In the olden days, all computer output went to the printer.

   C. Printing is the same whether it goes to the printer or to your PC's screen.

   D. The printf function *can* use the printer; it just chooses not to.

3. If you write a function to ring the printer's bell, what do you have to do?

   A. Send character code 0x07 (the "bell") to the printer.

   B. Declare the function to avoid those thorny prototyping errors.

   C. Make sure that the printer has a bell or beeper in the first place.

   D. All of the above.

4. *Mea culpa:*

   A. Sarah Culpa's sister.

   B. Italian for "I am a culp."

   C. A direction used in violin music, meaning to poke your neighbor's eye with your bow.

   D. A Latin phrase used by people who aren't bold enough to ever use the words "It's my fault."

Hmmm. Something salty would be nice right about now.

Lesson 8-5: I'm Outta Here!

Aside from the occasional loop (or the heinous `goto`), a C program runs and runs and then, eventually, it falls off the edge, beyond that last remaining curly bracket and into oblivion. Show's over. Fat lady's sung. DOS, Windows, OS/2, whatever takes over, and you're done. Thank you for coming.

You can bail out of a program before its time, however, in two ways. The first is covered in Lesson 5-4 in *C For Dummies,* Volume I. The `return` keyword can be used to quickly exit any function — including the `main` function — before that final curly bracket.

Better than the `return` keyword is the `exit` command. This command is perhaps the best way to bail out of a program. It's better than `return` because, unlike `return`, `exit` leaves the program at once — dives for the egress, in most cases. A silly `return` may merely eject you from a function inside a program. But `exit`? Hey, you're out the door and in the cold instantaneously.

Jumping out the window at any time with the `exit` function

A C program ends when the last line of source code in the `main` function is executed. That last, right curly bracket marks the end of the program and — with nothing else left to do, no instructions to follow — the program peaceably dies, and your computer's operating system takes over, wiping a false tear of sorrow from its cold, steely eyes.

Of course, you can always bail out early with the `exit` command, discussed in the following sidebar, "Command `exit`." That way, *you* are in control of when the program leaves. Want to bail out early in an `if` condition, sure! Or maybe you want to bail out in some function nested deep in the program's core. Fine, use `exit`. Ready, reliable, handy, and — unlike Dr. Kevorkian — it's not controversial.

- ✔ The `exit` command is similar to the END command in BASIC or the Fin command at the end of French films.

- ✔ If the `exit` command appears in the middle of a function, none of the commands after it is ever executed. That is, unless you skip over the `exit` command in some type of `if-then` structure.

- ✔ Refer to the programs REPT.C and MOON.C in Lesson 6-3 of Volume I of this book for some examples of the `exit` command in action.

Command exit

The exit command is used to quit any C program. It can appear in any function or module, anywhere, at any time — just like the camera crew from *60 Minutes*. Unlike a crooked businessman, however, your program has no place to hide; after executing the exit command, the program quits, right squat there. The format:

```
exit(n);
```

The *n* is a value, usually 0, that's sent back to the operating system in a Hail Mary-like pass that some high school basketball players use at the fourth-period buzzer. The operating system typically doesn't care what the value is,

though it can be anything from 0 to 255 in DOS. Mostly it's 0, as in

```
exit(0);
```

In DOS, the value returned is stored in the batch file ERRORLEVEL command. This would come in handy, if anyone ever sat down and decided to write a DOS batch file again.

The manual says that the exit requires the STDLIB.H include header file thing. However, most compilers require you to include only the standard STDIO.H file:

```
#include <stdlib.h>
#include <stdio.h>
```

At last, the infamous ASK program

Hey, this was hot stuff back in the late '80s. DOS batch file programmers yearned for a method of getting a Y or N keypress input from their users. The only way to do that was to "roll your own," which often resulted in a program very similar to the one that follows, ASK.C:

Start over with a clean sheet in your editor and type the following source code. Save the file to disk as ASK.C. Compile it.

Name: ASK.C

```c
#include <stdio.h>
#include <conio.h>
#define TRUE 1

void main(int argc,char *argv[])
{
  int x;
  char c;

  if(argc<2)                    //no options typed
  {
      printf("Here is the ASK program's format:\n");
      printf("ASK [Text]\n");
```

```
        printf("\"Text\" is displayed, then the PC\n");
        printf("waits for Y or N to be pressed. Y\n");
        printf("returns an ERRORLEVEL of 1; N is 2.\n");
        exit(0);
  }

/* Print all the arguments */

  for(x=1;x<argc;x++)
        printf("%s\x20",argv[x]);

  printf("(Y or N)?");      //print the YorN prompt

  while(TRUE)
  {
      c=getch();

      if(c=='y' || c=='Y')
      {
          printf("Y\n"); //Display their input
          exit(1);          //ERRORLEVEL=1
      }
      if(c=='n' || c=='N')
      {
          printf("N\n");
          exit(2);          //ERRORLEVEL=2
      }
  }
}
```

To run the program, you have to visit a DOS prompt near you. (Do this instead of running the program from your compiler's environment.) Begin by just typing the program's name:

```
C> ASK
```

Press the Enter key, and you see the text that's produced when fewer than two items are typed at the DOS prompt (Line 10 in the program):

```
Here is the ASK program's format:
ASK [Text]
"Text" is displayed, then the PC
waits for Y or N to be pressed. Y
returns an ERRORLEVEL of 1; N is 2.
```

Some things you already know about in ASK.C

The `#include <conio.h>` is required at the beginning of this C file for the `getch` function. The `#define TRUE 1` line is required by the program's `while` loop. Refer to Lesson 7-3 in Volume I of this book for more information about the "bizarre case of `while-true`."

The `main` function must be declared with the `argc` and `argv` variables for you to read in any text from the command line. Lesson 6-3 in Volume I tells you more about how they work. That lesson also shows you how the `if` comparison in Line 10 checks to see whether any text follows `ASK` on the command line.

```
void main(int argc,char *argv[])
```

The first `exit` command is used to quit the program if nothing is typed after `ASK` at the DOS prompt. The `exit` command passes the value 0 back to DOS. A 0 typically means that a program did not complete its task (at least, that the code returned from most DOS programs and utilities — it's not a hard-and-fast rule):

```
exit(0);
```

If any text appears after `ASK` at the DOS prompt, the `for` loop prints it. Lesson 4-5 in Volume I tells you more about how that works. The `printf` statement looks a little weird:

```
printf("%s\x20",argv[x]);
```

The `%s` is used to print the string indicated by the `argv[x]` variable. Immediately following the `%s` is the space character, which is shown using the `\x20` escape sequence. This stuff is demonstrated in Lesson 8-1. Without it, all the text `ASK` displays would appear bunched together. (That's usually one of those bugs you catch when you first run the program.) You could just stick a real space in there and it would mean the same thing, but I included the `\x20` in the source code because it doesn't leave any doubt about whether a space was supposed to be there.

The rest of the program works similarly to the guts of YORN.C, shown in Lesson 7-3 in Volume I of this book. The only additions are the `exit` commands, which return the value 1 or 2 to DOS, depending on which key is pressed.

Now that you know how the program works, try it out. Type the following line:

```
C> ASK IS IT SUPPOSED TO WORK THIS WAY?
```

Press the Enter key, and you see the following:

```
IS IT SUPPOSED TO WORK THIS WAY? (Y OR N)?
```

See how the "Y or N" prompt was added? Nifty, eh?

The computer then waits for you to press the Y or N key. Go ahead — try a Z or an M. Nothing. Then press Y. That works. You can try it again and press N. That works too. Nothing makes sense, however, until you run it in a batch file, which is done in the next section.

- ✔ If you already have the ASK.C program from Volume I, rename it to ASKOLD.C (refer to Lesson 7-3).

- ✔ Refer to Lesson 2-1, also in Volume I, to see how the \" escape sequence translates into a double-quote character.

- ✔ The nearby sidebar about ASK.C contains more highlights of the program, all of which are introduced in *C For Dummies,* Volume I.

A useless batch file example for you

Batch files became a thing of the past with DOS, yet they aren't truly useless. I know people who still run DOS menu systems on their Windows 95 computers simply because it's much easier than using anything Windows has to offer. But I digress.

The following batch file takes advantage of the ASK utility you just wrote. It's merely a demo; it doesn't do anything other than prove that ASK really works.

You can type this batch file text in your text editor, if you like. It's just text, though I'd double-check your typing if you've never messed with batch files.

Save the file to disk, naming it TEST.BAT or something similar (though it must have the BAT extension for DOS to run it):

```
@echo off
cls
ASK Do you want to format your hard disk?
IF ERRORLEVEL 2 GOTO NO
IF ERRORLEVEL 1 GOTO YES
GOTO END
:YES
ECHO Proceeding with format...
ECHO (Just kidding)
GOTO END
:NO
ECHO Okay, then. I won't. You're safe.
:END
```

Run the batch file program:

```
C> TEST
```

Press Enter and you see:

```
Do you want to format your hard disk? (Y or N)?
```

Try pressing any key other than Y or N. Nothing happens. That's the ASK utility in action.

If you press Y, you see the formatting message displayed (though your disk won't be formatted; that's for you to add later on your own). If you press N, the program gracefully exits without doing anything.

- ✔ Of course, it doesn't do anything to begin with, either.
- ✔ I wrote a nice book about batch files, titled *Advanced MS-DOS Batch File Programming*. It may still be in print, though you probably will have better luck picking it up on the remainder shelf at your bookstore or at the used-book booth at a computer show. Good luck!

Lesson 8-5 Quiz

1. How is } related to the exit command?

   A. Over a period of millions of years, the primitive } evolved into the exit command, though some of the } characters also evolved into monkeys.

   B. Both can be used to end a C program.

   C. The exit command ends a C program, and the final curly bracket in the main function also ends a program.

   D. The exit command does not require a curly bracket.

2. What value does the following exit command return to the operating system?

   ```
   exit(ZERO);
   ```

   A. The value zero.

   B. The value of zoro.

   C. The value of Zira.

   D. The value of the ZERO thing.

3. What happens if the following `return` statement is replaced by the `exit` command?

```
return(c);
```

   A. The `exit` command returns the value of c to the calling function.

   B. There's no difference.

   C. The program quits rather than return the value of c.

   D. You can't tell without looking at the rest of the code.

4. What color is coffee mold?

   A. Green.

   B. Beige.

   C. White.

   D. Black, so you can never tell.

Chapter 8 Final Exam

1. The `kbhit` function can be used to

    A. Find out whether any keys be hit.

    B. Find out how many kilobytes of brain cells are lost when someone hits you in the head.

    C. Find out how many keys have been pressed.

    D. Sell hit toys through the KayBee toy store chain.

2. One problem with `kbhit` is that

    A. It doesn't really *read* any characters from the keyboard.

    B. It can be used only in `while` loop text.

    C. It returns TRUE when the condition is really FALSE.

    D. It works only for keyboard keys, not for piano keys or car keys.

3. What makes toast turn brown?

    A. The toaster.

    B. The heat inside the toaster.

    C. The bread almost burning.

    D. A chemical in the bread changing color.

4. Which of the following functions raises 6 to the BAZILLIONTH power?

    A. `6^1,000,000,000,000,000,000,000,000,000,000,000`

    B. `6^BAZILLION`

    C. `6BAZILLION`

    D. `pow(6,BAZILLION)`

5. Which of the following symbols calculates the square root in C?

    A. √

    B. ^

    C. ~

    D. @

    E. None of the above.

6. If variable a is equal to 10, what happens to the variable x after the following statement?

```
x=++a;
```

A. The value of a is added to the value of x.

B. The value of a is added to the value of x twice.

C. The value of a is increased and then given to the value of x.

D. The value of a is given to the value of x.

7. Suppose that variable x is equal to 100. What are the values of variables x and y after the following statement?

```
y = ++x++;
```

A. x equals 101, and y equals 102.

B. x equals 100, and y equals 101.

C. x equals 102, and y equals 101.

D. The compiler generates an error.

8. Define California.

A. The fruit-and-nut state.

B. A fictitious paradise.

C. They're there because they could go no farther west.

D. The pace setter for those without pacemakers.

9. The goto keyword is unnecessary because

A. Other loops do things better.

B. It promotes sloppy programming.

C. Most people mispronounce it.

D. It's not unnecessary, or else they wouldn't have included it.

10. What does code 0x0c do to your printer?

A. Places it in a state of agitated excitement.

B. Causes it to spew out a sheet of paper.

C. Switches it to "shred" mode.

D. Resets it.

11. True or False: Real pirates buried their treasure.

12. How does Windows read the code returned to it by the `exit` function?

   A. It reads it as an ERRORLEVEL value, like DOS does.

   B. Windows couldn't care less.

   C. The `exit` function works only for the DOS prompt.

   D. Code 255 causes Windows to display an `Abnormal Termination` error.

13. Big Ben is the name of a

   A. Clock.

   B. Tower.

   C. Bell.

   D. Wrestler.

Bonus question!

Which of the following is *not* the title of a book published in 1995?

   A. *How to Avoid Huge Ships.*

   B. *The Joy of Chickens.*

   C. *Amputee Management: A Handbook.*

   D. *Highlights in the History of Concrete.*

   E. *Big and Very Big Hole Drilling.*

   F. *Simply Bursting — A Guide to Bladder Control.*

   G. *Proceedings of the Second International Workshop on Nude Mice.*

   H. All of the above.

   I. None of the above.

Chapter 9
Arrays and Strings and Things

• •

Lessons in This Chapter

▶ Asking for arrays

▶ Death arrays (strings and arrays)

▶ More input function madness

▶ Arrays of some sort

▶ Strings and characters

▶ Weaving a tapestry of text

▶ String-manipulation bedlam

▶ Arrays from beyond the first dimension

Programs in This Chapter

SAFE.C	HURRAY.C	LOTTO.C	SUSHI.C
WHORU.C	WHORU2.C	INPUT1.C	INPUT2.C
INPUT3.C	INPUT4.C	INPUT.C	SORTME.C
SORTBIG.C	SHOUT!.C	SCRAMBLE.C	SCRAM.C
INTRO.C	PASSWORD.C	RUDEDOS.C	BMUD.C
GRID.C	DWARFS.C	NAMES.C	DWARFS2.C

Vocabulary Introduced in This Chapter

`[]`	`strlen`	`putchar`	`isalpha`
`strcpy`	`strncpy`	`strcspn`	`strcmp`

• •

*D*o strings exist? Do you exist? Does anything exist?

Most things do exist. You exist too. Just try to prove to the IRS that you
don't exist, and it will offer a flood of evidence to the contrary. Strings,
however — they don't exist. In C, you have single-character variables and
you have numeric variables. Strings? Ha! They hold no significance in the
cosmic theme of things.

Oh, just toss it all out the window and take up gardening!

Actually, strings exist. They are merely an arrangement of single-character variables, all lined up in a contraption called an *array*. You can do the same with numeric variables too, creating arrays of them for various and sundry purposes. This chapter uncovers the mystery of arrays, with a concentration on strings. (C has no woodwinds, brass, or percussion instruments.)

Lesson 9-1: Asking for Arrays

Array is one of those words that loses its meaning the more you say it. Array. A ray. Air ray. Hairy. Hooray!

An array is nothing more than an organized collection of stuff. Suppose that you're decorating cookies, and, because you're obsessively neat, you have arranged them into two lines: one ready for decorating and another already decorated. Nerdy folk would say that you have two *arrays* of cookies. C programmers would say that you have an *initialized array* (decorated cookies) and an *uninitialized array* (undecorated cookies). Me? I would just eat the cookies and suck the raw frosting from the decorating tube.

What does all this mean? Nothing more than identifying a collection of stuff with the word *array*.

- An array is a collection of stuff, like a row of cookies or a list of items in a column or a line of cars backed up seven miles on the freeway.
- You can cheerfully ignore the terms *initialized* and *uninitialized* for now.
- Arrays open up the heretofore unexplored region of database programming in C. Because an array is essentially a collection of stuff in a database, you can do databasey things with arrays: List them, sort them, unsort them, create bogus databases for the IRS, and so on.
- It's the database manipulation that makes arrays so handy.

The whole deal with arrays

In the C language, an array is a collection of variables, all of the same type. You can have an array of integers, single-character variables, floats, doubles, and so on.

Alas, you can't have an array of strings — not yet, anyway. You have enough to do with integer arrays to keep you busy for this lesson.

Suppose that a bunch of football jocks are standing in line at the school café. Since you're standing behind them, they'll probably hoard all the good food before you get there. But that's not the point. What you should notice instead are the numbers printed across the back of their jerseys.

Unbeknownst to the football players, integers are printed on their jerseys. (They know that they have numbers on their jerseys, but not all of them know that the numbers are integers.) Standing there, they make up, in a way, an integer array, which you could write like this:

```
16, 88, 45, 99, 6, 33
```

Hike!

You could also make an array from their names — a string array:

```
Sherman, Fernan, Hastings, Harrison, Best, Hayden
```

Then you could make an array from the first letter of their girlfriend's names:

```
S, E, K, K, K, K
```

(Kelly is very popular.)

Each of these three examples is an array. The examples are a collection of items all of the same type: integers, strings, and characters.

Now for the nerdy terms:

Element: Each item in an array is called an *element*. The array can have as many elements as it needs (although in your computer the true size is limited by how much memory your PC has). In the preceding example, each of the arrays contains six elements: six jersey numbers, six names, six girlfriend's initials.

(Yes, even though Kelly appears four times in the last array, the K still counts as four elements. Not all the elements in an array have to be different.)

Here's something weird:

Zero: The first element in an array is numbered zero. Normally, if C were the least bit normal, the first element would be one. After all, all humans begin counting things as "One, two, three. . . ." Because C has to be different, though, the first element is zero.

- C says, "Zero, one, two. . . ." Get used to it.

- Please don't run away screaming just yet.

- Arrays contain all the same type of variable: all integers, all characters, all floats — all the same.

- Each item in an array is an *element*.

- Not every element has to be different. You can have an array of 52 items that are all the number 12, and it's still an array.

- The first item in an array is number zero. This requirement is very weird and will toss you for a loop more than once during your C programming career.

- Quite a few things in your PC begin numbering at zero. For example, the first memory address in your computer is address zero (written as 0x00000). The first *argument* typed at the DOS prompt is referred to as argv[0], which is also an array, as described in Lesson 6-3 in *C For Dummies,* Volume I. Also gander at the PRINTME1.C program in Lesson 8-4. See how the first printer port in your PC (called LPT1) is really zero, or 0x00? LPT2, the second printer port, is value 0x01. See? I'm not making this stuff up either.

The element zero deal (which you don't have to read)

This element zero thing can drive you nuts, but don't let it. For example, the first jock in line has 16 on his jersey. That's element zero of the array. Here's how you could type that up in a nerdy C language-like way, assuming that the array is named jock_array and the element numbers are in square brackets:

```
jock_array[0] = 16;

jock_array[1] = 88;

jock_array[2] = 45;
```

```
jock_array[3] = 99;

jock_array[4] = 6;

jock_array[5] = 33;
```

Although this stuff may look complex, it's just a way to write down how each of the jock's jersey numbers would fit into an array. The zeroth (yes, that's a real word) element is 16; then 88, 45, 99, and 6; finally, the fifth element is 33. Though 33 is the sixth item in the array, in weirdo C it's referenced as item 5.

A simple program before you get too bored

An array can hold any series of numbers, such as the numbers in a safe's combination. The following program, SAFE.C, is the same program the manager at my local bank uses to remind herself how to open the Big Safe. (I'm reprinting this program with her permission; as long as you don't know that it's the Bank of America on First Street, she said that it would be okay.)

Carefully type this source code into your editor. The integer array, which is discussed in the following sections, is the only new item in there. For now, just type carefully, and you'll be okay:

Name: SAFE.C

```c
#include <stdio.h>

void main()
{
    int numbers[] = { 36, 24, 12 };

    printf("The combination for the safe:\n");
    printf("1. Turn to %i left.\n",numbers[0]);
    printf("2. Turn to %i right.\n",numbers[1]);
    printf("3. Turn to %i left, open.\n",numbers[2]);
}
```

Compile and run. Here's what you should see:

```
The combination for the safe:
1. Turn to 36 left.
2. Turn to 24 right.
3. Turn to 12 left, open.
```

The array stored the three numbers, and then various `printf` statements reached into the array to grab the numbers back out.

- ✔ Like any other variable, an array must be declared before you can use it. This subject is covered in the very next section.

- ✔ Arrays are declared with the same words as any other variable: `int` for integer arrays, `float` for floating-point number arrays, and so on.

- ✔ Square brackets are big in Array Land.

- ✔ Elements in an array are referred to by the array name and then the element number. This subject is covered later in this lesson, in the section "Referring to elements in an array."

Properly declaring arrays in C

Like everything else in C, you can't pluck an array from thin air. No, as with other types of variables, you must *declare* it and type it in a proper and cryptic manner along with any other variables you plan to use in your program.

An array in C can be declared in two ways, depending on whether the array is empty or full.

A full array is one that already has information in it, like the numbers array in the SAFE.C program. It's defined like this:

```
int jock_array[] = {16, 88, 45, 99, 6, 33};
```

Table 9-1 tells you how each item fits into the big picture. Basically, there are three things: the type of array, int (integer); the array name, jock_array; and the values assigned to that array. The whole thing ends with a semicolon, just as any variable declaration does.

Table 9-1	Items You Need for a Full (Initialized) Array
Cryptogram	*What It Does*
int	Defines it as an array of integers
jock_array[]	The name of the array (square brackets are required and should be empty); the compiler figures out the array's size for you
=	Says "Set the contents of the array equal to the following values"
{	Curly brackets contain the array's info
16, 88, 45, 99, 6, 33	Numbers, separated by commas, to put into the array
}	Final curly bracket
;	Semicolon at the end of the variable declaration

The other type of array in C is empty, one you create to be filled in later. It's defined this way:

```
float coworker_IQ[20];
```

Rather than have numbers or other data assigned to this array, it merely has a size specified; 20 elements, in this example. It means that the `coworker_IQ` array has room for as many as 20 floating-point numbers.

The following check marks should answer most of the questions buzzing around in your head right now:

✔ In both cases, the array is declared similarly to any other variable. First comes the variable type and then the variable name. The first array in the preceding example is an *int*eger array named `jock_array`. The second array is a *float* array named `coworker_IQ`.

✔ A full array is also referred to as an *initialized* array. It means that all the data — each element in the array — is already there.

✔ An empty array is referred to as an *uninitialized* array.

✔ For an initialized array, the values in the array are listed when the array is defined — just as you can define any variable with a preset value, as explained in Lesson 3-3 in Volume I. Each element appears in curly brackets separated by a comma.

✔ Love them curly brackets.

✔ Commas appear after each number in the array, except for the last one. You will forget this statement often, and the compiler may or may not warn you, but your program will definitely screw up.

✔ The last item in the array *does not* have a comma by it.

✔ As always, a variable declaration must end in a semicolon, no matter which type of array you define.

✔ For an uninitialized (or empty) array, you simply state how many elements you want in the square brackets. In the preceding example, the number of elements in the `coworker_IQ` array is set equal to 20; that array can have as many as 20 elements in it.

✔ Technically speaking, when you declare an array like this:

```
int chairs[12];
```

you're telling the compiler to set aside space for an array that contains 12 elements of integer number size. It's the same as though you were throwing a dinner party and invited 12 people — you would need a long table with 12 chairs. (And then pray that no more than 12 people show up and each of them needs only one chair on which to sit.)

✔ No, you cannot readily change an array's size; you must set the value when you write the program and hope that you set it big enough. This challenge is something C programmers wrestle with every day.

✔ The square brackets are empty when you declare an initialized array. Fortunately, the compiler is smart enough to figure out the array's size and set it for you automatically. In the following declaration:

```
char cards[] = {'A', 'J', 'Q', 'K'};
```

the compiler creates a single-character array named cards that can hold four elements. Then the characters A, J, Q, and K are stuffed into the array.

Referring to elements in an array

Each element in an array is its own variable. It has to be. Otherwise, you would never be able to pluck out any individual item in the array, and then, well, what would be the point?

To refer to any item in an array, you have to know the array's name and the element's number. The array's name is like any other variable name in C. The element number, however, is weird because the first element is zero, not one. When you know those two things, you just write down the array name, stick the element number between the square brackets, and — presto! — you have a variable just like any other.

In the SAFE.C program, for example, the first item in the array is referred to as numbers[0]. Even though a funky square bracket is in there, the compiler sees the thing as a single integer variable.

✔ You can use array items throughout your program just as you would use any variable.

✔ Assign a value to an array element just as you would assign any variable:

```
orbit[1] = 53.449;
```

or

```
election[2000] = 78123;
```

or

```
input[7] = getch();
```

✔ Even the element number can be a variable:

```
loop[x] = counter();
```

Here, variable x is used to indicate an element in the loop array, an element that has the value returned by the counter function.

Sticking stuff into an array (initializing it)

Here's a truly meaningless program for you. It creates an empty (uninitialized) array that can hold 20 elements (numbered 0 through 19, natch). Then the program fills those elements with the numbers 1 through 20, then 20 through 1, and then random numbers.

Carefully type this program into your editor. It uses the random-number-generation routines from the program RANDOM4.C in Lesson 5-7 in Volume I. You can cut and paste that chunk of text (the rnd and seedrnd functions). Although the source code seems rather long, it's really the same for loop repeated three times. Cut and paste!

Name: HURRAY.C

```c
#include <stdio.h>
#include <stdlib.h>
#include <time.h>              //for seeding randomizer

#define ELEMENTS 20

int rnd(int range);
void seedrnd(void);

void main()
{
    int blorf[ELEMENTS];
    int x;

/* First pass, fill array with values 1 through 20 */

    printf("Initialize array from 1 to 20:\n");

    for(x=0;x<ELEMENTS;x++)
    {
        blorf[x] = x+1;
        printf("%i\x20",blorf[x]);
    }

/* Second pass, fill array with values 20 through 1 */

    printf("\nAnd now from 20 to 1:\n");
```

(continued)

(continued)

```
    for(x=0;x<ELEMENTS;x++)
    {
        blorf[x] = 20-x;
        printf("%i\x20",blorf[x]);
    }

/* Final pass, fill array with random values */

    printf("\nAnd now random numbers:\n");

    for(x=0;x<ELEMENTS;x++)
    {
        blorf[x] = rnd(20)+1;
        printf("%i\x20",blorf[x]);
    }

}

int rnd(int range)
{
  int r;

  r=rand()%range;                //spit up random number
  return(r);
}

void seedrnd(void)
{
  srand((unsigned)time(NULL));
}
```

Double-check your work. An error is bound to be in there somewhere — a missing semicolon or comment character.

Compile and run.

Here's the result:

```
Initialize array from 1 to 20:
1 2 3 4 5 6 7 8 9 10 11 12 13 14 15 16 17 18 19 20
And now from 20 to 1:
20 19 18 17 16 15 14 13 12 11 10 9 8 7 6 5 4 3 2 1
And now random numbers:
7 11 3 11 17 18 16 16 9 7 5 19 12 20 13 1 13 2 4 8
```

BLOW BY BLOW

Soothing words for the harried HURRAY.C program

Like most long programs, the HURRAY.C program contains a great deal of repetition. The idea is to fill the array and then display the results. Normally, your program might fill an array only once, either by itself or with user input. The array's contents may change, but probably not as shown in HURRAY.C.

The stdlib.h and time.h header files are included for the rnd and seedrnd functions, which are covered in Lesson 5-7 in Volume I. Notice that those functions are properly prototyped; refer to Lesson 5-1.

The define directive is used to set the size of the array, by assigning the shortcut word ELEMENTS to that value:

```
#define ELEMENTS 20
```

This shortcut is used throughout the program to represent the array's size. Oh, you could use the value directly, but by using the define directive, you can globally change the array size without having to go out and hunt down those references in the program's every nook and cranny.

The following line creates an array of integers named blorf (the array is named "blorf," not the integers). The array can hold 20 elements, as indicated by the ELEMENTS shortcut word:

```
int blorf[ELEMENTS];
```

The for loop repeats 20 times, raising the value of variable x from 0 to 19, which just also happens to be the way the elements are numbered in the array:

```
for(x=0;x<ELEMENTS;x++)
```

(See? Element zero *does* come in handy.)

Element x in the array is given the value of variable x plus one:

```
blorf[x] = x+1;
```

If x equals 0 (as it would the first time through the for loop), for example, element 0 of the array equals the value 1. Notice that the value of x is *not* incremented here. Incrementing x happens in the for loop. To display values 1 through 20, you must add 1 to the value of x. (Incrementing x is written as either x = x + 1 or x++.)

The printf statement displays element x's value for the blorf array:

```
printf("%i\x20",blorf[x]);
```

The value is displayed followed by the space character, \x20. Again, I do this because "%i " printed in a book doesn't make it clear whether a space follows the little i.

The second for loop reinitializes the array almost identically to the first for loop. The exception is the value assigned; it's 20 x, which puts values 20 through 1 into the array (the variable x loops from 0 through 19; 20 minus 0 is 1; 20 minus 1 is 19; and so on):

```
for(x=0;x<ELEMENTS;x++)
{
    blorf[x] = 20-x;
    printf("%i\x20",blorf[x]);
}
```

In the final for loop, random values from 1 through 20 are stuffed into the blorf array:

```
blorf[x] = rnd(20)+1;
```

Again, refer to Lesson 5-7 for details about the rnd(20)+1 construction.

The array named `blorf` is filled with three different sets of numbers, each of which can be changed like any other variable. See the previous sidebar, "Soothing words for the harried HURRAY.C program," for more detailed information about what's going on.

- ✔ Values can also be placed into an array by reading the information from the keyboard. You can use the `scanf` or `gets` functions for that; refer to Lesson 3-1 in Volume I for information about reading numerical values from the keyboard.

- ✔ Use `gets` to read information from the keyboard. More and more, I'm growing to hate the `scanf` function.

- ✔ Keep in mind that values read in from the keyboard must match the type of variable the array holds: `int`s for integer arrays, `float`s for floating-point arrays, and so on.

- ✔ The `#define` directive in this program sets the size of the `blorf` array to 20 elements. That's done so that the array size can be adjusted easily by editing that one line. Refer to Lesson 3-4 in Volume I for information about how handy the `#define` directive can be.

- ✔ The `\x20` escape sequence in the various `printf` statements inserts a blank (a space) between the array numbers. Refer to Table 2-1 in Volume I for more information about escape sequences.

An old but useful chestnut

The following program is a lottery-number picker, which is listed at the end of Volume I. Now that you're familiarizing yourself with arrays, the program should make a little more sense to you. It's listed next, minus the extensive comments from Volume I so that you can peruse the array aspects of the program:

Name: LOTTO.C

```
#include <stdio.h>
#include <stdlib.h>
#include <time.h>        //for the seedrnd() function

#define RANGE 50         //number of numbers
#define BALLS 6          //number of balls to draw
#define DELAY 1000000    //delay interval between picks

int rnd(int range);
void seedrnd(void);

void main()
```

```
{
  int numbers[RANGE]; //array that holds the balls
  int i,b;
  unsigned long d;     //delay variable

  printf("L O T T O    P I C K E R\n\n");
  seedrnd();           //seed the randomizer

/* initialize the array */

  for(i=0;i<RANGE;i++)        //initialize the array
      numbers[i]=0;

  printf("Press Enter to pick this week's numbers:");
  getchar();

/* draw the numbers */
  printf("\nHere they come: ");
  for(i=0;i<BALLS;i++)
  {
      for(d=0;d<=DELAY;d++);    //pause here

/* picks a random number and check to
see whether it's already been picked */

      do
      {
          b=rnd(RANGE);   //draw number
      }
      while(numbers[b]);  //already drawn?

      numbers[b]=1;       //mark it as drawn
      printf("%i ",b+1);  //add one for zero
  }
  printf("\n\nGood luck in the drawing!\n");
}

/* Generate a random value */

int rnd(int range)
{
  int r;
```

(continued)

(continued)

```
  r=rand()%range;          //spit up random number
  return(r);
}

/* Seed the randomizer */

void seedrnd(void)
{
  srand((unsigned)time(NULL));
}
```

Enter this source code into your editor (if you haven't already done so from Volume I). Compile and run.

```
L O T T O   P I C K E R

Press Enter to pick this week's numbers:
```

Press the Enter key.

```
Here they come: 35 11 49 34 26 37

Good luck in the drawing!
```

The program picks six numbers from 1 to 50 as your lucky lotto numbers this week. (You can change the range of numbers by entering a new value for the RANGE define, and you can choose more or fewer numbers by changing the BALLS define, both at the beginning of the source code.)

This lotto program works the same way any computer card game works. Like cards in a deck, balls in a lottery machine can be drawn only once. The object is not to generate the same random number twice. That is, you can't draw the same lotto ball, bingo ball, or card from a deck in the real world, so you shouldn't be able to do that in a computer program either.

The solution is to keep track of the numbers (cards or whatever) drawn by using an array. The array is initialized with all zeros to start, which is done in Lines 23 and 24 in LOTTO.C:

```
for(i=0;i<RANGE;i++)  //initialize the array
    numbers[i]=0;
```

Then, as the random numbers are drawn, a one is inserted into the array to indicate which numbers (cards, whatever) have already been used. The following snippet makes that happen:

```
do
{
    b=rnd(RANGE);          //draw number
}
while(numbers[b]);         //already drawn?

numbers[b]=1;              //mark it as drawn
printf("%i ",b+1);         //add one for zero
```

The variable b holds the number drawn, using the rnd() function introduced in Lesson 5-7 in Volume I. The rnd() function returns a value representing an element in the array. The do-while loop checks to see whether that value is equal to one — which is TRUE — if so, it keeps looping, generating new random numbers and checking the array for a zero or a one.

If the random number returned hasn't yet been drawn, the program continues; first, the value one (TRUE) is placed into the array with the numbers[b]=1; statement. That marks that number as "used." Then the number drawn is displayed on-screen. Note that the number displayed is b+1. That's because the rnd() function returns a value from zero through "RANGE." That's okay for filling the array, which also begins at element zero, but normally there's no zero ball in a lottery game.

The loop continues until the number of balls (represented by the shortcut word BALLS) has been drawn.

- ✔ All this nonsense is created to ensure that the same number isn't drawn twice. By sticking a 1 into the array, you ensure that that number isn't drawn again in your program.

- ✔ You could modify the LOTTO.C program to draw all 50 balls; just change the value of BALLS to 50 in the define statement. Notice that the program takes longer and longer to display the last few numbers as it waits for the random-number generator to produce a number that hasn't yet been drawn.

- ✔ Now you can write that card game! You need an array of 52 elements, each of which represents a card in the deck. You can use a do-while loop similar to the one in LOTTO.C to determine which cards have already been drawn.

- ✔ I could have initialized the array with values other than zero, and I could have used a value other than one to show that a ball had been drawn. In C, however, the values zero and one are typically used to represent FALSE and TRUE conditions, respectively. For more info, refer to Lessons 7-2 and 7-3 in Volume I.

✔ I've been called on this before. The value 1 is not *really* equal to TRUE in C. Any nonzero value could be taken to equal 1. This is a minor quibble, raised primarily by minor quibblers.

Lesson 9-1 Quiz

1. The first element in an array is

   A. The best element.

   B. Element numero uno.

   C. Element number one.

   D. The zeroth element.

2. *Zeroth* is a real word:

   A. TRUE.

   B. FALSE.

3. What can be said about the following?

```
int high_scores[] = { 99, 98, 99, 97};
```

   A. It's an integer array.

   B. The array has four elements.

   C. The array is named high_scores.

   D. Patrice Dabrowski was absent, so there is no 100 score.

   E. All of the above.

4. Which of the following statements defines a floating-point array that contains three elements?

   A. float ice_cream[3];

   B. float buoy[] = {1.0794, 33.0, 1678.5};

   C. float point[3] = { 1, 2, 3};

   D. float root_beer[2];

5. What was the name of Paul Bunyan's ox?

   A. Blue.

   B. Babe.

   C. Big Ox.

   D. Bovus.

Lesson 9-2: Death Arrays (Strings and Arrays)

All strings in C are basically single-character arrays. For example, the following string is just a bunch of single characters all marching one after the other:

```
sushi is mooshi
```

In Lesson 3-3 in *C For Dummies,* Volume I, you see the following variable declaration at the beginning of a program:

```
char menuitem[] = "Slimey Orange Stuff \"Icky Woka Gu\"";
```

Lo, it's a character array and also a string. You could do the same thing with `sushi is mooshi`:

```
char phrase[] = "sushi is mooshi";
```

You're essentially creating an array of single-character variables (`chars`). It's a string, and it's also an array. In fact, if you had lots of time to type, you could declare it as follows:

```
char phrase[] = { 's', 'u', 's', 'h', 'i', ' ', 'i', 's', '
', 'm', 'o', 'o', 's', 'h', 'i' };
```

Or you could even do the following, specifying the size of the array, which is redundant because the compiler does that for you anyway:

```
char phrase[16] = { 's', 'u', 's', 'h', 'i', ' ', 'i', 's',
' ', 'm', 'o', 'o', 's', 'h', 'i' };
```

Why 16 when the phrase is 15 characters long? Because every string in C ends in a NULL byte, character `0x00` (also written as `\0`). That's how C knows where to find the end of the string. Otherwise, it would keep looking for the NULL byte, scanning all through your PC's memory and crashing the program in a big, loud *thud!*

- ✔ See the next section for more information about the NULL byte.
- ✔ The entire string is referred to only by the array name; there's no need to specify the angle brackets when you refer to the string variable or array in the program. See ICKYGU.C in Lesson 3-3 in Volume I to find out how this stuff works.

- Single-character variables are declared using single quotes, not double quotes.

- Boy, isn't *sushi* hard to type?

Terminating a string (the NULL byte)

Don't call in Arnold! Strings in C can contain any number of characters — whatever you stick between the double quotes is part of the string. Even more than that: You can write a program to create a string that contains other, non-ASCII characters and control codes. C is very forgiving when it comes to stuffing things into strings.

The only character that doesn't live in a string is the NULL byte. That's character code zero (0x00), which the C language uses to mark the end of a string.

For example, consider this lesson's silly string *du jour:*

```
sushi is mooshy
```

This string is composed of 15 characters, including alphabetic characters and space characters. Although the string is 15 characters long, it occupies *16* bytes in memory. That's because the string has a NULL byte living at its end, right after the y in mooshy.

- All strings in C end in the NULL byte.

- The NULL byte is character code zero, written 0x00, or you can use the \0 escape sequence.

- You don't have to specify the NULL byte when you declare a string. The compiler automatically appends the NULL byte for you.

- At times, you do have to specify the NULL byte. I let you know when that happens. For declaring a string with double quotes (as is done throughout this chapter), you don't have to specify the NULL byte.

- You do have to set aside space for the NULL byte when you declare an empty string:

```
char input[80];
```

This string has room for only 79 characters; the 80th and last character *must* be the NULL byte.

- Your program goes nuts when a string goes off all loosey-goosey and forgets a NULL byte at the end. You may see a "NULL" type of error message, or your computer may grow stony and silent.

✔ Strings in C do not end with the Enter character. Although that may be true in other programming languages, in C the Enter character can be part of the string just like any other character.

✔ Even spaces in a string are part of the string. The string "sushi is mooshi" contains two spaces. Those spaces are as much characters in the string as the alphabetic characters. In fact, you can stock a string with just about any character except for the NULL byte; C doesn't really mind.

Dish me up some bait, mate

The following program draws out this sushi gag a little more. The array is declared, as shown in the preceding section, but then you get to see some strange things you can do with the string because, after all, it's really an array. The program uses a new string function, strlen, one of many fun string functions you read about later in this chapter.

Type this source code into your editor. See the nearby sidebar, "Some additional thoughts on SUSHI.C," for information about what the program does, though it's really similar to the integer array demos from the preceding lesson.

Name: SUSHI.C

```
#include <stdio.h>
#include <string.h>

void main()
{
    char phrase[] = "sushi is mooshi";
    int x,size;

    printf("\"%s\"\n",phrase);

    size = strlen(phrase);
    printf("That phrase is %i characters long.\n",size);

    for(x=0;x<size;x++)
        printf("phrase[%i] = '%c'\n",x,phrase[x]);

}
```

Function `strlen`

The `strlen` ("string length") function takes a look at a string or single-character array and returns the length — the number of characters in the string. The format:

```
v = strlen(string);
```

In this line, the value of v is equal to the number of characters in the string `string`. If `string` is "sushi is mooshi," then the value in v is 15, the number of characters in the string, including all characters in the string — even new lines and other weird stuff. It does not include the double quotes (which aren't part

of the string anyway), nor does it include the weird *NULL* character living in the caboose of every string in C.

For the `strlen` function to work, you have to include the STRING.H header file at the beginning of your source code. This popular header file contains lots of interesting string functions you probably will use from time to time.

If you forget the following line, your compiler gives you a giant "huh?" error when you try to link the program:

```
#include <string.h>
```

Compile and run. Here's the trite and predictable output:

```
"sushi is mooshi"
That phrase is 15 characters long.
phrase[0] = 's'
phrase[1] = 'u'
phrase[2] = 's'
phrase[3] = 'h'
phrase[4] = 'i'
phrase[5] = ' '
phrase[6] = 'i'
phrase[7] = 's'
phrase[8] = ' '
phrase[9] = 'm'
phrase[10] = 'o'
phrase[11] = 'o'
phrase[12] = 's'
phrase[13] = 'h'
phrase[14] = 'i'
```

The program mainly shows you the contents of each element in the `phrase` array, from 0 through 14 (15 elements). Of course, I don't really mean to bore you here. The purpose of this exercise becomes more apparent in the following section.

BLOW BY BLOW

Some additional thoughts on SUSHI.C

The STRING.H file is included so that you can use the `strlen` function later on. (The STRING.H file is mighty popular when you work with strings.)

The string array is declared like any string in C; the string's contents are held in double quotes. The program can then refer to the string by using the `phrase` variable name:

```
char phrase[] = "sushi is
   mooshi";
```

The integer variable `size` is set equal to the length of the string:

```
size = strlen(phrase);
```

That same variable is used in the following `for` loop to display each individual character in the string:

```
for(x=0;x<size;x++)
   printf("phrase[%i] =
   '%c'\n",x,phrase[x]);
```

The integer variable `x` is incremented from zero through the size of the string, minus one. It has to begin at zero because zero is the first element of the array. It prints the whole array because the `for` loop stops at exactly the string's length, thanks to the `size` variable.

✔ All strings in C are single-character arrays.

✔ The `strlen` function does not figure in the NULL byte when it gives you the length of the string. This behavior is logical because the NULL byte is not considered part of the string, just like the stop sign at an intersection is not considered part of the road.

✔ You can predefine any string in C by declaring it as an array. Use double quotes to enclose the string, just as you would in a `printf` or `puts` statement.

✔ You can also declare "blank" strings in C, a subject covered in the next section. This technique is similar to creating an empty array.

✔ As with all arrays, you can change the contents of a string array at any time.

TECHNICAL STUFF

Here's some extra credit for you. If you feel motivated, add the following code to the end of the program, just before the last curly bracket in the `main` function:

```
printf("Type a character and press Enter:");
phrase[9] = getchar();
printf("\n%s",phrase);
```

Compile and run. What you have done is read a character from the keyboard (*g*, for example) and then stick that character into the string. The final `printf` statement displays the result, something like

```
sushi is gooshi
```

Although the `getchar` function is inelegant, it's included with the STDIO.H file. You can use the `getch` function to read characters from the keyboard without pressing the Enter key, but you need the CONIO.H header file for that, as described in Lesson 3-6 in Volume I.

Foul ball!

Lesson 1-7 in Volume I introduces you to the program WHORU.C, which is pronounced "who-are-you-dot-see." Here's the source code again, just in case you loaned your Volume I to one of those people who never return things:

Name: WHORU.C

```c
#include <stdio.h>

void main()
{
  char me[20];

  printf("What is your name?");
  scanf("%s",me);
  printf("Darn glad to meet you, %s!\n",me);
}
```

The following variation on the program uses `gets` rather than `scanf`, which is more the way things operate in the real world:

Name: WHORU2.C

```c
#include <stdio.h>

void main()
{
    char me[5];

    printf("What's your name?");
    gets(me);
    printf("Darn glad to meet you, %s!\n",me);
}
```

You can edit the original WHORU.C source code into the new WHORU2.C source code. Basically, the size of the me array is changed to 5, and the `gets` function is used rather than `scanf` (which isn't anyone's favorite function).

Compile the program and run. Here's what you see:

```
What's your name?
```

Now type **Ishkabibble**, which may be your name already, but type it anyway, and then press the Enter key. You may see something like the following:

```
Darn glad to meet you, Ishkabibble
Divide Error
```

A `Divide Error` or `Divide Overflow` error may occur or maybe even no error at all. Even so, the result is considered the same; it's *unpredictable!* That's because you created a small-size array and filled it up with too much data. Technically, this is known as a *bounds error.*

Bounds errors occur when you try to stuff too much information into an array. For strings, this problem happens when a user enters more characters than the string array can hold.

You can get a bounds error on any program introduced so far in this book or in Volume I; whenever an empty string array is declared, if a user types more characters than the string can hold, weird things happen.

Exactly what weird things happen depends on each program. The program typically stops with some type of error. Some programs may run just fine. Some programs may lock up tight. It's *unpredictable!*

✔ The `gets` function, in addition to `scanf` and any other string-reading function in C, does not check to see whether the proper number of characters was typed. For that, you have to write your own function, which is covered next.

✔ The `gets` function is introduced in Lesson 2-4 in Volume I.

✔ The `scanf` function is introduced in, well, in Chapter 2 somewhere. I'd rather that you not use the `scanf` function, though. It's just too strange.

✔ Bounds checking is often something programmers never think about. Some older programs may not use it; a programmer instead creates a string array with, for example, 256 elements — more than anyone would ever type. The programmer thinks that the number is fine but never assumes that some doofus may actually put a program to the bounds-limit test. Just such a doofus did that with a common UNIX program a few years back. The famous Internet Worm virus worked because the old UNIX mail program didn't do any bounds checking on the e-mail address. In that case, the enterprising doofus overflowed the string variable with actual program code, which became the Internet Worm virus that shut down hundreds of computers across the world. Moral: Do your bounds checking!

Function putchar

The putchar function (pronounced "püt care," for "put character") is the opposite of the getchar function; getchar reads in a character from the keyboard, and putchar displays a character on-screen. Here's the format, though you probably could have guessed it:

```
putchar(c);
```

Here, c can be either a single-character variable or a character constant in single quotes.

The character represented by c is displayed on-screen:

```
putchar('c');
```

Most characters are displayed as symbols, just as you would expect. Some character codes, however (0 through 31), cause the cursor to jump around in various ways. These codes are listed later in this chapter, in Table 9-2. Most programs handle these characters in a special way, typically by using a switch-case loop, as demonstrated in the INPUT series of programs.

The putchar function is defined in the STDIO.H header file, which you must include at the beginning of your source code for everything to work:

```
#include <stdio.h>
```

Just as getchar has a companion, getch, the putchar function has a companion, putch. (Sounds like Klingon, eh?) This function is available in all Borland and Microsoft compilers and is really no different from putchar, though you do have to include the CONIO.H header file if you plan to use it instead.

Your very own string input function

The best and perhaps only way to do bounds checking on string input is to write your own string input function. That way, you're guaranteed that no one will ever overflow a single-character array with more characters than it was designed to hold.

Your primary goal behind writing your own input routine is to make sure that no more characters are typed than will fit in the array. You also have to scan for the Enter key, which is what tells you that a user is done typing. These are only two of many bothersome things that could cause you quite a headache, had I not already rounded them up in the following program, INPUT1.C (this program makes use of the putchar function, defined in the preceding "Function putchar" sidebar).

Be very careful of the indentation in this source code. It has many curly brackets to match up, and you may screw them up. (I did, when I first wrote it.) Otherwise, see the sidebar, "The secret inner workings of INPUT1.C," a few pages from here, for the program's details. This program basically handles text input from the keyboard, making sure that only the proper number of characters have been typed.

Enter the source code for INPUT1.C into your text editor. Double-check everything. Count them curly brackets!

Name: INPUT1.C

```c
#include <stdio.h>
#include <conio.h>

#define CR 0x0d        //carriage return
#define ESC 0x1b       //Escape key
#define TAB 0x09
#define LF 0x0a        //Line feed
#define BACKSPACE 0x08
#define NULL 0         //Empty character
#define TRUE 1
#define FALSE 0
#define LENGTH 15      //size of the string

void input(char *string, int length);

void main()
{
    char string[LENGTH];

    printf("What is your name?");
    input(string,LENGTH);
    printf("Darn glad to meet you, %s!\n",string);
}

void input(char *string,int length)
{
    int done = FALSE;
    int index = 0;
    char ch;

    string[0] = NULL;    //init the buffer

    do
    {
        ch = getch();

/* Check to see whether the buffer is full */
```

(continued)

(continued)

```
        if (index == length)
        {
            switch(ch)
            {
                case CR:
                    break;
                default:
                    ch = NULL;
                    break;
            }
        }

/* process the keyboard input */

        switch(ch)
        {
            case CR:          //Enter key
                string[index] = NULL;
                done = TRUE;
                break;
            case NULL:
                break;
            default:          //display & sto
                putchar(ch);
                string[index] = ch;
                index++;
                break;
        }
    }
    while(!done);

}
```

Compile. Fix up any messes: semicolons missing, semicolons rather than colons in the select-case structure, and those stupid middling curly brackets.

Run it.

```
What is your name?
```

Type **Bill** (even if it isn't your name) and press the Enter key. You see

```
What is your name?BillDarn glad to meet you, Bill!
```

Okay, so the program needs a little fixing. That will come. Before that's done, run the program again to test the bounds checking:

```
What is your name?
```

The size of the array is 15 characters. Type **I am the programmer**, which is more than 15 characters, to make sure that input stops properly:

```
What is your name?I am the progra
```

Can't type anymore? Good.

Press the Enter key to end the program.

The program doesn't display the "Enter" key because you haven't told it to do so. When you write your own input functions, you must handle *everything* at the keyboard.

- All strings in C end in the NULL byte, zero.

- Most programmers are named Bill.

- Table 9-2 shows you some of the stranger things that may happen when a user gets creative at the keyboard. Those characters behave as described in the table when you display them using the putchar function. Notice how some display strange characters and others control the cursor.

- The cursor can be controlled on the screen in other ways. Refer to the locate function in Lesson 5-6 in Volume I for the BIOS way to move the cursor around the screen.

- Refer to Lesson 5-3 in Volume I for more information about sending strings to functions, though you will never really understand it until you get into pointers, which I discuss in Chapter 10.

- Also see Lesson 5-3 for information about sending more than one value to a function.

- You don't have to return the string from the input function. This is another *pointer* trivia bit you find out about in Chapter 10.

- Refer to Lesson 7-5 in Volume I for a review of the switch-case structure.

- Lesson 7-3 discusses the while true (or "while not done") type of loop shown in INPUT1.C.

- Appendix B in Volume I lists the codes for the Enter key (CR for carriage return in the program), Escape, Tab, Backspace, and other keys on your keyboard. Yeah, I know that they're defined and not yet used in the program, but in later versions they are.

✔ String arrays that store keyboard input are often called buffers. A *buffer* is merely a storage place in memory, which is all any array is. You may say, in a whimsical way, "This program checks the size of the input buffer to prevent overflow." It just means that you're making sure that a user doesn't type more characters than will fit in the array. Nerdy, huh?

✔ You continue to modify and spruce up this program in the next lesson.

Table 9-2	Weird Codes You Can "Display" On-Screen	
Code	*Key(s)*	*What It Displays or What Happens*
0	Ctrl+@	Nothing (typically); NULL byte
1	Ctrl+A	☺
2	Ctrl+B	☻
3	Ctrl+C	♥
4	Ctrl+D	♦
5	Ctrl+E	♣
6	Ctrl+F	♠
7	Ctrl+G	Beeps the speaker
8	Ctrl+H (Backspace)	Moves cursor back one character (does not erase)
9	Ctrl+I (Tab)	Moves cursor forward to next tab stop or forward eight spaces
10	Ctrl+J	Line feed; moves cursor down one line
11	Ctrl+K	♂
12	Ctrl+L	♀; form feed on most printers and clears screen on some terminals
13	Ctrl+M (Enter)	Carriage return; moves cursor to beginning of line
14	Ctrl+N	♪
15	Ctrl+O	☼
16	Ctrl+P	►
17	Ctrl+Q	◄
18	Ctrl+R	↕
19	Ctrl+S	‼

Code	Key(s)	What It Displays or What Happens
20	Ctrl+T	¶
21	Ctrl+U	§
22	Ctrl+V	❑
23	Ctrl+W	↧
24	Ctrl+X	↑
25	Ctrl+Y	↓
26	Ctrl+Z	→; end-of-file marker in DOS
27	Ctrl+[(Escape)	←
28	Ctrl+\	∟
29	Ctrl+]	↔
30	Ctrl+^	▲
31	Ctrl+_	▼

The secret inner workings of INPUT1.C

This program is basically a modification of the WHORU.C and WHORU1.C (refer to Volume I) programs. The only difference is the addition of the input function, which reads a string of text from the keyboard and stuffs it into a character array (string variable). The function is protoyped at the beginning of the program:

```
void input(char *string, int
   length);
```

The asterisk before the string variable identifies it as a pointer variable, which is mainly how strings are passed to functions. (Secretly, only the string's memory location is passed, which is all the program needs to know.) The integer variable length is what tells the input function the maximum number of characters to get and stuff into the array.

The done variable is used to track whether the do-while loop is finished:

```
int done = FALSE;
```

As it starts, the do-while loop must work at least once because done is equal to FALSE and, therefore, the loop isn't done.

The index integer variable keeps track of two things at the same time — how many characters were typed and the array element in which to stuff the characters typed at the keyboard:

```
int index = 0;
```

(continued)

(continued)

The `index` variable is preset to zero, indicating the first element in the array, which is also the first character typed at the keyboard. This variable is incremented as more characters are typed.

Because a user may type nothing at all, the string variable must start out initialized to nothing. You do this by sticking a single NULL byte (zero) at the start of the array:

```
string[0] = NULL;    //init the
                     //buffer
```

If you don't do this, the array contains random characters in memory; if a user doesn't type anything, random "garbage" text may appear.

Inside the massive `do-while` loop, a character is read from the keyboard:

```
ch = getch();
```

First, an `if` test is done to see whether the array is full. The value of the `index` variable (which holds the number of characters typed) is compared to the size of the string array:

```
if (index == length)
```

If the values are equal, meaning that the array is full, really only one character can be typed: Enter, to end input. A `switch-case` structure tests that condition:

```
switch(ch)
{
    case CR:
        break;
    default:
        ch = NULL;
        break;
}
```

If Enter (CR) is pressed, the key is passed on through the rest of the function. Otherwise, the key (`ch`) is replaced with the NULL byte, which tells the rest of the function that nothing was read from the keyboard — after all, the array is full and nothing *can* be read from the keyboard.

The main `switch-case` structure is what really handles keyboard input. First, special characters are checked:

```
case CR:          //Enter key
        string[index] = NULL;
        done = TRUE;
        break;
```

If the Enter key is pressed, input is over. The NULL byte is placed at the end of the string, the `done` variable is set equal to `TRUE`, and the loop stops. The string is then ready for use by the rest of the program:

```
case NULL:
        break;
```

If the NULL key was entered, meaning that the array is full, nothing is done. A `break` command causes the loop to repeat, scanning for more characters. (This really happens only when the array is full and the silly user hasn't yet pressed the Enter key.)

The `default` condition is where whatever character was typed is displayed and then stored in the array:

```
putchar(ch);
```

The `putchar` function displays the character on-screen.

The character is then stored in the array.

```
string[index] = ch;
```

The `index` variable is then incremented so that it now points at the next element in the array:

```
index++;
```

If the first character typed is a B, it's stored in element zero of the array and the `index` variable is then incremented to point at element two. (Remember that the object of this routine is to make sure that only a certain number of characters are stored in the character array. The `index` variable is what keeps track of that number.)

Lesson 9-2 Quiz

1. A string in C is merely

    A. A thin piece of thread.

    B. A single-character array.

    C. A double-character array.

    D. A thin piece of character array.

Questions 2 and 3 refer to the following string declaration:

```
char whine[] = "I want a fur coat";
```

2. How many characters are in the string `whine`?

    A. Trivial question; the compiler figures it out for you.

    B. You could also use the `strlen` function to find out.

    C. Seventeen.

    D. All of the above.

3. What happens after the following statement?

```
whine[13] = 'b';
```

    A. The string is altered.

    B. Some idiot now wants a fur *boat*.

    C. The 13th element of the string, presently `c`, changes to a `b`.

    D. After this statement, the next statement in the program is executed, or, if the program is done, control returns to DOS or Windows.

4. What is bounds checking?

    A. Lining up the bumper of Dad's car with the Fulkerson's tree to see whether there are any foul balls.

    B. Checking to make sure that a character array is stuffed only with characters.

    C. Making sure that a user doesn't type more characters than a string can hold.

    D. Leaving your bounds with the nice lady at the front of the restaurant in exchange for a claim ticket.

Bonus question!

Which of the following is the best determination of a quality fruitcake?

A. Total mass.

B. Age in dog years.

C. Relative hardness on the Mohs scale.

D. Whether it was cooked by human labor or formed through some type of geological process.

Bonus bad joke!

Two strings go into a bar. The bartender shouts out, "Hey! We don't serve strings! You strings get out of here." So the strings leave. But then one of them gets an idea and ties a knot in himself and frays his ends. He walks back into the bar. The bartender shouts again, "I just told you to get out of here! You're a string." But the string said, "No, I'm a frayed knot."

Lesson 9-3: More `Input` Function Madness

Burdening yourself with writing all your program's input routines has its advantages and disadvantages.

As an advantage, you never have to worry about someone typing more input than your program was designed to accept. Yes, it's that bounds-checking nonsense again. The `input` function you're introduced to in the preceding lesson does a fair job of bounds checking for you.

The disadvantage is that you must take care of *everything* in your input routine. For example, when users press the Enter key, they expect a certain Enter-key-reaction on-screen. That is what you must take care of yourself.

The old carriage-return/line-feed business

When you press the Enter key, you expect one of two things to happen. First, you expect that the program will accept, swallow, and digest whatever it is you typed. This, the INPUT1.C program does fine. The second thing you expect — that the cursor will hop down to the beginning of the next line — doesn't yet happen in INPUT1.C. That's because, when you write your own input routine, you must *make* it happen. You are the *programmer,* remember?

In most text-based programs, pressing the Enter key produces what's known as a CR-LF, a carriage return (CR) and line feed (LF). This is old typewriter lingo. Pressing the carriage return used to mean whacking the carriage-return bar on a typewriter, which brought the carriage back to the first column on the page. The line feed referred to the second part of that action, where the platen rolled up a line so that you could begin typing again — without typing over your work. The same thing is necessary on a computer screen.

On your PC's display, the CR character is code 13, or 0x0d in hexadecimal. This code is produced when you press the Enter key. In fact, in the source code for INPUT1.C, you see it defined at the beginning of the program:

```
#define CR 0x0d  //carriage return
```

Press the Enter key, and the getch function returns that value.

The LF, line feed, character is code 10, or 0x0a in hex. This code is produced by pressing the Ctrl+J key combination on your keyboard. (J is, coincidentally, the tenth letter of the alphabet; refer to Table 9-2.) It's also defined at the beginning of the INPUT1.C source code:

```
#define LF 0x0a  //line feed
```

Problem: Pressing the Enter key does only half the job. As the programmer, it's up to you to supply — or rather, *display* — the line-feed character on-screen. That way, the program does what it's expected to do.

- ✔ You don't pronounce CR-LF as "curliff." It's "carriage return – line feed."

- ✔ Displaying the CR code, 0x0d, on-screen causes the cursor to jump to the beginning of the line.

- ✔ Displaying the LF code, 0x0a, on-screen causes the cursor to hop down a line of text.

- ✔ The Enter key produces only the CR character. You must display the LF on-screen (if that's what you want) in your source code. This process is demonstrated in the next section.

- ✔ The CR always comes first. Though you could LF and then CR, it's traditionally done CR and then LF.

- ✔ This CR-LF stuff is specific to the PC. On some UNIX systems, only the CR is required; the computer interprets code 13 (0x0d) as moving the cursor to the beginning of the line *and* down one line. That's why some text you may have downloaded from the Internet appears all on one line when you display it on your PC screen; it's missing line-feed characters.

Sprucing up your input *routine*

Return to your editor and load the INPUT1.C source code.

Scroll down to line 55 or so, where you see the `case CR:` statement in the middle of the `input` function. (It's the second `case CR:` statement.) Here's what it should look like:

```
case CR:          //Enter key
   string[index] = NULL;
   done = TRUE;
   break;
```

Change that chunk of code by adding the following two lines after `case CR:`

```
putchar(ch);
putchar(LF);
```

These lines display the carriage-return character, held in the `ch` variable, and then the line-feed character, `LF`. That chunk of code should now look like this:

```
case CR:          //Enter key
   putchar(ch);
   putchar(LF);
   string[index] = NULL;
   done = TRUE;
   break;
```

Save the source code to disk under a new name, INPUT2.C.

Compile and run.

Here's what you may see as the output:

```
What is your name?George McFly
Darn glad to meet you, George McFly!
```

The program behaves as you would expect: Pressing the Enter key drops the cursor down to the beginning of the next line. But this isn't the only improvement necessary to the program.

(Refer to the preceding lesson for the full details of the INPUT1.C program.)

Here's what happens inside the `case CR:` part of the program — the thing you just modified:

```
case CR:          //Enter key
```

This part of the code is executed only when a user presses the Enter key. That means that he or she is done with the input. First, display the carriage return, which just happens to be in the `ch` variable:

```
putchar(ch);
```

Second, display the line-feed character, code 0x0a, which is referenced by the `LF` shortcut word:

```
putchar(LF);
```

Third, because input is done, you have to mark the end of the string. You do this by putting a NULL byte (character code 0x00) at the end of the string. You do not put a carriage return there because in C the NULL byte marks the end of the string:

```
string[index] = NULL;
```

Finally, the loop ends by setting the `done` variable equal to TRUE and breaking the `switch-case` structure:

```
done = TRUE;
break;
```

- ✔ The NULL byte, character code 0x00, is what ends a string in C.

- ✔ If you want to include the carriage-return character in your string, you can do so, of course. For this program, it's not necessary.

- ✔ If you did include the carriage-return character in your string, you still have to tack on a NULL byte at the end of the array.

- ✔ It's not a string without that NULL byte.

- ✔ The \n escape sequence produces both a CR and an LF on your screen. You could replace both the extra lines added to the program with the following, if you like:

```
putchar('\n');
```

On the screen, this line has the same effect as displaying the CR and then LF codes. In fact, it makes the program more compatible with some UNIX computers, where the LF would be displayed as an extra blank line and just annoy the boogers out of everyone.

Taking care of Backspace

Go ahead and run the INPUT2.C program again:

```
What is your name?
```

Now type **Sylvester**, but don't press Enter yet:

```
What is your name?Sylvester
```

Oops! Your name is really Bud. Better backspace over Sylvester and type Bud.

Press the Backspace key to erase Sylvester and then type **Bud**.

Oops! You can't do it! The cursor is stuck under the V in Sylvester. In fact, you can't type anything now — you can only press the Enter key. Why? Because, according to the program, you have already used up your 15 characters. Yes, the INPUT2.C program counts the Backspace key as a character and stores it in the array. This probably isn't what you intended.

Press Enter to end the program:

```
Darn glad to meet you, Syl!ester
```

Ugh.

Just as users expect a certain reaction from the computer when the Enter key is pressed, they also expect a certain reaction from the Backspace key: They expect the cursor to move backward and gobble up the preceding character. In your program, you have to not only "display" the backspace character but also adjust the value of the index variable to account for characters being removed from the array. Not a major job, but something that must be done.

Load the source code for INPUT2.C into your editor.

Add the following new case statement in the last switch-case structure (around Line 61). Put it between the case CR: and case NULL: statements:

```
case BACKSPACE:
  putchar(ch);
  putchar(' ');
  putchar(ch);
  index--;
  break;
```

The BACKSPACE shortcut word is defined early in the program, set equal to the backspace character code, 0x08. Then the program uses the putchar function to display the backspace character. That action backs up the cursor but does not erase. The next putchar displays a space character, which erases whatever's on-screen. Then another putchar displays the backspace code again. Three steps, but the screen is erased.

Finally, the index variable is decremented, which backs it up one spot in the array — exactly what's happening visually on-screen, but this is for character storage in the array. The break statement then breaks the switch-case structure, and the program loops again, looking for more characters.

Enough explanations!

Save the source code to disk as INPUT3.C. Compile. Run:

```
What is your name?
```

Type **Sylvester**. Don't press Enter:

```
What is your name?Sylvester
```

Back up and erase Sylvester. Then type **Bud**:

```
What is your name?Bud
```

Press Enter:

```
Darn glad to meet you, Bud!
```

- ✔ The backspace character code, 0x08, moves the cursor back one space on the screen. It does not erase characters; it only moves the cursor backward.

- ✔ Most programs display three characters when you press the Backspace key: backspace, to back up; the space character, to erase; and then backspace again to back up again.

- ✔ Refer to Lesson 4-7 in *C For Dummies,* Volume I, for information about the -- (decrementing) operator.

- ✔ Pressing the Backspace key backs up and erases characters on the screen but not in the array. It could, but it doesn't have to. The reason is that new characters that are typed automatically replace the older, erased characters still living in the array. When a user presses the Enter key, a NULL byte is tacked on to the end of the string anyway. Yup, the program handles the whole deal rather nicely.

Move 'em on back — whoa!

Here's another wrinkle — another nut in the bag you must deal with when you write your own input functions. Run the INPUT3.C program again:

```
What is your name?
```

Now do something that only a six-year-old would do: Start pressing the Backspace key to see what happens.

Slowly, the prompt disappears. Not only that — internally, the `index` variable is being decremented from zero. Cripes! What could it be? If you press Backspace four times, the value of the `index` variable could be 65,531! Or –4! Where does the program store characters when the `index` variable is that huge?

The answer: Don't think about it! The program will probably crash because — and you probably didn't see this coming — you didn't do bounds checking.

Yes, you already have bounds checking on the high end: You still can't fill the array with more characters than it was designed to hold. But you haven't yet checked to see whether the array is empty and the user presses the Backspace key. Ugh. More coding.

Just press the Enter key to quit the program. It may hang your computer or shut down the program's window in Windows 95. Restart your PC if you need to. I know — that's a stupid thing for me to put in a book, but get used to this resetting nonsense if you ever plan to write any programs on your own.

To finish the Backspace job, load the INPUT3.C source code into your editor and focus your eyeballs on the `case BACKSPACE:` part of the code.

The program should not process the Backspace keystroke if nothing has been typed. That condition can be checked by testing to see whether the value of the `index` variable is equal to zero. Modify the `case BACKSPACE:` part of the code to read this way:

```
case BACKSPACE:
  if (index==0)
  {
      break;
  }
  else
  {
```

```
        putchar(ch);
        putchar(' ');
        putchar(ch);
        index--;
        break;
    }
```

Yes, it's your old pal, `if-else`. If the `index` variable is equal to zero, a `break` is executed and the program's loop spins again — nothing happens! Otherwise, if `index` isn't equal to zero (and you can then assume that something has been typed), the backspace routine is executed.

Save the changes to disk as a new file, INPUT4.C. Compile and run.

Now test the program to make sure that you can't over-erase. Type some text. Erase it. Type something else. Check the bounds on *both* sides of the input. Everything works peachy keen.

- ✔ You need *two* equal signs in an `if` comparison.

- ✔ Refer to Lesson 4-2 in Volume I for more information about `if-else` in C.

- ✔ Tables 3-1 and 3-2 in Volume I show the ranges for integer variables, such as `index`. When you decrement `index` below zero, its value is interpreted by the program as 64,000-something. Then, if you try to type a character, it's stored at some memory address way off in outer space. This situation is usually what causes the program to crash.

The final, final, final `input` *function*

The following is the full source code listing for the `input` function. Double-check it with what you have on disk as INPUT4.C:

Name: INPUT.C

```
#include <stdio.h>
#include <conio.h>

#define CR 0x0d       //carriage return
#define ESC 0x1b      //Escape key
#define TAB 0x09
#define LF 0x0a       //line feed
#define BACKSPACE 0x08
#define NULL 0        //Empty character
```

(continued)

(continued)

```
#define TRUE 1
#define FALSE 0
#define LENGTH 15    //size of the string

void input(char *string, int length);

void main()
{
    char string[LENGTH];

    printf("What is your name?");
    input(string,LENGTH);
    printf("Darn glad to meet you, %s!\n",string);
}

void input(char *string, int length)
{
    int done = FALSE;
    int index = 0;
    char ch;

    string[0] = NULL;    //init the buffer

    do
    {
        ch = getch();

/* Check to see whether the buffer is full */

        if (index == length)
        {
            switch(ch)
            {
                case CR:
                    break;
                default:
                    ch = NULL;
                    break;
            }
        }

/* Process the keyboard input */

        switch(ch)
```

```
    {
            case CR:            //Enter key
                putchar(ch);
                putchar(LF);
                string[index] = NULL;
                done = TRUE;
                break;
            case BACKSPACE:
                if(index==0)
                {
                    break;
                }
                else
                {
                    putchar(ch);
                    putchar(' ');
                    putchar(ch);
                    index--;
                    break;
                }
            case NULL:
                break;
            default:            //display & sto
                putchar(ch);
                string[index] = ch;
                index++;
                break;
        }
    }
    while(!done);
}
```

You use the input function elsewhere in this book, so be sure to save it somewhere for easy copying and pasting later.

Lesson 9-3 Quiz

1. What happens when you press the Enter key?

   A. It makes a clicking noise.

   B. It generates a carriage-return character, code 0x0d.

   C. It moves the cursor back to the beginning of the line.

   D. All of the above.

2. What's a line feed?

   A. Same thing as "letting out some slack."

   B. About twice the cost of chicken feed.

   C. The Line Feed button on your keyboard.

   D. A command that moves the cursor down one line, probably code 0x0a, but I'd have to look back in the lesson to know for sure.

3. How can the Backspace key be used to back up and erase?

   A. By pressing it.

   B. By pressing it down and somewhat to the left.

   C. Because the backspace code, 0x08, merely backs up the cursor, you also have to display a space to erase and then back up again. It's an annoying process, but it works.

   D. Back Space Key, Francis Scott's obscure younger brother, used to drive a milk wagon during the War of 1812.

4. What does the head writer do?

   A. He writes on people's heads.

   B. He writes about people's heads.

   C. He's the writer with the biggest head.

   D. He shifts all the blame and takes all the credit.

Bonus program! (Which you probably won't do anyway)

Most users expect the Escape key to act as a Cancel key. How you deal with the Escape key in your input function is up to you and what your program wants done. Although you could have the key erase all input and start over, it's more likely that a user would expect it to act as a Cancel key.

Your task: Write another edition of the INPUT.C program and call it INPUT5.C. Add a chunk of code to handle the Escape keystroke. You have to reprototype the input function so that it returns a value: TRUE if Escape was pressed to cancel or FALSE if Escape was not pressed. (A solution is in Appendix A in this book if you're too lazy to try it on your own.)

If you haven't taken a break since the beginning of this chapter, do so at once!

Lesson 9-4: Arrays of Some Sorts

Arrays are similar to databases, and one of the nifty database-like things you can do with them is sort them. Got a bunch of numbers? Hey, put 'em in order! A through Z. One through one bazillion. Although the computer does the work, it's up to you to tell it how to do the sorting.

Arrays can be sorted in lots of ways. This book shows you only a few of the simpler methods. Advanced C programming books show you some fast and nifty tricks for sorting. One of them is the QuickSort, which you can find in a highly technical book called *Algorithms in C*, by Robert Sedgewick (Addison-Wesley).

Sort me, quickly!

Even though lotto balls may be drawn in random order, they're always listed in ascending order in the next day's paper. Sounds like a complex job — something they probably have an intern do. But your computer is better than any old intern.

The following program is named SORTME.C. It contains the sort function, which organizes the elements in an array in ascending order:

Name: SORTME.C

```
#include <stdio.h>

#define SIZE 6        //size of the array

void sort(int *array,int size);

void main()
{
    int lotto[] = { 10, 48, 1, 37, 6, 24 };
    int i;

    printf("Here is the array unsorted:\n");

    for(i=0;i<SIZE;i++)
        printf("%i\t",lotto[i]);

    printf("\nAnd here is the sorted array:\n");

    sort(lotto,SIZE);
```

(continued)

(continued)

```
    for(i=0;i<SIZE;i++)
        printf("%i\t",lotto[i]);

}

void sort(int *array,int size)
{
    int a,b,temp;

    for(a=0;a<size-1;a++)
        for(b=a+1;b<size;b++)
            if(array[a] > array[b])
            {
                temp=array[b];
                array[b] = array[a];
                array[a] = temp;
            }
}
```

Carefully type the source code for SORTME.C into your editor. Unlike a true lotto program, this one uses a fixed array — same numbers every week. At least it sorts them in order. Save the file to disk and name it SORTME.C.

Compile and run.

Here's a sample of the output:

```
Here is the array unsorted:
10      48      1       37      6       24
Here is the sorted array:
1       6       10      24      37      48
```

Understanding how the sort function works isn't important. Well, maybe a little. All you have to know is that it works and how to use it. That's covered in the next section.

- ✔ Ascending. (uh-SEN-ding). *adj.* 1. Rising, going upward. From littlest to biggest. From A to Z. Like that.

- ✔ The \t escape sequence is used in the printf statements in SORTME.C to shove a tab between each of the numbers (refer to Table 2-1 in *C For Dummies,* Volume I).

✔ The sort subroutine essentially compares each element in the array with all the elements after it. If one is larger than the other, the values are swapped.

✔ If you like, you can merge the sorting routine in SORTME.C with the source code from LOTTO.C, introduced earlier this chapter. That way, you can display the results in newspaper-like ascending order — and save yourself the $5 per hour an intern would cost.

✔ I am informed by my journalist friends that interns actually work without pay. Strange world, eh?

Sorting things out

Sorting anything involves making comparisons. When you sort an array, you're comparing one value with every other value in the array. An if command and various symbols, such as <, >, ==, <=, and => make it all happen. And two for loops ensure that every value is compared to every other value in the array.

Hey! A figure would sure help!

Figures 9-1 through 9-5 graphically illustrate how the SORTME.C program goes about its business. In each progressing figure, the first (outer) for loop's variable a points to the first element of the array, and the second (inner) for loop's variable b points to the next (and subsequent) elements in the array. At each step of the process, a comparison is made: "Is 10 greater than 48?" If so, the numbers are swapped, which is what happens in the second step in Figure 9-1.

As soon as variable b equals the last element, the first (outer) for loop spins again, starting at the array's second element (see Figure 9-2). Again, each item in the array is compared with the second element, and, if one is greater than the other, they're swapped.

Figure 9-3 shows the next turn of the first for loop. More comparing. More swapping.

Figures 9-4 and 9-5 show the final two turns of the first for loop. Everything wraps up nicely — a fine denouement, if you ask me.

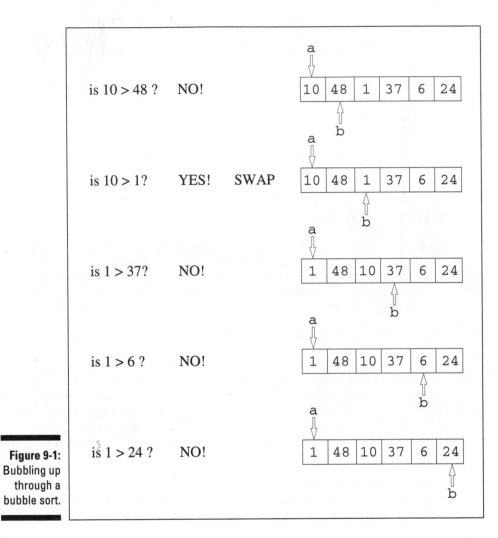

Figure 9-1:
Bubbling up
through a
bubble sort.

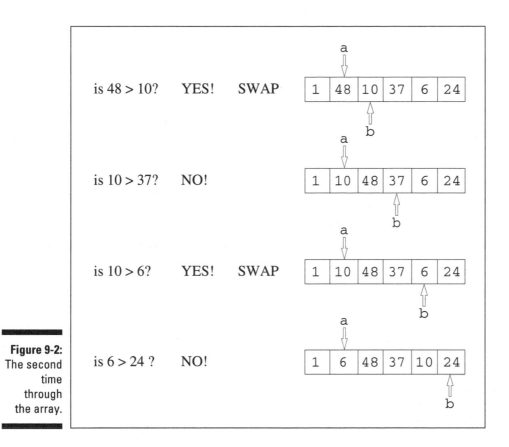

Figure 9-2:
The second time through the array.

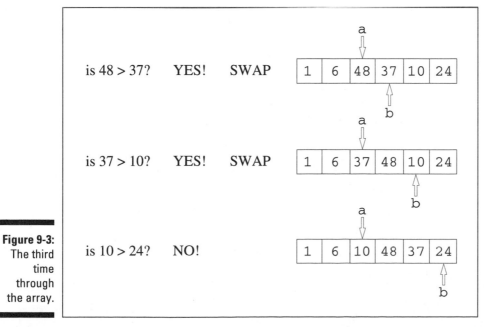

Figure 9-3:
The third time through the array.

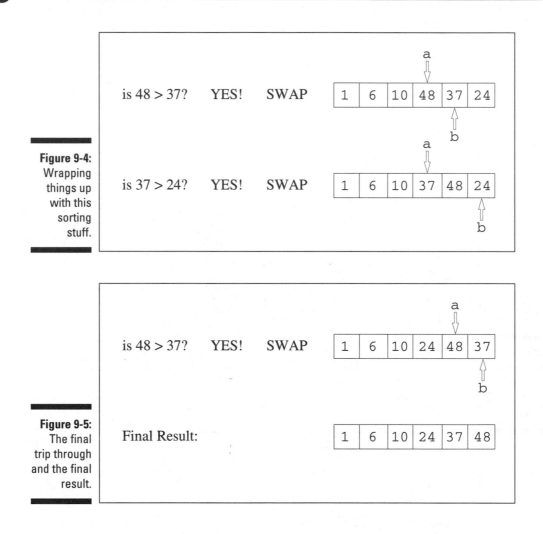

Figure 9-4:
Wrapping things up with this sorting stuff.

Figure 9-5:
The final trip through and the final result.

- *Denouement* (day-noo-MAH). *n.* The wrap-up or conclusion of events, like tying up the loose ends in a murder mystery. (Literally, it's French for "untying the knots." Oh, those French. . . .)

- The programs in this lesson (SORTME.C from the preceding section and SORTBIG.C in the following section) use what's called a *bubble sort,* named after those round things that spontaneously emerge from champagne.

- A bubble sort essentially compares each item in the array with all the other items, one at a time. In these examples, if one value is less than another, they're swapped in the array. Then the comparison continues until every value has been checked with every other value.

- Yes, it really works.

✔ You shouldn't waste brain molecules trying to suss out a bubble sort. All you have to do is copy the technique shown in the preceding `sort` function and employ it in your own programs. No license fee required. Offer valid in all 50 states, even Tennessee.

✔ Sorting a set of strings with a bubble sort is possible, but it's not something you can do at this stage of the game.

✔ Honestly, I have no idea why it's called a "bubble" sort.

✔ No, this has nothing to do with "bubble memory," whatever that is.

✔ The problem with the bubble sort is that it's slow. The program in the next section demonstrates that to you.

Sorting an obscenely huge series of numbers

Nothing impresses some bean counters like a computer's vast capability to sift through endless numbers. Number crunching, they call it. Sounds boring to me. But there's a point to be made here: A bubble sort sorts out — yessiree — thousands of numbers for you. It just doesn't do it quickly.

For example, the following program, SORTBIG.C, uses the `rnd` random-number-generation routine to fill an array with 100 random integers. Then the same bubble sort shown to you in SORTME.C is used to put the array in order.

Type this source code into your editor. You can copy and paste the `rnd` and `seedrnd` functions from the old RANDOM4.C program; also paste in the `sort` function from `sortme`. Remember to properly prototype each function — oh, just make it all look like the following listing, and you'll be fine:

Name: SORTBIG.C

```
#include <stdlib.h>
#include <time.h>          //for the seedrnd() function
#include <stdio.h>

#define SIZE 100           //size of the array

void sort(int *array,int size);
int rnd(int range);
void seedrnd(void);

void main()
```

(continued)

(continued)

```
{
    int r[SIZE];
    int i;

    printf("Here is the array unsorted:\n");

  seedrnd();              //seed the randomizer
    for(i=0;i<SIZE;i++)
    {
        r[i] = rnd(1000)+1;
        printf("%i\t",r[i]);
    }

    printf("\nPress Enter to see the sorted array:");
    getchar();
    printf("\n");

    sort(r,SIZE);

    for(i=0;i<SIZE;i++)
        printf("%i\t",r[i]);

}

void sort(int *array,int size)
{
    int a,b,temp;

    for(a=0;a<size-1;a++)
        for(b=a+1;b<size;b++)
            if(array[a] > array[b])
            {
                temp=array[b];
                array[b] = array[a];
                array[a] = temp;
            }
}

int rnd(int range)
{
  int r;
```

```
  r=rand()%range;              //spit up random number
  return(r);
}

/* Seed the randomizer */

void seedrnd(void)
{
  srand((unsigned)time(NULL));
}
```

Save the source code to disk as SORTBIG.C.

Compile and run.

Here's a sample of what you may see on your screen:

```
Here is the array unsorted:
868     320  756  44   106  192  596  909  287  100
977     40   842  424  993  380  502  17   924  727
500     792  112  367  184  53   501  219  759  741
813     241  392  87   816  41   858  99   238  578
725     379  732  435  204  527  603  732  473  467
670     973  546  612  243  671  572  67   653  754
854     672  824  583  568  2    301  206  605  109
647     666  837  766  695  315  622  107  292  93
901     334  237  175  24   403  266  830  911  919
336     851  251  788  917  721  157  818  460  283

Press Enter to see the sorted array:
```

Press the Enter key:

```
2       17   24   40   41   44   53   67   87   93
99      100  106  107  109  112  157  175  184  192
204     206  219  237  238  241  243  251  266  283
287     292  301  315  320  334  336  367  379  380
392     403  424  435  460  467  473  500  501  502
527     546  568  572  578  583  596  603  605  612
622     647  653  666  670  671  672  695  721  725
727     732  732  741  754  756  759  766  788  792
813     816  818  824  830  837  842  851  854  858
868     901  909  911  917  919  924  973  977  993
```

Now, before you run off and show your mother-in-law how quick your computer can sort a batch of nonsense numbers, return to your editor with the source code for SORTBIG.C.

Change Line 5 to read

```
#define SIZE 1000          //size of the array
```

That's 1,000 random numbers in the array.

Save. Compile. Run.

Maybe you'll notice it running slower on your PC; maybe you won't. Either way, a hint of a pause occurs after you press the Enter key.

To be certain that a bubble sort is really kind of slow, reedit the source code for SORTBIG.C and change Line 5 again, this time to 10,000:

```
#define SIZE 10000          //size of the array
```

Save it to disk. Compile. When you run it, a noticeable pause should occur after you press the Enter key. That's the computer sorting the array, which takes approximately five seconds on my Pentium 120; it could take minutes to do on a 386 or older 286 PC!

- Though the computer can sort, and can sort faster than any human, it takes time. Expect your programs to slow to a crawl when you have to sort a large amount of information. You may consider displaying a warning message about this situation to let users know that the PC isn't having an out-of-body experience.

- Refer to Lesson 5-7 in Volume I for more information about random numbers in C programs.

Lesson 9-4 Quiz

1. Sorting is done primarily by

   A. People at the post office.

   B. Little old librarians with 3 x 5 cards.

   C. Using the if command with one of those symbol things.

   D. Men, although 65 percent of women. . . . Wait. Oh, it says *sorting*. I thought it said *snoring*.

2. A bubble sort is

    A. A Hubble sort.

    B. A simple sort you can do in C because all you have to do is copy the proper routine from the programs listed in this lesson.

    C. Like, when you blow soap bubbles on a really cold day and, like, they freeze and then you can arrange them in order, y'know.

    D. I refuse to answer the question on the grounds that it's a fragment.

3. The problem with sorting huge arrays is that

    A. The array can get heavy and dent your hard disk.

    B. They eat you out of house and home.

    C. You have to write your source code using a very large font.

    D. Sorting them can take lots of time, and quality time at that.

4. Which of these does not belong?

    A. `if(array[a] > array[b])`

    B. Banana.

    C. Bicycle.

    D. Zebra.

Bonus question (worth .75 points)!

Cagney and Lacey. Which is which, and does it matter?

Lesson 9-5: Strings and Characters

Because a string is just a character array, it's quite possible to scan through it by using a `for` loop and mess with the characters in the string along the way. Well, maybe not exactly "mess," but you can churn through the string to see what's in it and, well, *modify* it, if you like.

To help you examine or change a string, you can use the smattering of C language functions defined in the CTYPE.H header file. All these functions are listed in the following two tables. Table 9-3 shows functions that can be used to check for certain characters with an `if` statement; Table 9-4 shows the functions you can use to modify characters in other devious ways.

It's utter character mayhem!

Table 9-3	CTYPE.H Test Functions
Function or Macro	**Returns TRUE When Character Variable c Is This**
isalnum(c)	A number or letter of the alphabet
isalpha(c)	A letter of the alphabet, either upper- or lowercase
isascii(c)	A character code less than 128 (ASCII codes range from 0 through 127; the PC uses character codes 0 through 255, but codes 128 and up are not official ASCII characters)
iscntrl(c)	A control character, ASCII code 0 through 31 and code 127
isdigit(c)	A number character 0 through 9
isgraph(c)	A printable character, code 32 through 126 (which are all the characters on your keyboard)
islower(c)	A lowercase letter (a through z) only
ispunct(c)	A punctuation character (period or comma, for example)
isspace(c)	A space character (tab or spacebar, for example)
isupper(c)	An uppercase letter, A through Z
isxdigit(c)	A hexadecimal digit character, A through F, a through f, and 1 through 9

Table 9-4	CTYPE.H Character-Changing Functions
Function or Macro	**Changes Character Variable c to This**
toascii(c)	A true ASCII code (it basically lops off the top bit in any 8-bit character code — techy stuff)
tolower(c)	A lowercase letter (other characters are ignored)
toupper(c)	An uppercase letter (other characters are ignored)

✔ Pronunciation guide: The functions in Tables 9-3 and 9-4 consist of two words jammed together. The first word is either *is* or *to,* so *isascii* is pronounced "is ask-ee," not "eye-sask-eye." The tolower function is pronounced "to lower," not "toll hour."

✔ The CTYPE.H header file contains functions that let you examine or modify characters. These characters can be single-character variables or individual characters in an array (string).

✔ All the CTYPE.H functions that check for certain characters return either TRUE or FALSE (TRUE is any nonzero value, and FALSE is zero).

✔ Those CTYPE.H functions that don't check for certain characters typically change the character being examined. For example, the `toupper` function changes lowercase letters to uppercase (changes lower- *to upper*case).

✔ For messing with whole strings, you use the functions in the STRING.H header file. This subject is covered in the next lesson.

✔ Officially, the functions in the CTYPE.H header file are called *macros*. That's because they're simple shortcut techniques used to examine characters. You could write your own macros to do the same thing, but that would be stupid because someone else has already done the work and put the macros in the CTYPE.H header file.

The droll "make me uppercase" program

Changing characters from upper- to lowercase in a string is a handy thing to do. For example, you may be using one of the string-comparing functions (introduced in the next lesson) to make sure that what a user types is proper. The best way to do that is to make the entire string uppercase and compare it to other uppercase strings (that way, you eliminate the possibility of wise guys who TyPe Like TheY hAVe TOO mUCH tImE oN THeiR HaNDs).

This source code is for SHOUT!.C, a program that uses the `toupper` function to convert characters in a string to uppercase. Carefully type that code into your editor. Save the file to disk as SHOUT!.C.

Name: SHOUT!.C

```c
#include <stdio.h>
#include <ctype.h>

void main()
{
    char string[] = "You don't have to shout!";
    char c;
    int x;

    x = 0;

    puts(string);

    while(c!='!')
    {
        c = string[x];
```

(continued)

(continued)

```
        c = toupper(c);
        string[x] = c;
        x++;
    }

    puts(string);

}
```

Compile and run.

```
You don't have to shout!
YOU DON'T HAVE TO SHOUT!
```

Notice how the `toupper` function converts only letters of the alphabet? The punctuation marks and spaces were not changed.

Trivial information about how to do uppercase

Converting letters of the alphabet from upper- to lowercase isn't as hard as it seems. The `toupper` function (and its companion, `tolower`) are merely taking advantage of a cute little trick set up by the ASCII character codes.

If you look at Appendix B in *C For Dummies*, Volume I, you see that all the upper- and lowercase letters of the alphabet live in two clumps: uppercase letters starting at ASCII code 65 and lowercase starting at code 97. Therefore, one of the simplest ways to convert to uppercase is to subtract the difference between the two codes. For example, the ASCII code for a is 97. Subtract 32 from 97 and you get 65, the code for uppercase A.

In the `toupper` macro, the calculation is done like this:

```
c = c - ('a' - 'A');
```

Because the compiler sees all characters as numbers (it merely displays them as characters), (`'a' - 'A'`) is really 97 – 65, or 32. The value of variable c is decreased by 32, which magically makes it an uppercase character. This system works for all lowercase letters because each one is exactly 32 places away from its uppercase counterpart (refer to the ASCII table).

Oh, and the `toupper` macro also checks to make sure that the character is a letter of the alphabet, and a lowercase one at that. This is done by an `if` statement:

```
if(c >= 'a' && c <= 'z')
```

This line reads, "if c is greater than or equal to `'a'` and less than or equal to `'z'`." If that's true, c holds a lowercase letter.

- The SHOUT!.C program uses the `toupper` function, which is introduced in Lesson 7-3 in Volume I. Refer there for more information.

- The `!` in C means "not." So `while(c != '!')` could read, "While the contents of variable c are not not," but it doesn't. Instead, the program uses the exclamation point as the last character in the string to signal a stop to the `while` loop.

- The program's name, SHOUT!.C, also has an exclamation point in it. This is a perfectly legitimate filename character in DOS and Windows, but not in UNIX. On the off chance that you're ever writing programs on a UNIX machine, don't put an exclamation point in your program's name.

A better way to scan through a string

The program SHOUT!.C uses the exclamation point in the string `You don't have to shout!` as a flag. When the program's `while` loop encounters the exclamation point, the `while` loop stops looping. That's perfectly okay for the SHOUT!.C program because its string never changes and you can rely on the `!` being there. It's a rather inelegant solution, however, for working with strings typed at the keyboard or read from disk or just about any string anywhere that may or may not end in an exclamation point.

A better solution is to take advantage of a feature *every* string in C has: the NULL byte at the end of the string.

No matter what, whenever you define a string in C or whenever a user types a string at the keyboard, the string must have a sole NULL byte — value 0x00 — at the end. This process had to be done manually in the INPUT.C series of programs shown earlier in this chapter. It's just one of those C things.

To take advantage of the NULL byte, you could change Line 14 in the SHOUT!.C source code to read

```
while(c)
```

This line means that the program loops as long as the c variable doesn't hold the NULL byte. To make sure that c doesn't begin with the value zero, it should be preset to something (anything) else in Line 7:

```
char c = '!';
```

(The compiler doesn't assign any value to variables you create. However, some "garbage" or leftover program may remain in memory, and your variable assumes whatever value it finds there. If that value is the NULL byte, the program doesn't work, so it's best to preassign the variable a value, as shown in the preceding example.)

Another thing you can do is tighten up a bit of redundancy in the program. To witness:

```
c = string[x];
c = toupper(c);
```

As you may remember from Lesson 5-5 in Volume I, C functions work from the inside out. It's possible to easily combine those two statements into one:

```
c = toupper(string[x]);
```

You could combine statements even more and the program would work, but the result would be harder to read — and debug. Avoid the temptation to write a one-line C program "just because," and stick with just the elegant shortcuts, such as the one function inside the other in the preceding example.

Save SHOUT!.C to disk again. Compile and run.

Everything works the same; on the program's "outside," you don't notice any difference, but the inside has been made more elegant and versatile. You see another variation on this theme in the next section.

✔ All strings in the C language end in a NULL byte.

✔ The NULL byte registers as a "FALSE" in an if test or in a while or while-do or do-while test.

✔ The NULL byte is the same as zero, 0x00, or \0 (refer to Table 2-1 in Volume I).

✔ About the only time a string doesn't end in a NULL byte is when some bozo programmer writes an input routine and forgets to add the NULL byte. Of course, this situation will never happen to you (refer to Lesson 9-2).

✔ If you're going to use any variable in a while loop (or an if text), be sure that you initialize its value to something not FALSE before the loop starts. If you don't, the program may run just fine, but there's an outside chance that it may not. It's voodoo, I tells ya!

✔ Generally speaking, although you can collapse many C language statements into a single line, it's not a really good idea. It gives the program no real speed advantage, and it makes the source code more difficult to read and debug.

Rotate that dirty string

The English alphabet has exactly 26 characters. That's 13 plus 13, which is where you get the 13 in the term *rot13*. The *rot* part is pronounced "rote," not "rot." It comes from *rotate,* which means to rotate the letters of the alphabet 13 places — like on those old secret decoder rings of yore. When you rot13 something, A becomes N, B becomes O, C becomes P, and so on. Although the system isn't clever enough to fool enemy spies, it can be used to disguise a message (see the nearby sidebar labeled "Lurid details on rot13 you don't have to remember").

The following source code is for a program that scrambles a string of text by using a rot13 function. The rot13 function uses the isalpha function to look for letters of the alphabet, and then it uses an if-else if-else function to "rotate" characters 13 places (much easier than a decoder ring).

Carefully type the following source code into your editor. Save the file to disk as SCRAMBLE.C (any comments about what's going on appear in the nearby sidebar, "There's a Wankel engine inside SCRAMBLE.C"):

Name: SCRAMBLE.C

```
#include <stdio.h>
#include <ctype.h>

void rot13(char *string);

void main()
{
    char phrase[] = "A pig fell in the mud.";

    printf("The phrase is:\n");
    puts(phrase);

    rot13(phrase);        //rot13 the phrase

    printf("The scrambled phrase is:\n");
    puts(phrase);

    rot13(phrase);        //rot13 it again

    printf("And unscrambled:\n");
    puts(phrase);
}

void rot13(char *string)
```

(continued)

(continued)

```
{
    int count = 0;
    char c = '!';        //initialize c

    while(c)
    {
        c = string[count];
        if(isalpha(c))
        {
            if(toupper(c)>='A' && toupper(c)<='M')
                c+=13;
            else
                c-=13;
        }
        string[count] = c;
        count++;
    }
}
```

Compile it. Run it. See it:

```
The phrase is:
A pig fell in the mud.
The scrambled phrase is:
N cvt sryy va gur zhq.
And unscrambled:
A pig fell in the mud.
```

Function isalpha

The isalpha function tests to see whether a character is a letter of the alphabet, in the range A through Z as well as a through z. Here's the format:

```
int = isalpha(c);
```

The single-character variable c is examined by isalpha. If it's a letter of the alphabet, the function returns a TRUE (nonzero) value as int. Otherwise, the value returned is FALSE, or zero.

The isalpha function does not change the value of the c variable. It merely tests whether the variable is a letter of the alphabet. Most often, you see isalpha used in an if statement or sometimes in a while loop.

To use the isalpha function, you must include the following line in your source code (without it, the compiler thinks that you're just plain nuts):

```
#include <ctype.h>
```

The phrase churns through the rot13 function twice. The first time, the phrase is scrambled: N cvt sryy va gur zhq. The second time, the phrase returns to normal. See? It really does work.

✔ Refer to the preceding section for information about the while(c) loop.

✔ Refer to Lessons 4-1 and 4-2 and Tables 4-1 and 4-2 in Volume I for more information about the if statement, if-else, and other strange decision-making tools.

✔ Yes, a for loop could have been used instead, but because the rot13 function doesn't know when the string ends, it would be hard to figure out when the for loop would end.

✔ Two CTYPE.H functions can tell you whether a character is upper- or lowercase; isupper and islower, respectively. However, these functions could not be used in the SCRAMBLE.C program because it merely searches out characters in the A-through-M range.

✔ You can use come character-conversion functions, such as toupper in SCRAMBLE.C, for-on-the-fly if comparisons. For more information, see the box on the next page and Lesson 7-3 in Volume I.

Lurid details on rot13 you don't have to remember

Rot13 has its roots in the UNIX operating system, and you may find it used occasionally in some of the Internet humor newsgroups. Someone may rot13 a message that others may find offensive. What may be a nasty joke looks like this:

Naq gur frpbaq aha fnvq, 'Vg
  zhfg or gur jngre.'

That won't offend anyone.

To unscramble the message, you rot13 it and see what it really says. Likewise, you could write a dirty ditty and then rot13 it and send it off to a newsgroup. That way, it wouldn't offend the easily offended without their deliberately re-rotating the message.

As shown in the SCRAMBLE.C program, because the alphabet is 26 letters long, you can rot13 something once to scramble it and rot13 it again to unscramble it. That process works just like a decoder ring: If you *rot26* something, you're merely lining up A with A, B with B and so on. It's a nifty way to scramble and unscramble text, though it's not considered good cryptography.

There's a Wankel engine inside SCRAMBLE.C

No true secrets lurk in the SCRAMBLE.C source code, but the heart of the code is the `rot13` function, which rotates letters of the alphabet like the Wankel engine rotates its piston. (The Wankel engine was the original "rotary" engine featured in early Mazda automobiles.)

The `rot13` function's `while` loop essentially just churns through the string, waiting for the NULL character at the end. Along the way, characters are read from the string and stored in the `c` variable:

```
c = string[count];
```

A test is then made to see whether the string is a letter of the alphabet:

```
if(isalpha(c))
```

If so, more tests are done to determine how to rotate the character. Although this process could be complex, with a 26-letter alphabet, it's rather cinchy: The rule is that if the character is in the range of A through M, you add 13. Otherwise, you subtract 13. That's all a `rot13` really is. An `if-else` structure handles the details:

```
if(toupper(c)>='A' &&
    toupper(c)<='M')
```

```
        c+=13;
else
        c-=13;
```

The first `if` tests to see whether the character is in the A-through-M range: "If character `c` is greater than or equal to A and (a logical AND) `c` is less than or equal to M." If `c` is in that range, the contents of variable `c` are increased by 13. (Refer to Lesson 4-8 and Table 4-5 in Volume I for the details of `c+=13`.)

Note that the `toupper` function in the `if` comparison doesn't change the value of variable `c`; it just *replaces* it with an uppercase letter for the comparison. For example, if `c` holds a lowercase letter h, the `toupper` function converts it into a big H, which is then compared with A and M. If you write it as `c=toupper(c)`, the contents of variable `c` change. In this example, it's merely converted on the fly for a quick comparison.

The `else` part of the structure is executed if `c` holds a letter in the N-to-Z range, in which case you decrease it by 13.

The final result is re-stored into the string:

```
string[count] = c;
```

Lesson 9-5 Quiz

1. Which CTYPE.H function would you use to determine whether a character is a letter of the alphabet or a number?

   A. `isalnum`

   B. `islam`

   C. `island`

   D. `izzanum`

2. What's the difference between the `toupper` and `isupper` functions?

   A. Nothing; they're both CTYPE.H functions.

   B. You mean aside from the spelling?

   C. One changes a character to uppercase, and the other returns TRUE or FALSE depending on whether a character is upper- or lowercase.

   D. You must journey through `toupper` before attaining `isupper`.

Questions 3 through 5 deal with this snippet of code:

```
if(toupper(c) == 'Y')
```

3. TRUE or FALSE: The contents of variable `c` are changed by the preceding expression.

4. TRUE or FALSE: The `if` statement is true when `c` contains `'y'`.

5. TRUE or FALSE: If the moon were a beach ball, the House of Representatives could inflate it in less than a month.

Lesson 9-6: Weaving a Tapestry of Text

When it comes to working with strings, the best thing you can do is include the handy STRING.H header in your programs. It enables you to use lots of fun string-manipulation functions, some of which you probably wouldn't think that you would need but which come in handy.

For example, consider the following source code, SCRAM.C. It's a modification of the SCRAMBLE.C program introduced in Lesson 9-5. The program has two additions: First, it accepts keyboard input; second, it retains the original string — only a copy of the string is sent to the `rot13` function. Third, it utterly ignores some of the handy tools found in the STRING.H header file.

Use your editor to combine elements from SCRAMBLE.C and the final INPUT.C program to help you copy and paste and create this source code for SCRAM.C. The major difference in this program is that around Line 28 (or so), the string `phrase` is copied to the string `scrambled` so that the original string remains unchanged; only the `scrambled` version (the copy) is sent to the `rot13` function.

Name: SCRAM.C

```
#include <stdio.h>
#include <conio.h>
#include <ctype.h>
```

(continued)

(continued)

```
#define CR 0x0d        //carriage return
#define ESC 0x1b       //Escape key
#define TAB 0x09
#define LF 0x0a        //line feed
#define BACKSPACE 0x08
#define NULL 0          //Empty character
#define TRUE 1
#define FALSE 0
#define LENGTH 128     //size of the string

void rot13(char *string);
void input(char *string, int length);

void main()
{
    char phrase[LENGTH];
    char scrambled[LENGTH];

    puts("Type a phrase to be scrambled:");
    input(phrase,LENGTH);

/* copy the phrase before scrambling */

    scrambled = phrase;

    rot13(scrambled);      //rot13 the phrase

    printf("The scrambled phrase is:\n");
    puts(scrambled);
}

void rot13(char *string)
{
    int count = 0;
    char c = '!';          //initialize c

    while(c)
    {
        c = string[count];
        if(isalpha(c))
        {
            if(toupper(c)>='A' && toupper(c)<='M')
```

```
                        c+=13;
                else
                    c-=13;
            }
        string[count] = c;
        count++;
    }
}

void input(char *string, int length)
{
    int done = FALSE;
    int index = 0;
    char ch;

    string[0] = NULL;    //init the buffer

    do
    {
        ch = getch();

/* Check to see whether the buffer is full */

        if (index == length)
        {
            switch(ch)
            {
                case CR:
                    break;
                default:
                    ch = NULL;
                    break;
            }
        }

/* process the keyboard input */

        switch(ch)
        {
            case CR:            //Enter key
                putchar(ch);
                putchar(LF);
                string[index] = NULL;
```

(continued)

(continued)

```
                done = TRUE;
                break;
        case BACKSPACE:
            if(index==0)
            {
                break;
            }
            else
            {
                putchar(ch);
                putchar(' ');
                putchar(ch);
                index--;
                break;
            }
        case NULL:
            break;
        default:            //display & sto
            putchar(ch);
            string[index] = ch;
            index++;
            break;
        }
    }
    while(!done);
}
```

Save the file to disk and name it SCRAM.C. Compile:

```
Lvalue required
```

Oops! It's the dreaded `Lvalue` error! This message means that you tried to work some calculation and the compiler believes that nothing is there to calculate. Uh-oh. If your compiler is smart, it should tell you on which source-code line the boo-boo took place. On my screen, it says `Line 28`, which is where the strings are duplicated:

```
scrambled = phrase;
```

For any — *any* — variables in C, the equal sign should work. If both `scrambled` and `phrase` were single-character variables, it would work. If they were both any type of numeric variables, stuff would happen. For strings, however, this is a major boo-boo.

- ✔ The next section tells you how to fix the problem.

- ✔ You cannot copy or duplicate strings in C, not with an equal sign anyway.

- ✔ You cannot duplicate strings by putting an asterisk in front of them or by declaring them as pointer variables. (You will understand this concept better after reading Chapter 10, but it's a rule I have to mention now, right here in the string-copying lesson.)

- ✔ Refer to Lessons 9-2 and 9-3 for more information about the `input` function.

Copying a string in C

Because a string is actually an array, you can duplicate it only by copying each element into another array. Just setting the two arrays equal to each other doesn't work in C. (It may work in other programming languages, but not in C.)

You could write your own string-copying routine, but your compiler, fortunately, comes with a string-copying routine. It's `strcpy`, which I pronounce "string copy." This gem is defined in the STRING.H header file and described in the following "Function `strcpy`" sidebar.

Function `strcpy`

The `strcpy` function copies or duplicates one string into another. Here's the format:

`strcpy(doop,org);`

Both `doop` and `org` are strings of equal size. After the preceding function, the contents of string `org` are copied into string `doop`. Both strings are then identical, containing the same text or characters.

You must include the STRING.H header file in your source code for the `strcpy` function to work:

`#include <string.h>`

If you don't, the compiler goes bonkers.

Reedit the source code for SCRAM.C. Near the top, add the following line:

```
#include <string.h>
```

Then edit Line 28, or whichever line in your source code contains the offending Lvalue error, to read

```
strcpy(scrambled,phrase);
```

This function copies the contents of string phrase into string scrambled. That way, the original input is retained.

Save. Compile. (Yes, it compiles, unless you made a typo.) Run.

```
Type a phrase to be scrambled:
```

Jab your fingers at the keyboard and write something pithy. For example:

```
It's always darkest when the lights are out.
```

Press Enter.

```
The scrambled phrase is:
Vg'f nyjnlf qnexrfg jura gur yvtugf ner bhg.
```

✔ This sample program doesn't really *need* two copies of the string. However, other programs you write may require that.

✔ Don't be concerned about having "too many" #include lines at the beginning of your source code. Some complex C programs have dozens of them. When you need them, you need them. You get no penalty for tossing in too many, though your programs are fatter.

Chopping up a string into wee li'l bits

A variation of the strcpy function is strncpy. The strncpy function copies only a given number of characters from one string to another, which is what the *n* means: "Copy *n* characters from this string to that." The strcpy function shown in the preceding section copies *all* characters from one string to another.

To determine how many characters *n* represents, of course, you have to know something about the string you're copying. For that, you need one of the string-peeking functions, one that can peer into a string and tell you where certain characters live. One such function is strcspn. Both strncpy and strcspn are formally introduced in the following two sidebars and demonstrated in the following program, INTRO.C.

Function `strncpy`

The `strncpy` function copies a certain number of characters from one string into another. It works similarly to the `strcpy` function. Here's the format:

`strncpy(doop,org,length);`

Both `doop` and `org` are strings. `length` is an integer value or variable. After the function in the preceding line, the number of characters specified by `length` are copied from string `org` into string `doop`.

If `length` is greater than the length of string `org`, string `doop` is appended with NULL characters.

If `length` is less than the length of string `org`, no NULL is stuck on the end of the string `doop`. You *must* append a NULL there yourself (see the INTRO.C program for an example).

As with all string functions, the `strncpy` function requires the STRING.H header file in your source code lest the compiler stick its tongue in your direction:

`#include <string.h>`

Function `strcspn`

The `strcspn` function is one of a trio of STRING.H functions that scans for characters inside a string. In this case, `strcspn` looks for one string inside another. Here's the format:

`loc = strcspn(string,chars);`

`string` is a character array, the string to be searched. `chars` is another character array, one that contains one or more characters to be found in `string`. `loc` is the offset (the array element, actually) where the characters represented by `chars` are found in `string`.

Both `string` and `chars` can be either string constants or variables. `chars` is typically one or more characters or an entire string constant, enclosed in double quotes. The characters in `chars` must appear together, in sequence in `string` for a match to be found.

If the string is not found, the `strcspn` function returns a value equal to the length of `string`.

When `strcspn` returns zero, it means that the string was found at the first position (element zero, remember?).

Here's a sample call using string constants:

`pos = strcspn("Click me, you fool!","me");`

The `strcspn` function looks for the string `"me"` in the string `"Click me, you fool!"` Because `"me"` appears in the first string at Position 7, the `strcspn` function returns the value 6. Remember that arrays begin numbering their first element at zero:

`01234567...`

`Click me...`

The value 6 is stored in the `pos` variable.

As with all string functions, you must include the STRING.H header file at the beginning of your source code, lest you offend some such programming god or another:

`#include <string.h>`

Type the following source code into your editor. The nearby sidebar, "That tricky middle part of INTRO.C," explains the middle section. Save the program to disk as INTRO.C:

Name: INTRO.C

```c
#include <stdio.h>
#include <string.h>

void main()
{
    char name[25];
    char first[25];
    char space[] = " ";
    int pos;

    printf("Type your name, first and last?");
    gets(name);

    pos = strcspn(name,space);
    strncpy(first,name,pos);
    first[pos] = '\0';

    printf("Pleased to meet you, %s.\n",name);
    printf("Or should I call you %s?\n",first);
}
```

Compile and run. Here's some sample output:

```
Type your name, first and last?Ned Grep
Pleased to meet you, Ned Grep.
Or should I call you Ned?
```

The program fishes out your first name from the name string by using the strcspn and strncpy functions. That method works as long as the string that's typed is two words with a space in the middle.

✔ All strings in C end with the NULL byte, 0x00 or \0.

✔ Because the strncpy function does not copy or append a NULL byte to the end of a string, you must do it manually. That's what happens in Line 16 of the program.

✔ If you do not remember to append a NULL byte to the end of the duplicated string, your program will goof up from here 'til Tuesday. All strings in C *must* end with a NULL byte. After a strncpy function, you must append a NULL to the duplicated string.

That tricky middle part of INTRO.C

The INTRO.C program snips out the first word from the string variable name and places it in the string variable first. In this case, the first word should be the first name of the person typing at the keyboard:

```
pos = strcspn(name,space);
```

The strncspn function scans the string name for the characters in the string variable space. That's just one character, the space. The function easily could have been written this way:

```
pos = strcspn(name," ");
```

Remember that because strcspn requires a string as input, you must enclose the string in double quotes. If the space is found in the string name, the position (or element number) is returned in the pos integer variable. If you type Ned Grep, pos is set equal to 3, which is the element number for the space between Ned and Grep.

The strncpy function copies pos number of characters from the string name into the string first:

```
strncpy(first,name,pos);
```

Continuing the example, strncpy copies three characters from name to first, which are N, e, and d. (See how having zero as the first array element comes in handy here?)

```
first[pos] = '\0';
```

Finally, and most important, you must finish off the new string created by strncpy. Remember that the function does not append a NULL byte to the end of the new string. In this example, the NULL byte is tacked on the string perfectly, again using the pos variable; element 3 of the new array is set equal to the NULL byte.

✔ Don't let the offsets inside a string throw you off. If you remember that a string is an array and that arrays begin numbering their elements with zero and not with one, everything comes out in the wash. If you overthink the problem, though, and begin converting numbers and offsets and positions in your head, you're bound to screw something up.

✔ The strcspn function returns zero if a match is found at the *beginning* of the string. If that would happen in the INTRO.C program, a new chunk of code would be required to copy over the proper number of bytes into the new string. This mental exercise is too large to handle in this wee li'l lesson.

✔ The functions in the STRING.H header are perhaps some of the most difficult to type in all the C language. The strcspn is a particular booger.

Open sesame!

Another fun string function is `strcmp`, the string compare function. It returns zero (which is, oddly, FALSE) if two strings match up identically. The `strcmp` function is fully described in the sidebar "Function `strcmp`," a little earlier in this chapter. The following program, PASSWORD.C, demonstrates how you can use `strcmp`:

Name: PASSWORD.C

```
#include <stdio.h>
#include <conio.h>
#include <string.h>

#define CR 0x0d       //carriage return
#define ESC 0x1b      //Escape key
#define TAB 0x09
#define LF 0x0a       //line feed
#define BACKSPACE 0x08
#define NULL 0        //Empty character
#define TRUE 1
#define FALSE 0
#define LENGTH 15     //size of the string

void input(char *string, int length);

void main()
{
    char string[LENGTH];
    char password[] = "please";
    int result;

    printf("Enter your secret password:");
    input(string,LENGTH);

    result = strcmp(string,password);

    if(result==0)
        printf("Entry granted!\n");
    else
    {
        printf("Sorry. Wrong password.\n");
        printf("Security has been notified.\n");
        printf("We will find you...\n");
```

```
    }
}

void input(char *string, int length)
{
    int done = FALSE;
    int index = 0;
    char ch;

    string[0] = NULL;    //init the buffer

    do
    {
        ch = getch();

/* Check to see whether the buffer is full */

        if (index == length)
        {
            switch(ch)
            {
                case CR:
                    break;
                default:
                    ch = NULL;
                    break;
            }
        }

/* process the keyboard input */

        switch(ch)
        {
            case CR:            //Enter key
                putchar(ch);
                putchar(LF);
                string[index] = NULL;
                done = TRUE;
                break;
            case BACKSPACE:
                if(index==0)
                {
                    break;
```

(continued)

(continued)

```
            }
            else
            {
                putchar(ch);
                putchar(' ');
                putchar(ch);
                index--;
                break;
            }
        case NULL:
            break;
        default:        //display & sto
/* Do not display input */
            putchar('*');
            string[index] = ch;
            index++;
            break;
        }
    }
    while(!done);
}
```

Function `strcmp`

The `strcmp` function compares two strings. If the strings are identical, the function returns zero (FALSE). If the strings are not identical, the function returns values less than zero or greater than zero, depending on how the two strings compare (which isn't important, so don't ask me why I brought it up). Here's the format:

```
result = strcmp(gumby,pokey);
```

This statement compares the contents of the strings `gumby` and `pokey`. They both can be string variables, or one can be a string constant (though having both as string constants is kinda dorky). If both strings contain the exact same information and are the exact same length, the function returns zero, which is saved in the `result` variable.

Two variations on the `strcmp` function are `strcmpi` and `stricmp`. The only difference between them and `strcmp` is that both `strcmpi` and `stricmp` ignore the case of any letters being compared. The `strcmpi` or `stricmp` functions may not be available on certain UNIX and ANSI C compilers.

If you want the `strcmp` function to work, you're going to have to include the STRING.H header file at the tippy-top of your source code:

```
#include <string.h>
```

The easiest way to create the source code for PASSWORD.C is to edit the INPUT.C program created earlier in this chapter. Load that file into your editor and make these changes:

Include the STRING.H header file at the beginning of the source code.

Change the main function as shown in the preceding example.

Finally, you have to adjust the way the input function displays the text you typed. It's a good idea for asterisks to be displayed rather than keyboard input, which is what most password programs do. To make that change in the input function, locate the *default* part of the last switch-case structure and change the putchar function to read

```
putchar('*');
```

This line displays an asterisk no matter what was typed at the keyboard, yet it leaves untouched the true input, held in the character variable ch. (Refer to the preceding source code listing if you need more help locating this line of code.)

Use your editor's Save As command to save the finished product to disk as PASSWORD.C.

Compile. Fix up any errors.

Run dat program!

```
Enter your secret password:
```

Type **please** (in lowercase) and press the Enter key.

```
Entry granted!
```

Now run the program again and type **nothing** as the password:

```
Enter your secret password:*******
Sorry. Wrong password.
Security has been notified.
We will find you...
```

The if structure in the program checks to see whether the strings match using the following statement:

```
if(result == 0)
```

If the value of the `result` variable is zero, the strings matched. `Else` handles the situation when the strings don't match, but you could also write the comparison like this:

```
if(!result)
```

When `result` equals zero, the value of `result` is considered a "logical FALSE" by the compiler. To change that to TRUE, you put a ! or "NOT" in front of the variable. The program still works the same, but it requires more thought when you're reading the source code.

✔ The PASSWORD.C program is a little strict. PC users normally don't expect passwords to be typed in lower- or uppercase; as with DOS commands, you should be able to type a password in upper-, lower-, or mixed case and still have it match. To make it happen, simply change Line 26 of the program to read `strcmpi` rather than `strcmp`.

✔ The `strcmp` function works by comparing each character in the two strings. As long as the strings are the same, the function keeps comparing characters. After a difference is found, `strcmp` returns a value less than zero if the first character's ASCII value is less than the second character's; otherwise, the value returned is greater than zero.

Lesson 9-6 Quiz

1. How do you copy a string in C?

    A. It just can't be done.

    B. No, it can be done with a simple equal sign.

    C. You need the `strcpy` function.

    D. You need a Xerox 9000.

2. That figure-eight thing on most globes and maps is called a

    A. Sundial.

    B. Sunatron.

    C. Analemma.

    D. Anasolar.

3. What is `strcspn`?

    A. The function that enables WebTV to see the C-SPAN channel.

    B. The function that enables you to find one string inside another.

C. The String Capture and Print function.

D. The Stop Traffic Run Counterclockwise Spit and Perspire Nonchalantly function.

4. If the `strcmp` function discovers that two strings are identical, it returns which value?

A. The length of the strings.

B. TRUE (nonzero).

C. FALSE (zero).

D. The first string compared.

Bonus question (worth one gold star!)

5. Who invented radio?

A. Guglielmo Radio.

B. Guglielmo Marconi.

C. Guglielmo Macaroni.

D. Guglielmo Phillips.

Time for something tasty before the next lesson.

Lesson 9-7: String-Manipulation Bedlam

Suppose that you want to stick one string on the end of another string. If you're a DOS person, you might use the word *append*. It's techy. Normal humans may say "glue," as in "glue two strings together" (or maybe "tie two strings together"). Then there's the word *stick* and its past tense, *stuck*. I like those myself. In C, though, the word is *concatenate*.

Gads, isn't concatenate an ugly word? "Kon-KAT-un-ate." Could you ever see Uncle Vern use the term? "Come help me concatenate the trailer to my truck." Nope. In computer science, however, especially UNIX-like things, such as the C language, you get to *concatenate* a bunch of things — primarily strings.

✔ *Concatenate* has its roots in some Latin term or something like that. It means to chain together.

✔ Aside from writing good code, programmers are concerned about saving time, so they say "cat" rather than "concatenate."

✔ A certain UNIX command, `cat`, is also short for *concatenate*. It displays files on the console, similar to the old TYPE command in DOS.

Concatenating strings

If you're into all this cat nonsense, you can probably guess that the C language function used to stick one string on the end of another is cat-something. Specifically, it's strcat, which is formally introduced in the following sidebar, "Function strcat."

The following program, RUDEDOS.C, is a fake DOS prompt program that spits out a nasty message for every command you type. I'm not recommending that you run this program on anyone else's DOS computer, but then again I have no moral control of what programs you write and how you use them. The RUDEDOS.C program also introduces the strupr function, detailed in a sidebar box somewhere around here.

Carefully hunt and peck this source code into your editor. Count your parentheses — I tend to goof them up in tiny programs more often than in big programs. Save the text to disk under the name RUDEDOS.C:

Name: RUDEDOS.C

```
#include <stdio.h>
#include <string.h>

void main()
{
    char command[64];
    char oh[] = "Oh, so it's \"";
    char now[] = "\" now, hmmm?\n";
    char new[128];

    for(;;)
    {
        printf("C:\\>");
gets(command);

        strcpy(new,oh);
        strcat(new,strupr(command));
        strcat(new,now);
        puts(new);
    }
}
```

Compile. Run.

```
C:\>
```

Function strcat

The strcat (*string cat*) function takes one string and sticks it on the butt end of another string. Here's how it works:

```
strcat(start,end);
```

After this function, the contents of string end are stuck to the end of string start. The string start then contains the contents of both strings, one after the other.

You must make sure that enough room has been set aside for the start string to hold both itself and the contents of whatever string you append to it.

The strcat function generates results that can be used as a string in your program. For example:

```
puts(strcat(alpha,beta));
```

This statement displays the results of sticking the contents of string beta on the end of string alpha.

As with all string functions, you must include the STRING.H header file in your source code to ensure copious amounts of goodwill between you and the compiler:

```
#include <string.h>
```

Function strupr

When you want to convert a string into ALL CAPS, use the strupr (*string upper*) function. It converts all lowercase characters in a string to uppercase. It changes the original string but does not create a new copy. The format is shown here:

```
strupr(string);
```

After this function, the contents of the variable string are converted to uppercase. That's it.

You can also use the strupr function as a string itself. For example:

```
puts(strupr(string));
```

This statement displays the results of strupr, making the variable string uppercase. The string is still converted, but the function can be used as a string itself. This is a wacky concept you don't have to get right away, but it's demonstrated in RUDEDOS.C in a minute.

The strupr function has a counterpart, strlwr (*string lower*), which, as you may guess, converts strings to lowercase.

This function (and strlwr) may not be available in some UNIX or ANSI C compilers.

Like all its siblings, the strupr function requires the presence of its mother, STRING.H, included at the tippy top of your source code:

```
#include <string.h>
```

Dissertation on the guts of the RUDEDOS.C program

The silly RUDEDOS.C program starts off with four string variables. The command variable holds keyboard input; oh and now hold text that doesn't change (called "static text," though it has nothing to do with "static cling"); and new is designed to hold the final string concatenated from the other three.

The for(;;) statement causes the program to loop endlessly. Then a fake C prompt is displayed and input grabbed from the keyboard and stored in the command string variable. After a user presses the Enter key to end input, the program takes over with its rudeness:

```
strcpy(new,oh);
```

The oh string is first copied into the new string. This has two effects. First, it zeroes out any previous contents of the new string and sets

up RUDEDOS's first response to begin with the text Oh, so it's" (including the double quote).

Because C functions work from the inside out, first the contents of the command string (which were typed at the keyboard) are converted to uppercase by the strupr function. Then the strcat function is used to append that string to the end of the new string. Slowly, this is building up the RUDEDOS response:

```
strcat(new,strupr(command));
```

Finally, a second strcat function appends the last of the rude response to the string:

```
strcat(new,now);
```

The results are then displayed with a puts function:

```
puts(new);
```

Don't be fooled into thinking that you're at a DOS prompt. (I left the program running on my PC once, and it me took a while to remember what I had done.) Type a command, such as **dir**. Press Enter:

```
Oh, so it's "DIR" now, hmmm?
```

Another "DOS prompt" is displayed, and the madness continues. . . .

Press Ctrl+C to stop the program. (That keystroke combination works because gets uses DOS functions to read the keyboard and Ctrl+C cancels the program just as it cancels some DOS commands.)

- ✔ The strcat function appends one string to the end of another.
- ✔ Always make sure to have enough room in the first string so that you can append the second string. If you don't or if the second string is too large, your program may crash or the system may lock up.
- ✔ Lesson 4-6 in *C For Dummies,* Volume I, has information about the for(;;) loop, which I always pronounce "for-ever."

> ↙ The strupr function converts a string to uppercase.
>
> ↙ To convert only a single character to uppercase, use the toupper function, discussed in Lesson 9-5 and introduced in Lesson 7-3 in Volume I.

And how's this for weird?

C has an abundance of string-manipulation functions. Most string functions are very useful. Some functions are really complex. Some are specific. Some are just weird.

Type the following source code into your editor. It uses only one new string function, strrev. Save the source code to disk as BMUD.C:

Name: BMUD.C

```
#include <stdio.h>
#include <string.h>

void main()
{
    char phrase[64];

    puts("Backwardland Translator");
    printf("Type your phrase:");
    gets(phrase);
    puts("\nHere is the translation:");
    puts(strrev(phrase));
}
```

Function strrev

The strrev (*string reverse*) function reverses a string, tossing the thing out backward. Here's the format:

strrev(forward);

This function reverses the contents of the string represented by the string variable forward. (You can also use a string constant enclosed in double quotes.) The output of strrev can be displayed directly, as in

puts(strrev("stack cats"));

This statement displays stac kcats on the screen.

Don't forget the following line at the top of your source code if you expect the strrev function to work for you:

#include <string.h>

Compile. Because BMUD.C is such a short program, you probably will make some errors. Fix any, if need be.

Run.

```
Backwardland Translator
Type your phrase:
```

Type something clever, such as **My but that's a fine hat**. Press the Enter key:

```
Here is the translation:
tah enif a s'taht tub yM
```

- The strrev function reverses all the characters in a string.

- The strrev function does not reverse the NULL character at the end of the string. If it did, every string it reversed would be very, very short.

- Try typing the following into the Backwardland Translator:

  ```
  I did evil
  ```

- A phrase that can be read both forward and backward is called a *palindrome*.

All them string functions

The last several lessons have introduced you to a gaggle of string functions. Each of them is listed and described briefly in Table 9-5. Go back through the past few pages for more details about how each one works.

Table 9-5	An Assorted Gaggle of String Functions
Function	*Overly Brief Description*
strcat	Sticks two strings together, one at the end of the other
strchr	Searches a string for a specific character; returns a string starting at the character's location
strcmp	Compares one string to another; returns zero if both match
strcmpi	Compares two strings and ignores upper- and lowercase differences
strcpy	Copies one string into another string
strcspn	Searches one string for characters found in another string
stricmp	Same as strcmpi

Function	Overly Brief Description
strlen	Returns the length of a string (but does not count the NULL byte at the end of the string)
strlwr	Converts a string to lowercase
strrev	Reverses the characters in a string and spits it out again
strupr	Converts a string to uppercase

✔ Yeah, C has tons more string functions. This book touches on only a few of them.

✔ The problem with some string functions is that they require a knowledge of *pointers,* which haven't been introduced yet in this book. Chapter 10 has the lowdown.

✔ Refer to your C language library guide or online documentation for more STRING.H functions. If you're using one of the newer C language packages in Windows, use the Help system to search for *string.h* and then point-and-click to read about the various functions and their examples.

✔ It's always a good idea to write a quick-and-dirty little program to demonstrate a STRING.H function *before* you stick it in the middle of some gargantuan program.

Lesson 9-7 Quiz

1. Can you concatenate an elephant?

   A. No, you concatenate a duck.

   B. No, you need more than one elephant.

   C. Yes, if both the elephant and the cat are over the age of consent.

   D. Yes, and the elephant will enjoy it.

2. What happens to the string variable noodle in this statement?

   ```
   strupr(strlwr(noodle));
   ```

   A. Nothing; the two functions cancel each other out. Like, duh!

   B. Noodle is converted to uppercase.

   C. Noodle is converted to lowercase.

   D. Because noodle contains only symbols, nothing happens.

3. What do you call a bit of text that reads the same forward as it does backward?

   A. A palindrome.

   B. A palimony.

   C. A palimpsest.

   D. A palinode.

4. Define *smurf:*

   A. A noun.

   B. A verb.

   C. An adjective.

   D. An emetic.

Lesson 9-8: Arrays from Beyond the First Dimension

All the arrays you've seen so far in this chapter are of the one-dimensional variety. They're all basically a bunch of numbers one after the other or a string of characters. That's one-dimensional — like most characters in a Steven Seagal movie. But C is capable of more: It also uses two-dimensional arrays.

A two-dimensional array is no big deal. In fact, you probably will never use one in any of your programs. There are just better ways to do things with many numbers in C, most of which don't involve the hassle or mental overhead of creating a two-dimensional array. Even so, prudence dictates that I discuss it here anyway, so I try to make it fun.

✏ Because this subject is so obtuse, I have decided to pepper the chapter with inane Viking jokes.

✏ Q: Why did the Viking wear a sheep around his neck?

A: Because he couldn't grow a beard.

Declaring a two-dimensional array

A two-dimensional array is essentially a grid. For example, a checkerboard is a two-dimensional array. It has eight squares going across and eight going up and down — a giant grid of 64 squares ($8 \times 8 = 64$).

In C, you declare such an array as follows:

```
int checkers[8][8];
```

This line reads, "Create an array of integers that has two dimensions, eight rows of eight items each."

Here are a bunch of check marks to review what you know thus far:

✔ You can think of a two-dimensional array as a giant grid.

✔ Two-dimensional arrays have rows and columns.

✔ Two-dimensional arrays are declared like regular arrays, but with two numbers in two square brackets.

✔ Some other programming languages may declare two-dimensional arrays like this:

```
pascal[8,8]
```

This technique is horrifically unkosher in C. The compiler will think that you've had one too many of Aunt Velma's rum balls.

✔ As with one-dimensional arrays, the first element is always zero. For two-dimensional arrays, the first "row" is always zero.

✔ Zero! Zero! Zero!

✔ *All* the array elements are of the same variable type. You cannot have a two-dimensional array with one dimension being ints and the other chars. In that case, what you need is a *structure,* which is covered in Chapter 11 somewhere.

✔ Q: Why do Viking hats have pointy horns on the outside?

A: Pointy horns on the inside would be too painful — even for Vikings.

Declaring an initialized two-dimensional array

C programmers get all fancy-schmancy when they declare an initialized two-dimensional array. It's time to show off your prowess with the Tab key and curly brackets!

Essentially, the declared two-dimensional array is splayed out in the source code to look like a grid, as shown in the following program, GRID.C:

```
int array[3][3] = {
    1, 8, 6,
    5, 3, 7,
    9, 4, 2
    };
```

You could easily declare the array like this:

```
int array[3][3] = { 1, 8, 6, 5, 3, 7, 9, 4, 2};
```

Still, that's kind of confusing, especially if you're copying something from a book and trying to double-check the numbers. It also ruins the spirit of the two-dimensional array, which has been known to induce missing } errors in some compilers.

Wantonly type the source code for this program into your editor. Save it to disk as GRID.C. Those extra \n things in Lines 13 and 31 are to help clean up the program's output:

Name: GRID.C

```c
#include <stdio.h>

void main()
{
    int a,b,r1,r2,r3,c1,c2,c3;
    int array[3][3] = {
        1, 8, 6,
        5, 3, 7,
        9, 4, 2
        };

    puts("Presenting the Magic Square:\n");

    for(a=0;a<3;a++)
    {
        for(b=0;b<3;b++)
        {
            printf("%i\t",array[a][b]);
        }
        printf("\n");
    }

    r1 = array[0][0] + array[0][1] + array[0][2];
    r2 = array[1][0] + array[1][1] + array[1][2];
```

```
        r3 = array[2][0] + array[2][1] + array[2][2];
    c1 = array[0][0] + array[1][0] + array[2][0];
    c2 = array[0][1] + array[1][1] + array[2][1];
    c3 = array[0][2] + array[1][2] + array[2][2];

    printf("\nSum for row 1 is %i.\n",r1);
    printf("Sum for row 2 is %i.\n",r2);
    printf("Sum for row 3 is %i.\n",r3);
    printf("Sum for column 1 is %i.\n",c1);
    printf("Sum for column 2 is %i.\n",c2);
    printf("Sum for column 3 is %i.\n",c3);
}
```

Compile and run.

```
Presenting the Magic Square:

1    8    6
5    3    7
9    4    2

Sum for row 1 is 15.
Sum for row 2 is 15.
Sum for row 3 is 15.
Sum for column 1 is 15.
Sum for column 2 is 15.
Sum for column 3 is 15.
```

Try that with a one-dimensional array!

> ✔ The magic square is a grid of numbers that has the same totals up and down for all rows. An even more magic square is one in which the totals also add up to the same numbers diagonally.

> ✔ The magic square in the GRID.C program uses all the numbers, 1 through 9.

> ✔ The curly brackets around the inner for loop are not necessary. I included them in the source code only to make it more readable.

> ✔ The \t escape sequence displays a tab character on-screen.

> ✔ You could also use a for loop to display the results of adding each row and column. This method would, however, make the program unduly complex.

✔ If you're declaring an initialized array, you don't always have to specify a count for the first part of the array. As with declared one-dimensional arrays, the compiler figures it out for you. In GRID.C, the array could also be declared this way:

```
int array[][3] = {
  1, 8, 6,
  5, 3, 7,
  9, 4, 2
  };
```

The compiler guesses that the first value should be three because the total number of items divided by three is equal to three. I recommend against setting up arrays like this because it tends to make people scrunch up their faces when they read your source code.

Referencing items in a two-dimensional array

Each item in a two-dimensional array has both a "row" and "column" reference — just like squares on a bingo card or chunks of ocean in a Battleship game. The set of square brackets is the "row," and the next set is the "column." (These items have no official names in C, though I'm sure that they would be overly complex and utterly nondescript if there were names.)

Suppose that you have a 5 x 5 array of integers. Here's how it's declared:

```
int bingo[5][5];
```

The array holds 25 items: 5 rows and 5 columns. Here's how you reference the first item:

```
bingo[0][0]
```

Element zero is the first item in any array. The same holds true for arrays beyond the first dimension. In this example, you have item zero of row zero. Here's how the next four items in the array are referenced:

```
bingo[0][1]
bingo[0][2]
bingo[0][3]
bingo[0][4]
```

No `bingo[0][5]` is listed here because you didn't declare the array to be that big. Instead, the next element of the array is in the next "row," which is referenced as

```
bingo[1][0]
```

The final element of the array is referenced as

```
bingo[4][4]
```

The "free" square? How about

```
bingo[2][2]
```

Figure 9-6 shows how the grid works out in referencing elements in the `bingo` array.

bingo[0][0]	bingo[0][1]	bingo[0][2]	bingo[0][3]	bingo[0][4]
bingo[1][0]	bingo[1][1]	bingo[1][2]	bingo[1][3]	bingo[1][4]
bingo[2][0]	bingo[2][1]	bingo[2][2]	bingo[2][3]	bingo[2][4]
bingo[3][0]	bingo[3][1]	bingo[3][2]	bingo[3][3]	bingo[3][4]
bingo[4][0]	bingo[4][1]	bingo[4][2]	bingo[4][3]	bingo[4][4]

Figure 9-6:
Referencing
elements in
a two-
dimensional
array.

- ✔ Refer to the source code for the GRID.C program for more examples.
- ✔ Most programs use two nested `for` loops to wade through the items in two-dimensional arrays.
- ✔ Q: What did the Viking call his pillaging and looting?

  A: "My job."

An array of strings

Strings were born for two-dimensional arrays. A string by itself is a one-dimensional array. It's just plain unfair that it can't be more. After all, think of the things you can do with multiple strings — things like the tepid little game I dreamt up called DWARFS.C, something Disney should have included on its *Snow White and the Seven Dwarves* CD-ROM but somehow overlooked.

Use your best typing fingers to enter this source code into your editor. Beware of the long lines in the listing; they may be split in two here, but they should be typed as one line in your editor. Save the mess to disk as DWARFS.C:

Name: DWARFS.C

```
#include <stdio.h>
#include <string.h>

void main()
{
    char dwarf[7][8] = {
        "bashful",
        "doc",
        "dopey",
        "grumpy",
        "happy",
        "sneezy",
        "sleepy"
    };
    char input[64];
    int named=0;
    int x;

    puts("See if you can name all seven dwarfs:");
```

```
    while(1)
    {
        if(named==1)
            printf("\nSo far you've named %i
            dwarf.\n",named);
        else
            printf("\nSo far you've named %i
            dwarfs.\n",named);

        printf("Enter a name:");
        gets(input);

        if(strcmp(input,"")==0) //no input, end
            break;

        for(x=0;x<7;x++)
        {
            if(strcmpi(input,dwarf[x])==0)
            {
                printf("Yes! %s is right.\n",input);
                named++;
            }
        }

        if(named==7)
            break;          //game over!
        else
            puts("Try again:");
    }

}
```

Compile. Fix any errors, and don't forget doodads and missing semicolons.

Run.

```
See if you can name all seven dwarfs:

So far you've named 0 dwarfs.
Enter a name:
```

Go ahead and play the game. Press Enter by itself to quit if you get bored.

✔ See the nearby "Hi-ho, hi-ho" sidebar for a discussion of the details about how the DWARFS program works.

✔ A one-dimensional character array is a single string. A two-dimensional character array is a set of several strings.

✔ You can declare a two-dimensional character array as empty or "full." The DWARFS.C program declares a "full" or initialized two-dimensional string array.

✔ An empty string array is declared like this:

```
char newideas[4][128];
```

This string array has room for four strings, each of which can be as long as 127 characters (plus one extra item for the NULL at the end of the string).

✔ Generally speaking, with a two-dimensional string array, the first item in square brackets tells you the number of strings in the array, and the second item tells you how long each string can be.

✔ You reference the string by mentioning only the first array element:

```
puts(states[49]);
```

Assume that `states` is a two-dimensional array. Here, `states[49]` refers to the 50th string in the array. (Remember that `states[0]` is the first string in the array.)

✔ Do not reference strings in a two-dimensional array like this:

```
puts(uhoh[9][0]);
```

You may assume that `uhoh[9][0]` refers to the tenth string in the array — but it does not! It refers to the first *character* of the tenth string — a single-character variable, not a string. When you use the two brackets with the array name, you're treating the array like a two-dimensional character array, not an array of strings.

✔ The following variable refers to a specific character in a two-dimensional string array:

```
pickypicky[3][4]
```

This variable represents the fifth character of the fourth string in the array.

✔ The DWARFS game has a flaw in it: You can type the name of the same dwarf seven times to win. A fix for this bug is offered in the section "Fixing the dwarves," later in this lesson.

BLOW BY BLOW

Hi-ho, hi-ho, it's a DWARFS.C source code blow-by-blow

The DWARFS.C program declares a two-dimensional string array designed to hold seven strings (the first item in square brackets), with each string as long as seven characters; an 8 is put in the second set of square brackets because a seven-character string must also have a NULL at the end:

```
char dwarf[7][8] = {
    "bashful",
    "doc",
    "dopey",
    "grumpy",
    "happy",
    "sneezy",
    "sleepy"
};
```

The named variable is initialized to zero, which means that the program starts out with the user not having made any correct guesses.

The main part of the program is an endless loop:

```
while(1)
```

A while loop with 1 as its condition loops forever. Various break statements get out of the loop. (You can work the loop in other ways, including while(named<7), which you can try on your own if you have tons of time and are in a cheerful mood.)

The next chunk of code merely serves to avoid one of those "(s)" things. You know, like when DOS says "25 file(s)" or something. A simple if-else avoids the situation:

```
if(named==1)
    printf("\nSo far you've
    named %i dwarf.\n",named);
else
    printf("\nSo far you've
    named %i dwarfs.\n",named);
```

If nothing was entered, the program breaks out of the loop and ends:

```
if(strcmp(input,"")==0) //no
                        //input, end
                        break;
```

The strcmp function compares the input with nothing; "" in C means an empty string. It's still a string, but it contains only the NULL byte. If that's what was entered as input, the break command breaks out of the loop.

Next, a for loop compares input with all seven of the strings in the dwarf array. The strcmpi function is used, which ignores the case of the input. (It works just like strcmp, introduced in Lesson 9-6.) If the result is zero, there's a match:

```
if(strcmpi(input,dwarf[x])==0)
```

Notice that the array is referenced by only its first dimension, dwarf[x]. That works for a two-dimensional array of strings. The x variable (which is incremented by the for loop) represents each of the seven items in the array. The second dimension is implied.

You cannot use the following:

```
if(strcmpi(input,dwarf[x][0])==0)
```

(continued)

(continued)

The compiler does not read `dwarf[x][0]` as a string. The variable `dwarf[x][0]` can be read as a single character because the whole thing is, after all, a character array. But `strcmpi` requires a string. The only string reference is `dwarf[x]`, where `x` is the number of one of the strings in the two-dimensional array.

If the proper string was typed, and `strcmpi` returns zero in that case, the `if` structure executes the following two statements. The proper answer is displayed and the value of the `named` variable is incremented:

```
printf("Yes! %s is
    right.\n",input);
named++;
```

Finally, an `if` structure tests to see whether all seven dwarves were mentioned. If so, the loop stops with a `break` command; otherwise, the user is urged to "try again":

```
if(named==7)
        break;         //game over!
else
        puts("Try again:");
```

Arrays in the twilight zone

Just as two-dimensional arrays are rare in C, three-dimensional arrays are almost unheard of. I don't know whether you can have four or more dimensions in an array. I haven't seen it in any book, and, honestly, I'm too tired to test it now.

If you can reenergize those dozen or so brain cells you have left over from high school geometry, you probably remember that a two-dimensional square becomes a cube in the third dimension. That's exactly what happens in C when you create a three-dimensional variable. It's mind-boggling, as the following declaration proves:

```
int boggle[3][3][3] = {
  1, 2, 3,
  4, 5, 6,
  7, 8, 9,

  10, 11, 12,
  13, 14, 15,
  16, 17, 18,

  100, 101, 102,
  103, 104, 105,
  106, 107, 108,
  };
```

Keeping in mind that element zero thing, the variable `boggle[1][0][2]` refers to the second "page" of numbers — first row, last item, or the value 12.

- ✔ Egads!

- ✔ Yeah, you could visualize the data as a cube. Personally, I believe that such a process should be in violation of the Geneva Convention on the treatment of prisoners of war.

- ✔ If you have trouble working with three-dimensional spreadsheets, give up on the concept of three-dimensional arrays right here and now.

- ✔ Don't forget all those commas after each number. Your pretty formatting is merely for human eyes. The compiler expects a comma after each number, except for the last one in the array. This statement holds true for arrays of any dimension.

Guard your eyes from the dirty truth about multidimensional arrays

Allow me to let you in on a little secret: C really doesn't have any such things as multidimensional arrays. Nope. They don't exist. The compiler merely creates a long *one-dimensional* array, no matter what type of information you store in it or how pretty you format it. The secret to all the brackets and nonsense is how the compiler *finds* information in the array.

For example, the preceding `boggle` example can really be written like this:

```
int boggle[27] = { 1, 2, 3, 4,
   5, 6, 7, 8, 9, 10, 11, 12,
   13, 14, 15, 16, 17, 18, 100,
   101, 102, 103, 104, 105,
   106, 107, 108};
```

When you declare it as `boggle[3][3][3]`, the compiler divides the numbers into three chunks, and then three chunks again, and finally the smallest three chunks.

The first number in brackets, `[3]`, represents chunks of nine numbers.

The second number, `[3]`, represents chunks of three numbers (which is the third number).

Follow along with me (it helps to do this while you're listening to the radio because the entire concept is distracting anyway): The variable `boggle[1][0][2]` refers to `[1]` chunk of 9, `[0]` chunks of 3, plus 3 (because `[2]` is the third element in an array). So 9 + 3 is the 12th element of the array, which just happens to be 12.

Don't try to go figuring all that in your head. The compiler does the work for you. My point here, aside from shattering your multidimensional array dreams of glory, is to show you how the brackets are used as shorthand to reference elements in an array.

Remember that the compiler does the work. Because of that, you can cheerfully forget everything mentioned in this sidebar.

Three-dimensional string arrays

String arrays are already two-dimensional. If you add a third dimension, you're basically creating a grid of strings — like the answer squares in *Jeopardy!*

The following program example shows how to declare a three-dimensional array of strings, how to reference them, and how to drive yourself nuts trying to use them in a program.

Type this program into your editor. Watch the quotes and commas in the three-dimensional string array. Save this mess to disk as NAMES.C:

Name: NAMES.C

```
#include <stdio.h>

void main()
{
    char names[4][3][10] = {
        "Bob",    "Bill",  "Bret",
        "Dan",    "Dave",  "Don",
        "George", "Harry", "John",
        "Mike",   "Steve", "Vern"
    };
    int a,b;

    for(a=0;a<4;a++)
        for(b=0;b<3;b++)
            printf("%s\n",names[a][b]);
}
```

Compile and run:

```
Bob
Bill
Bret
Dan
Dave
Don
George
Harry
John
Mike
Steve
Vern
```

- ✔ When you create a multidimensional array of strings, the first and second items are the rows and columns. The last item is the maximum size for every string in the array. For names[4][3][10], the array holds four rows of three strings, and each string can be no more than nine characters long (plus the NULL byte).

- ✔ As with an array of strings, you do not specify the last number in square brackets when you reference the array. To reference John, you specify names[2][2] and not names[2][2][0].

- ✔ Isn't this messy?

- ✔ No curly brackets are required around the nested for loops because each of them holds only one statement. If you think that it looks odd, you can put curly brackets around them, but it's not necessary.

- ✔ If you read the sidebar "Guard your eyes from the dirty truth about multidimensional arrays," a little earlier in this chapter, you realize that the array declaration names[4][3][10] can also be written as names[12][10]. The [4] and the [3] are merely for your own reference.

Fixing the dwarves

A bug in the DWARFS program introduced earlier in this lesson enables a sharp-witted user to simply type the same dwarf's name over and over to win the game. Obviously, it would be nice if the program somehow kept track of which names had already been guessed.

Welcome to three-dimensional array land! It's just behind Cinderella's castle in Disneyland. To get there, you just have to make a few modifications to your DWARFS.C source code. First, a brief discussion.

To keep track of which names have been guessed, each name grows another element, which is a short string containing either a question mark or an exclamation point. If the string contains a question mark, it means that the name hasn't been guessed. If the string contains an exclamation point, the name has already been guessed. That should foil the rascals!

Here's how to redeclare the dwarf array in three dimensions:

```
char dwarf[7][2][8] = {
  "bashful", "?",
  "doc",     "?",
  "dopey",   "?",
  "grumpy",  "?",
  "happy",   "?",
  "sneezy",  "?",
  "sleepy",  "?"
};
```

The dwarf array has seven [7] lines with two [2] strings. Each string can have as many as ten [10] characters in it. (Although this technique wastes some space because the second string is only one character long, I think that most PCs can handle a few extra bytes of program bloat.)

The if statement that uses the strcmpi command to compare a user's input with the dwarves' names must also be changed to reflect the added dimension:

```
if(strcmpi(input,dwarf[x][0])==0)
```

Now dwarf[x][0] refers to the row represented by variable x and then the first string in that row. You do not write this as dwarf[x][0][0], which points to a single character and not a string.

Finally, an if-else structure must be added (or modified from the existing if statement) to determine whether a name has already been guessed:

```
if(dwarf[x][1][0]=='!')
   printf("You already named that dwarf!\n");
else
{
   printf("Yes! %s is right.\n",input);
   named++;
   dwarf[x][1][0]='!';
}
```

The reference dwarf[x][1][0] is acceptable here; it's a single character, and the if command compares it to a single character, '!' (the exclamation point). If the first character [0] of the second string [1] for name [x] is an exclamation point, the user has already guessed that name.

The final line in the else part of the if-else structure sets the character to an exclamation point when a user guesses a name. It's a simple variable assignment, just like you would find in a one-dimensional array:

```
dwarf[x][1][0]='!';
```

This line reads, "Set the first character [0] of the second string [1] for name [x] to an exclamation point. (Single quotes are used for single-character variables.

The following is the finished, touched-up source code for DWARFS.C. Make the proper changes to the source code on your computer, and then compile and run the program. It cannot be fooled!

Name: DWARFS2.C

```
#include <stdio.h>
#include <string.h>

void main()
{
    char dwarf[7][2][8] = {
        "bashful", "?",
        "doc",     "?",
        "dopey",   "?",
        "grumpy",  "?",
        "happy",   "?",
        "sneezy",  "?",
        "sleepy",  "?"
    };
    char input[64];
    int named=0;
    int x;

    puts("See if you can name all seven dwarfs:");

    while(1)
    {
        if(named==1)
            printf("\nSo far you've named %i
            dwarf.\n",named);
        else
            printf("\nSo far you've named %i
            dwarfs.\n",named);

        printf("Enter a name:");
        gets(input);

        if(strcmp(input,"")==0) //no input, end
            break;

        for(x=0;x<7;x++)
        {
            if(strcmpi(input,dwarf[x][0])==0)
            {
                if(dwarf[x][1][0]=='!')
                    printf("You already named that
        dwarf!\n");
```

(continued)

(continued)

```
            else
            {
                printf("Yes! %s is right.\n",input);
                named++;
                dwarf[x][1][0]='!';
            }
        }
    }

    if(named==7)
    {
        puts("You got 'em all! Snow would be proud!");
        break;        //game over!
    }
    else
        puts("Try again:");
    }
}
```

✔ Be wary of long lines split in two in the DWARFS.C source code listing. You do not have to split those lines in your editor.

✔ Feel free to go gonzo with this source code and splash it up with fancier displays and whatnot.

✔ Q: How did Vikings refer to their enemies?

A: "Customers."

Lesson 9-8 Quiz

1. Which of the following declares a two-dimensional array?

A. `int two_dimensional_array;`

B. `int pick_me[2][2];`

C. `int pick_me[0][2];`

D. `int no_pick_me[2,2];`

2. How would you refer to the second item in the second row of the theatre **array?**

    A. theatre[1][1];

    B. theatre[2][2];

    C. theatre[0][0];

    D. "The lady with the big hair who's blocking my view."

3. In this string array, what does the 12 refer to?

    ```
    char violins[12][40];
    ```

    A. The number of people who are playing violins.

    B. A dozen of something.

    C. The first axis.

    D. The number of strings in the array.

4. In the preceding example, what does the number 40 refer to?

    A. The maximum length of each string (which is 39 because you have to have one place for the NULL byte).

    B. The median age of the violin players.

    C. The number of strings.

    D. The size of the longest string on a violin.

5. A three-dimensional array is

    A. An array with rows, columns, and pages.

    B. A pain in the butt.

    C. A joke.

    D. All of the above.

6. In 1702, when New York colonists went to visit the new governor, Lord Cornbury, they found him doing what?

    A. "Entertaining" a neighbor woman.

    B. Counting stolen gold bullion.

    C. Wearing a dress and knitting a doily.

    D. Gardening.

Chapter 9 Final Exam

1. What is the first element of every array?

    A. Zero.

    B. One.

    C. Primo.

    D. It depends on the array's size.

2. What is the first person in line at an all-you-can-eat restaurant?

    A. Fat.

    B. Slow.

    C. Hungry.

    D. An employee.

3. An array declared with stuff already in it is called

    A. An initialized array.

    B. A stuffy array.

    C. A prêt-à-porter array.

    D. Nothing because that's the way arrays come out of the box anyway.

4. Which element of the array `fish` does the following statement refer to?

```
guppy = fish[2];
```

    A. The first element.

    B. The tooth element.

    C. The second element.

    D. The third element.

5. Every string in C ends with what character?

    A. A NULL byte.

    B. Mr. Roper from *Three's Company*.

    C. The Enter character.

    D. The final double-quote character.

    E. A semicolon.

6. How big is the string created by the following declaration?

```
Char string[80];
```

   A. The string is 80 characters long.

   B. The string is 81 characters long.

   C. The string can be 79 characters long because you need a NULL byte in there somewhere.

   D. The string isn't any length because only space for the string is set aside.

7. Which comes first, the carriage return or the line feed?

   A. It's CR-LF.

   B. It depends on what you're doing.

   C. Carriage Return came first during their vaudeville act. Later, when Line Feed joined up with a singing group, he came first. During their reunion tour and subsequent film in 1963, they were given double billing.

   D. The egg.

8. A bubble sort works by

   A. Comparing each element in the array with every other element and swapping those that are out of sorts.

   B. Sorting bubbles.

   C. Tying balloons to the first elements so that they rise to the top.

   D. Carbonation.

9. The bigger the database, the longer it takes to

   A. Sort.

   B. Print.

   C. Collect money from the client.

   D. Climb up a steep hill.

10. What does the following function return?

```
isupper(toupper(c));
```

   A. Always TRUE.

   B. Always FALSE.

   C. Always MAYBE.

   D. Always `Lvalue required`.

11. Which set of letters does the following statement prove true for?

```
if(toupper(c)>='A' && toupper(c)<='M')
```

A. `'B'` through `'L'`.

B. `'A'` through `'M'`.

C. `'A'` through `'M'` and `'a'` through `'m'`.

D. `'A'` through `'Z'` and then down the ramp and out the door.

12. Carbon dioxide poisoning is most often caused by

A. Carbon dioxide.

B. Soft drinks.

C. Leaky furnaces and stoves.

D. Smoking.

13. Suppose that both `eta` and `potata` are strings. What's wrong with the following?

```
eta = potata;
```

A. Absolutely nothing is wrong.

B. The square brackets are missing.

C. Although the statements appear to be copying strings, only the first character in each string is copied.

D. You need a separate function to copy one string to another.

14. The `strcmp` function, which compares two strings, returns what value if the strings are, in fact, equal?

A. Zero.

B. TRUE.

C. FALSE.

D. It returns the length of both strings.

15. Where did the term *taxi cab* come from?

A. From the Latin *taxiambulus,* for a hired means of transportation, and *cab,* from *caballarius,* for an enclosed compartment.

B. From the term *cabriolet,* a two-wheeled carriage, and *tax,* which referred to the burdensome taxes on the first for-hire cabriolets in early New York City.

C. From the term *taximeter cabriolet,* the *taximeter* being a device that measures the fare.

D. *Taxi Cab* was an early Boston cab company, the name eventually applied to all cabs and cars for hire.

16. Concatenation is

A. Illegal in many southern states.

B. The art of copying one string to another.

C. The art of appending one string to another.

D. The art of creating cats from string, similar to macramé.

17. Most functions that manipulate strings can be found in

A. Your grocer's freezer.

B. A yarn store.

C. Your C language library reference.

D. The STRING.H header file.

18. What happens to the string porkrind after the following statement has run its course?

```
strrev(strlwr(porkrind));
```

A. The string comes out backward in lowercase.

B. The string comes out in lowercase and backward.

C. The string is unchanged.

D. Hmmm. Pork rinds. . . .

19. A two-dimensional character array is really

A. An array of strings.

B. An array of a whole mess of characters.

C. It depends on how the array is defined.

D. Another term for a police artist sketch.

20. Which of the following variables refers to the third string in a two-dimensional character array:

A. array[3];

B. array[2];

C. array[3][0];

D. array[2][0];

21. In which dimension was the *Twilight Zone?*

    A. First.

    B. Third.

    C. Fifth.

    D. Sixth.

"THE ARTIST WAS ALSO A PROGRAMMER AND EVIDENTLY PRODUCED SEVERAL VARIATIONS ON THIS THEME."

Chapter 10
The Ugliest Aspect of C: Pointers

● ●

Lessons in This Chapter

▶ Basic boring computer memory stuff

▶ Location, location, location

▶ More pointers, more memory, more madness

▶ And now, the asterisk, please

▶ Pointers and arrays

▶ Pointers are out to destroy arrays

▶ Pointers and strings

▶ Passing pointers to functions

▶ Arrays to and from functions

▶ Arrays of pointers

▶ Sorting strings with pointers

Programs in This Chapter

WHATEVER.C	SIZEOF.C	METRIC.C	USELESS.C
ROMAN.C	TEENY.C	PRIMES.C	LOVYDOVY.C
FISH.C	STRING.C	LINDA1.C	LINDA2.C
LINDA3.C	ULINE.C	STRLEN.C	NOVOWELS.C
ARRAYADD.C	SEVEN.C	CMDLINE1.C	CMDLINE2.C
CMDLINE3.C	PSORT1.C	PSORT2.C	PSORT3.C

Vocabulary Introduced in This Chapter

sizeof	* (pointer)	& (address-of)	static

● ●

*T*here's this bug. It's called a *fly* in English. That's also what the bug does — it *flies*. So a *fly flies*. Most people don't find that confusing, probably because everyone has had their share of flies buzzing around their heads. Saying that a fly flies makes perfect sense, and no one goes into brain lock. (Unless you get into fleas that flee.)

There's this thing in C. It's a variable called a *pointer*. That's also what the variable does — it *points* at something. *Pointers point.* Therein lies the rub: If pointers were called something else, budding C programmers would probably not sit and stew and suffer from brain lock over the concept.

This chapter tackles what many consider to be the most awkwardly presented part of the C programming language — *pointers*. The chapter introduces the subject and explains it in such a lucid manner that after reading it you may wonder what all the fuss was about.

Lesson 10-1: Basic Boring Computer Memory Stuff

Type the following program into your editor.

After you enter the text into your editor, save the file to disk as WHATEVER.C:

Name: WHATEVER.C

```
#include <stdio.h>

void main()
{
    char c;
    int i;
    long x;
    float f;
    double d;

    printf("char variable c = %c\n",c);
    printf("int variable i = %i\n",i);
    printf("long variable x = %l\n",x);
    printf("float variable f = %f\n",f);
    printf("double variable d = %f\n",d);
}
```

Compile. Run.

Your output may look something like this:

```
char variable c = w
int variable i = 18295
long variable x =
float variable f = 0.000000
double variable d = 0.000000
```

You may see other, random values there. That's the whole point: The values are meaningless and random. Why? And why didn't the program crash? After all, the variables were used but never assigned anything. Won't that vex the compiler?

 ✔ Answers coming up!

 ✔ You don't have to assign a variable any data. Only if you create a variable and never use it does the compiler give you one of those "Variable x is never used" warning errors.

 ✔ Variables can be used before they have been assigned any information. There's no reason to do this, but the compiler doesn't complain. It may laugh at you, but it doesn't complain.

Buying the land but not building the house

When you declare a variable in C, you're telling the compiler to set aside space for it. This process works just like building your dream house. First you buy a piece of land, and then you build the house. You can't build the house first, just as you can't assign a value to an undeclared variable.

In your computer, the land is memory.

When you need variables, you tell the compiler how many and of what type. The computer then builds a program that goes out and talks to the computer's real estate agent, who dishes up the proper portions of memory for your program.

 ✔ Variables must be stored somewhere. Computer memory is that somewhere. It's designed to hold information.

 ✔ Memory also holds the program while it's running.

 ✔ Memory is also referred to as RAM.

 ✔ Most people use the term RAM when they're writing a song about their computer, because more words rhyme with *RAM* than with *memory*.

Refer to the WHATEVER.C program. That program creates variables but never assigns them any values, which is similar to buying a lot and not building a house on it. What do you have in that case? You may call it a vacant lot, but something is always there: trees, scrub, garbage, muck, radioactive waste — whatever. The same thing holds true for your computer's memory.

When your program assigns a variable some memory space, it doesn't clear out whatever information may already be stored there. Instead, the variable *assumes* that random information, just as a vacant lot *assumes* the scrub and trees and such. That's what the WHATEVER.C program displays; the random data already stored in your computer's memory. What that could be is anything.

The moral of the story is that you should always assign data to your variables *before* you use them. Otherwise, they assume random information in your PC, which is different from computer to computer. And that's not the end of the story.

- ✔ The compiler does not initialize new variables to zero. In other programming languages, variables that are declared may be assigned zero to begin with, but not in C.

- ✔ Where does the random information come from? It's usually junk left over from programs you have run. DOS (or Windows) doesn't "clean up" memory when a program quits; it just makes that memory available to other programs that need it.

- ✔ The compiler is not only the real estate buyer in your computer, it's also the real estate agent. (Sounds illegal.) The compiler buys lots (memory) for variables based on the variable's needs. Some variables need a great deal of memory; some need only a byte. The compiler sets everything up, assigns memory to variables, and keeps track of their location in memory as well as what type of data they hold.

- ✔ Although your *program* assigns the variable's memory locations and such, the compiler is what *creates* the program. So sue me.

- ✔ The amount of space a variable needs is referred to as its *size* in memory. More about this in the next section.

- ✔ The actual location of the variable in memory is called its *address* — just like the address on your house or on the ugly vacant lot on the corner where the drug dealers hang out.

- ✔ The compiler does all this work. You merely tell it to create a variable; it does the rest.

Some variables are more greedy than others

In your PC, memory space is measured in bytes. Your computer has millions of bytes of RAM, all of which can be used to store variables. That's exactly what Lotus 1-2-3 did in DOS: It used *all* of the memory for its variables. That annoying little MEM thing on the screen, telling you that no more memory was available, was the bane of every 1-2-3 user.

Each variable you declare in your program consumes one or more bytes of memory. Sure, your program may start out innocently enough, but eventually those little bytes add up to kilobytes and megabytes, and then you're writing the routine to flash the letters MEM on-screen. It's vicious.

This program, SIZEOF.C, divulges how much memory each variable is allocated by the compiler. It uses the keyword sizeof to determine how many bytes each variable sucks up. Type the source code into your compiler and save it as SIZEOF.C:

Name: SIZEOF.C

```c
#include <stdio.h>
#include <stdlib.h>

void main()
{
    char a;
    int b;
    long c;
    float d;
    double e;

    puts("Variable sizes:");
    printf("Size of a character = %i\n",sizeof(a));
    printf("Size of an integer = %i\n",sizeof(b));
    printf("Size of a long = %i\n",sizeof(c));
    printf("Size of a float = %i\n",sizeof(d));
    printf("Size of a double = %i\n",sizeof(e));
}
```

Compile and run.

```
Variable sizes:
Size of a character = 1
Size of an integer = 2
Size of a long = 4
Size of a float = 4
Size of a double = 8
```

The program's output tells you how many bytes each type of variable requires. All this is calculated by the sizeof keyword; the details of how it works are covered in the following sidebar, "Keyword sizeof."

✔ Table 3-1 in *C For Dummies,* Volume I, lists the whole assortment of C numeric data types, including a column describing how many bytes each of those variables gobbles up. If you look at the table, it confirms the values returned by the sizeof function.

✔ Not every computer uses the same storage space for its variables, which is why the sizeof keyword was created. You can't assume that your PC and a UNIX computer store an integer using two bytes. The sizeof keyword always returns the proper amount of storage required, no matter on what computer your program was compiled.

✔ Yes, there's a point to knowing how many bytes a variable gobbles up, but that's not the point of the sizeof keyword. You use sizeof primarily in Chapter 11, when you have to manually allocate memory for new variables you create.

✔ Table 1-1 in Volume I of this book has a list of all the C language keywords. Yup, sizeof is there.

Keyword sizeof

The sizeof keyword returns the amount of memory a variable uses. It's used mostly for allocating memory for structures or buffers, typically coupled with the malloc function (see Lesson 11-4). Here's the format:

```
int = sizeof(something);
```

The sizeof keyword is followed by a set of parentheses, inside of which is a variable or structure (something, in the preceding example). sizeof returns the size, in bytes, of the something *variable.* The value returned can be used directly, as in the SIZEOF.C program, or stored in an integer variable (int, in the preceding example).

You may occasionally see sizeof used without the parentheses. It may or may not be okay on your compiler; to be sure, always use the parentheses.

Because sizeof is a keyword, it does not require an include statement or header file in order to work properly.

✔ The size of the program has little to do with how many bytes it uses. I wrote a tiny program — 10K — that sorts all the files on a hard disk. Because thousands of files may be on the disk, the program uses several kilobytes of storage for the sort. On an old 512K PC AT, the sort would run out of memory every time.

✔ Nope, `sizeof` does not return the size of your program.

✔ Nope, `sizeof` does not return the size of memory inside your computer either.

✔ You can give a program the name of a C language function. SIZEOF.C is kosher, as are PRINTF.C and even CHAR.C. You just cannot name a variable after a reserved word. Lesson 3-3 in Volume I of this book discusses what's verboten (and not) with variable names.

Calculating the size of an array

Aside from single variables, you can use the `sizeof` keyword to return the size of an array. Make the following changes to the SIZEOF.C program.

First, add a new variable declaration:

```
char temp[8];
```

That's a character array — a string — consisting of as many as eight characters.

Second, under the `puts` statement, add the following `printf` statement:

```
printf("Size of the array = %i\n",sizeof(temp));
```

This `printf` statement displays how many bytes the character array (string) takes up. Yes, `sizeof` works on arrays as well as on single variables.

Save your changes to disk.

Compile and run. Among the output, you see a line that reads

```
Size of the array = 8
```

An array of eight characters is eight bytes long — which follows because character variables measure one byte each.

Now edit the SIZEOF.C source code and change the array to an array of integers:

```
int temp[8];
```

(You don't have to edit the `printf` statement because it measures only the size of the array and doesn't use the array's data.)

Compile and run. You see a new amount for the size of the array:

```
Size of the array = 16
```

Integers are bigger than character variables. On your screen right now, in fact, you should see that an integer is two bytes in size:

```
Size of an integer = 2
```

Therefore, the array of integers requires 16 bytes of storage; an array of eight 2-byte integers (2 × 8 elements in the array) is 16 bytes long.

One more change!

Edit the SIZEOF.C source code a third time. This time, change the array definition as follows:

```
double temp [8];
```

That's now an array of double-precision floating-point numbers — something NASA probably uses every day to calculate the price of Tang. (You can probably guess what the new output will look like). Save SIZEOF.C to disk again.

Compile. Run. Here's the new size of the array:

```
Size of the array = 64
```

Whoa! Sixty-four bytes are required to hold an array of eight double-precision numbers. That may not be a *ton* of space, but you can see how a spreadsheet program such as Lotus 1-2-3 can gobble up memory quickly.

✔ Even though Chapter 9 deals primarily with character arrays (strings), you can have an array of any variable type in C.

✔ The compiler sets aside memory for variables even if you don't use them. For example, you may create a huge array, but the program ends up using only a small part of it. Even so, the program still hogs up excess memory. This information is important to keep in mind if you're running low on memory: Double-check the size of your arrays.

✔ Honestly, programs that require lots of memory usually dish it up to themselves a little at a time. This process is done by the `malloc` (*m*emory *alloc*ation) function, which is covered in Chapter 11.

It all boils down to this

The compiler really saves you a great deal of work. Look what it does so far:

- ✔ Sets aside a certain chunk of memory for each variable you declare
- ✔ Knows exactly how much memory to set aside for the variable
- ✔ Knows how to organize an array so that it can find variables in the array — even though not every type of array holds variables of the same memory size
- ✔ Accesses the information stored in the variables and interprets that data properly (chars are characters, and ints are integers)
- ✔ Never calls you dirty names or says nasty things about you behind your back

So far, you have only half the equation. You know how much real estate (computer memory) variables and arrays require, but you don't yet know where the real estate is. Where's the address?

C has a special way of discovering exactly *where* in memory variables live. It's the second part of the real estate equation — the location, location, location part. This subject is covered in the next lesson.

How big? Where? Why would I want to know?

"If the compiler is so darn good to me, why would I have to know how big a variable is or where it's stored in memory?"

Obviously, you *don't* have to know that stuff, but it has advantages. Remember that C is a mid-level programming language. That's because C has the capability to directly examine computer memory and the variables stored there. This stuff may seem ambiguous to you now, but it makes some things very easy.

For example, it would be hell on earth to sort a huge array of strings, moving all those bytes back and forth as you do in a bubble sort (refer to Lesson 9-4 in Chapter 9). However, if you sort an array of memory addresses — the locations of those strings and not the strings themselves — you save yourself tons of time and headaches.

Other examples flow throughout the rest of this book and in other C references and advanced tutorials. Although you can use basic C programming to create interesting things, you don't really *know* C until you use memory addresses and the special variables that hold those addresses. The variables are called *pointers.*

Lesson 10-1 Quiz

1. Using a variable before assigning it a value gives you what?

    A. Anything.

    B. A compiler error.

    C. A very willing variable.

    D. A constant.

2. Memory in your computer is measured by which yardstick?

    A. The yardstick of RAM.

    B. The yardstick of bytes.

    C. The yardstick the Welcome Wagon people left.

    D. Computer memory is measured in the metric system.

3. A variable in memory has which two descriptions?

    A. Length and breath.

    B. Uh, that's length and *breadth*.

    C. Size and location.

    D. Résumés and letters of recommendation.

4. *Ping-Pong* is Chinese for

    A. Bounce-ball.

    B. Ping game (Ping is the region in China where Ping-Pong was invented).

    C. Ball [and] paddle.

    D. Irritating battle.

    E. All of the above.

    F. None of the above.

5. The `sizeof` keyword measures the size of what?

    A. The size of a variable.

    B. The size of the programmer's ego.

    C. The size of the table the computer sits on.

    D. The size of underpants the planet Earth would wear, considering that the equator is approximately 40,000 kilometers in girth:

```
Underpants = sizeof(girth);
```

Lesson 10-2: Location, Location, Location

The three rules of real estate are

- ✔ Location
- ✔ Location
- ✔ Location

What they're trying to tell you is that *where* the real estate is located is more important than what's on it or the price or the view or something like that. I always ponder this concept because our neighborhood real estate guy lives in a house that gets a face full of headlights whenever someone drives down the street.

In your computer, location is a spot in memory — what's called an *address.*

Everything in your computer's memory has its own address, which tells everything else in the computer where that something lives and keeps things from living in the same spot.

In C, you can keep track of where your program's variables live by using *pointers.*

- ✔ A *pointer* is a variable that holds a memory address.
- ✔ Better repeat that: *A pointer is a variable that holds a memory address.*
- ✔ A pointer is also a good hunting dog.
- ✔ The Pointer Sisters are a musical act.
- ✔ Harry Nilsson wrote a musical called *The Point,* the story of a little boy named Oblio who had a dog named Arrow.
- ✔ "Oh-blee-oh."
- ✔ Different types of variables have different types of pointers. This statement makes sense when you figure that a character variable takes up one byte in memory, an integer uses two bytes, and so on.

- ✔ Pointer dogs point at things, but the Pointer Sisters point only if it's part of the act. And Oblio didn't have a point on his head, though everyone else did.

A boring program suitable as an example

You never know when the United States may suddenly convert to the metric system. My guess: never. When we finally do succumb to world pressure, you will have the following program ready to help you make the switch.

Type this silly program into your editor. It's just simple, dopey math, multiplying a distance in miles by 1.609 to get the distance in kilometers (which is what my reference book tells me to do). Save the dopey thing to disk as METRIC.C:

Name: METRIC.C

```
#include <stdio.h>
#include <math.h>

void main()
{
    char input[20];
    double miles,kilometers;

    printf("Enter a value in miles:");
    miles=atof(gets(input));

    kilometers = miles*1.609;

    printf("%.2f miles works out to\
    %.2f kilometers",miles,kilometers);
}
```

Compile and run.

```
Enter a value in miles:
```

Try to impress your metric-literate friends by telling them how long your commute is every day. Suppose that you trek 8$\frac{1}{2}$ miles every day. Type **8.5** and press the Enter key:

```
8.50 miles works out to      13.68 kilometers
```

Wow. Much impressive.

- ✔ *Doubles* are double-precision floating-point numbers. Don't let them scare you.

- ✔ In case of a water landing, double-precision variables can be used as a flotation device.

✔ This program requires floating-point numbers because it multiplies one of them by a floating-point number (1.609) and probably gets a floating-point result.

✔ Name a number you could multiply by 1.609 and *not* get a floating-point result. No, better not. This book isn't about math puzzles.

✔ The atof function requires a string as input and returns a double floating-point number as output. That's why the program's miles and kilometers variables are doubles rather than plain floats.

✔ C functions work from the inside out, as explained in Lesson 5-5 in *C For Dummies,* Volume I. That's why the gets function is nested inside the atof function in METRIC.C. You could put those functions on separate lines, but it's not necessary — unless a bunch of parentheses bother you.

✔ Don't let the \ in the middle of the printf statement toss you for a loop. (And, no, it's not a looping statement.) It merely enables you to split a long printf between two lines.

Hello, Mr. Pointer!

The compiler knows four things about any variable:

✔ Its name

✔ Its type (char, int, and so on)

✔ Its size (in bytes)

✔ Its location in memory (address)

You, O program creator, know the variable's name and type because you were the one who entered that information into your editor. You can use the sizeof keyword to find out the variable's girth in memory. To find out where in memory the variable lives, you need a pointer.

Pointer: Don't lean on your elbows at the dinner table, especially at Grandma's house.

A *pointer* is a variable that holds a memory address. Suppose that you have a pointer variable named Arrow and an int variable named Oblio. In your PC's memory, Oblio lives at address 14355 in memory. (Because Oblio is an integer, he takes up two bytes, so Oblio really lives at 14355 and 14356. He's his own neighbor.) After performing the proper pointer magic, the pointer variable Arrow would contain 14355, Oblio's address in memory.

A pointer is like this amazing letter carrier who knows where everyone lives!

So you can use a pointer to find out where variables live in memory. To do that, you must declare the pointer variables just as you declare any variable and then tell the pointer to divine some other variable's address — a two-step process. The first step, declaring the pointer variable, is discussed in the following sidebar about the pointer declaration thing. The second step is covered in the next section.

- Pointers are variables that hold memory addresses.

- Pointer variables are declared with an asterisk, which identifies them as pointers to the compiler.

- If you ever want to access your PC's memory, you need a pointer.

- Yes, someday you will — truly — want to access your PC's memory.

- Why declare pointers of a specific variable type? Because each variable type uses a different amount of memory (see the preceding lesson, about the sizeof keyword). The pointer has to know what it's pointing at.

- The asterisk is the key. When you're declaring a pointer, stick an asterisk before its name. That way, the compiler knows that you're asking for a pointer and not another dumb variable type.

- Though you need the asterisk when you declare a pointer variable, when you *use* the pointer variable, it may or may not have its asterisk. Don't let this bother you now. Just remember that pointers need asterisks when they're declared.

---

* (Pointer declaration thing)

Declaring a pointer works like declaring any type of variable, but with an * (asterisk) in front of the variable name. Here's the format:

type *pointervar;

type is any type of variable: char, int, double, float, long, and so on. It tells you which type of variable the pointer snatches memory addresses for. If the pointer is looking at Oblio, an integer, it must be declared as an int. It can be declared on the same line as any other int in your program.

pointervar is the name of the pointer variable. It's always prefixed by an asterisk when it's declared, which identifies the variable as a pointer to the compiler. You can name the pointer variable as you would name any variable, and the same rules and limits apply. (Pointers cannot be given names used by other variables in the program, which is true of any variable.)

The converted metric-conversion program

Summon the source code for METRIC.C back into your editor. Modify the program so that you can discover the secrets of where the program sticks the miles variable in memory. That requires a pointer variable, specifically one that likes to snoop at double-precision floating-point numbers (doubles).

Here's what you have to do:

- ✔ Declare the pointer; it must exist before you can use it.
- ✔ Assign the pointer an address in memory; like other variables, it must be equal to something, or else it contains "garbage."
- ✔ Use the pointer (which is like, duh); a printf statement displays its value and the memory location of the miles variable.

Creating a pointer variable

First, add the following pointer variable declaration, just below the line that declares the miles variable:

```
double *m_address;
```

Like miles, the pointer must be a double. Then comes a space and then an asterisk (a pointer variable, remember) and the variable's name, m_address; the pointer gives you the address of the miles variable.

Assigning the pointer variable a value (memory address)

Like all variables, pointers must be given values before they do anyone any good (refer to the WHATEVER.C program in Lesson 10-1).

To get a variable's address, you assign a pointer variable to it. Add the following line at the end of the main function:

```
m_address = &miles;
```

This line slides the memory location — the address — of the miles variable through the equal sign and into the m_address pointer variable. Two weird things: The pointer doesn't have its asterisk, and the variable it's examining grows this & thing.

Pointer variables don't always need their asterisks. That's because pointers have, like many famous criminals, split personalities. Used without the asterisk, they consume and represent memory locations. (Lesson 10-4 discusses how they're used with an asterisk.) Either way, you must declare the pointer with an asterisk — always.

Operator & (address of)

The & (address-of) operator is used to pluck the memory location — and not the contents — from a variable. Here's the format:

&var

When the compiler sees the & in front of any variable (var), it coughs up the variable's address (its location in memory) rather than the variable's value.

The & operator is used primarily when you're assigning pointers to variables. It's also required in the scanf function for reading in values and strings.

By the way, & is an ampersand, which is pronounced "AMP-er-sand." When it's used as the address-of operator, I say "address of" in my head (but never out loud).

The & is the address-of prefix operator (see the nearby sidebar about the & operator). It tells the compiler to read the variable's *address,* not its contents. That address is then stored in the pointer variable, which, in its asterisk-less state, is designed to store memory addresses.

Pointers hold memory addresses. They literally *suck* them out of other variables.

Using the pointer as a memory address holder

For the third step in the program's modification, you have to use the pointer. The m_address pointer variable already contains the address of the miles variable. All you have to do is display that value.

First, some output formatting stuff — to clean up the display. Add the following line at the end of the program, just below the m_address = &miles; statement you just added:

```
puts("\nVariables:");
```

This line separates the program's normal output from the informational output you're about to add.

Second, on the line right after the puts statement, add the following:

```
printf("miles is %i bytes at address\
%u\n",sizeof(miles),m_address);
```

The printf statement (split on two lines with the \ character), displays both the size of the miles variable and its location in memory. Because both values are integers, the %i and %u placeholders are used in the printf statement.

Pointer variables are *not* integers. They hold an integer value, which is the memory location of another variable. The pointer variables themselves are *pointers* of a certain type, char, int, double, and so on. (Call this Weird Pointer Thing #472.) For example, the m_address pointer is a double pointer variable. It holds the address of a double variable in memory. That address just happens to be an integer value. But the pointer variable is not an int!

So what does the program know?

Save the modified source code for METRIC.C to disk.

Compile. You may see some warning errors, depending on how your compiler is set up. That's okay. See the check mark list at the end of this section for more information.

Run the program. Type any old value for miles; you're more interested in the latter part of the output:

```
Enter a value in miles: 8.5
8.50 miles works out to    13.68 kilometers
Variables:
miles is 8 bytes at address    13720
```

The Variables section of the output tells you that the miles variable is 8 bytes in size and resides at memory address 13,720. (You may see a different address on your screen.)

The sizeof keyword calculates the variable's size, and 8 bytes is the size of a double-precision floating-point number.

The pointer variable, m_address, holds the address of the miles variable in memory. It sits at address 13,720 — not a bad neighborhood.

✓ The size of a variable never changes, but its memory address does. If you change the METRIC.C program and recompile, the location of miles in memory may change. Of course, the m_address pointer variable always contains the proper address.

✓ The addresses at which variables can be found range from 0 through 65,535. If you refer to Table 3-1 in *C For Dummies,* Volume I, however, you see that only an *unsigned* integer can display a value as high as 65,535. The %i placeholder is a *signed* value. If your compiler stores a variable at address 65,522, for example, the %i placeholder displays it as –14, which doesn't look like a good address. Therefore, the %u placeholder is used in METRIC.C's final printf statements to display unsigned values.

- ✔ An address of –14 surely would incense the post office.

- ✔ More than any other part of C, pointers generate the most warning errors. Under normal circumstances, this program *should not* produce any of them. If it does, adjust your compiler so that it doesn't display the type of warning messages you see on-screen.

- ✔ Suppose that you omit the & in the following statement:

```
m_address = &miles;
```

In that case, you're assigning the value of the `miles` variable to the `m_address` pointer variable. Right away, you get an "incompatible type" error and the compiler doesn't compile. If it didn't give you that error, `m_address` wouldn't point to the location of `miles` in memory; it would contain some other value, not what you want.

- ✔ This is wrong:

```
*m_address = &miles;
```

Not that it doesn't work, but it isn't what you intended. To initialize a pointer, you *do not* use the asterisk. (Lesson 10-4 describes how to use a pointer with its asterisk.)

A scary, on-your-own exercise

This section doesn't have to be *too* scary. Go back into your editor and modify the METRIC.C source code. Repeat the steps you followed earlier, but create, assign, and display the value of a pointer variable, `k_address`, that contains the memory location of the `kilometers` variable.

You have 20 seconds to complete the exercise.

(Just kidding.)

When you're done, keep reading.

No. Don't read this until you're done. Now do it!

Now. I'm not kidding.

(Music plays.)

Done? Save the source code to disk.

Compile. Did you get an error? Remember the & thing? If you got an error, compare your new lines with those listed earlier for the `miles` and `m_address` variables. Your stuff should look the same, except for the different variable names.

Run. Here's what the output may look like:

```
Enter a value in miles: 8.5
8.50 miles works out to      13.68 kilometers
Variables:
miles is 8 bytes at address      13752
kilometers is 8 bytes at address      13720
```

The address numbers you see may be different, but your output should look similar to this example: Each variable is eight bytes in size and sits at a different spot in memory.

Snagging the address of the last variable

One more modification! The METRIC.C program contains one more variable, the input array. Here are the steps you have to take to assign a pointer variable to it and read its address:

First, declare the pointer variable. Insert the following line just below the array declaration at the beginning of the source code:

```
char *i_address;
```

Because this new pointer leers at a string, which is an array of chars, it must be a char pointer. The pointer's name is i_address and has the obligatory "I am a pointer" asterisk.

Second, you have to assign the input array's address to the pointer. You may think that this line would work:

```
i_address = &input[0];
```

or maybe even this one:

```
i_address = &input;
```

Both are wrong.

Initializing a pointer to an array is a special thing — another darned exception! Add this line to your source code, just above the other two pointer assignments you've added:

```
i_address = input;
```

The missing ampersand is yet another one of those few weird exceptions in the C language — not as many exceptions as you get in French, but an exception anyway. For some reason, the compiler knows that an array name is an address already, so the ampersand becomes unnecessary. Here's the rule all spelled out:

When you snag the address of an array into a pointer, you don't need the & operator.

This rule holds true for all types of arrays, not just for `char` arrays. For some reason, by its very nature the array's name is enough for the pointer to get what it needs. (You still need an & when you use an array in a `scanf` function, but that's another story.)

Third, and finally, you need another `printf` statement to display the results. Stick the preceding line before the other two `printf` statements you added:

```
printf("input is %i bytes at address\
%u\n",sizeof(input),i_address);
```

Nothing new there.

Compile and run. Here's how the output may look:

```
Enter a value in miles: 8.5
8.50 miles works out to    13.68 kilometers
Variables:
input is 20 bytes at address    13770
miles is 8 bytes at address     13750
kilometers is 8 bytes at address    13758
```

The `input` array is 20 bytes long and lives at address 13770. Whew! Congratulations. You passed your first pointer lesson.

✔ You may not see this in your output, but look at the preceding example. Notice the addresses displayed by the program: `input` is found at address 13770 and is 20 bytes long. The sum of 13770 and 20 is 13750, which is where `miles` is found. Now `miles` is 8 bytes long, and 13750 + 8 = 13758, which is where `kilometers` lives. This may or may not happen with your program, or the variables may be stored out of order, but it shows you how the compiler packs the variables in memory.

✔ If your variable addresses aren't that close, you may notice that they're two, four, or six bytes from each other. Those bytes represent the storage space taken by the pointer variables themselves. Consider this information for trivial purposes only.

TECHNICAL STUFF

Sleep heavily after reading this memory address information

In the midst of this overwhelming lesson, you may have caught on to the peculiarity of the memory addresses held in pointer variables. For the most part, the memory addresses returned are all integers in the range of 0 to 65,535. Never mind that pointers themselves aren't integers. But why, with all the megabytes of RAM in your PC, does the pointer return a value in the (unsigned) range of 0 to 65,535? Isn't 65,535 bytes of memory only 64K? Your PC has way more memory in it than 64K.

The answer is, as you expect, funky. The PC's memory is divided into 64K chunks called *segments.* If you have set up your compiler to

create silly little DOS programs (the kind this book specializes in), the compiler optimizes itself to produce output that runs in 64K segments. That's why the memory addresses for your variables are something less than 65,535.

Another part of the memory address, called the *offset,* is used to tell the compiler *exactly* where in memory (from address zero on up through address *x* megabytes) a variable exists. You can mess with that value in C if you like, but only an advanced C programming book tells you how it works. (Yes, it's that trivial.)

Here's a final listing of the METRIC.C program, in case you're totally flummoxed:

```c
#include <stdio.h>
#include <math.h>

void main()
{
    char input[20];
    char *i_address;
    double miles,kilometers;
    double *m_address,*k_address;

    printf("Enter a value in miles:");
    miles=atof(gets(input));

    kilometers = miles*1.609;

printf("%.2f miles works out to\
    %.2f kilometers",miles,kilometers);
```

(continued)

(continued)

```
    i_address = input;
    m_address = &miles;
    k_address = &kilometers;

    puts("\nVariables:");

    printf("input is %i bytes at address\
%u\n",sizeof(input),i_address);
    printf("miles is %i bytes at address\
%u\n",sizeof(miles),m_address);
    printf("kilometers is %i bytes at address\
%u\n",sizeof(kilometers),k_address);
}
```

Lesson 10-2 Quiz

1. Which of the following things is weird about pointers?

    A. They're declared with a * in front of their names.

    B. They may or may not use the * in front of their names in the program.

    C. They are declared of a certain type, though the memory address values they hold are integers.

    D. All of the above.

2. Which of the following is an *improper* way to declare a pointer variable arrow to hold the address of the character variable oblio?

    A. char *arrow; char oblio;

    B. char *arrow,oblio;

    C. char *arrow, &oblio;

    D. char arrow, *oblio;

3. Which of the following assigns the address of variable oblio to pointer variable arrow?

    A. arrow = &oblio;

    B. arrow = *oblio;

C. `*arrow = oblio;`

D. `arrow = oblio;`

4. Match the pointer variable with the type of `printf` statement required to print it:

A. `char *groucho`   1. `printf("%u\n",groucho);`

B. `int *chico`   2. `printf("%u\n",chico);`

C. `float *harpo`   3. `printf("%u\n",harpo);`

D. `double *zeppo`   4. `printf("%u\n",zeppo);`

5. Why did Columbus have trouble funding his voyage?

A. Bad credit.

B. They thought that the Orient was too far away.

C. They thought that the world was flat and that he would fall off.

D. Because the Portuguese had sworn to sink his fleet, no one would put up the insurance money.

Lesson 10-3: More Pointers, More Memory, More Madness

Please type into your editor the following silly program, which I promise is not the last silly program in this book.

After you type all this source code into your editor, save the beast as USELESS.C:

Name: USELESS.C

```
#include <stdio.h>

void main()
{
    int i,v,x;
    int *address;

    i = 1;
    v = 5;
    x = 10;
```

(continued)

(continued)

```
    address = &i;
    printf("var i = %u\n",address);

    address = &v;
    printf("var v = %u\n",address);

    address = &x;
    printf("var x = %u\n",address);
}
```

Compile and run. Here's the useless output:

```
var i = 65524
var v = 65522
var x = 65520
```

You may see different memory addresses on your screen. You may even see them all two bytes apart, which is the size of an integer variable.

The point of the program — if you can believe that it has a point — is twofold.

Pointer: Guys, never wear white socks with dark formal wear.

First, the program shows that one pointer variable can reference several other variables. In USELESS.C, the address pointer variable is used three times, each time being set equal to the address of the program's three variables. Pointers, like any other type of variable, can hold different values. That's why they're variables and not constants.

Second, and not really that obvious, the program shows that pointer variables must be initialized before they can be used. Actually, they should be initialized before they can be *useful,* because an uninitialized pointer variable is like any other uninitialized variable: It contains garbage.

Figure 10-1 illustrates how the address pointer variable works in the USELESS.C program. It accesses each of the integers stored in memory, pointing to their memory locations. (Each square in the figure represents a byte of memory; integers take up two bytes.)

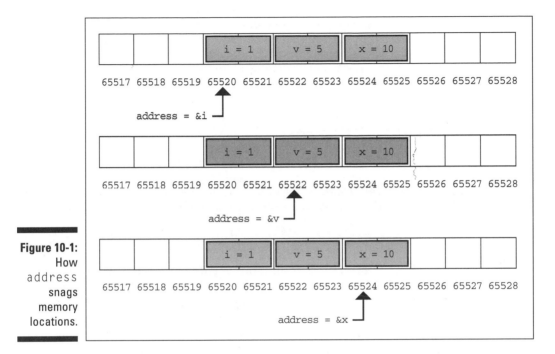

Figure 10-1:
How
address
snags
memory
locations.

All the information following should be familiar to you:

A pointer variable must be declared, assigned a value (initialized), and then used. The USELESS.C program does that in three steps. First, the pointer is declared:

```
int *address;
```

Then it's initialized:

```
address = &i;
```

Then it's used:

```
printf("var i = %u\n",address);
```

- ✔ Pointers must be declared with the asterisk.
- ✔ When a pointer is used without its asterisk, it refers to a memory location.
- ✔ When a pointer is used with its asterisk is covered in the next lesson.
- ✔ To assign a pointer a memory location, you must prefix the other variable with the & (address-of) operator.

✔ Though pointers are declared of a certain type (the same type as the variables they examine), the values they contain are memory addresses, which are displayed as integers. The %u placeholder is used in the printf statement to display the address held in the pointer as an unsigned integer value.

Roamin' numerals (and another exception!)

From the preceding lesson, you should know that when you use a pointer to grab a variable's address, you need the ampersand:

```
m_address = &miles;
```

When you grab the address of an array, you don't need the ampersand:

```
i_address = input;
```

Here, input is an array. It can be any type of array. The & isn't needed. However. . . .

Oh no, please, not *another* exception!

When you access individual elements in the array, you need the ampersand. The elements are, after all, different from the array name itself. For one, they have square brackets and numbers. That makes them different internally to the compiler, and that's enough nudging to require the &, lest you get an ugly error — like the one you see when you enter the following program:

Name: ROMAN.C

```
#include <stdio.h>

void main()
{
    char rn[] = {'I', 'V', 'X', 'L', 'C', 'M'};
    char *r;
    int x;

    for(x=0;x<6;x++)
    {
        r = rn[x];
        printf("%i. %u = %c\n",x+1,r,rn[x]);
    }

}
```

This program should make sense to you. A character array is created, along with a character pointer and an integer. Then a loop is used to display all the characters in the array, along with their memory locations.

Save the file to disk as ROMAN.C, from the roman numerals in this program's array.

Compile.

The error on a Borland compiler is `Nonportable pointer conversion`.

Microsoft compilers yield a `Different levels of indirection` error.

The problem? You cannot grab the address of an array element unless you prefix it with an & (address-of) operator.

Don't run that program — change it!

Load the source code for ROMAN.C into your editor. Find Line 11. Rewrite it as follows:

```
r = &rn[x]
```

Save it back to disk.

Recompile. It should do so smoothly, minus any errors:

```
1. 65520 = I
2. 65521 = V
3. 65522 = X
4. 65523 = L
5. 65524 = C
6. 65525 = M
```

Although the addresses you see may be different, the results should be similar.

- ✔ Each address is only one byte apart. How come? Character variables use only one byte in memory.
- ✔ All the addresses are sequential because the array is stored that way in memory.
- ✔ The rn array could also have been declared as follows:

  ```
  char rn[] = "IVXLCM"
  ```

- ✔ Either way, it's still an array of single characters.
- ✔ Another pointer: Ladies, never wear a red bra under a white blouse.

More Roman tweaking

Here's another view of the ROMAN.C program:

```c
#include <stdio.h>

void main()
{
    char rn[] = {'I', 'V', 'X', 'L', 'C', 'M'};
    char *r;
    int x;

    r = rn;

    for(x=0;x<6;x++)
    {
        printf("%i. %u = %c\n",x+1,r,rn[x]);
        r++;
    }

}
```

Return to your text editor and rearrange your ROMAN.C source code as shown here. Two items:

First, the pointer variable is set equal to the array before the for loop:

```c
r = rn;
```

This example works without the & because rn is the name of the array, not an individual element.

Second, the pointer variable is incremented in the for loop, which should point it at each successive element in the array:

```c
r++;
```

This line works because pointers are like any other variable. In fact, you can even do math with pointers — a subject I put off until much, much later.

A cloud of puzzlement about this may be circling your head. Even so, it should work: The pointer is initialized to a memory location, the start of the array. Then, for every element displayed in the array, the pointer is incremented. The program's output should be completely unaffected by these changes.

Save the file to disk.

Compile.

Cross your fingers and run it:

```
1.  65520 = I
2.  65521 = V
3.  65522 = X
4.  65523 = L
5.  65524 = C
6.  65525 = M
```

The output you see on-screen should be identical to the output before you modified the program. It worked!

      ✔ You do not need an & when you're getting the address of an array name.

      ✔ You can increment a pointer just as you would increment any other variable.

Utterly corrupting the ROMAN program

As a final change to the ROMAN program, consider converting the char array over to an int array. Fire up the source code in your editor, and make the following change to the array declaration:

```
int rn[] = { 1, 5, 10, 50, 100, 1000 };
```

Now rn is an array of the values of the six roman numerals.

You also have to change the pointer declaration because it is now pointing at an integer array rather than at a character array:

```
int *r;
```

Finally, you have to change the printf statement to display integers (%i) rather than characters (%c):

```
printf("%i. %u = %i\n",x+1,r,rn[x]);
```

Save the changes to disk.

Compile. No errors? Did you think that you would get errors? Never mind.

Run it:

```
1. 65514 = 1
2. 65516 = 5
3. 65518 = 10
4. 65520 = 50
5. 65522 = 100
6. 65524 = 1000
```

Just look at the results; don't think about the program for a second.

Each number in the int array was properly displayed, 1 through 1000. The memory locations look just fine: They're all in a row, which makes sense for an array, and they're each two bytes apart because integers use two bytes in memory.

Now for the interesting part: The numbers 65514 through 65524 were obtained by repeating the following statement:

```
r++;
```

You may think that if the memory address in r were equal to 65514, r++ (which is really r + 1) would equal 65515. Wouldn't it?

The answer is no! Remember that r is an *integer* pointer and that integers take up *two* bytes in memory. The compiler is smart enough to know that. If you increment a pointer to an integer in memory — to point at the next integer stored in memory — you must add *two* to the pointer's value.

The same holds true for other variables of different sizes. For example, a double eats up eight bytes in memory. If r is a double pointer, r++ really adds 8 to the value of r, which points to the next double in memory.

That's why it's very important to declare a pointer variable as the proper type. It's also why pointer variables of one type cannot snoop on variables of another type.

✔ You don't have to remember exactly what incrementing (or decrementing) a pointer variable adds or subtracts to or from the memory address. The compiler keeps track of that for you.

✔ Truly, a pointer of one variable type is designed to point only at variables of the same type. You cannot randomly assign pointers to variables. Your program would make no sense.

✔ Refer to Lesson 10-1 for more information about how much space variables occupy in memory.

✔ The Romans had no symbol for zero. In fact, a group of historians claim that the Roman Empire fell because all their accountants went nuts.

Lesson 10-3 Quiz

1. Pointer variables can hold the address from any other variable.

   A. True.

   B. False.

   C. True, as long as the other variables are of the same type as the pointer.

   D. False, as long as the dog-food companies refuse to tell us what exactly "meat byproducts" are.

2. Who is the bad guy in Nilsson's *The Point* (the album that features Oblio and his dog, Arrow)?

   A. The Overlord.

   B. The Baron.

   C. The Count.

   D. Mr. Cone.

3. Assuming that t is a pointer variable, what is wrong with the following?

   ```
   t = sun[22];
   ```

   A. The programmer wanted to read element 22 but forgot that the first element in any array is zero.

   B. The array variable needs an ampersand for t to read its address.

   C. The t variable needs a bowtie or something.

   D. Trick question: Nothing is wrong.

4. Suppose that a pointer variable contains a memory location. What happens after you increment the pointer variable?

   A. The contents of that memory location increase.

   B. The memory location changes places with the next byte in memory.

   C. The variable points at the next chunk of memory that would hold the kind of variables it's designed to look at.

   D. The pointer variable increments itself by one.

Take a break! A good two-hour nap, followed by some ice cream, would be an excellent treat.

Lesson 10-4: And Now, the Asterisk, Please

A great deal is going on with pointers, and you have a great deal to keep in your head. Right now, you're about one-third of the way through your pointer odyssey, so it's a good time for a review.

A review

Make sure that you know the following things. If you're fuzzy on any one of them, review Lessons 10-1, 10-2, and 10-3 until you have this stuff pretty much inside your head:

✔ Variables take up different amounts of space in memory. The `sizeof` keyword tells you how much space each variable hogs up.

✔ Pointer variables are declared of the same type as the variables they examine, `char` for `char`, `int` for `int`, and so on.

✔ Pointer variables must be assigned an address before they can be used. They must be *initialized*.

✔ That preceding point gets more C programmers in trouble than anything, so let me repeat it:

Pointer variables must be assigned an address before they can be used. They must be *initialized*.

✔ To get the address of any variable, you need the & (address-of) operator. The address is then given to the pointer variable like any assignment in C:

```
pvar = &whatever;
```

✔ You do not need the & when you're assigning a pointer to an array.

✔ You need the & when you're assigning a pointer to an array element.

✔ The value contained inside the pointer is a memory address, which can be displayed with the `printf` function and the `%u` placeholder. Even so, the pointer itself is not considered an integer variable.

✔ When pointers are incremented or decremented, they point at the next chunk of memory, not at the next memory location. If the pointer is a `float` and you increment the pointer's value, it points at the next memory address that would hold a float, usually four bytes away. (Review Chapter 9 if this stuff still bugs you.)

✔ A floating pointer would be called a *buoy*.

✔ The Cheat Sheet inside the front cover of this book contains a summary of pointer information. Look there when you want a quick summary or reminder of how something works.

Pointers that point and peek

Pointers are a difficult concept to grasp for many budding C programmers. Sure, you've already been through some monster concepts, especially when you're assigning a pointer to a variable. Perhaps the main reason pointers drive C programmers bonkers is that pointers have a dual nature. Consider pointer arrow:

```
arrow
```

By itself, pointer arrow represents a memory location — if it has been properly initialized. (Otherwise, like any other variable, it holds garbage.)

```
*arrow
```

After the pointer has been initialized and it holds the memory location of some variable, the variable's *value* can be accessed with the asterisk — the same asterisk you use to declare the pointer. In this mode, the pointer takes on a new nature. The asterisk means, "Show me what lives at. . . ."

The asterisk in front of a pointer variable means, "Show me what lives at. . . ." or "Show me the contents of. . . ."

What lives at where? Contents of what? Pointers hold addresses. To see what value is held at that address, you use the asterisk.

Time for a demo program!

✔ Read the next two bullet points only if you've ever programmed in BASIC.

✔ If you're familiar with the BASIC programming language, a pointer with an asterisk is similar to the peek command: It displays the contents of some memory location. A pointer is more than peek; peek returns only tiny integers, and a pointer returns whatever value is stored in memory, which can be any variable type.

✔ 'Nother BASIC similarity: A pointer with an asterisk can also be used like the poke command to change the contents of memory.

✔ Technically, a pointer in C is similar to the VARPTR function in BASIC. No one really uses the VARPTR function, so I'm just wasting valuable typing molecules telling you this.

The pointer is a snoopy mailman

Here's another silly demo program.

Type the following source code into your editor. The only new thing is the pointer variable used with its asterisk in the final `printf` statement. Otherwise, this stuff should all be old hat to you. Save this trivial little program as TEENY.C:

Name: TEENY.C

```
#include <stdio.h>

void main()
{
    int teeny;
    int *t;

/* initialize variables */

    teeny = 1;
    t = &teeny;

/* use and abuse variables */

    printf("Variable teeny = %i\n",teeny);
    printf("Memory address = %u\n",t);
    printf("Contents of memory = %i\n",*t);
}
```

Compile and run. Here's a sample of the output — the part I dwell on at length in this lesson:

```
Variable teeny = 1
```

The variable `teeny` has a value of 1. No biggie. I mean, little kids are reading about this stuff in Lesson 3-1 in Volume I of this book.

The program has conveniently stored the variable `teeny` at memory address 65,524:

```
Memory address = 65524
```

On your computer, it's probably in another, better neighborhood. Even so, the pointer served its function; it knows where `teeny` lives in memory.

Finally:

```
Contents of memory = 1
```

What you see displayed is the value of the *t variable. It's a pointer that contains a memory address. The integer value at that address is 1. The pointer with its asterisk shows you what lives at that address in memory.

✔ The content of variable t (65524) is a memory address.

✔ The content of variable *t (1) is an integer value.

✔ It's that funky dual nature of pointers again! They can be memory addresses or values, depending on whether you use the asterisk.

✔ In the TEENY.C program, the `teeny` variable lives at address 65,524. The t pointer holds that address, but it can also look there to see what value is stored.

✔ The final `printf` uses a `%i` placeholder to tell you the value of the *t variable. That's because *t is an integer pointer and the values it references are `int`s.

✔ The pointer variable t does not change in the program; it's merely used in two different ways. Without the asterisk, t contains the address of the `teeny` variable. With the asterisk, *t shows you what lives at that address: the integer value 1.

✔ When you initialize a pointer to look at a specific variable in memory:

```
t = &teeny;
```

then the following is true:

```
*t = teeny;
```

✔ The value of the *t pointer variable is equal to the value of the `teeny` variable. This concept works for *any* pointer and variable of the same type: Initialize the pointer to the variable, and then both can be used the same, as just shown.

More messin' around with *pointers

Edit the TEENY.C source code again. Duplicate the final three printf statements: Copy and paste them just below those already in the program.

Between the two sets of printf statements, add the following line:

```
teeny = 64;
```

The whole program should now look like this:

```c
#include <stdio.h>

void main()
{
    int teeny;
    int *t;

/* initialize variables */

    teeny = 1;
    t = &teeny;

/* use and abuse variables */

    printf("Variable teeny = %i\n",teeny);
    printf("Memory address = %u\n",t);
    printf("Contents of memory = %i\n",*t);

    teeny = 64;

    printf("Variable teeny = %i\n",teeny);
    printf("Memory address = %u\n",t);
    printf("Contents of memory = %i\n",*t);
}
```

Compile and run.

Here's the output:

```
Variable teeny = 1
Memory address = 65524
Contents of memory = 1
Variable teeny = 64
Memory address = 65524
Contents of memory = 64
```

The second set of `printf` statements tell you that the value of `teeny` has changed from 1 to 64. The memory location stays the same (65524) because of this line:

```
teeny = 64;
```

What was stored at that memory location has changed. The `*t` pointer reflects that.

Reload the TEENY.C source code back into your editor. (Don't worry about all this reloading; your disk drive doesn't get tired.)

Change the `teeny = 64;` line to

```
*t = 64;
```

The value 64 is slid through the equal sign and stored at the memory address in pointer `t`. The memory address is not changed, because `*t` is used, but what lives at that address is changed to 64. (Because `*t` is the same thing as the variable `teeny`, you haven't changed anything at all in the program.)

Enough talk!

Save. Compile. Run.

The output is the same. Why? Because you didn't really change anything. Using the variable `*t` is the same as using `teeny` in the program. That's basically the point of pointers.

- ✔ After a pointer has been initialized, using the pointer with its asterisk is the same as using the variable it was initialized to. Weird concept, but you learn to live with it.

- ✔ In the final rendition of TEENY.C, both `*t` and `teeny` are essentially the same thing.

- ✔ Don't do this:

```
t = 64;
```

This example sticks memory location 64 into variable `t`. It's initializing a pointer to a specific address. What lives at address 64? I don't know, but it's probably very creepy.

- ✔ Always initialize a pointer before you use it. Every program with pointers needs a statement similar to the following:

```
t = &teeny;
```

✔ Only with the pointer's asterisk can you store a value in memory and then only after you have initialized the pointer variable.

✔ C gurus say that *t accesses the contents of variable teeny "indirectly." That makes sense: The pointer snuck around the neighborhood, found out teeny's address, and then peeked in the window to see what value was there.

One pointer, several variables

Load the source code for the USELESS.C program into your editor.

If you can't recall (because so much material is in your brain), the USELESS.C program uses one pointer variable, address, to access three different integer variables in the program.

"No biggie," you say. "Child's play," you chortle.

Fine. Change every printf statement in the program, sticking an asterisk in front of the address pointer variable. You don't have to change anything else; you're just changing the nature of what address displays. Change this:

```
address
```

to this:

```
*address
```

Save. Compile. Run.

```
var i = 1
var v = 5
var x = 10
```

Each time, the *address variable reads the proper value from memory. Again, after it's properly initialized, the pointer variable with its asterisk can be used to replace the variable it points at.

✔ The advantage here is that you were able to snoop on three different integer variables by using only one pointer variable. This is beginning to show you a little bit of how useful pointers can be.

✔ You don't have to change the %u to %i in the printf statements. Both placeholders display integer values.

WARNING!

✔ Don't do this:

```
*address = &i
```

This line does not initialize the address variable. Instead, it stores the memory location of the i variable somewhere else in memory. Where? Who knows! The address variable hasn't been initialized. Oops! (Your compiler should spot this error and not build the program.)

TECHNICAL STUFF

✔ Both the values referenced and held in the address variable can be displayed — that annoying dual-nature thing of pointers again. All it takes is more modification to the printf statements to show both sides of the pointer's face. For example:

```
printf("var I = %i at address %u\n", *address, address);
```

The first *address represents the contents; the second address represents the memory location.

Lesson 10-4 Quiz

1. After you initialize the blorf pointer to the zing variable, which of the following is true?

   A. blorf = zing

   B. *blorf = zing

   C. *blorf = &zing

   D. cheesecake = 500 calories

2. Explain the following printf thing:

   ```
   printf("%f fathoms at %u bytes\n",*sub,sub);
   ```

   A. The pointer must be a floating-point pointer, a buoy.

   B. The output will be garbled.

   C. Oh, that shows the dual nature of a pointer, as the memory location and what's stored at that location.

   D. You cannot explain a printf statement. Instead, the masters teach that you should stare at the statement and absorb it into your soul. Become one with printf. Sing the song of the mute elf. Ommmm!

3. Which of the following is *not* a real Japanese holiday?

    A. January 15, Adult's Day.

    B. February 3, the Bean-Throwing Festival.

    C. September 15, Respect-for-the-Aged Day.

    D. November 23, The Peacock Feast.

4. Assuming that `tpr` is a pointer variable, which of the following is probably not what the programmer intended?

    A. `tpr = 64;`

    B. `*tpr = &whatever;`

    C. `*tpr = 64;`

    D. `tpr = &whatever;`

5. What is the following?

```
T = 4*alpha;
```

    A. Variable `t` equals four times the contents of `alpha`.

    B. Variable `t` equals four pointers named `alpha`.

    C. Variable `t` equals four times `alpha`.

    D. Variable `t` is a drink with jam and bread.

Take a short snack break here before the next lesson!

Lesson 10-5: Pointers and Arrays

Pointers and arrays were made for each other. Then one day the pointer woke up and realized that almost everything an array did he could do. So he accused the array of not even existing.

Scandalous!

The pointer is right: What you find out in Chapter 9 about using arrays is really a shorthand notation for using pointers. All those brackets and such — they're just abbreviated pointer language. This stuff will make sense to you soon, of course — probably some time after you finish this lesson and the next.

✔ Pointers can do *everything* an array does. Although you can use pointers as a substitute for array notation, you cannot use pointers to declare an array. For the most part, you cannot substitute something like int array[24] with pointers.

✔ Don't forget array notation! Even advanced programmers set up and use arrays all the time. True, you can use pointers to do the same thing, but there's nothing wrong or backward about using arrays the old-fashioned way.

✔ I honestly believe that this is the last time I'll ever tell you that something about the C language is untrue.

Zipping through an array with a pointer

The following program, PRIMES.C, displays the first ten prime numbers. This is a big thing with computer programmers. They all clamor for programs that hunt down prime numbers. Me? I just stick them in an array.

Type the source code for PRIMES.C into your editor. The array declaration is a little long, so it wraps around in this book; make sure that it's all on one line in your editor. Save the program to disk as PRIMES.C:

Name: PRIMES.C

```c
#include <stdio.h>

void main()
{
    int primes[] = { 1, 2, 3, 5, 7, 11, 13, 17, 19, 23 };
    int *p;
    int x;

/* initialize the pointer */

    p = primes;

    for(x=0;x<10;x++)
    {
        printf("%i\n",*p);
        p++;
    }
}
```

Compile and run.

What you see are the ten numbers in the array displayed in order. What displayed them was a pointer, not the array variables or elements or whatever you call the bracket things.

First, the pointer was initialized to the array:

```
p = primes;
```

No & here because primes is the name of the array. No * because p is being initialized. (You cannot use the asterisk until *after* a pointer variable has been initialized.)

Second, the pointer is used:

```
printf("%i\n",*p);
```

The %i placeholder in the printf statement gets its value from *p. At this point, p is equal to the memory address of the array's first element, and the * tells the program to fetch whatever lives at that address; the first element in the array holds the value 1.

Finally, inside the loop, the value of the pointer variable (the address) is incremented:

```
p++;
```

As you saw in the ROMAN.C example, this line increments the pointer to the next memory address for a given size of variable. It does not add one to the value of p, nor does it increment the contents of that memory location.

Figure 10-2 illustrates what happens to p++. First, p is initialized to the same memory address as the beginning of the primes array. Then *p is used to grab whatever lives at that address. Finally, p is incremented one integer-size chunk with p++. This step ensures that p is incremented that way through each array item, as shown in the figure.

- As a pointer variable is incremented through an array, it contains the address of each successive variable in the array.

- Incrementing a pointer variable does not change the value of whatever is stored at that location. You need the * in front of a pointer to see what lives at a given address as well as to change that value.

- The PRIMES.C source code is very similar to the ROMAN.C series of programs you worked on in Lesson 10-3 (the final incarnation of ROMAN.C).

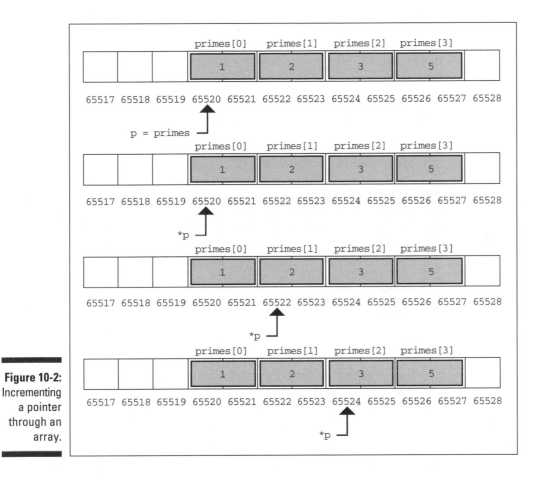

Figure 10-2: Incrementing a pointer through an array.

 A prime number is any number that can be divided evenly by only 1 and itself. Five is a prime number, for example, because when you divide it by any numbers other than 1 or 5, you get severe decimal-place action. The number 12 is not a prime number because it can be divided evenly by 2, 3, 4, and 6.

And now, something to truly drive you nuts

 I'm putting a snack break right here because you're going to want to start this section fresh. Go get something to eat. Go walk outside and enjoy nature for a bit. Then come back to face this horror:

```
*p++
```

Strange things happen when you use incrementation with a pointer and its asterisk. Actually, it's not *that* strange. You can tell that a memory address is being examined and that something is being incremented. Which of those happens to what and when is the big question.

Start off by making the PRIMES.C program tighter. Get rid of the curly brackets, and stick only one statement inside the for loop:

```
for(x=0;x<10;x++)
    printf("%i\n",*p++);
```

What you're doing is combining the *p with the p++ statement that follows it. Put them both in a vise, and it comes out like *p++. The truly odd thing is that the program and its output are not affected: Because the ++ follows p, that memory address is incremented *after* the variable was read and used. This makes the program harder to read, of course; *p++ is awfully cryptic.

Save. Compile. Run.

The program's output is the same.

- ✔ You may think that *p++ would cause the pointer to increment the variable at that memory location and not the pointer's address value. This situation is another befuddlement about pointers — something the next section touches on.

- ✔ Don't bother glossing over this stuff. Incrementing pointers, and pointer math in general, happens frequently in C. The following sections explain this subject carefully, so pay attention!

- ✔ Pointers, like variables, are not islands unto themselves. They must be used somehow. The following statement:

```
*p;
```

generates one of those annoying Lvalue required errors. It's just as silly as if you wrote

```
total;
```

You must *do* something with the variable or use it somehow.

- ✔ Doing math with pointers does not work like normal math. Whenever you add, subtract, or otherwise mess with a pointer, you're working with chunks of memory equal in size to the pointer's variable type. Adding 10 to an integer pointer, for example, actually adds 20 bytes to the memory location stored there.

- ✔ The preceding check mark discusses a rather dreary subject. Don't read it again.

An ugly can of worms

I'd rather not show you the *p++ pointer thing, but it crops up and slaps you in the face sooner or later. When I want to deal with something like that, I cheat. I feel that it's only fair that I tell you how to cheat too.

Several things are working in a contraption such as *p++ or ++*p or *(p++) or — take your pick. Remember that pointers are variables and that you can manipulate them just like any other variable. They're also subject to two weird C language rules:

The order of precedence

The weird ++ or -- before or after the variable

Knowing both of these rules tells you whether the pointer's memory location or variable is incremented and whether it's incremented before or after it's read.

Why memorize rules when you can cheat!

When I want to know what's happening with a pointer variable and incrementation or decrementation, I just whip out a handy table, exactly like the one shown in Table 10-1. This table illustrates many of the pointer knot problems you may encounter. Refer to the table when you're puzzled or when you need a quick reference without hurting your brain.

Table 10-1	**Pointers, Parentheses, and Math**	
Pointer Thing	*Memory Address*	*Memory Contents*
p	Yup	Nope
*p	Nope	Yup
*p++	Incremented after value is read	Unchanged
*(p++)	Incremented after value is read	Unchanged
(*p)++	Unchanged	Incremented after it's used
*++p	Incremented before value is read	Unchanged
*(++p)	Incremented before value is read	Unchanged
++*p	Unchanged	Incremented before it's used
++(*p)	Unchanged	Incremented before it's used
p*++	Not a pointer	Not a pointer
p++*	Not a pointer	Not a pointer

Table 10-1 tells you whether the pointer's memory location or variable (memory contents) are being manipulated. It also explains whether the contents are manipulated before or after a value is read from memory.

- ✔ Table 10-1 is also on the Cheat Sheet inside the front cover of this book. Tear out the Cheat Sheet and keep it close to your computer.

- ✔ Table 10-1 uses the ++ (incrementation) operator, though any mathematical manipulation can replace it.

- ✔ The order of precedence for *, ++, and -- is the same. The compiler takes them in order, but from *right* to *left*.

- ✔ The sacred order of precedence (My Dear Aunt Sally) is covered in Lesson 3-8 in Volume I of this book.

- ✔ Also remember that a ++ following a variable increments it *after* it's used; a ++ before a variable increments it *before* it's used, as explained in Lesson 8-2 in Chapter 8.

- ✔ A great way to always ensure that a pointer behaves the way you want is to enclose the vital parts of it in parentheses. For example:

```
*(p++)
```

The value at address p is read, and then p is incremented. No argument. No right-to-left reading. As long as you remember that p is incremented *after* it's used, you'll be okay.

- ✔ Whatever appears in the parentheses happens first.

- ✔ I'm not going to go into any more detail here because you're probably in a hurry and this pointer stuff won't make sense until later. Please, if you glossed over this lesson, return and reread this lesson after you finish this chapter.

Lesson 10-5 Quiz

1. If pointer p is initialized to array `primes`, what's the value of *p?

    A. The first element in the array.

    B. The memory location of the first element.

    C. I don't know; I keep saying "star-pee" in my head.

    D. Nine.

2. Incrementing an integer pointer does what?

    A. Adds one to it.

    B. Makes it point to the next integer stored in memory.

C. Makes it point to the next element of an array.

D. Both B and C.

3. How would you combine the pointers used in the following two statements?

```
a = *zot;
zot++;
```

A. I wouldn't.

B. a = *zot++;

C. a = zot*++;

D. a = ||*zot*||*.*

E. @#$%^&!!

4. How can you tell what goes on in the following?

```
++*p
```

A. Read for order of precedence from right to left, and then see which side of the thing the ++ is on.

B. Put parentheses around everything.

C. Write the author of this book some e-mail.

D. Look it up in Table 10-1.

5. Who was not an Andrews Sister?

A. Maxene.

B. Laverne.

C. Patty.

D. Julie.

Lesson 10-6: Pointers Are Out to Destroy Arrays

Pointers and arrays are so alike that it makes you sick. They're not exactly in love, because you can use pointer things to utterly do away with array notation.

Utterly?

Yes, utterly. You still need array notation to declare the array. After that, you can use the much more versatile pointer to crawl all over the array, accessing values and changing things with nary a square bracket in sight.

A romance novel is in there somewhere, as demonstrated by the following program.

Type this source code into your editor. The pointer is declared and initialed but so far unused. That will change. Save it to disk as LOVYDOVY.C:

Name: LOVYDOVY.C

```c
#include <stdio.h>

void main()
{
    int array[8];
    int *a, x;

/* initialize the pointer */

    a = array;

    for(x=0;x<8;x++)
    {
        array[x] = x*100;
        printf("array[%i] = %i\n",x,array[x]);
    }
}
```

Compile. You may see a "value not used" error because pointer a is assigned a value that the program never bothers with. That's okay for now.

Run it. Here's what you should see as output:

```
array[0] = 0
array[1] = 100
array[2] = 200
array[3] = 300
array[4] = 400
array[5] = 500
array[6] = 600
array[7] = 700
```

The first value is zero because x*100 equals zero when *x* is zero. Other than that, this should be a relatively straightforward array program, the kind that little kids win medals for during the summer fair and livestock exhibition.

Now . . . time to cut!

After a pointer has been initialized to an array, you can use that pointer to examine or change any element in the array. The program PRIMES.C from the preceding lesson showed how you can read array elements with a pointer. You can change LOVYDOVY.C to fill an array with a pointer.

To remove the first instance of pointer notation from the program, load the source code for LOVYDOVY.C into your editor. Change the `for` loop as follows:

```
for(x=0;x<8;x++)
{
    *a = x*100;
    printf("array[%i] = %i\n",x,*a);
    a++;
}
```

The first line fills the first element of the array with the value of x times 100; *a represents the array element. The *a is also used in the `printf` statement to display the element's value. Finally, the last line increments a as a memory location one integer-size notch, which points at the next element in the array.

Save the program to disk.

Compile. (You don't see a warning error this time because the a variable is finally used in the program.)

Run. The output is the same. All you did was replace the array notation with pointers.

> ✔ So far, the pointer solution is rather inelegant. After all, you used three pointer statements to replace two array-bracket-things. The program got bigger! That's not very efficient.

> ✔ The next section discusses a better way to replace array notation with pointers.

The weird relationship between pointers and array brackets

Although it's possible to rewrite any array program with pointers, there's a tried-and-true way to do it. It involves the simple conversion methods listed in Table 10-2. It shows you a straight-across way of replacing any array-thing with a pointer-thing in a program.

Table 10-2	Pointers and Array Brackets
Array Notation	*Pointer Equivalent*
`array[0]`	`*a`
`array[1]`	`*(a+1)`
`array[2]`	`*(a+2)`
`array[3]`	`*(a+3)`
`array[x]`	`*(a+x)`

In the table, `array` is the name of any array in C and `a` is a pointer variable. It's assumed that `a` is initialized to point to the `array` as follows:

```
a = array;
```

Each element in the array can be accessed using pointers as shown in the table. (Though Table 10-2 shows only elements 0 through 3, you can access any array element as shown here.)

The final item in Table 10-2 shows how to access an element based on a variable, *x*, rather than on a constant. It all really works the same.

   ✔ When you add a number to a pointer, you're adding a memory-size chunk and not a value. Adding 4 to an integer pointer actually refers to the fourth element in an array.

   ✔ The parentheses are important here. What happens inside the parentheses happens first in C, so

```
*(p+2)
```

In this variable, two memory chunks are added to the address stored in `p` (making it equivalent to `array[2]`). The two chunks are added first. Then whatever value lives there is fetched by the `*` that lives outside the parentheses.

✔ Using array-equivalent notation does not change the value of the memory address in the pointer:

```
*(a+6)
```

In this line, the memory address stored in a is not changed. Instead, it has six memory-size chunks added to it, from which a value is read.

✔ Two-dimensional arrays? They can be accessed with pointers as well, which I touch on in Lesson 10-10. However, this is an aspect of C considered "advanced" by all programmers. It's really beyond the scope of this book, so stick with array notation for multidimensional arrays.

Removing all vestiges of array notation

The LOVYDOVY.C program's conversion to pointers from array notation was rather clumsy. To make a better stab at it, you should replace the old array notation directly with the pointer notation shown in Table 10-2.

Open up your editor and load LOVYDOVY.C once again.

Restore the for loop to its original state, but with pointers rather than with array notation. Here's how it should look:

```
for(x=0;x<8;x++)
{
    *(a+x) = x*100;
    printf("array[%i] = %i\n",x,*(a+x));
}
```

You're essentially taking the array[x] from the program's original listing (see the beginning of this lesson) and replacing it with *(a+x) from Table 10-2.

Notice how the actual value stored in pointer a — the base where the array starts in memory — is not changed with this notation. Because the value remains the same, the program is smaller and the direct array to pointer notation works like a dream.

Save the source code to disk. Compile and run. The program's output remains the same.

Proof for disbelievers

You can thank your friends the parentheses for ensuring that the value fetched by pointer notation comes from the proper place. Witness the following flashback to beginning algebra:

```
*(a + 5)
```

If a is the address of the array's starting point in memory, a + 5 is the fifth integer-size chunk (*element*) in the array. No problem. If you omit the parentheses, you get something else:

```
*a + 5
```

Then it works out to whatever value lives at *a plus 5. If *a points at the first array element and that element is zero, for example, *a +5 evaluates to 5 — not the fifth array element.

This may seem strange, until you work another demo program. . . .

Load the source code for LOVYDOVY.C into your editor. Change the printf statement to read as follows:

```
printf("array[%] = %i\n",x,*a+x);
```

You're removing the parentheses from the *(a+x) at the end of the statement. Rather than display the value stored at element x, the program should now just do some math.

Save. Compile. Run.

```
array[0] = 0
array[1] = 1
array[2] = 2
array[3] = 3
array[4] = 4
array[5] = 5
array[6] = 6
array[7] = 7
```

These results are misleading. The array holds the same values as it did before. What you see here is the result of *a + x, which simply adds the value of *x* to zero for each loop in the array.

More proof!

Load the source code into your editor again. Change the `printf` statement once more:

```
printf("array[%] = %i\t%i\n",x,array[x],*a+x);
```

The output displays the array element number, the contents of that array element, and then the results of *a + x. Save it to disk.

Compile and run.

```
array[0] = 0     0
array[1] = 100   1
array[2] = 200   2
array[3] = 300   3
array[4] = 400   4
array[5] = 500   5
array[6] = 600   6
array[7] = 700   7
```

The array's element still holds their so-far traditional values. The result of *a + x is completely different.

See? Your friends the parentheses truly are your pals.

One, final, major difference between arrays and pointers

Although many similarities exist between pointers and arrays, they have one key difference: An array isn't a variable.

Pointers are variables. You can change their contents and change what lives at the memory addresses they point to. Arrays, on the other hand, are pretty much stuck in memory. You can't move them. You can't reassign them. You can change their variables, but that's about it.

In a way, this situation makes pointers a more versatile method of accessing arrays in memory. You see this concept demonstrated especially with character arrays (strings), as covered in the next lesson.

✔ Even though pointers could replace array notation, you still have to declare an array as you always have.

✔ Pointers cannot be used to declare an initialized array:

```
int *p = { 1, 2, 3, 4, 5 };
```

The compiler will just hate you if you try that.

✔ Pointers cannot be used to declare an empty array:

```
int *p[8];
```

This example declares an array of *pointers,* not integers. (Gadzooks!) Nope, you *must* declare your arrays the old-fashioned way. Then declare a pointer and assign it to the array.

Lesson 10-6 Quiz

1. Match the array notation to its pointer notation equivalent:

   A. `array[0]`   1. `*a`

   B. `array[1]`   2. `*(a+1)`

   C. `array[i+2]`   3. `*(i+2)`

   D. `array[x]`   4. `*(a+x)`

2. Assuming that `a` is initialized to point at array `circus`, which element does `a` refer to in the following statement?

   ```
   *(a+5+6)
   ```

   A. The fifth element.

   B. The sixth element.

   C. The eleventh element.

   D. The fifty-sixth element.

   E. The circus elephant.

3. Which of the following actors has not played Batman on film?

   A. Jing Abalos.

   B. Robert Lowery.

   C. Lewis Wilson.

   D. Kevin Conroy.

4. Can you replace all vestiges of array notation with pointers?

    A. You betcha.

    B. Most, but not all.

    C. You still have to declare the array using array notation.

    D. As a God-fearing person, I'm not taken to using words such as *vestiges*.

Grab a quick snack!

Lesson 10-7: Pointers and Strings

Pointers *really* make sense when you begin dealing with strings. Pointers and strings have a special relationship, which buds from the cozy pointer-array thing. Pointers don't just love strings — they *love* strings.

An odd way to display a string

You should know two basic things about strings in C: They're arrays, and the character marking the end of the string is the NULL byte. Armed with that knowledge, you could create a program that uses the putchar function to display all the characters in a string — something like the following program.

Type the source code for FISH.C into your editor. Save it to disk:

Name: FISH.C

```
#include <stdio.h>

void main()
{
    char string[] = "Is it supposed to smell that way?";
    char ch = '!';
    int x = 0;

    while(ch != '\0')
    {
        ch = string[x];
        putchar(ch);
        x++;
    }
}
```

Compile and run.

```
Is it supposed to smell that way?
```

The program uses a simple `while` loop to scan through and display each character in the string. The following sidebar, "The hows and whys of a FISH.C program," elaborates on some of the more interesting parts of the program, if any.

BLOW BY BLOW

The hows and whys of a FISH.C program

All the program's variables are initialized; `string`, `ch`, and `x`:

```
char string[] = "Is it supposed
    to smell that way?";
```

`string` is initialized to a string constant. No problem — you've been doing this for years now. The only reason that `ch` and `x` are initialized is to save yourself two steps in the program. Otherwise, you would have to write the following:

```
ch = '!';
```

```
x = 0;
```

There's nothing wrong with that; it's just that you save time by initializing them as they're declared.

Why initialize them? If you don't initialize `ch`, it contains "garbage," and that garbage just may be the NULL character. In that case, the program doesn't display anything because the `while` loop never loops. `ch` must be initialized so that the `while` loop works at least once. The `x` is initialized, well, just because.

The `while` loop repeats as long as the value of the `ch` variable is *not* equal to the NULL character:

```
while(ch != '\0')
```

Remember that the NULL character marks the end of a string.

Inside the loop, each character is fetched from the string:

```
ch = string[x];
```

Variable `x` is used as a counter. Because it's already initialized to zero, the preceding statement grabs the first character in the string, element zero, the first time the `while` loop spins.

A `putchar` function displays the character in the string, and then the `x` counter is incremented and the loop repeats, grabbing and displaying the next character in the string:

```
putchar(ch);
```

```
x++;
```

This happens until the last character, the NULL, is encountered.

- ✔ All strings in C end with a NULL character. That's how the `while` loop is able to step through every character in the string and know exactly when to stop.

- ✔ The escape sequence for the NULL character is \0.

- ✔ You could use a `for` loop instead — but only if you know the length of the string. The FISH.C program is smarter than that. It relies on that NULL byte tucked away at the end of every string to tell the `while` loop when to end.

- ✔ Overall, this is a truly clunky way to do things in C. True, the program works, but things can be made to work much more efficiently by employing pointers.

- ✔ Pointers work for cheap.

A better way to display a string

Reload the source code for FISH.C into your editor. Change it so that it resembles the following, pointer-improved version of the program:

```
#include <stdio.h>

void main()
{
    char string[] = "Is it supposed to smell that way?";
    char *s;

/* initialize the pointer */

    s = string;

    while(*s != '\0')
    {
        putchar(*s);
        s++;
    }
}
```

Many things have changed: Gone are the `ch` and `x` variables. Also the clunky array notation is missing. And the program is shorter, sweeter, and more to the pointer.

Save your changes to disk.

Compile. Run.

```
Is it supposed to smell that way?
```

Here's a rundown of the program's improvements:

- The program's pointer variable, s, is initialized to be equal to the start of the array in memory:

```
s = string;
```

  Remember that the & is not required here because string is the name of an array.

- The nature of the while loop's condition changes as well:

```
while(*s != '\0')
```

  You have no need to initialize *s because it's already pointing at the first character in the string. That saves the step of setting ch equal to ! in the first version of the program. By using a pointer, you're already set up and ready to loop.

- The putchar function displays the character the s variable points at:

```
putchar(*s);
```

  Variable s contains a memory location, and *s represents the character stored at that location.

- Then the address of the s variable is incremented to the next character-size chunk of memory:

```
s++;
```

- Character chunks are equal to one byte of memory, and a char is the only type of pointer that has this one-to-one relationship (at least on a PC).

- The program continues to loop through the string until the NULL byte is encountered.

More tricks!

The NULL byte is zero. Because zero is sometimes known as FALSE, you could rewrite the while loop as follows:

```
while(*s)
```

This line reads, "While the value represented by pointer s is not equal to zero (the NULL byte), keep looping." As long as the character at memory location s is not the NULL byte, the while loop repeats.

Make the preceding modification to the FISH.C source code. Save your work to disk, and then compile and run it.

> ✔ A while loop repeats as long as the value between the parentheses is not zero. Because the NULL byte is a zero value, while(*s) repeats until *s contains the NULL byte.
>
> ✔ If Zero is FALSE, would Zero Mostel be False Mostel?
>
> ✔ Sure looks cryptic, eh? You haven't seen the half of it. . . .

Even more tricks!

Consider the following two lines in the program:

```
putchar(*s);
s++;
```

If you completed Lesson 10-5, you agonized over the fact that these two lines can really be combined:

```
putchar(*s++);
```

No, that's not pretty to look at, but it still works: The value stored at memory location s is read and displayed, and then memory location s is incremented.

Edit the source code again, replacing the existing while loop with the following:

```
while(*s)
  putchar(*s++);
```

You don't need the curly brackets because only one statement is in the while loop.

Save. Compile. Run.

> ✔ Better refer to Table 10-1 to prove that *s++ does what it's supposed to do. The Table Never Lies.
>
> ✔ The program looks much tighter, eh? Contrast the FISH.C program with the original, clunky version shown at the beginning of this lesson. Elegant, eh?

✔ This same `while`-and-pointer method was used in the PRINTME3.C program in Chapter 8. In that program, a `while` loop plods through a string to send characters off to the printer.

One last, crazy trick

Those insurance company diet charts are all screwed up. For example, a person of my height — a big-boned, large-frame type of person (really big-boned, I mean) — should weigh in at 179 pounds. I haven't weighed 179 since I was 17. Doctors tell me that it's always possible to lose more weight, but those doctors just aren't as big-boned as I am.

Losing weight is also possible for FISH.C, even though it's big-boned and looks skinny enough already.

Here's one last, final notch on the belt for FISH.C:

```
while(putchar(*s++))
    ;
```

Never mind why or how this is possible; just make this change to your source code. Save, compile, and run.

Amazing. The program still works.

Here's the final version of FISH.C, which looks little like how the program began at the beginning of this lesson:

```
#include <stdio.h>

void main()
{
    char string[] = "Is it supposed to smell that way?";
    char *s;

/* initialize the pointer */

    s = string;

    while(putchar(*s++))
        ;
}
```

✔ Don't ever expect that you can write something like `while(putchar(*s++));` right off the top of your head. Most programmers start out the long way and work things back together as they mess with the program.

✔ Or you might just store a chestnut like `while(putchar(*s++));` in a bunch of commonly used routines and forget how it evolved. That's what I do.

✔ There's nothing wrong with writing out the `while` loop long-ways. Both versions still work.

✔ As long as a pointer is initialized to a string, you can use the preceding `while` loop to display the string.

✔ Personally, I'd rather look like the Buddha than have small children run in horror pointing at my protruding rib cage.

The lowdown on compiler definitions

C functions may work from the inside out, but the `while` keyword is not a function. It's a control statement — a loop. How exactly does the compiler know what's inside? Or, better still: How would you as a programmer know that `putchar(*s++)` not only displays a character but also returns that same character?

The answer is in your C language library. It lists all the C language functions and how they're defined.

Most functions return a value. For some functions, such as the `sqrt` (square root) functions, the value returned is obvious. For other functions, it's not apparent that the function returns a value, even though it might.

To see what exactly each function returns, refer to your C language library. For example, the following is the format for the `putchar` function:

```
int putchar(int c);
```

The `putchar` function requires an `integer` value c, which is the character to be displayed. (Most libraries use `int` when they might mean `char`, because a `char` is like a tiny `int` — don't ask me why.)

The `putchar` function also returns an `integer` value, which is the character displayed. Therefore, you can use `putchar` in a `while` or `if` comparison because it returns what it displays.

Consider the following definition:

```
char *gets(char *p)
```

The gets (get string) function requires one string as input and generates another string as output. char *p is the same thing as a string; it's a character pointer to a string in memory. Same thing. The function is prototyped as a string because it returns a string.

Even though you may *think* that you understand this stuff, don't get all cocky. In memory, a pointer variable is equal to a string only *without* its asterisk. With an asterisk, the pointer is only a character — not a string. (What? Did you think that this could possibly make sense right away?)

Why is char *gets considered a character? Because strings don't exist in C! Strings are merely character arrays. If I were running things, I'd go ahead and format the library reference like this:

```
string gets(string)
```

Nobody voted me in charge, though, so you have to put up with the traditional method of declaring functions in your C library.

- In your C library, an int is often used to represent a single character. (Why they don't use char is beyond me.)

- Also in your C library, strings are referred to as char *something. That's really a string, and it means that whatever is being declared either accepts a string as input or returns a string as output.

- The following section shows how you could potentially get in trouble with this stuff.

Oh! String! String! String!

Here's another demo program, STRING.C, which should drive you nuts. Prepare to dash away all your assumptions!

Name: STRING.C

```
#include <stdio.h>

void main()
{
    char text[] = "Going! Going! Gone!";
```

```
    char *t;

/* initialize the pointer */
    t = text;

    puts(*t);
}
```

Type this source code into your editor. This is a wee li'l program you may concoct on your own some day. After all, the definition for puts (put string) in your library reference goes something like this:

```
int puts(char *string)
```

Hmmm. Makes sense. Confidently save that sucker to disk and give it the name STRING.C.

Compile and . . . er, uh?

Microsoft calls it "different levels of indirection" or "different types for formal and actual."

Borland refers to it as a "type mismatch error." Plus, you may receive notice that variable t is never used. Uh-oh.

What the error message means is that you fed a function one thing when it was expecting another. In this case, you fed the function what it looked like it wanted: *t, which is what char *string looks like in the library definition. But it just ain't so.

In a library definition, char *string refers to a string in memory — a character array. Your variable *s is a single character in the array — not the whole string. A *big* difference exists between a single variable and an array, as your compiler just informed you.

To make amends, change Line 11 in the program to read

```
puts(t);
```

By itself, t is a memory location. Because the pointer has been initialized to point to the address of the string, it's really the *same doo-dah deal* as the string itself.

Save STRING.C to disk. Compile . . . and no errors!

Run:

```
Going! Going! Gone!
```

This really shouldn't be a surprise to you. First, if you declare a string `text`, you should know that the following statement displays that string:

```
puts(text);
```

Second, if you set pointer `t` equal to `text` — which is done in the program — then you should know that the following line also displays the string:

```
puts(t);
```

After all, `t` = `text`. It says so right in your program.

- A string pointer variable `*s` is a single character, not an entire string in memory. No, it really doesn't matter what the library definition says it is (refer to the preceding section).

- The string pointer variable without its asterisk *and* properly initialized is the same thing as a string in memory.

- Don't let the formats in your C language library reference confuse you. A `char *string` definition means a string of characters, not a single character.

And another weird thing about strings

A key point about pointers is that they're variables. Because of that, you can mess with them, as shown by the following modifications to the STRING.C program.

Whip the source code for STRING.C into your editor. Change the program to reflect the addition of a `while` loop as shown here. Save the file back to disk, and then compile and run it:

```
#include <stdio.h>

void main()
{
    char text[] = "Going! Going! Gone!";
    char *t;
```

```
/* initialize the pointer */
    t = text;

    while(*t)
    {
        puts(t);
        t++;
    }
}
```

Here's what the output should resemble:

```
Going! Going! Gone!
oing! Going! Gone!
ing! Going! Gone!
ng! Going! Gone!
g! Going! Gone!
! Going! Gone!
 Going! Gone!
Going! Gone!
oing! Gone!
ing! Gone!
ng! Gone!
g! Gone!
! Gone!
 Gone!
Gone!
one!
ne!
e!
!
```

The while loop scans through the text array one character at a time. Each time it scans, it displays the string. Because the t variable is incremented, the string gets shorter and shorter with each iteration of the loop. This is possible only with pointer variables.

✔ Array notation just doesn't work in this program. Even if you could finagle it, you cannot increment an array:

```
text++;
```

This example generates one of those annoying Lvalue errors. Arrays are constants; pointers are variables.

 ✔ The `while` loop in STRING.C works because `*t` represents each successive character in the array. When `*t` finally points to the NULL byte marking the end of the string, the `while` loop stops.

 ✔ The `puts(t)` statement works because `t` holds the address of a string in memory. However, because `t` is incremented after the string is displayed, the string gets shorter and shorter (as shown by the output).

 ✔ The program MARQUEE.C in Appendix B uses a pointer similar to the one in STRING.C to scroll a message across the screen.

Declaring a string by using a char pointer

This whole chapter is about how close strings and pointers are.

Audience: How close are they?

Host: If they were any closer, they'd be arrested for tailgating.

Ba-dum-dum.

You don't really have to use array notation to declare a string in your program. You can do the following:

```
char *s = "This is a string";
```

This is the same as doing this:

```
char string[] = "This is a string";
```

and then this:

```
s = string;
```

The difference is that a pointer is declared and assigned a value immediately. I have only one warning here:

This trick works only with strings.

You cannot declare any other variable type this way:

```
int *n = 37;
```

This example does not create an integer variable. Likewise:

```
char *c = 'I';
```

This example does not create a character variable. Most compilers utterly gag if you attempt this type of boner — and that's good because if they didn't gag, your program would not work as expected.

Another thing that doesn't work:

```
char *s;
gets(s);
```

The first line declares a string pointer, s. The second line attempts to use that pointer like an array — but no array space has been allocated! In fact, the pointer hasn't even been initialized, so if the compiler doesn't spit an error at you, the program bombs big-time.

Strings, arrays, and other variables must be *allocated* before they can be used. When you declare a pointer as a string, it's the same as allocating it because the string must be placed in memory. It doesn't work for any other type of variable or array.

To prove that this new pointer thing really works, change the source code for STRING.C a final time. Make it look like this:

```
#include <stdio.h>

void main()
{
    char *t = "Going! Going! Gone!";

    while(*t)
    {
        puts(t);
        t++;
    }
}
```

There's no need to initialize the pointer. It's already done! Save the source code, compile, and then run.

This trick works *only* with strings. I normally wouldn't show it to you, but the pointer-string declaration is common in other books and references. Just remember that it's an exception, not the rule.

Lesson 10-7 Quiz

For this quiz, I'm doing something different. Here are the answers, and the questions are listed in Appendix A. Just as on *Jeopardy!*, you must think of the correct *question* for each of the following answers (good luck!):

A. Because all strings end with the NULL byte.

B. It eats strings.

C. You can only declare strings that way.

D. *Midnight Cowboy.*

Lesson 10-8: Passing Pointers to Functions

Lessons 5-3 and 5-4 discussed sending variables to functions and getting something back — basic C language stuff. Because pointers are variables, you can send them to functions as well. It involves a little more brainwork on your part because you have to keep track of whether you're sending the pointer as an address or the pointer's value to the function.

Oh, and then there's the subject of returning pointers from functions, which can drive even the bravest programmer stark-raving mad.

Basic pointer nonsense review

Don't let your head spin 'round like a possessed 13-year-old. It's easy to get overwhelmed by pointers and functions and such. I've seen programmers go through their source code and randomly place asterisks and ampersands to try to get things to work right. As long as you keep in mind the basic rules of pointers, you'll be okay:

Initialize a pointer before you use it.

Without the asterisk, the pointer is a memory address.

With the asterisk, the pointer represents what lives at that address.

Those are the pointer basics from bonnet to boot. Passing a pointer to a function? Allow the following program to help explain it:

Name: LINDA1.C

```
#include <stdio.h>

void peasoup(int green);

void main()
{
    int turn;

    turn=13;

    peasoup(turn);
}

void peasoup(int green)
{
    while(green--)
        puts("Blech!");
}
```

Okay, the program has no pointers. Yet. Just copy this code into your text editor and save it to disk as LINDA1.C.

Compile and run.

The program essentially passes the value 13 to the peasoup function, which spews out the word Blech! that many times.

I'll bet that a pointer could do the same thing. . . .

Modify the source code so that the head integer pointer variable is declared. Then head is initialized to the turn variable and finally passes the value of head to the function. Can you do that on your own? See whether you can.

(Music plays.)

Done?

I'll bet that you declared the pointer just fine:

```
int *head;
```

I would also bet that you assigned the head variable to the turn variable just fine:

```
head = &turn;
```

(Did you forget the ampersand? That may have happened if you got used to working with arrays.)

And I'll bet that you may have done the following:

```
peasoup(head);
```

Did you?

Save the change to disk and rename the program as LINDA2.C.

Compile and. . . .

```
Type mismatch in parameter 'green' in call to 'peasoup' in
                function main
```

```
different levels of indirection
different types for formal and actual parameter
```

(The ghastly thing is that my Visual C++ compiler actually *made* the program. *Don't run it!*)

What you're experiencing are the joys of prototyping. The compiler knows that the peasoup function hungers for an integer. Yet you fed it a pointer — a raw pointer — which is a memory address and not an integer at all.

Solution? The asterisk.

```
peasoup(*head);
```

The asterisk tells the compiler to use what lives at a memory address, not the memory address itself.

Reedit your source code and change the call to the peasoup function to read as just shown. (I commend you if you already did this and didn't get an error when you compiled.) Here's the final rendition of LINDA2.C as it should appear in your text editor:

```
#include <stdio.h>

void peasoup(int green);

void main()
{
    int turn;
    int *head;
```

```
    turn=13;
    head = &turn;

    peasoup(*head);
}

void peasoup(int green)
{
    while(green--)
        puts("Blech!");
}
```

Save it to disk. Compile and run.

The output should be the same: 13 Blech!s on your screen. It was a pointer passed to the function that did it, though, not a plain integer variable.

- ✔ Remember that an initialized pointer with its asterisk is the *same thing* as the variable it's set equal to:

```
turn=13;
head = &turn;
```

After this transition, the variable *head is the same dang-doodle thing as the variable turn. The same!

- ✔ The function requires an integer as input. You can pass an integer pointer to the function — no problem — as long as the pointer has been properly initialized first.

- ✔ The peasoup function uses a while loop to count down how many times to repeat the word Blech! on the screen:

```
while(green--)
```

Each spin through the loop decrements the value of green until it's zero. Zero is FALSE, so the loop stops.

- ✔ The program is named LINDA1.C after actress Linda Blair, who played the head-turning, demon-possessed adolescent in *The Exorcist* — one of the funniest movies of all time.

Messages from beyond

Functions can swallow *and* spit up! You can send a value to a function, the function can func, and a value can be returned. This is basic function stuff you should have absorbed from Chapter 5 in *C For Dummies,* Volume I.

Typically, a value is returned from a function by a `return` command. For example:

```
int peasoup(int green)
```

If `peasoup` were to mangle the value `green` and return it, it would have to be prototyped and declared as shown here.

But, ah-ah! You don't really have to return a value if you pass a pointer to a function. You can modify the pointer and not have to return it because the pointer is merely a memory location. The modified variable *stays* in memory, right where it was created. This sounds sneaky, but I'll bet that it works:

Name: LINDA3.C

```c
#include <stdio.h>

void peasoup(int green);

void main()
{
    int turn;
    int *head;

    turn=13;
    head = &turn;

    peasoup(*head);

    printf("Oh, no, it's %i!\n",*head);
}

void peasoup(int green)
{
    while(green--)
        puts("Blech!");

    green = 13 * 51 + 3;
}
```

Create the preceding source code. It's a subtle modification of the LINDA2.C program. This time, though, the value passed to the `peasoup` function is modified inside that function. The last statement changes the value of the variable to `13 * 51 +3`. Because `green` represents a pointer, that new value should reappear in the `main` function, displayed by the last `printf` statement there:

```
printf("Oh, no, it's %i!\n",*head);
```

Nothing needs to be returned because green represents a pointer. Save it to disk as LINDA3.C.

Compile and run:

```
Blech!
Blech!
Blech!
Blech!
Blech!
Blech!
Blech!
Blech!
Blech!
Blech!
Blech!
Blech!
Blech!
Oh, no, it's 13!
```

Okay, it didn't work. Don't think that you goofed up if your output looks the same as shown here. The value 13 is *not* the product of 13 * 51 + 3.

What went wrong? *Pointers,* that's what. You didn't pass a pointer to the program — you passed an integer variable. Remember that the pointer is variable head. The variable *head is what lives at a specific address, an integer value.

You have to pass the pointer to the function. "Logically then," you say, because you're sort of a pointer expert, " I just pass along the pointer with the asterisk thing."

Okay. Do it: Change your source code so that Line 15 reads as follows:

```
peasoup(head);
```

Save! Compile! Uh-uh-uh!

Wait a second. Déjà vu! Did you try this before, earlier in this lesson? The problem isn't that you picked the wrong thing to send to the function. The problem is that you haven't yet told the function that it's working with a *pointer* and not with a plain integer.

Remember the dual nature of pointers: If you need a value, you use the asterisk — as you did in the LINDA2.C program. If you're going to pass a pointer to a function, you pass the pointer without the asterisk *and* you redeclare the function so that it swallows pointers.

The peasoup function must be redefined this way:

```
void peasoup(int *green)
{
    while(*green--)
        puts("Blech!");

    *green = 13 * 51 + 3;
}
```

Now peasoup knows that it's getting a pointer rather than an integer. Furthermore, the function itself has been modified to deal with the pointer rather than with a regular variable. See those *green things in there? They be pointers in action.

It works like this:

```
peasoup(head);
```

The function is called with the pointer in memory address mode. You're passing the location of an integer variable in memory (head, in this example).

Inside the function, you declare the variable as a pointer:

```
void peasoup(int *green)
```

This line is required for the same reason it's required at the start of the main function; you must declare a pointer with its asterisk.

Inside the function, the pointer is *still* used with its asterisk:

```
while(*green--)
```

and

```
*green = 13 * 51 + 3;
```

Why? Because you want to manipulate the *value* at a memory location, not the memory location itself. (Incidentally, the same type of manipulation takes place with strings in a function. More of that in the following lesson.)

Here's how the source code for LINDA3.C should look in your editor; the source code also has the newly prototyped peasoup function (which you may have forgotten to change):

```
#include <stdio.h>

void peasoup(int *green);

void main()
{
    int turn;
    int *head;

    turn=13;
    head = &turn;

    peasoup(head);

    printf("Oh, no, it's %i!\n",*head);
}

void peasoup(int *green)
{
    while(*green--)
        puts("Blech!");

    *green = 13 * 51 + 3;
}
```

(Did you remember to prototype the peasoup function?)

Save! Compile! Run?

```
Blech!
Blech!
Blech!
Blech!
```

and on and on, until finally:

```
Blech!
On, no, it's 13!
```

The program runs, but it doesn't do what you want it to because of a subtle misunderstanding that can be cleared up if you look back at Table 10-1.

Yes! It's that ugly pointer math again!

Keep one thumb in this book at Table 10-1, and with the other nine thumbs examine the following:

```
while(*green--)
```

In Table 10-1, you can compare this function to *p++. Both work the same way. According to the table, the *memory address* is affected, not the value. Why? Who knows? The table tells the truth. What the peasoup function does is to decrement the memory address and ignore the contents at that address — not what you wanted.

Looking farther down in the table, you see the function you want, (*p)++. In that format, the memory address is unchanged, but the contents are changed. Simply apply that to the peasoup function in LINDA3.C:

```
while((*green)--)
```

Make the change. Save to disk. Compile. Run.

```
Blech!
Blech!
Blech!
Blech!
Blech!
Blech!
Blech!
Blech!
Blech!
Blech!
Blech!
Blech!
Blech!
Oh, no, it's 666!
```

Finally.

- Is a value returned from the peasoup function? No. A pointer is modified. Only the contents of a memory location are changed. The net result is the same as though the function returned a value, but because pointers were used, nothing needed to be returned.

- If you want to send a pointer to a function, send the memory address.

- Inside a function you pass a pointer to, declare the variable as a pointer (which is done with peasoup in the preceding example).

- Inside the function, use the pointer with its asterisk to get the value; use the pointer without its asterisk to access a memory location. (This is standard pointer stuff.)

- To return a value from a function, simply modify the pointer. You don't need a return statement because the pointer is modified in memory.

- Honestly, this is all basic pointer stuff.

- At times, you will encounter a problem like the while loop test in the peasoup function. Don't let it bug you! Just keep Table 10-1 handy, or use the duplicate reference on the Cheat Sheet inside the front cover of this book. Chances are, if you *just know* that everything is working, you're probably faced with a pointer math problem and not any misuse of the pointer variables themselves.

- As long as the program compiles without any pointer errors or warnings, you should be on the right track.

- Please don't think that there's anything satanic about this program or this book. I'm just working from the exorcism theme. (Maybe it's time to switch to another great Linda Blair movie, *Sarah T. — Portrait of a Teenage Alcoholic.*)

- Oops! Too late. The lesson is over.

Lesson 10-8 Quiz

1. Which of the following films did not star Linda Blair?

   A. *Victory at Entebbe.*

   B. *Red Head.*

   C. *Roller Boogie.*

   D. *Fatal Blood.*

2. If `smell` is a `float` pointer, how would you pass the proper value to the following function:

```
void socks(float stinky);
```

A. `socks(smell);`

B. `socks(*smell);`

C. `socks(&smell);`

D. `socks((float *)smell);`

3. Assume that you're passing the `float` pointer `smell` to the following function:

```
void socks(float *stinky);
```

A. `socks(smell);`

B. `socks(*smell);`

C. `socks(&smell);`

D. `socks((float *)smell);`

4. What does the following function do?

```
void socks(float *stinky)
{
    *stinky*=100;
}
```

A. Nothing; you cannot have asterisks on *both* sides of a pointer.

B. Nothing; the function is of type `void` and therefore cannot return a value, even a pointer.

C. It changes the value of the `stinky` variable but does nothing with that variable.

D. The value of `stinky` is changed in both the function and the main program.

Lesson 10-9: Arrays to and from Functions

One thing you're taught in Lessons 5-3 and 5-4 in Volume I of this book — something you probably didn't know — is that sending a string to a function involves sending a string *pointer* and not some other type of `char` variable.

Of course, the way this book teaches, you just nod your head and obey. Passing a pointer is nothing more than remembering to tack the asterisk to the front of the string's variable name. No biggie. It's still really no biggie. Just remember the following:

To pass any array to a function, you pass its memory address.

A memory address is, after all, what a pointer contains. Passing the array name to a function is simple. No ampersands. No asterisks. No mess like you saw in the preceding lesson.

For example, to assign the array stuff[] to a pointer s, you do the following:

```
s = stuff;
```

No brackets. No ampersand.

To pass the array stuff to the mangle function, you do the following:

```
mangle(stuff);
```

No brackets. No ampersand.

In fact, if you've already initialized a pointer variable s to an array stuff, you can pass the pointer instead:

```
mangle(s);
```

It all looks the same to the compiler.

Meanwhile, in the function you declare the array as a pointer:

```
void mangle(int *some_array)
```

Don't get confused! The function requires an array as input; in this case, an array of integers. But you have to define the array as a pointer. Why? Because, to the compiler, the pointer is merely an address. That's all you passed — the starting address of the array in memory.

Yes, this process works just like sending a pointer to a function in the preceding lesson. The difference is that the pointer represents a whole array in memory, not a single value.

Inside the function, you can use array notation to access the elements in the array. For example:

```
printf("Element zero = %i",some_array[0]);
```

No asterisk. No pointer nonsense. The compiler recognizes the array for what it is. The only difference is that the array is known as some_array inside the function. Otherwise, everything works just fine.

Yeah, you could use pointer notation as well. But, eh, why bother?

See the next section for a demo program.

Gander at the program LILJERK.C from Lesson 5-3 in Volume I of this book. It contains the following function:

```
void jerk(char *name)
{
    int i;

    for(i=0;i<3;i++)
        printf("%s is a jerk\n",name);
}
```

The char *name thing is a string pointer. From reading Lesson 10-7, you also know that it's C language notation for "a string." Basically, the function desires a string as input, and it uses the name variable to represent the string inside the function.

(Secretly — which is why this information is in parentheses and why you should be whispering it if you're reading aloud — all that's passed to the function is the string's starting address in memory. The entire string never moves; only its address is passed along to the function. Shhh!)

Passing a character array to a function

The following program, ULINE.C, contains a function, underline, that swallows a string — which is the same as any other array in C. See whether you can figure out what it does before you run it. (Don't let the *string++ thing bug you; just refer to Table 10-1, which is conveniently replicated on the Cheat Sheet inside the front cover of this book.)

Enter the source code. Save it to disk as ULINE.C:

Name: ULINE.C

```
#include <stdio.h>

void underline(char *string);

void main()
{
    char text[] = "1998's Starting Line-up";

    puts(text);
    underline(text);
}

void underline(char *string)
{
    while(*string++)
        putchar('=');

    putchar('\n');
}
```

Compile and run.

```
1998's Starting Line-up
=======================
```

The underline function takes a string and underlines it with a bunch of equal signs. No, the string isn't really read; it's *used*. (This isn't string abuse, so don't go sending e-mail off to Mr. Ritchie.)

✔ Puzzling over the while(*string++) thing? Here's how it works out in long notation:

```
while(*string != '\0')
{
    putchar('=');
    string++;
}
```

The while loop's condition checks for the end of the string, whether or not the current character is the NULL byte. Inside the loop, an equal sign is displayed by the putchar function. Next, the string memory address is incremented. The while loop then uses *string to read the next character in the string.

TIP

✔ Unlike in the preceding lesson, here you want the memory location to increment, not just the value at that memory location (refer to Table 10-1).

✔ Whenever you see a `while` loop with `*string++` (or something similar) as its condition, you can bet your bonnet that the loop repeats until no more characters are in the string.

✔ This really isn't anything new. Strings are just passed to functions as pointers.

✔ Once inside a function, of course, you can mess with a pointer just like you can anywhere else in a program. The following section shows an example.

One more of those `*string++` *things for you*

I just can't get over how handy the ugly `*string++` thing is, especially with strings. Even if you have utterly given up on figuring out how it works, you must get used to it. Consider the following program:

Name: STRLEN.C

```
#include <stdio.h>

void main()
{
    char string[] = "Mmmm! Love them pork rinds!";
    char *s;
    int x = 0;

/* initialize the pointer */
    s = string;

    while(*s++) x++;

    printf("The string \"%s\" is %i characters
            long.",string,x);
}
```

Carefully enter the source code for this program. The final `printf` statement is kind of long and may be split on two lines in this book; don't do that in your editor. Save it to disk as STRLEN.C.

Compile and run.

```
The string "Mmmm! Love them pork rinds!" is 27 characters
            long.
```

The `while(*s++)` loop incremented an integer variable x to count the
length of the string.

The following line in the program:

```
while(*s++) x++;
```

could also have been written as

```
while(*s++)
{
    x++;
}
```

or even longer as

```
while(*s != '\0')
{
    s++;
    x++;
}
```

- ✔ The `while` loop ticks through every character in the string. While it's looping, you can use the `*s` variable to represent each character in the string and then do something strange or useful to that character.

- ✔ This program is named STRLEN.C, just like the `strlen` (string length) function. No problem with that.

- ✔ This section is kind of off the track from the rest of the lesson, so go ahead and take a snack break now.

The forbidden vowels!

In its effort to control information, the government of Fredonia decides to outlaw vowels. As the government's chief programmer, you're ordered to write a special function to remove all vowels from any string and replace those vowels with non-offensive characters. This task shouldn't be a problem for you, especially because the solution is shown right here.

Carefully type the following source code into your editor. Watch those curly brackets! Also, those are colons after the case statements, not semicolons. Save the monster to disk as NOVOWELS.C:

Name: NOVOWELS.C

```c
#include <stdio.h>
#include <ctype.h>

void novowels(char *string);

void main()
{
    char *phrase = "No more vowels in Fredonia!";

    puts("Before purification:\n");
    puts(phrase);

    novowels(phrase);

    puts("\nAfter purification:\n");
    puts(phrase);
}

void novowels(char *string)
{
    while(*string++)
    {
        switch(toupper(*string))
        {
            case('A'):
                *string = '&';
                break;
            case('E'):
                *string = '@';
                break;
            case('I'):
                *string = '#';
                break;
            case('O'):
                *string = '$';
                break;
            case('U'):
                *string = '%';
                break;
```

```
            default:
                break;
        }
    }
}
```

Compile. Fix any errors, things you forgot — stuff like that.

BLOW BY BLOW

Soothing words of wisdom about the novowels function

The only strange part of the NOVOWELS.C program is the novowels function. It searches through a string of text for any vowel. When a vowel is found, it's replaced in the string with another character.

The following contraption (and you should get used to it) helps the while loop march through the string:

```
while(*string++)
```

Without referring to the past few lessons (again), it works out as follows:

```
while(*string != '\0')
```

While the character pointed to by the string variable is not the NULL character. . . .

```
string++
```

Increment the memory address to the next location. Because the ++ appears after the variable, its value isn't incremented until after every other statement in the while loop is executed. A tough delay, but useful.

Inside the loop, the switch statement examines every character in the string:

```
switch(toupper(*string))
```

*string represents each character in the string, and the toupper function converts it to uppercase.

Each of the case statements compares the current character in the string with each vowel: A, E, I, O and U. (Only uppercase letters need to be compared, thanks to the toupper function.)

When a vowel is encountered, it's replaced with another character, like this:

```
*string = '&';
```

Remember that a pointer variable with its asterisk is the same as any other variable. Here, *string is a char variable and is being filled with a new value: the ampersand.

```
default:
```

The default part of the switch-case structure handles all non-vowels in the string. A single break; statement tells the program to ignore those characters.

The amazing stuff is that the string doesn't have to be returned from the function. All the function's modifications are done in memory, thanks to the pointer variable.

Even more amazing: This program doesn't need array notation. Sure, you could have referred to characters in the string as string[0] and so on, but you didn't have to because you could use the far more versatile pointer variables.

Run. Here's what you should see:

```
Before purification:

No more vowels in Fredonia!

After purification:

N$ m$r@ v$w@ls #n Fr@d$n#&!
```

In case you were wondering about what you were supposed to be wondering about: This program uses a function to modify a string, *but it does not return the string!* The underline function is a void type. It takes advantage of the pointer so that it doesn't have to return the string; the string is modified in memory. Sneaky.

- ✔ See the previous sidebar, "Soothing words of wisdom about the novowels function," for more information.
- ✔ Refer to Lesson 7-5 in Volume I of this book for more information about those sneaky switch-case loops.
- ✔ Refer to Lesson 10-8, the LINDA3.C program, in Chapter 10 for information about not returning pointers from functions.
- ✔ You probably should use a switch-case loop whenever your program has to make more than one decision — especially if those decisions are about single values (chars or ints). Sure, an if-if else-else structure would work as well, but that's not as straightforward or easy to read as the switch-case structure.
- ✔ You have to include the CTYPE.H header file because this program uses the toupper function, described in Lesson 9-5 in Chapter 9.
- ✔ I apologize for the NOVOWELS.C filename. It's a bear to type.

Passing nonstring arrays to functions

Don't let other types of arrays throw you for a loop. You can pass them to a function just like you pass strings.

As an example, Lesson 9-4 in Chapter 9 shows you how arrays are passed to functions: They're passed as pointers. The SORTME.C program contains the following function:

```
void sort(int *array,int size)
{
    int a,b,temp;
```

```
    for(a=0;a<size-1;a++)
        for(b=a+1;b<size;b++)
            if(array[a] > array[b])
            {
                temp=array[b];
                array[b] = array[a];
                array[a] = temp;
            }
}
```

No pointer variable was declared or initialized in the main program. Instead, the array is just passed to the function like this:

```
sort(lotto,SIZE);
```

Inside the function, the array must be declared as a pointer. Why? Because pointers and arrays hold a special relationship. The declaration int *array tells the program that array is an integer pointer. It's already initialized because the program passes the lotto array to the function — the same as array = lotto;.

You could use pointer notation inside the function, but you don't have to. Either way, the same job gets done.

The following program passes two integer arrays to a function. It then adds their elements together and stores the results in a third array, which is "returned" from the function.

The ARRAYADD.C program takes two arrays and adds each element together, storing the result in a third array. The print_array function displays each array's contents. The caffeine function adds the arrays and stores the result in a third array. Type the following source code into your editor to make all that happen. Save it to disk as ARRAYADD.C:

Name: ARRAYADD.C

```
#include <stdio.h>

#define SIZE 9

void print_array(int *array,int size);

int *caffeine(int *array1,int *array2,int size);

void main()
```

(continued)

(continued)

```
{
    int joe[] = { 1, 2, 3, 4, 5, 6, 7, 8, 9 };
    int java[] = { 9, 8, 7, 6, 5, 4, 3, 2, 1 };
    int *coffee;

    puts("First array:");
    print_array(joe,SIZE);

    puts("\nSecond array:");
    print_array(java,SIZE);

    coffee = caffeine(joe,java,SIZE);

    puts("\nThird array:");
    print_array(coffee,SIZE);
}

void print_array(int *array,int size)
{
    int x = 0;

    while(size--)
    {
        printf("#%i = %i\n",x+1,array[x]);
        x++;
    }
}

int *caffeine(int *array1,int *array2,int size)
{
    int total[SIZE];
    int x;

    for(x=0;x<size;x++)
            total[x]=array1[x]+array2[x];

    return(total);
}
```

Compile! You get an error because the program isn't right yet. (I do that to you on purpose, in case you haven't noticed.)

```
Suspicious pointer conversion in function caffeine
```

Don't bother looking it up: It's the `return` statement. Nothing is truly wrong, but you see in a few paragraphs why the compiler is so wise.

```
ARRAYADD.EXE - 0 error(s), 0 warning(s)
```

Dumb old Microsoft compiler! Don't worry — the program contains a goof. Apparently, only the people at Borland have the foresight to notify you about it.

Run it. Here's a sample of the output:

```
First array:
#1 = 1
#2 = 2
#3 = 3
#4 = 4
#5 = 5
#6 = 6
#7 = 7
#8 = 8
#9 = 9

Second array:
#1 = 9
#2 = 8
#3 = 7
#4 = 6
#5 = 5
#6 = 4
#7 = 3
#8 = 2
#9 = 1

Third array:
#1 = 2580
#2 = 8
#3 = 1
#4 = -56
#5 = 801
#6 = 246
#7 = 6
#8 = 6
#9 = 2580
```

Two out of three ain't bad. From the output, you can divine the following:

- The print_array function works just dandy!
- The caffeine function doesn't work just dandy!
- The next two sections explain how to get it right.
- Both functions accept arrays as pointers. Inside the functions, though, the arrays are referenced as arrays.
- You could even modify the array in the function, and it would stay changed throughout the program. That's because you're modifying a memory location in the function and not a variable. Thank you, Mr. Pointer!
- The caffeine function is an integer pointer function. Because it returns an integer pointer value, it's prototyped like this:

```
int *caffeine(int *array1,int *array2,int size);
```

In this case, it returns a whole array (or just the starting memory location of the array). This example shouldn't freak you out; it's basically passing back the array in reverse — opposite of the way you pass an array to a function.

For example, to pass the blorf array to the spittoon function, you use the following:

```
spittoon(blorf);
```

spittoon is declared like this:

```
void spittoon(int *blorf)
```

Going backward, to return the little_brother array from the pest function:

```
return(little_brother)
```

The function is declared like this:

```
int *pest(void)
```

Likewise, a function returning a pointer needs a pointer variable in the main function to receive that value. That's where the coffee pointer comes in:

```
int *coffee;
```

That variable holds the address of the array returned from the caffeine function. It all should work forward as well as backward.

I apologize if this description is inadequately brief, but that's basically how it works. You can sort out the memory address and value of that address stuff later, if you like.

Analyzing the caffeine *function*

It's unfair to say that the caffeine function doesn't work. In reality, it does work as you planned. It does, in fact, create an array and fill it with the proper values. Rewrite the function to call the print_array function in the middle, and you can see my point:

```
int *caffeine(int *array1,int *array2,int size)
{
    int total[SIZE];
    int x;

    for(x=0;x<size;x++)
            total[x]=array1[x]+array2[x];

    puts("\nThe total array:");
    print_array(total,SIZE);

    return(total);
}
```

Make these modifications to the ARRAYADD.C source code. (Add the puts and print_array statements.) Save. Compile. Run.

In the output, you see the new section that displays the contents of the total array:

```
The total array:
#1 = 10
#2 = 10
#3 = 10
#4 = 10
#5 = 10
#6 = 10
#7 = 10
#8 = 10
#9 = 10
```

Alas, the third array in the output is still all wacky.

Reedit your source code to remove the two lines you added to the caffeine function.

The horror of functions murdering their variables (and how to put a stop to it)

Something happens between the `return` statement and the `main` function. It's something that happens to every variable in every function you call. It's something I haven't told you because, well, you've never had to access variables in a called function. Here's what happens:

After a function is done, in an act of sadistic terror, it kills off all its own variables.

Sad but true. Because the function has no need for its variables after it's done func-ing, it releases that memory space back to the computer. The variables, once proud and strong, are laid utterly to waste.

In the `caffeine` function, the `total` array is, well, totaled after the function returns control to the `main` function. What you see displayed in the program's output is garbage — the remnants of the `total` array.

To order a function to retain its variables, you must use the keyword `static` when you're declaring the variable. The `static` keyword tells the compiler to build the program so that the variable's value is retained even after the function is done with its func.

Edit the source code for ARRAYADD.C again. Change the `total` array's declaration in the `caffeine` function as follows:

```
int static total[SIZE];
```

That's it! This line makes the array permanent so that its contents can be accessed with the `coffee` pointer in the `main` function.

Save. Compile. (You Borland people don't see any errors this time.)

Run it. The third chunk of the output looks like this:

```
Third array:
#1 = 10
#2 = 10
#3 = 10
#4 = 10
#5 = 10
#6 = 10
#7 = 10
#8 = 10
#9 = 10
```

Keyword static

The static keyword enables a function to retain its variables and their data even after the function is done running. Without that declaration, the variable's value is changed or reassigned after the function quits or returns.

Variables are declared static using the following format. First comes the variable type

(char, int, float, and so on), then the word static, and then the variable name:

type static varname;

There's no need to declare a variable as static unless you want to retain its value, as covered in this lesson.

The array was created in the function and then returned to the main program. From there, it's accessed via the coffee pointer and displayed just like any other array.

- ✔ This demo program has been the only time in my C programming life that I've needed to use the static keyword. It's just not that common.

- ✔ Another way to have variables available to all functions is to declare them *externally.*

- ✔ Keep in mind one simple thing: The total array was not created with a pointer. You cannot create arrays or any other variables with pointers. You must create a variable first and then assign a pointer to it. The caffeine function does that in a roundabout way because it's the function that eventually declares the array as a pointer (caffeine is a pointer function that returns an array). But an array is never declared as a pointer. That's just not the way it works.

Lesson 10-9 Quiz

1. Which of the following is spelled correctly?

   A. Kwantzit Hut.

   B. Cuaonsut Hut.

   C. Quonset Hut.

   D. One of those cheesy-looking corrugated metal ugly things the military is fond of.

2. To pass a string to a function, you declare what type of variable in the function?

  A. A `char`.

  B. A `*char`.

  C. A string variable.

  D. A `char` pointer.

3. An advantage of passing pointers to a function is what?

  A. Only people who have gotten this far in the book know what's going on.

  B. Because pointers weigh less than other variables, the program won't get clogged arteries.

  C. You can change a pointer variable without having to return anything from the function.

  D. Trick question: Passing a pointer to a function has in fact several disadvantages.

4. To pass the `yolk` array to the `egg` function, you do what?

  A. `egg(yolk);`

  B. `egg(&yolk);`

  C. `egg(*yolk);`

  D. `egg(yolk[]);`

5. How would the `egg` function be declared if it were to accept an array as input?

  A. `void egg(int some_array);`

  B. `void egg(int &some_array);`

  C. `void egg(int *some_array);`

  D. `void egg(int some_array[]);`

6. Declare a variable to properly absorb the output of the following function:

```
int *troubles(void)
```

  A. `int something;`

  B. `int *something;`

  C. `int &something;`

  D. `int something[];`

Bonus question!

Who won the 1953 World Series?

    A. Yankees.

    B. Dodgers.

    C. Giants.

    D. Indians.

 Take a break now! Then go back and redo both this and the preceding lesson. Honestly, it makes much more sense the second time through. (At this stage, you're probably rushing a little too much anyway.)

Lesson 10-10: Arrays of Pointers

 This lesson borders on "advanced" material. Most beginner books don't go into pointer arrays because they induce headaches and agony just at the point that you really think you understand what pointers are all about. (And, honestly, you're probably eager to move on to the next chapter anyway.)

If you want to skip this lesson and the next, feel free. This section has no quiz, and the final exam in this chapter does not cover these topics. Even so, these lessons do explain how to sort strings, which is something I promised in Chapter 9 I would talk about.

Pointers and arrays

In your efforts to believe that you know everything about pointers, one day you declare an array as follows:

```
int *nifty[6];
```

At first glance, it looks like you have created an integer array of six elements and a pointer to that array all at the same time.

Wrong. Wrong. Wrong.

That trick works only with strings. The following example is okay:

```
char *string = "I believe I'm okay."
```

Just about everything else you can think of is wrong or just misdirected. For example, the `int *nifty[6];` declaration creates an array of six integer pointers. Why you would want that is beyond me, but it can be done.

- ✔ It's better to use multidimensional arrays than pointer arrays (refer to Chapter 9). Array notation can easily handle most things you need a pointer array for.

- ✔ There's only one instance in which you may possibly find a pointer array handy: strings. Because each string is considered an array, an array of strings — which is a two-dimensional character array — is similar to (if not the same thing as) an array of string pointers.

Saving some space with string pointer arrays

Lesson 9-8 introduces you to a two-dimensional string array, `dwarf`:

```
char dwarf[7][8] = {
    "bashful",
    "doc",
    "dopey",
    "grumpy",
    "happy",
    "sneezy",
    "sleepy"
};
```

The seven strings sit in a two-dimensional character array — a giant grid that's seven rows by eight columns. That's what's needed because the longest dwarf name (`"bashful"`) is seven characters long, and you need an extra character for the NULL byte at the end of the string.

Figure 10-3 illustrates the character array the DWARFS.C program creates and how it's filled.

The array is a grid of 56 bytes (7×8, as declared in the program). Yet, because only the longest string needs 8 bytes of storage, the rest of the strings waste space. It's not much space — 11 bytes total — but imagine how bad it could be for the following array:

```
char prompts[3][16] = {
    "Type something:",
    "C:\>",
    "."
};
```

b	a	s	h	f	u	l	\0								
d	o	c	\0												
d	o	p	e	y	\0										
g	r	u	m	p	y	\0									
h	a	p	p	y	\0										
s	n	e	e	z	y	\0									
s	l	e	e	p	y	\0									

Figure 10-3: Two-dimensional string arrays can be inefficient.

Three ([3]) strings of 16 ([16]) characters each must be declared in order to properly initialize this array. Figure 10-4 shows how that wastes space in your computer's memory.

T	y	p	e		s	o	m	t	h	i	n	g	:	\0
C	:	\	>	\0										
.	\0													

Figure 10-4: Lots of space is wasted in this array.

The point here really isn't wasted memory. Your PC has megabytes of RAM in it, so being sloppy with a string array is forgivable. As is often the case with C, however, you can just find better ways to do things. In this case, it's better to create a string array with pointers rather than create a multidimensional array.

✔ The NULL byte, shown using its escape sequence \0 in Figures 10-3 and 10-4, ends every string in an array. You must account for that character when you set up the size of the array.

✔ You cannot use a character pointer array to point to strings that don't yet exist. For example:

```
char input[80];
```

Here, a storage space of 80 bytes is created for a future string array. No pointer equivalent exists for this statement.

Making a string pointer array

Because the compiler lets you get away with declaring a character pointer string, you can also get away with declaring an array of character pointers to a whole bunch of strings.

Okay. You never really "get away" with anything in C. It's just something you can do with strings and not with any other type of variable. (I don't want to lead you down The Path of Having Too Much Fun here.)

As an example of declaring a pointer-string thing, this one is perfectly okay:

```
char *snow = "White";
```

The following pointer array thing is also okay:

```
char *seven[] = {
    "bashful",
    "doc",
    "dopey",
    "grumpy",
    "happy",
    "sneezy",
    "sleepy"
};
```

The declaration *seven[] tells the compiler to do two things. First, a character pointer array is created, as shown in Figure 10-5. The pointers each take up two bytes of memory and can hold the addresses of strings stored elsewhere in memory. Whatever. It's all done by the compiler, so you don't have to think about it.

Figure 10-5 shows how the compiler allocates the array, creating storage space for seven pointers to hold the address of seven strings elsewhere in memory.

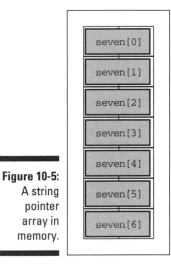

Figure 10-5:
A string
pointer
array in
memory.

The second thing the `*seven[]` declaration tells the compiler is to initialize the pointers to hold the addresses of the seven strings declared in the array — two steps in one. What's really created in memory looks like Figure 10-6.

seven[0]	⇨	b	a	s	h	f	u	l	\0
seven[1]	⇨	d	o	c	\0				
seven[2]	⇨	d	o	p	e	y	\0		
seven[3]	⇨	g	r	u	m	p	y	\0	
seven[4]	⇨	h	a	p	p	y	\0		
seven[5]	⇨	s	n	e	e	z	y	\0	
seven[6]	⇨	s	l	e	e	p	y	\0	

Figure 10-6:
A string
pointer
array and
its strings.

✔ The initialized string pointer array works because you can use a pointer to create a string. The compiler simply sticks the strings into memory and then plugs those strings' addresses into the proper pointer variable slots.

✔ Declaring a string pointer array can save some memory, but that's not the reason you use them; the advantage to an array of pointers is that pointers, because they're variables, are more easily manipulated than a plain Kmart-variety two-dimensional array.

✔ Remember that pointer arrays are created to be more handy, not specifically to save memory. For example, the seven array uses more memory than the dwarfs array. The pointers in the seven array take up two bytes of memory apiece. Those 14 total bytes are more than the 11 bytes lost by declaring the dwarfs array the old-fashioned way (compare Figure 10-3 with Figure 10-6).

A redundant demo program to prove that it works

re•dun•dant (*ri-dun'dent*) *adj.* **1.** *See* redundant.

The following program uses both array notation and pointer notation to declare an array of strings. It illustrates how both methods work similarly, which is kind of redundant, but that's sort of been the point of this whole book.

Type this source code into your editor. Save it to disk as SEVEN.C:

Name: SEVEN.C

```
#include <stdio.h>

void main()
{
    char dwarf[7][8] = {
        "bashful",
        "doc",
        "dopey",
        "grumpy",
        "happy",
        "sneezy",
        "sleepy",
    };

    char *seven[] = {
        "bashful",
        "doc",
        "dopey",
        "grumpy",
```

```
        "happy",
        "sneezy",
        "sleepy"
    };
    int x;

    for(x=0;x<7;x++)
        printf("%s\n",dwarf[x]);

    putchar('\n');

    for(x=0;x<7;x++)
        printf("%s\n",seven[x]);
}
```

Compile and run.

The program displays the contents of both arrays, showing that pointer and array notation are basically the same.

Check marks to cheer you up:

- ✔ Both an array of pointers and a standard two-dimensional array display strings in the same manner: dwarf[0] is the first string in the dwarf array, and seven[0] is the first string in the seven array.

- ✔ The preceding check mark is true only for strings. If you have an integer pointer array, for example, it works differently (which is one reason I'm not touching integer pointers — the "third rail" of pointers).

- ✔ What's the difference between dwarf[0] and seven[0]? Nothing. They're both memory addresses of the first string in the array. dwarf is an array you declared, and seven is a pointer whose value was assigned by the compiler.

Pointer array déjà vu

One major reason for bringing up this pointer array nonsense is the following doodad from way back in Lesson 6-3, in *C For Dummies,* Volume I:

```
*argv[]
```

Armed with your now potentially deadly knowledge of pointers, you should recognize that *argv[] is, in fact . . . a pointer array!

(Heavy disaster-movie music plays.)

The `argv[]` thing, which represents stuff typed after the program name at the DOS prompt, is an array of pointers. Each pointer contains the address of one item typed at the DOS prompt. This is the same deal as the `seven[]` array, though the input comes from the DOS prompt.

Type the following source code into your editor. It's just a silly little program that displays all the options you type after the program name at the DOS prompt. Save the source code to disk as CMDLINE1.C:

Name: CMDLINE1.C

```
#include <stdio.h>

void main(int argc,char *argv[])
{
    int x;

    puts("Command line arguments:");

    for(x=0;x<argc;x++)
        puts(argv[x]);
}
```

Compile.

To run the program, you need a DOS prompt. If you're in a Windows environment, you have to start up a DOS window and run the program there. (You may have to recompile CMDLINE1.C as a DOS-prompt program.)

Run it:

```
Command line arguments:
C:\WORK\CSTUFF\CMDLINE1.EXE
```

Run it again, and this time type something after `cmdline` at the DOS prompt:

```
Command line arguments:
C:\WORK\CSTUFF\CMDLINE1.EXE
I
am
not
an
argument
```

✔ The argc variable contains the number of items typed at the DOS prompt. It always equals at least 1, which represents the name of the program.

✔ The puts function can use each element in the argv array as a string. Because each element is a character pointer (part of the pointer array) and that pointer holds the address of a string, it all works.

✔ Refer to Lesson 6-3 in Volume I of this book for more info about command-prompt argument type issues.

✔ Yes, they're called "arguments." If I were in charge of naming things, I would have chosen "doodads" instead (then again, everything is a doodad to me).

Now, what the heck is that thing?

Sit back and think of multiple layers of illogic for a second. Because a pointer array is a collection of memory addresses, each element in the array is a memory address:

```
argv[1]
```

This variable is a string, but it's also merely a memory address — and a pointer. What happens if you do this to it?

```
*argv[1]
```

Uh-oh!

That kind of thing shouldn't boggle you at all. It's really no different from *s or *string or any other pointer variable with an asterisk in front of it. Basically, the pointer variable is now the same as a single character variable. It works the same as the following:

```
s = string;
putchar(*s);
```

If string is a string and s is a pointer variable, the putchar function displays the first character in the string:

```
putchar(*argv[1]);
```

Because argv[1] is a string, *argv[1] is merely the first character in that string. This putchar function displays the first character in string argv[1].

Want to display the second character in the string? Then you increment the string pointer. Here's how it works with the s pointer example:

```
s = string;
putchar(*s);
s++;
putchar(*s);
```

Because s is the address of the string, incrementing it one character-size chunk (s++) moves it up to the next memory address, which holds the next character in the string. This should be old-hat pointer stuff to you.

The pointer argv[1] is also a memory address. Incrementing it points to the next character in the string, which is then displayed by the putchar function:

```
putchar(*argv[1]);
argv[1]++;
putchar(*argv[1]);
```

Yes, you can increment argv[1]. It's not an array — it's a pointer. This is the advantage of using pointers rather than a two-dimensional array to declare multiple strings.

The following program is a modification of CMDLINE1.C. It uses the *argv[x] contraption to display the command-line arguments one character at a time.

Type this source code into your editor. Save it to disk as CMDLINE2.C:

Name: CMDLINE2.C

```
#include <stdio.h>

void main(int argc,char *argv[])
{
    int x;

    puts("Command line arguments:");

    for(x=0;x<argc;x++)
    {
        while(*argv[x])
        {
```

```
            putchar(*argv[x]);
            argv[x]++;
        }
        putchar('\n');
    }
}
```

Compile it. Run it and type **Kiss me, Titus** after cmdline2 at the DOS prompt:

```
Command line arguments:
C:\WORK\CSTUFF\CMDLINE2.EXE
Kiss
me,
Titus
```

Although the output is the same, it was a putchar function and not puts that displayed the string's contents.

- ✔ The statement while(*argv[x]) loops through each string in the array one character at a time (refer to the preceding lesson).

- ✔ The putchar function displays each character in the string. The notation *argv[x] stands for a single character in the string.

- ✔ The statement argv[x] increments the memory address held in the argv[x] pointer variable, which points at the next character in the string.

- ✔ A for loop is required in order to loop through every string held in the pointer array.

You may be wondering (though you're probably not) why the while loop couldn't look like this:

```
while(*argv[x]++)
    putchar(*argv[x]);
```

After all, that while convention was beaten into your brain in the preceding lesson. The problem here is that argv[x] is incremented before the putchar function has a chance to print the first character in the string. The true solution is shown in the following monster:

```
while(putchar(*argv[x]++))
    ;
```

Although this solution works, it's not the prettiest thing to look at. The character is read from string `argv[x]`, and then the string is incremented. Egads! Enough!

Pointers (even in an array) are variables

Because pointers are variables, you know that they can change. Or, more accurately, they can be changed. They don't just change impulsively.

Array of pointers can be changed as well. Because you can swap elements in a pointer array, exchanging their values without changing what those values are, it's possible to mess up the order of character pointers in an array without moving any of the strings they point to.

Type this program into your editor. Save it to disk as CMDLINE3.C:

Name: CMDLINE3.C

```c
#include <stdio.h>
#include <stdlib.h>

void main(int argc,char *argv[])
{
    char *temp;

    if(argc!=3)
    {
        puts("Type two items after CMDLINE3");
        exit(0);
    }

/* swap the arguments */

    temp = argv[1];
    argv[1] = argv[2];
    argv[2] = temp;

/* display arguments */

    printf("argv[1] = %s\n",argv[1]);
    printf("argv[2] = %s\n",argv[2]);
}
```

Compile and run:

```
C> Type two items after CMDLINE3
```

Okay. Type **cmdline3 first second** at the DOS prompt and press the Enter key:

```
C> cmdline3 first second
argv[1] = second
argv[2] = first
```

What you typed hasn't changed, but the pointers that hold those memory addresses have changed. They've been swapped in the array — just as you would swap two array elements in a sort.

It really doesn't take much to swap the elements. First, you must have a character pointer to help store one element during the swap:

```
char *temp;
```

In the program, this statement creates a temporary character pointer, temp, to help store the pointers held in the argv array. Then the following three statements can do the swap:

```
temp = argv[1];
argv[1] = argv[2];
argv[2] = temp;
```

You're not moving strings here; you're moving the addresses of the strings. You could move the strings, but why bother? What the program really cares about is the string's starting address and not the string itself. Here, you're just moving the string's starting address. Yes, this is how you sort strings in C.

> ✔ Swapping pointer variables in an array does not change the strings they point to (just as if you shuffle your property cards in a game of Monopoly, it doesn't rearrange where the properties live on the game board).

> ✔ Refer to Lesson 9-4 in Chapter 9 for more information about sorting and swapping elements in an array.

> ✔ Sorting strings is the subject of the next lesson.

Lesson 10-10 Quiz

This quiz has been canceled. It's 15 minutes after class started. The professor isn't here. You're gone!

Lesson 10-11: Sorting Strings with Pointers

I'm certain that someone along the line has written a C program that sorts strings without using pointers. It can be done, but *I* wouldn't want to do it. After all, Lesson 10-11 shows you how cinchy it is to swap pointers in an array. That's an effective way to sort entire strings without moving the clunky things around in memory.

- ✔ You may want to review Lesson 9-4 on sorting integer arrays.
- ✔ The idea here: You sort the strings by swapping pointers to them. The strings themselves don't move.

A simple, though incorrect, string-sorting program

The following program sorts eight characters. (It really sorts eight strings, but the strings happen to be the names of Disney cartoon characters). To accomplish this task, the program borrows the bubble-sort technique used in Lesson 9-4 and the pointer-swapping trick you read about in the preceding lesson:

Name: PSORT1.C

```
#include <stdio.h>

#define SIZE 8

void main()
{
    char *names[] = {
        "Mickey",
        "Minnie",
```

```
        "Donald",
        "Daisy",
        "Goofy",
        "Chip",
        "Dale",
        "Pluto"
    };
    char *temp;
    int x,a,b;

    for(a=0;a<SIZE-1;a++)
        for(b=a+1;b<SIZE;b++)
        {
            if(*names[a] > *names[b])
            {
                temp = names[a];
                names[a] = names[b];
                names[b] = temp;
            }
        }

    for(x=0;x<SIZE;x++)
        printf("%s\n",names[x]);
}
```

Save this program to disk as PSORT1.C. Compile and run:

```
Chip
Daisy
Donald
Dale
Goofy
Minnie
Mickey
Pluto
```

It works! Well, sort of. The program did effectively swap the pointers in the array so that the array now points to the strings in alphabetical order — but only alphabetical order as far as the first character of each string is concerned. See how the D names and M names are not in alphabetical order?

What went wrong

The PSORT1.C program uses a bubble sort to sift through each string in the array. Strings are swapped based on an `if` comparison — which is all standard stuff. Because pointers are being swapped, the following `if` statement is used:

```
if(*names[a] > *names[b])
```

This example works, and it makes sense: `names[a]` is the address of one string in the array, and `names[b]` is the address of another string. The `*` is used to represent the contents of the strings. Alas, `*names[a]` and `*names[b]` are *character* variables. They are not entire strings.

A string is a *character* array. The C compiler references the string by the memory location of the first character. The variable `*names[a]` is a character variable, not a string.

When you put an asterisk before a pointer in an array (and I'm talking about `char` pointers here), you get a single character and not the entire string. The preceding lesson tried to drive this issue home.

So

```
*names[a]
```

is really the same as

```
names[a][0]
```

But you can't do that in this program. This is a `pointer` array program, and the preceding line is a no-no.

To sort the strings, you must make comparisons beyond the first character in the string. Before you can do that, you have to know how to reference those characters. You're going to have to take a dip in the toxic pond of Ugly Pointer Array Notation.

- ✔ You should know that `*argv[1]` is a pointer variable representing the first character of the string `argv[1]`. In Lesson 10-9, you see that the second character in the string can be accessed as follows:

```
argv[1]++;
putchar(*argv[1]);
```

> ✔ In a string-sorting program, unfortunately, you can't go around incrementing your pointer; if you do that, when you swap pointers, you won't be swapping the start of the string.
>
> ✔ "Oh, bother" — Winnie the Pooh.

Ugly pointer array notation

In the land of creepy C notation, you find the following etched into a pillared monument:

```
**array
```

Before you faint, allow me to rule out an obvious possibility: The ** is not from the same planet as ++ and --. It's not some type of multiplication-incrementation. I shudder to think of any mathematical concept along those lines. (Hey, I use *Quicken* to balance my checkbook!)

The ** is actually a set of pointers. Evil twins. Ugly. Imposing.

There's only one way to deal with the ** monster. . . .

No — put away the torches and pitchforks. The only (and best) way to deal with it is to use your pals the parentheses. Tucking anything in parentheses makes it easily understood. It also enables you to control what happens first:

```
*(*array)
```

This notation isn't that heinous. If array is an array of strings, array itself is the first element, the address of the first string. Then *array would be the string itself — what the first element in the array points to in memory. The final * on the outside points to the first character of the first string because strings are character arrays.

It's an array of arrays! Hooray!

Here's another way to put it:

```
*(*array)
```

is the same thing as

```
*array[0]
```

which is exactly the same thing as

```
array[0][0]
```

Now you can see why most people use array notation rather than pointers. Remember, though, with array notation comes a certain lack of flexibility: You can't swap array notation variables like you can swap pointers, which makes sorting strings a major hassle.

Don't even bother trying to figure out how to access the second character of a string just yet. Worry first about accessing the next *element* in the pointer array. Keep in mind that the array is composed of pointers, not honest variables. With pointers, you can do strange arithmetic. Here's how:

```
**(array+1)
```

This is the same thing as

```
*array[1]
```

which is the same thing as

```
array[1][0]
```

(It's the first character of the second array.)

Here's how `**(array+1)` breaks down:

```
*(*(array+1))
```

On the inside, you have `array+1`. From your basic pointer arithmetic, you should know that `array+1` points to the second element in a pointer array. The 1 adds a pointer-size chunk to the start of the array in memory. So `array+1` really equals the second element in the array, which is the address of the second string in memory.

`array+1` does *not* equal the string — just its address. It's a memory location, like 134 or something. It's not a string!

To make `array+1` represent the string whose address it contains, you need the * doodad:

```
*(array+1)
```

Now, that's a string! More precisely, it's the address of a string in memory, but the * causes the compiler to see what's at that address as an array of characters.

Remember that pointers have a dual nature. By themselves, they hold a memory location, the address of some value in memory. Only with the asterisk do they tell you what that value is.

Moving right along:

```
*(*(array+1))
```

By putting the second asterisk before the pointer-string thing, you force the compiler to see the whole thing as a *character* and not as a string.

Table 10-3 breaks everything down for you from the inside out. Keep in mind that you're still working with strings and their first characters in this notation. The table should clear up how it all works.

Table 10-3	How the Ugly ** Notation Works Itself Out	
Doodad	**What It Is**	**How the Compiler Sees It**
array+1	An address	A pointer
*(array+1)	Contents of address, or what lives there	A string
((array+1))	Contents of a character array	A character
**(array+1)	Same as preceding entry	Same as preceding entry

Oh, why not finally drive the point home by rewriting the PSORT1.C program using this beastly notation!

Load the PSORT1.C source code into your editor. You have to change two types of references in the program:

```
*names[a]
```

becomes

```
**(names+a)
```

This is how the program references the *characters* in the strings in the pointer array. And then

```
names[a]
```

becomes

```
*(names+a)
```

This is how the program references the string's address (pointer) in the program:

Name: PSORT2.C

```c
#include <stdio.h>

#define SIZE 8

void main()
{
    char *names[] = {
        "Mickey",
        "Minnie",
        "Donald",
        "Daisy",
        "Goofy",
        "Chip",
        "Dale",
        "Pluto"
    };
    char *temp;
    int x,a,b;

    for(a=0;a<SIZE-1;a++)
        for(b=a+1;b<SIZE;b++)
        {
            if(**(names+a) > **(names+b))
            {
                temp = *(names+a);
                *(names+a) = *(names+b);
                *(names+b) = temp;
            }
        }

    for(x=0;x<SIZE;x++)
        printf("%s\n",*(names+x));
}
```

Save the file to disk as PSORT2.C. Compile and run.

The output is identical. All you've done is change from array notation to pointer notation. The compiler itself doesn't see any difference. In fact, the compiler is really wondering what you're up do.

What you're up to, of course, is sorting the *characters* in the strings, which is covered in the next section.

> ✔ The ** thing is not really that common. I've seen it used only in C language books and seldom in any programs.

> ✔ The program uses **(name+x) notation for comparison but *(name+x) notation for swapping. Why? Because **(name+x) is a character, and *(name+x) is a string. You cannot compare strings in an if statement. (You can compare them using the strcmp function, but that would cut short this lesson.)

> ✔ The pointer variable temp does not change in the program. It's simply a storage place for another pointer variable. Because *(names+a) is the same as names[a], there's no need to gussy up the temp variable with any external doodads.

Sorting a string by its characters

Now that you know how to access arrays using full-power (and full-on butt-ugly) pointer notation, you're ready to access the characters in memory. After all, the characters in a string must be compared before you can say that you have sorted the entire string.

To access those characters with pointer notation, you have to pull together two tricks. Don't be concerned that you didn't think of this on your own; it's not terribly obvious.

From Table 10-3, you should know that the following is the string itself, the start of the character array in memory:

```
*(name+a)
```

Variable a represents the element in the array pointer — a specific string in the array. (Variable x was used in the PSORT2.C program.)

Go back to Table 10-2, which discusses the relationship between arrays and pointers. To get to character *x* in a string, you use the following pointer notation:

```
*(n+x)
```

Variable n is an array pointer to the start of the string. n plus x points to the *x*th character of the string, element x.

Now combine the two. After all, variable n is the same as *(name). Both are pointers to the start of a string in memory. Because they're identical, you can replace one with the other. Figure 10-7 shows how the replacement is made and the monster you end up with.

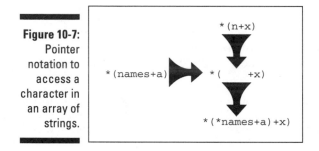

Figure 10-7: Pointer notation to access a character in an array of strings.

The monster you end up with is

```
*(*names+a)+x)
```

This is the same as the following array notation:

```
n[a][x]
```

That's array n, string number a, character number x. With pointer notation, it's pointer array names, element number a, character x. Both the same.

Golly, array notation surely is easier. With array notation, though, you can't sort and swap the strings, as you can in the following program:

Carefully enter the following source code into your editor. The nearby Blow-by-Blow sidebar, "Twisty, mazelike secrets of PSORT3.C," explains the guts of the program — though aside from the pointer notation, it's nothing you don't already know. Save the beast to disk as PSORT3.C:

Name: PSORT3.C

```
#include <stdio.h>

#define SIZE 8
```

```
void main()
{
    char *names[] = {
        "Mickey",
        "Minnie",
        "Donald",
        "Daisy",
        "Goofy",
        "Chip",
        "Dale",
        "Pluto"
    };
    char *temp;
    int x,a,b;

    for(a=0;a<SIZE-1;a++)
        for(b=a+1;b<SIZE;b++)
        {
            x = 0;
            while(*(*(names+a)+x))
            {
                if(*(*(names+a)+x) > *(*(names+b)+x))
                {
                    temp = *(names+a);
                    *(names+a) = *(names+b);
                    *(names+b) = temp;
                    break;
                }
                else if(*(*(names+a)+x) < *(*(names+b)+x))
                    break;
                else
                    x++;
            }
        }

    for(x=0;x<SIZE;x++)
        printf("%s\n",*(names+x));
}
```

Compile it! You may get some errors, considering that the program has many, many semicolons and curly brackets to goof up. And those parentheses! Miss one of them, and the compiler gags. It's ugly. Make sure that all your parentheses match up.

Twisty, mazelike secrets of PSORT3.C

The PSORT3.C program sorts strings using a standard bubble sort. Each string in the array is compared to every other string — *but on a character-by-character* basis.

Two nested loops creep through the whole array, comparing one string against every other string in the array:

```
for(a=0;a<SIZE-1;a++)
    for(b=a+1;b<SIZE;b++)
```

The first string is `*(names+a)`, and the second is `*(names+b)`. (This is pointer notation for `*names[a]` and `*names[b]`.)

To compare the characters in each string, a `while` loop is used. The variable *x* serves as an index to each character in the string.

The condition is the same one used in a `while` loop to display a string:

```
while(*(*(names+a)+x))
```

Because the ugly `*(*names+a)+x)` variable represents each character in string `a` of the array, the `while` loop repeats once for each character in the string (refer to Lesson 10-8 for more information).

The `if` comparison now is between the first character of the two strings. The following ugly variables are really pointer notation for `names[a][x]` and `names[b][x]`:

```
if(*(*(names+a)+x) >
  *(*(names+b)+x))
```

If the first character is greater than the second, the two strings are swapped:

```
temp = *(names+a);
*(names+a) = *(names+b);
*(names+b) = temp;
```

This is standard bubble-sort stuff, and it's the beauty of pointers. If you were using array notation, you probably would call a function here that swaps the strings. Messy, messy, messy.

After the strings are swapped (actually, after their memory locations are swapped), a `break` command halts the `while` loop, and the program continues by comparing the next two strings in the array.

If the first character is less than the second, there's no need to swap them, and the loop ends with a `break` statement.

```
else if(*(*(names+a)+x) <
   *(*(names+b)+x))
```

The final `else` is what makes comparing strings like `Daisy` and `Dale` work. If both strings are equal, `x` is incremented to point at the next character in the string:

```
else
    x++;
```

Eventually, one character should be less than or equal to the next. If not and the `while` loop stops, both strings are considered equal and are not swapped.

Run:

```
Chip
Daisy
Dale
Donald
Goofy
Mickey
Minnie
Pluto
```

The program successfully sorted all the strings. Look at the *D*s. Even Daisy and Dale are sorted correctly.

- ✔ If you have the time (and I know that you probably do — I mean, you *sleep* and waste time, right?), you may try to rewrite this program using array notation.

- ✔ PSORT3.C sorts shorter strings before longer ones. If you have Goof and Goofy in the array, for example, Goof sorts out first.

- ✔ Yes, it would be a heck of a lot easier to use the strcmp function to compare the strings. If you did, though, you would never learn the proper pointer notation for accessing characters. Refer to Lesson 9-6 for more information about strcmp.

- ✔ The following notation is incorrect:

```
**(names+a)+x
```

Never mind trying to figure that one out. It's not the same as this monster:

```
*(*names+a)+x)
```

- ✔ You have a number of different ways to sort strings in C. What you see here is the way I do it, which doesn't mean that it's the best way or the only way.

Lesson 10-11 Quiz

No quiz for this stuff because it's kind of advanced. If you can just remember that sorting strings is merely a matter of sorting pointers to those strings, however, I would be very happy.

Chapter 10 Final Exam

1. Why use a variable before it's initialized?

   A. Why not?

   B. To show how the sizeof keyword operates.

   C. Uninitialized variables hold garbage, so using them is kinda dumb.

   D. Uninitialized variables reserve memory space for new variables to be created later.

2. How can you tell how much storage space a double uses in memory?

   A. Look at Table 3-3 in Volume I of this book.

   B. Look in your compiler's reference manual.

   C. Use the sizeof keyword.

   D. A double uses twice as much storage space as a single.

3. The most maddening things about pointers is that

   A. They have a dual nature: memory address and the contents of that address.

   B. They are declared with the asterisk but not always used with the asterisk.

   C. It has something to do with * and also with &.

   D. Well, just about everything is maddening with pointers.

4. Before a pointer can be used, it must be

   A. Worshipped.

   B. Sharpened.

   C. Initialized.

   D. Adorned with * things.

5. Which of the following initializes the pointer ding to the variable dong?

   A. `ding = dong;`

   B. `ding = &dong;`

   C. `*ding = &dong;`

   D. `ding = *dong;`

   E. `&ding = dong;`

6. What were Albert Einstein's last words?

    A. "God *does* play dice!"

    B. "It's all relative."

    C. "Tell Mother I'm coming home."

    D. "What truck?"

    E. Unknown.

7. For what one type of variable do you not need the ampersand for initializing a pointer?

    A. String arrays.

    B. Array elements.

    C. Arrays themselves.

    D. You always need the ampersand.

8. If you increment a pointer variable, what happens to it?

    A. It grows by one.

    B. It grows by one chunk of memory (the chunk is the same size as the pointer's variable type).

    C. The contents of that memory location are incremented.

    D. The memory location increases, but the compiler produces an error.

9. After pointer variable pooh is initialized to variable piglet, what does variable *pooh contain?

    A. Honey.

    B. No, it's hunny.

    C. Variable *pooh contains the same value as variable piglet.

    D. Variable *pooh contains piglet's memory location.

10. If the pointer variable pope is initialized to the variable vatican and pope equals 345, what does that tell you about variable vatican?

    A. Variable vatican must live at address 345 in memory.

    B. Variable vatican is an integer.

    C. Variable vatican is a large chunk of tax-exempt property in downtown Rome.

    D. Variable vatican must be guarded by variable swiss and sell stamps for income.

11. What should you do if you ever see something like *p++ in a program?

    A. Smother it with parentheses.

    B. Work it from right to left and then inside out.

    C. Chuck it all and refer to Table 10-1.

    D. Give up and relearn Visual Basic.

12. Match the state with its postal abbreviation:

    A. Maine   1. MA

    B. Maryland   2. MD

    C. Massachusetts   3. ME

    D. Michigan   4. MI

    E. Minnesota   5. MN

    F. Mississippi   6. MO

    G. Missouri   7. MS

    H. Montana   8. MT

13. Supposing that pointer buzz has been initialized to array moon, which of the following variables represents the value of the eighth element in the array?

    A. `buzz[8];`

    B. `*buzz+7;`

    C. `*(buzz+7);`

    D. The answer cannot be determined until you know what type of array (and pointer) you're dealing with.

14. Which of the following declarations is not forbidden in all 50 states?

    A. `char *string = "Thing";`

    B. `char *string[] = "Thing";`

    C. `int *tedger = 45;`

    D. `float *onthe_c = 3.141;`

15. How many times does the following while loop repeat itself?

```
while(*s++)
```

    A. Infinitely.

    B. As long as the variable *s never contains a NULL byte.

C. For as many characters as there are in the string represented by s.

D. s.

16. What kind of input does the following function require?

```
void long_stick(int *pointer)
```

A. None; it's a void function.

B. Like, duh, a pointer. Specifically, an integer pointer.

C. Any pointer value.

D. Any integer value.

17. How would you call the long_stick function shown in Question 16, assuming that variable p is a pointer?

A. long_stick(&p);

B. long_stick(*p);

C. long_stick(p);

D. long_stick(int *p);

18. If the long_stick function (see Question 16) modifies the variable pointer, is that new value available in the main function?

A. If you have done everything right, of course.

B. Nope!

19. The following function returns which type of value?

```
float *coconut(int meat,int milk,int oil)
```

A. A floating-pointer point, or point pointer.

B. A float.

C. A memory address.

D. Something to do with coconuts.

20. What does the static keyword do?

A. Prevents your disks from being accidentally erased by static electricity.

B. Causes the socks variables to stick together.

C. Makes sure that an array doesn't wiggle around in memory.

D. Prevents a function from committing murder.

The 5th Wave   By Rich Tennant

Chapter 11

The Whole Deal with Structures

- -

Lessons in This Chapter

▶ Multivariables

▶ Arrays of structures

▶ Structures and functions

▶ Making sacrifices to Malloc

▶ Structures and (gasp!) pointers

Programs in This Chapter

OZ1.C	OZ2.C	INFOSTO.C	MORESTO.C
LOGIN.C	OZ3.C	OZ4.C	OZ5.C
LETS_GO!.C	LETSGO!.C	OZ6.C	MBDAY.C
BDAYS.C	HOWDY.C	STDB.C	

Vocabulary introduced in This Chapter

```
struct        .        malloc        ->
```

- -

*F*or a program to be truly useful, it must do something. This action typically involves mangling information somehow, such as how the phone company bills you $10,000 for one long-distance call to Albuquerque. Some refer to the process as "number crunching." I prefer the term "massaging data." Whatever, it's the earmark of a program that does something.

If you plan to write a program that crunches or massages (or even mangles), you need a device called a *structure*. Arrays can't do it. Ten thousand variables of matching types can't do it. Only with a well-built structure can you properly mangle information, turning and tweaking it to appease the greedy or fool the oblivious.

This chapter tackles the lumbering structure monster. This stuff isn't hard, not like the battle with pointers in Chapter 10. No, structures are lovable beasts — solid, ground-hugging, easily understandable — the kind of doowaddles you wish everything was made of.

Lesson 11-1: Multivariables

Imagine how dull life was before the invention of the 3 x 5 card.

"Oh, here's that meat loaf recipe you wanted. I just knotted it out using Morse code on this piece of string. . . ."

"Card catalog? No, you just stand here and shout out the name of the book you want. We have librarians stationed throughout the building. See? Just say, 'Anyone know where Mark Twain is?' and then someone will shout, 'He's over here!' and you just follow that person's voice. . . ."

"Are you the new applicant? Just tell me your name and employment history. I remember everything. . . ."

In the C language, structures are similar to 3 x 5 cards. They hold a combination of information tidbits — like a fill-in-the-blank something or other. They keep related information together and easily accessed.

> ✔ Structures are used primarily for database applications. Anything where a clump of information must be kept is an ideal place for a structure to be used.
>
> ✔ If you're familiar with the Pascal programming language, a structure in C is similar to a *record* in Pascal.
>
> ✔ If you're not familiar with the Pascal programming language, well then, aren't *you* the lucky one!

Life without structures

Not knowing anything about structures, you may one day sit down and start that *Wizard of Oz* database you've always dreamed of. The following program, OZ1.C, is a step in this direction; it keeps tabs on actors, their roles, and their age at the time they appeared in *The Wizard of Oz* (1939).

Type the following source code into your editor. The long `printf` statement is wrapped in this book; you don't have to type it on two lines in your text editor. Save it to disk as OZ1.C:

Name: OZ1.C

```
#include <stdio.h>

void main()
{
    char *actor = "Judy Garland";
```

```
    char *character = "Dorothy";
    int age = 17;

    puts("Wizard of Oz Database!");

    printf("%s played %s, and was %i years old\n",
actor,character,age);
}
```

Compile and run:

```
Wizard of Oz Database!
Judy Garland played Dorothy, and was 17 years old
```

Ho-hum.

It can get sloppy, of course. Assume that you grow to love your program and want to catalog the three main male actors. If so, you probably would end up with something like the following example.

Modify the OZ1.C source code and, using a great deal of copy and paste, create the following. Save it to disk as OZ2.C:

Name: OZ2.C

```
#include <stdio.h>

void main()
{
    char *actor1 = "Judy Garland";
    char *character1 = "Dorothy";
    int age1 = 17;

    char *actor2 = "Ray Bolger";
    char *character2 = "Scarecrow";
    int age2 = 35;

    char *actor3 = "Bert Lahr";
    char *character3 = "Cowardly Lion";
    int age3 = 44;

    char *actor4 = "Jack Haley";
    char *character4 = "Tin Woodsman";
    int age4 = 40;
```

(continued)

(continued)

```
    puts("Wizard of Oz Database!");

    printf("%s played %s, and was %i years old\n",
            actor1,character1,age1);
    printf("%s played %s, and was %i years old\n",
            actor2,character2,age2);
    printf("%s played %s, and was %i years old\n",
            actor3,character3,age3);
    printf("%s played %s, and was %i years old\n",
            actor4,character4,age4);
}
```

Compile. Fix any errors. This is Missing Semicolon Season, so double-check for any statements that lost their semicolons.

Run:

```
Wizard of Oz Database!
Judy Garland played Dorothy, and was 17 years old
Ray Bolger played Scarecrow, and was 35 years old
Bert Lahr played Cowardly Lion, and was 44 years old
Jack Haley played Tin Woodsman, and was 40 years old
```

This program is just a fount of information. Go ahead: Stun your neighbors with it.

Yeah, but the OZ2.C program as it stands is *ugly* as sin. Don't all the redundant variables strike you as awkward? And this program displays only the variables' values. No searching or sorting or nerdy things like that. Imagine what a nightmare that would be!

- ✔ Your bank obviously doesn't store its account information using a system like this one. Or maybe it does, if you bank where I do.
- ✔ These programs take advantage of the string-creation shortcut you found out about in Lesson 10-7:

  ```
  char *actor1 = "Judy Garland";
  ```

- ✔ Just think of this ruse as a shortcut, not a pointer. No sense in mentally struggling with pointers in this chapter. (At least, not yet!)

Arrays are not the answer

You may think that you can solve the Wizard of Oz program's problems by sticking everything into an array. (Or just give the Wizard the witch's broomstick and be done with it.)

Unfortunately, arrays are a half-solution, really. The following program shows how you would work it if you tried to stuff all the information into arrays. Don't bother typing the program. It's a bear!

```c
#include <stdio.h>

void main()
{
    char *actor[] = {
        "Judy Garland",
        "Ray Bolger",
        "Bert Lahr",
        "Jack Haley"
        };

    char *character[] = {
        "Dorothy",
        "Scarecrow",
        "Cowardly Lion",
        "Tin Woodsman"
        };

    int age[] = { 17, 35, 44, 40 };

    int x;

    puts("Wizard of Oz Database!");

    for(x=0;x<4;x++)
    {
        printf("%s played ",actor[x]);
        printf("%s, and was ",character[x]);
        printf("%i years old\n",age[x]);
    }
}
```

Although it's true that three arrays can hold the data and a `for` loop prints everything nicely, the whole thing still smells. There must be a better solution. . . .

✔ The preceding program's output is the same as for OZ2.C, shown earlier in this lesson.

✔ This program would work fine — if only all the data were of *one* variable type. For example, if you were working with just actors and their roles, you could slap it all down in a nice two-dimensional string array.

✔ "I'll take Actors and Their Roles for 100, Alex."

✔ Alas, even the multidimensional array solution is cumbersome. Using all that array notation to access each element is clumsy. If you want to sort or search, you had better be adept at using pointers. Yikes! Time to find another solution.

✔ The solution to the Wizard of Oz program problem is offered in the next lesson.

Why, what you need is a 3 x 5 card!

In real life (remember that?), you probably would store complex information on a 3 x 5 card. As any salesperson can tell you, computers are just big 3 x 5 card things anyway. Remember the old advertisements? You could store your recipes on the computer, put your CD collection there, organize your checkbook, yada-yada, and so on.

In the C language, a 3 x 5 card is known as a *structure*. It's a collection of variable types all stored in one compact unit. Each unit is similar to a record in a database, which you can access and tweak just like any other variable in C.

Rather than bore you with the format right away, just type the following program into your editor. Double-check your typing because some new doohickeys are in there that you haven't seen. Save it to disk as INFOSTO.C:

Name: INFOSTO.C

```
#include <stdio.h>
#include <conio.h>
#include <stdlib.h>

void main()
{
    char input[10];

    struct stuff
    {
        char c;
        int n;
```

```
    };

    struct stuff mystuff;

    puts("Your Own Stuff");

    printf("Enter your favorite letter: ");
    mystuff.c = getche();
    putchar('\n');

    printf("Enter your favorite number: ");
    mystuff.n = atoi(gets(input));

    printf("Okay. Your favorite letter is %c\n",mystuff.c);
    printf("And your favorite number is %i.\n",mystuff.n);
}
```

Compile and run.

```
Your Own Stuff
Enter your favorite letter:
```

Type an **M** — no need to press the Enter key.

```
Enter your favorite number:
```

Type **42** and press the Enter key.

```
Okay. Your favorite letter is M
And your favorite number is 42.
```

This program probably should win the Big Deal award for the whole book. After all, what it did could easily be done without structures. As usual, that's not the point.

The point is to get you used to three things:

✔ Before a structure can be used, it must be defined. In the INFOSTO.C program, Lines 9 through 13 declare the structure named `stuff`:

```
struct stuff
{
    char c;
    int n;
};
```

✔ After the structure is defined, variables of that type of structure are declared. In INFOSTO.C, a structure variable named `mystuff` of the type `stuff` is declared in Line 15:

```
struct stuff mystuff;
```

✔ Finally, the structure's variables are used, employing the dot thing that makes them look like an Internet address. Notice that although the variables look funky, they're still used like normal variables.

Declare! Define! Use!

✔ Define a structure and give it a name. The structure contains variables, such as the `char` and `int` variables in the INFOSTO.C program.

✔ Declare a structure variable of a certain structure type. If you define the `blech` structure, you must then declare a variable of that type. Call it `yech`.

✔ Finally, use the structure variable you declared.

✔ The dot variables aren't really that weird. For example:

```
mystuff.c
```

This line tells you that variable `c` is a member of the `mystuff` structure variable. If you look to see how `mystuff` is declared, you see that `c` is a normal `char` variable. (More on this subject in the next section.)

✔ You declare two things with structures. First, the structure itself is defined, and then a structure variable is declared.

General notes about the INFOSTO.C program:

✔ The `getche` function reads one character from the keyboard, such as `getch`. Unlike `getch`, however, the `getche` function also *echoes* that character to the screen. That must be what the extra *e* stands for.

✔ Oh, and you have to include the CONIO.H header file to make the `getche` function work.

✔ The STDLIB.H header file is required for the `atoi` function to work.

The lowdown on structures

A *structure* is a collection of differing variable types, all of which typically describe something similar. For example, your name, address, weight, and favorite cartoon character could be stored in a structure.

Keyword struct

The struct keyword is used to create a *structure,* a single unit that holds several different variable types. Here's the format:

```
struct name {
    type name;
    type name;
};
```

name is the name of the structure. It defines the structure but doesn't create any structure variables.

Within the structures, curly brackets are variable declarations; type is a variable type (char, int, float, and so on), and name is the name of that variable — just like any normal variable you would declare in a function. These variables are the "members" of the structure, just as obsessively skinny people are members of a gym.

After the structure is defined, a structure variable is usually declared. The following format is used:

```
struct name variable;
```

The keyword struct is followed by the name of a declared structure (name) and then the name of the structure variable itself (variable).

Structures variables can also be defined "on the fly" by using this format:

```
struct name {
    type name;
    type name;
} variable;
```

Multiple structure variables can be declared like this:

```
struct name {
    type name;
    type name;
} var1, var2, var3;
```

where var1, var2, and var3 are each variables of the name type of structure.

To access the elements of a structure, the dot format is used:

name.var

The name is the name of a structure variable. That's followed by a dot (or period) and then the variable name (var) as declared inside the structure.

By themselves, structures are only mildly useful. Their true power comes from creating arrays of structures for storing similar information about lots of things — such as in a database.

Structures are created by using the struct keyword, as described in the nearby "Keyword struct" sidebar.

✔ Structures must be defined and then variables for that structure created. Only after the structures' variables have been created can you store information in the structure. Merely creating the structure is only half the job.

- ✔ After you create a structure, you can create as many variables for that structure as you need.

- ✔ Structures can hold an almost infinite amount of variables in any combination.

- ✔ Variables inside a structure are used just like any other variables in C. Just because a char variable is named person.name doesn't mean that it's any different from a char variable named orville.

- ✔ You often use structures when you're accessing specialized information. For example, a program that reads GIF graphics files from disk uses a structure to see how the graphical information is stored.

More stuff

By itself, the INFOSTO.C program's job could be done by any other program in C, but not when you try to juggle a second set of information, as shown in the MORESTO.C program.

Load the INFOSTO.C program in your editor and make the following changes, which adds a second variable of the stuff type. Save the program to disk as MORESTO.C:

Name: MORESTO.C

```
#include <stdio.h>
#include <conio.h>
#include <stdlib.h>

void main()
{
    char input[10];

    struct stuff
    {
        char c;
        int n;
    } mystuff, hisstuff;

/* Here's someone else's info */

    hisstuff.c = 'Y';
    hisstuff.n = 199;
```

```
        puts("Your Own Stuff");

        printf("Enter your favorite letter: ");
        mystuff.c = getche();
        putchar('\n');

        printf("Enter your favorite number: ");
        mystuff.n = atoi(gets(input));

        printf("Okay. Your favorite letter is %c\n",mystuff.c);
        printf("And your favorite number is %i.\n",mystuff.n);
        printf("His favorite letter is %c\n",hisstuff.c);
        printf("And his favorite number is %i.\n",hisstuff.n);
}
```

Compile and run.

Type your favorite letter and number again. In the last part of the output, you see the preset information for the hisstuff structure variable as well:

```
Okay. Your favorite letter is M
And your favorite number is 42.
His favorite letter is Y
And his favorite number is 199.
```

You see similar information, but from two different structure variables.

After structures are defined, they are variables just like any other variables in C. In MORESTO.C, two variables of the stuff type of structure are declared: mystuff and hisstuff.

The MORESTO.C program declares its structure variables along with the structure itself:

```
struct stuff
{
    char c;
    int n;
} mystuff, hisstuff;
```

This example could also be written as

```
struct stuff
{
    char c;
    int n;
};

struct stuff mystuff;
struct stuff hisstuff;
```

Or the last two lines can be combined:

```
struct stuff mystuff, hisstuff;
```

The secret password program (again)

As with every other type of variable in C, you can also create a structure variable that contains predefined data. The only weird part is that you must define the structure first and then declare a structure variable filled with data. The following program, LOGIN.C, shows how it's done.

Type this source code into your editor. Save it to disk as LOGIN.C:

Name: LOGIN.C

```
#include <stdio.h>
#include <string.h>
#include <stdlib.h>

void main()
{
    char input[20];

    struct login
    {
        char id[9];
        char password[9];
    };

    struct login user1 = {
        "bclinton",
        "bubba"
        };

    puts("White House Computer");
```

```
    printf("Login Mr. President:");
    gets(input);

    if(strcmp(input,user1.id)!=0)
    {
        puts("Incorrect login!");
        exit(0);
    }

    printf("Password:");
    gets(input);

    if(strcmp(input,user1.password)!=0)
    {
        puts("Incorrect password!");
        exit(0);
    }

    puts("Hello, Mr. President!");
}
```

Compile and run.

```
White House Computer
Login Mr. President:
```

Oh, play around here if you like. Otherwise, type **bclinton** and press the Enter key.

```
Password:
```

Type **bubba** and press Enter.

```
Hello, Mr. President!
```

Think of the fun you will have looking at the files in *that* computer!

🖙 The login structure is declared first.

🖙 The information for the user1 structure is initialized when the user1 structure is declared:

```
struct login user1 = {
    "bclinton",
    "bubba"
    };
```

The first string is set equal to `bclinton`; the second, to `bubba`.

I used a different structure format in the LOGIN.C source code from what I used in the INFOSTO.C and MORESTO.C programs. It doesn't really matter to the compiler where you put the curly brackets in your programs; use whatever is most readable to you. Refer to Lesson 4-4 in *C For Dummies, Volume I*, which discusses this whole "pretty printing" issue.

"Pretty printing" is the name given to source code that's overly formatted. Because the compiler doesn't really care how it looks (only that all the pieces are there and in the right order), the fancy formatting is up to you.

You cannot define the structure *and* assign variables to it at the same time. Defining the structure is merely telling the compiler, "Hey! Here's a strange, new type of variable." Only after that's done can you declare variables of that type of structure and, optionally, initialize them with data.

Now you can, if you like, declare everything together. For example:

```
struct login
{
    char id[9];
    char password[9];
} user1 = {
    "bclinton",
    "bubba"
};
```

This example essentially combines both steps into one statement: The `login` structure is defined and then the `user1` variable declared *and* filled with data. This method works, but it's ugly. It also limits you to initializing only one variable. My advice: Don't bother.

✔ A true login program displays asterisks when the password is entered. Refer to the PASSWORD.C program in Lesson 9-6 in Chapter 9 for a sample input routine (which you can add to the LOGIN.C program if you want, but you probably don't).

✔ The STRING.H file is included to make the `strcmp` function work.

✔ The `strcmp` function compares two strings, returning a value of zero if both strings match up, as shown in Lesson 9-6.

✔ You may consider using the `strcmpi` function if you plan to write a compare-input type of program. Unlike `strcmp`, the `strcmpi` function ignores upper- and lowercase letters in comparing strings.

✔ The STDLIB.H file is included to make the exit function work. Don't you think that exit should be part of the STDIO.H header file? I do. To whom do I complain, though?

Lesson 11-1 Quiz

1. What do structures hold?

    A. Hands.

    B. Jolly variables.

    C. People.

    D. Objects of art.

2. What are the three steps to using a structure, in order?

    A. Define the structure; declare a structure variable; use the dot-variable things.

    B. Open the door; walk into the lobby; take the elevator up.

    C. Denial; guilt; acceptance.

    D. The two-step; the foxtrot; the waltz.

3. Which of the following is not a Greek or Roman deity?

    A. Aeolus.

    B. Chloris.

    C. Nike.

    D. Pompous.

4. How would you display the character variable initial from the following structure?

```
struct pals {
    int jersey;
    char initial;
    char name[20];
};
```

    A. putchar('initial');

    B. putchar('pals.initial');

    C. printf("%c",pals.initial);

    D. None of the above.

Lesson 11-2: Arrays of Structures

Meanwhile, back in the merry old land of Oz. . . .

Structures provide the means by which you can continue to work on your Wizard of Oz database program. The following is a modification of the OZ1.C program, done with a structure rather than with scattered variables.

Type this source code into your editor. Save it to disk as OZ3.C:

Name: OZ3.C

```c
#include <stdio.h>
#include <string.h>

void main()
{
    struct oz {
        char actor[30];
        char character[30];
        int age;
        };

    struct oz actor;

    strcpy(actor.actor,"Judy Garland");
    strcpy(actor.character,"Dorothy");
    actor.age = 17;

    puts("Wizard of Oz Database!");

    printf("%s played %s, and was %i years old\n",\
        actor.actor,actor.character,actor.age);
}
```

Compile and run.

The output is the same as the OZ1.C program, but the method was much better, much more organized. The following sidebar, "The Wizard of Oz program done in structure mode," elucidates things.

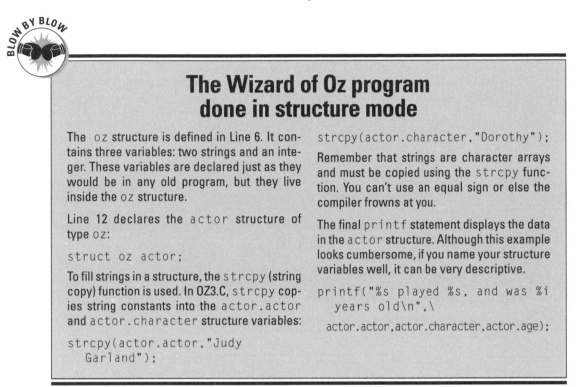

BLOW BY BLOW

The Wizard of Oz program done in structure mode

The oz structure is defined in Line 6. It contains three variables: two strings and an integer. These variables are declared just as they would be in any old program, but they live inside the oz structure.

Line 12 declares the actor structure of type oz:

```
struct oz actor;
```

To fill strings in a structure, the strcpy (string copy) function is used. In OZ3.C, strcpy copies string constants into the actor.actor and actor.character structure variables:

```
strcpy(actor.actor,"Judy
   Garland");
```

```
strcpy(actor.character,"Dorothy");
```

Remember that strings are character arrays and must be copied using the strcpy function. You can't use an equal sign or else the compiler frowns at you.

The final printf statement displays the data in the actor structure. Although this example looks cumbersome, if you name your structure variables well, it can be very descriptive.

```
printf("%s played %s, and was %i
   years old\n",\
   actor.actor,actor.character,actor.age);
```

- ✔ The STRING.H header file is included so that the strcpy function doesn't drive the compiler nuts (refer to Lesson 9-6 in Chapter 9).

- ✔ The structure oz and the actor variable could also have been defined and declared like this:

```
struct oz {
    char actor[30];
    char character[30];
    int age;
    } actor;
```

- ✔ Frank Morgan had five roles in *The Wizard of Oz:* In addition to playing the Wizard and Professor Marvel, he was the doorkeeper, the Wizard's guard, and the horseman for the horse of a different color.

Structures all stuffed into an array

A database program isn't truly useful unless you have more than one record. In C, a structure is similar to a record. An array of structures, well, that's looking more and more like a database.

Creating an array of structures is cinchy. After all, struct variables are just like any other in C; the only difference is that you define the variable — the *multivariable* — yourself. Then you can declare a structure variable as an array just as you would declare a char or int array. For example, here's the stuff structure definition from Lesson 11-1:

```
struct stuff
{
    char c;
    int n;
};
```

After that's defined, you can create variables of the struct stuff type just like any other variable declaration in C:

```
struct stuff mystuff;
int x;
```

In this example, the mystuff structure variable is created — just like the x variable is created after it:

```
struct stuff mystuff[20];
int x[20];
```

In this example, an array of 20 stuff structures named mystuff is created, just like an array of 20 integers named x is created after it. Same deal.

To access the elements in the array, you also use a similar format:

```
mystuff[0].c
```

In this example, character c of the first element (the first structure) in the array is accessed. The array notation comes first, then the period, and then the variable in the structure:

```
mystuff[x].n
```

Here, variable x represents an element in the mystuff structure array. Whatever element that is, the preceding variable represents the n integer value of that structure thing.

- ✔ The first element of any array is always zero.
- ✔ This is still the same weird dot-format used by structure variables, but with the array notation thing stuck in there too.

Bring on the rest of the Oz crew!

The following program expands the Wizard of Oz database to include the three main male actors as well as Judy Garland. This program is the structure-array equivalent of the OZ2.C program.

Type this source code into your editor. It's very messy, so please be careful. Save it to disk as OZ4.C:

Name: OZ4.C

```
#include <stdio.h>
#include <string.h>

void main()
{
    struct oz {
        char actor[30];
        char character[30];
        int age;
        };

    struct oz actor[4];
    int x;

    strcpy(actor[0].actor,"Judy Garland");
    strcpy(actor[0].character,"Dorothy");
    actor[0].age = 17;

    strcpy(actor[1].actor,"Ray Bolger");
    strcpy(actor[1].character,"Scarecrow");
    actor[1].age = 35;

    strcpy(actor[2].actor,"Bert Lahr");
    strcpy(actor[2].character,"Cowardly Lion");
    actor[2].age = 44;

    strcpy(actor[3].actor,"Jack Haley");
    strcpy(actor[3].character,"Tin Woodsman");
    actor[3].age = 40;

    puts("Wizard of Oz Database!");

    for(x=0;x<4;x++)
```

(continued)

(continued)

```
        printf("%s played %s, and was %i years old\n",\
            actor[x].actor,actor[x].character,\
            actor[x].age);
}
```

Compile. Fix any errors. Because this program has so many doodads, you probably will miss one or two.

Run:

```
Wizard of Oz Database!
Judy Garland played Dorothy, and was 17 years old
Ray Bolger played Scarecrow, and was 35 years old
Bert Lahr played Cowardly Lion, and was 44 years old
Jack Haley played Tin Woodsman, and was 40 years old
```

The output is the same as OZ2.C, but it was produced by structures.

If you venture back and look at the OZ2.C source code, you see that the OZ4.C version is, unfortunately, much clunkier. It takes numerous `strcpy` functions to move the data into the variables. In fact, the only clean advantage to using structures is that you need only a `for` loop and one `printf` statement to display the database, and not the ugly gang-of-four `printf` statements at the end of OZ2.C.

If it's elegance you're into and if you know what's in your structure array, you can, of course, preload it. The following program shows how that looks.

Type this source code into your editor. (It's easy to modify the OZ4.C source code and convert it into this format.) Save it to disk as OZ5.C:

Name: OZ5.C

```
#include <stdio.h>

void main()
{
    struct oz {
        char actor[30];
        char character[30];
        int age;
        };
```

```
struct oz actor[4] = {
    "Judy Garland", "Dorothy",  17,
    "Ray Bolger", "Scarecrow",  35,
    "Bert Lahr", "Cowardly Lion",  44,
    "Jack Haley", "Tin Woodsman",  40
    };

int x;

puts("Wizard of Oz Database!");

for(x=0;x<4;x++)
    printf("%s played %s, and was %i years old\n",\
        actor[x].actor,actor[x].character,\
        actor[x].age);
}
```

Pretty spiffy, eh? Compile and run.

The output is the same as for OZ4.C. The program itself, however, is much more elegant.

Welcome to the way things typically work in the C language. Whenever you find your source code growing messy, repetitive, or ugly, a better solution for your problem probably exists. Recompare the OZ2.C source code with OZ5.C to see what I'm talking about.

Again, don't let the split printf statement at the end of the source code freak you out. Splitting up the lines by using the backslash character is a pretty solution for the long, ugly structure array of variable names.

In real life, information is loaded into a structure array either by a user, who types merrily at the keyboard, or by reading the information from a file on disk. Rarely do you pack a structure array as shown in OZ5.C.

The actor structure array is filled just like any initialized multidimensional array in C. The only difference is that the "rows" of information are each members of the structure — which means that they can contain information of different types. For example, if actor were a three-dimensional character array, all the values would have to be strings.

All arrays begin with element zero. That's why array[0].actor is the first item filled in the structure array.

Copying one structure element to another

I have to add this "bonus section" to this lesson to deal with a problem you may encounter (which turns out *not* to be the compiler's problem, but really *your* problem).

Structure arrays are composed of many different pieces. One element in a structure array can hold dozens of variables. As with a string, you probably would guess that you have to be careful if you ever have to duplicate a structure array element.

Here's a demo program for you to stew over. Type this horribly long and detailed source code into your editor. The program creates an array of structures and then swaps two of the structure elements. It takes up a number of keyboard molecules on your part, so type carefully. Save the thing to disk as LETS_GO!.C:

Name: LETS_GO!.C

```c
#include <stdio.h>
#include <string.h>

void main()
{
    struct solarsystem {
        char planet[8];
        double population;
    };

    struct solarsystem planets[9] = {
        "Mercury", 0,
        "Venus", 0,
        "Earth", 5.5E9,
        "Mars", 0,
        "Jupiter", 0,
        "Saturn", 0,
        "Uranus", 0,
        "Neptune", 0,
        "Pluto", 0
        };
    struct solarsystem temp;

    int x;
```

```
        puts("Solar System Data");

        for(x=0;x<9;x++)
            printf("Planet %i: %s, Population: %.0f\n",\
                x+1,
                planets[x].planet,
                planets[x].population);

        puts("\nAfter we swap with Jupiter:");

/* Copy Jupiter's data to temp */

        strcpy(temp.planet,planets[4].planet);
        temp.population = planets[4].population;

/* Copy Earth to Jupiter */

        strcpy(planets[4].planet,planets[2].planet);
        planets[4].population = planets[2].population;

/* Copy temp to Earth */

        strcpy(planets[2].planet,temp.planet);
        planets[2].population=temp.population;

        for(x=0;x<9;x++)
            printf("Planet %i: %s, Population: %.0f\n",\
                x+1,
                planets[x].planet,
                planets[x].population);
}
```

Compile. Fix those errors!

Run:

```
Solar System Data
Planet 1: Mercury, Population: 0
Planet 2: Venus, Population: 0
Planet 3: Earth, Population: 5500000000
Planet 4: Mars, Population: 0
Planet 5: Jupiter, Population: 0
Planet 6: Saturn, Population: 0
```

(continued)

(continued)

```
Planet 7: Uranus, Population: 0
Planet 8: Neptune, Population: 0
Planet 9: Pluto, Population: 0

After we swap with Jupiter:
Planet 1: Mercury, Population: 0
Planet 2: Venus, Population: 0
Planet 3: Jupiter, Population: 0
Planet 4: Mars, Population: 0
Planet 5: Earth, Population: 5500000000
Planet 6: Saturn, Population: 0
Planet 7: Uranus, Population: 0
Planet 8: Neptune, Population: 0
Planet 9: Pluto, Population: 0
```

The point here is not that Earth is changing places with Jupiter. That would make it much colder than it is already, and, honestly, after last winter, I really don't need that. No, the point is that in order to swap two structure array elements, you probably will jump through some flaming hoops.

The program creates two variables using the solarsystem structure: First comes the planets array, which is initialized to contain vital data about all nine planets in our solar system:

```
struct solarsystem planets[9]
```

Second comes the temp variable, which isn't an array but just a storage place for the swap to happen later:

```
struct solarsystem temp;
```

Yes, you can create an array and a stand-alone variable from one structure. No one will be cross with you for doing so.

The heavy-duty part (which you might come up with on your own) is the swapping of the elements. It happens the same way elements are swapped in a bubble sort (refer to Lesson 9-4 in Chapter 9). It also takes place with a great deal of individual element swapping. To wit:

First, Jupiter's data is saved in the temp variable:

```
strcpy(temp.planet,planets[4].planet);
temp.population = planets[4].population;
```

Each item must be copied over. Strings must be copied with the `strcpy` function. There's no other way!

Then Earth is copied to Jupiter's position:

```
strcpy(planets[4].planet,planets[2].planet);
planets[4].population = planets[2].population;
```

Then Jupiter, saved in the `temp` variable, is copied back to Earth's position:

```
strcpy(planets[2].planet,temp.planet);
planets[2].population=temp.population;
```

Do you have to do that? You may think so. In fact, this whole exercise is based on what you already know in C. To sum it up: C doesn't let you get away with anything.

But that's not true!

Structures, even though they contain various different members, are still seen by the compiler as *one* variable. It's perfectly legitimate, for example, to have the following exchange:

```
temp = planets[4];
planets[4] = planets[2];
planets[2] = temp;
```

You still can't copy strings with an equal sign, but you can copy structures and any strings they contain. Bring up the LETS_GO!.C source code in your editor again, and replace the nonsense in the middle of the program with the preceding three statements.

Here's how your source code should look when you're done:

Name: LET's Go! .C

```
#include <stdio.h>

void main()
{
    struct solarsystem {
        char planet[8];
        double population;
    };

    struct solarsystem planets[9] = {
```

(continued)

(continued)

```
            "Mercury", 0,
            "Venus", 0,
            "Earth", 5.5E9,
            "Mars", 0,
            "Jupiter", 0,
            "Saturn", 0,
            "Uranus", 0,
            "Neptune", 0,
            "Pluto", 0
            };
    struct solarsystem temp;

    int x;

    puts("Solar System Data");

    for(x=0;x<9;x++)
        printf("Planet %i: %s, Population: %.0f\n",\
            x+1,
            planets[x].planet,
            planets[x].population);

    puts("\nAfter we swap with Jupiter:");

/* Copy Jupiter's data to temp */

    temp = planets[4];

/* Copy Earth to Jupiter */

    planets[4]= planets[2];

/* Copy temp to Earth */

    planets[2]=temp;

    for(x=0;x<9;x++)
        printf("Planet %i: %s, Population: %.0f\n",\
            x+1,
            planets[x].planet,
            planets[x].population);
}
```

It's almost *shameful* that you can get away with this stuff. Anyway, save this new file to disk as LETSGO!.C (which is only moderately easier to type).

Compile and run!

The output is the same because you have changed only the program's guts. You did two things, though: You made the program easier to read, and you discovered that you can copy structure array elements without a ton of overhead.

Don't think that the last `printf` statement is really more than one statement. I've split it on several lines to make it more readable. Because it's only one statement, you do not need curly brackets after the `for` statement.

Even though a structure contains various variables of different types, you can copy one structure variable to another with an equal sign. Both structure variables must be of the same type, like the `solarsystem` types in LETSGO!.C.

✔ You still cannot copy strings using an equal sign. Use the `strcmp` function for that, as covered somewhere else in this book.

✔ Somewhere else, like Lesson 9-6.

✔ The name LETS_GO!.C is a valid DOS (and Windows) filename. It is not a valid UNIX filename. If you're using UNIX, name the source code LETS_GO.C and then LETSGO.C (they're the same as the Dos filenames, but without the exclamation points).

✔ The number 5.5E9 is the population of the earth, $5^{1/2}$ billion people. Lesson 3-5 in Volume I of this book has more information about E notation "big" numbers.

✔ Unfortunately, the `printf` function does not put commas in very large numbers. The following example:

```
5500000000
```

really should appear as

```
5,500,000,000
```

Alas, if you want it to look that way, you have to write a comma-inserting routine yourself.

✔ If you used a `float` rather than a `double`, random information may appear in the output:

```
5500000256
```

The reason is simply that a `float` isn't as precise as a `double`, as explained in Lesson 3-5 in *C For Dummies,* Volume I.

✔ Using a `float` in Microsoft C produces some weird type of mismatch error. That's why I used `double` for the type of the `population` variable.

✔ Please don't let the vital data about all nine planets in our solar system fall into Klingon hands.

Lesson 11-2 Quiz

1. To fill string data in a structure, you have to

    A. Read the information from disk.

    B. Read it from the keyboard.

    C. Use `strcpy` to fill the structure's strings with constant values.

    D. Most likely, all of the above.

2. You can initialize an array of structures very similarly to the way you initialize an array of any other type of variables. What's the big difference?

    A. There is no big difference.

    B. The big difference is the money you save by shopping at Target.

    C. The big difference is that structures hold variables of different types.

    D. You must enclose each structure array element within its own set of curly brackets.

3. Is the following statement allowable?

```
array[1] = array[2];
```

    A. No.

    B. Yes.

    C. Allowable for structure arrays, but not for any other type of array.

    D. Only in France.

4. Identify the proper glasses.

    A. Champagne glass.

    B. Red wine glass.

    C. Water goblet.

    D. White wine glass.

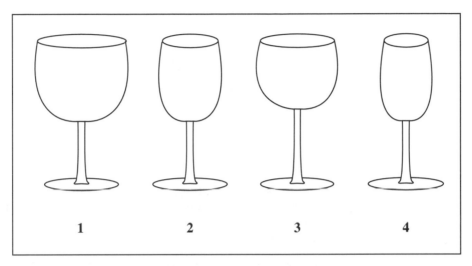

Walking around for ten minutes or so will work the blood that's been pooling up in your legs back into your body and make you feel better. Trust me.

Lesson 11-3: Structures and Functions

You can send and receive structure variables to and from functions, no problem. No hang-ups, no pointers, no multiple declarations, no new funky characters to prefix or append. After all, a structure — even a structure array — is simply another type of variable, just like a char or an int. Passing it to a function or getting it back is not a big deal.

The only big deal is that the structure's definition must be known to the entire program. You can't redefine or re-create the structure inside a function. That would create a cluttered-looking program, and, as you well know, that's the sign of not doing something properly in the C language.

As an example, the following is a no-no:

```
void main()
{
   struct dumb {
        int ent;
        char chair;
   } dumber;

/* something happens */
```

(continued)

(continued)

```
  display_struct(dumber);
}

void display_struct(struct d)
{
  printf("%i and %c",d.ent,d.chair);
}
```

The `dumb` structure is defined in the `main` function. Then a `dumber` variable of the `dumb` structure type is created. Assume that something happens and that the structure is filled with data. Then it's sent to the `display_struct` function. So far, so good.

The `display_struct` function has a problem. The `struct d` thing is never defined. The compiler should give you a big "What the heck is this `struct d` thing?" type of error. And, no, it doesn't help to redefine the structure inside the function. That creates a different structure.

What you need is a structure definition that's known to the entire program — all your functions. From near and far! From the hills and into the valleys! A global broadcast!

Hey! A *global variable!*

Special review section: Declaring a global variable

A *global* variable is something that's available to every function in your program. It's defined *outside* of any function, which, through the quirkiness of C, makes it available to every function in the program.

A global variable is typically listed just before the `main` function, along with the prototypes, `defines`, and `includes`. (Those things have no specific order, though most programmers put their global variables last.)

With a structure, you have to define only the structure outside the program's functions. Oh, you could declare the structure's variables out there too, but only if you need to. You're essentially defining the structure in No Man's Land so that every function can use it.

- For a review of this global variable stuff, see the section "Making a global variable" in Lesson 5-2 in Volume I of this book. That information also applies to structures.

- The next section contains a sample program, in case you're utterly lost.

- Here are some examples of global variables:

```
the weather
stupidity
bad Chinese food
neighbors' dogs
telemarketing
```

Hey, function! Here's a structure!

The following program is (yet another) modification to the Wizard of Oz database. This time, the printf statement that displays the information has been put into its own function.

Type this source code into your editor. (You can use the OZ5.C program as a base from which to edit.) Save the code to disk as OZ6.C. Then compile and run:

Name: OZ6.C

```c
#include <stdio.h>

    struct oz {
        char actor[30];
        char character[30];
        int age;
        };

void print_oz(struct oz info);

void main()
{
    struct oz actor[4] = {
        "Judy Garland", "Dorothy",  17,
        "Ray Bolger", "Scarecrow",  35,
        "Bert Lahr", "Cowardly Lion", 44,
        "Jack Haley", "Tin Woodsman",  40
        };
```

(continued)

(continued)

```
    int x;

    puts("Wizard of Oz Database!");

    for(x=0;x<4;x++)
        print_oz(actor[x]);
}

void print_oz(struct oz info)
{
    printf("%s played %s",info.actor,info.character);
    printf(", and was %i years old\n",info.age);
}
```

- ✔ The output is the same as the OZ5.C program, though the way that output was displayed was by passing each element in the structure array to a routine — insidiously clever stuff.

- ✔ The following sidebar, "The techy tidbits behind the OZ6.C program," describes all the juicy tidbits.

- ✔ The print_oz function can be used to print individual struct variables as well as elements in a struct array. The only limitation is that the struct variables must all be of the oz type.

- ✔ Don't be tempted into the land of pointers by the following function call:

```
    print_oz(actor[x]);
```

After being brainwashed with pointer functions, you may believe that the print_oz function requires a *pointer* as input. It does not. The variable actor[x] is a struct oz type of variable; you're passing along a *single item* to the function — just as though you were passing an element from an integer array.

- ✔ Another point along the same lines as the preceding check mark: The variable actor[x] is not an entire array. It's only an array element, a single variable. It is *not* the same as passing an array name or a string to a function. In that case, you would need a pointer, but not otherwise.

- ✔ See how pointers can drive you mad? And they're not even the subject here — not even related to it!

BLOW BY BLOW

The techy tidbits behind the OZ6.C program

To pass a structure variable to a function, you must declare the variable's structure as a global variable. Just take the structure definition from the `main` function and plop it down in free space, as shown in OZ6.C:

```
struct oz {
    char actor[30];
    char character[30];
    int age;
    };
```

This example means that structure variables of the `oz` type are defined and available for every function in the program. Although you could also declare the structure array here, that's not necessary for this program. (If you did, the array would be available to every function, and you wouldn't have to send or receive anything from a function.)

The `print_oz` function is prototyped at the beginning of the preceding program:

```
void print_oz(struct oz info);
```

As input, the function requires a structure variable of type `oz` (and because `oz` is global, it knows what that is). Internally, the function refers to the structure using the `info` variable.

A `for` loop churns through each element in the array, passing it off to the `print_oz` function with the following line:

```
print_oz(actor[x]);
```

The single structure variable `actor[x]` is passed along to the `print_oz` function.

Inside the `print_oz` function, the `printf` statements display the values held in the structure. The structure is referred to as `info` here:

```
printf("%s played
    %s",info.actor,info.character);
printf(", and was %i years
    old\n",info.age);
```

Each member of the structure is displayed, and then the function ends with control returning back to the `main` function.

Structures for the birds (nested structures)

Defining a structure is just like creating another type of variable, a multivariable. If your insanity level has been keeping up with the C language, you may have assumed that one structure can live inside another structure.

Then again, you may be a stable person and not used to thinking like the C language. (Me? I try not to imagine what other horrors this programming language could possibly dream up.)

Consider the following structure:

```
struct date {
  int month;
  int day;
  int year;
  };
```

This example is simple enough: It's a structure that contains information about a birthdate. This structure could be a part of a larger structure:

```
struct family {
  char name[20];
  struct date birthday;
  };
```

Don't go running from the computer! All you're doing is sticking a structure variable of type date into the family structure. This example is known as a *nested structure*.

A nested structure variable is declared just like any other variable:

```
struct family people;
```

The structure variable people is created.

The only craziness with a nested structure comes when you're referring to the nested variables. The following printf statements display the contents of each item in the people family structure:

```
printf("Your name = %s\n",people.name);
printf("Birth month = %i\n",people.birthday.month;
printf("Birth day = %i\n",people.birthday.day;
printf("Birth year = %i\n",people.birthday.year;
```

It's just more dots! The variable people.birthday.day is the structure people, member birthday (which is a structure) and then day (which is a member of the birthday structure). Whew!

Here's all of that in a program you can type into your editor and delight over. Substitute your own vital statistics for those shown here (enter your name and birthday information). Save the code to disk as MYBDAY.C:

Name: MYBDAY.C

```
#include <stdio.h>
#include <string.h>
```

```
void main()
{
    struct date {
        int month;
        int day;
        int year;
        };

    struct family {
        char name[20];
        struct date birthday;
        } me;

/* Fill in your own data here */

    strcpy(me.name,"Dan");
    me.birthday.month = 10;
    me.birthday.day = 19;
    me.birthday.year = 1960;

    printf("%s was born on %i/%i/%i\n",\
        me.name,\
        me.birthday.month,\
        me.birthday.day,\
        me.birthday.year);
}
```

Compile and run:

```
Dan was born on 10/19/1960
```

(Your output should reflect your information, of course, and not mine.)

- ✔ Do the dots drive you crazy? They shouldn't. If you have named your structures well, in fact, you can instantly tell what a variable represents: `me.birthday.year` is fairly self-explanatory.

- ✔ Yeah, `my.birthday.year` would be more self-explanatory — and proper English.

- ✔ The structure is declared inside the `main` function in the MYBDAY.C program. You have no need to make it global because no other functions access the structure (or even exist, for that matter).

- ✔ You have to use the `strcpy` function to copy a string constant into a structure's string variable (Line 19).

Yes, you can easily avoid nested structures. For example, the `family` structure could be redefined as follows:

```
struct family {
  char name[20];
  int month;
  int day;
  int year;
   };
```

I have never seen a circumstance in which a nested structure has actually been used (other than in a book about C), but that doesn't rule them out of existence.

The structure you nest inside must be declared as a variable. For example:

```
struct family {
  char name[20];
  struct date;
   };
```

This declaration is wrong. The `struct date` item must have a variable name after it. This makes sense when you also observe that the `char name[20]` variable isn't written as just `char`. Variables must be named inside structures.

Returning a structure from a function

To have a function chew up a structure and return it is no different from having a function chew up an integer and return it. For example:

```
int mangle(void)
```

The `mangle` function is now defined. It requires no input (`void`) and produces an integer output.

```
struct vital_data mangle(void)
```

The `mangle` function requires no input and produces a structure of type `vital` as output. That structure, along with all its members, is returned to whichever part of the program called the `mangle` function.

As you may suspect, you must declare your structure as global if you plan to return it from a function. Again, this process should be no big deal.

The following program is a modification of the MYBDAY.C program. In this one, you enter information for the birthday of everyone in your family. One function (getdata) handles the input and returns a structure variable. Another function (print_data) displays output. Functions and structures are both coming and going in the following program example.

Crack your fingers and get to work! Type this massive amount of source code into your editor. Be careful. Double-check everything. When you have it all down, save it to disk as BDAYS.C:

Name: BDAYS.C

```c
#include <stdio.h>
#include <stdlib.h>

    struct date {
        int month;
        int day;
        int year;
        };

    struct family {
        char name[20];
        struct date birthday;
        };

struct family getdata(int member);
void print_data(struct family person);

void main()
{
    int x,f;
    char numb[3];
    struct family myfamily[10];

    printf("How many people in your family?");
    f = atoi(gets(numb));

    puts("Enter information about each family member");

    for(x=0;x<f;x++)
        myfamily[x] = getdata(x);

    puts("\nHere is your family data:");
```

(continued)

(continued)

```
    for(x=0;x<f;x++)
        print_data(myfamily[x]);
}

/* Fill in each "record" in the structure */

struct family getdata(int member)
{
    struct family new;
    int temp;           //temp integer storage
    char input[5];      //temp string storage

    printf("Family member %i:\n",member+1);

/* Get their name */

    printf("Name:");
    gets(new.name);

/* Get birthday info */

    puts("Birthday information:");

    printf("Month:");
    temp = atoi(gets(input));
    new.birthday.month = temp;

    printf("Day:");
    temp = atoi(gets(input));
    new.birthday.day = temp;

    printf("Year:");
    temp = atoi(gets(input));
    new.birthday.year = temp;

    return(new);
}

void print_data(struct family person)
{
    printf("%s was born on %i/%i/%i\n",\
```

```
        person.name,\
        person.birthday.month,\
        person.birthday.day,\
        person.birthday.year);
}
```

Compile. Fix those errors! Forgotten semicolons, missing curly brackets, and quotes are all the bane of C programmers the world over!

Run.

```
How many people are in your family?
```

Type the number of people in your family. Don't get cute and type a huge amount, because the program uses this number to determine how many structures you need in the array. (Don't type more than ten, because that's the size of the array.)

If you're an only-child orphan, type **3** just because.

Type your name because you're obviously family member 1:

```
Enter information about each family member
Family member 1:
Name:
```

Enter the month in which you were born:

```
Birthday information:
Month:
```

Enter the day of the month you were born:

```
Day:
```

Enter the year you were born. If you're very old and were born B.C., enter a negative number:

```
Year:
```

Continue typing information. You have to do this for each member of your family, which is why I warned you earlier not to be cute:

```
Family member 2:
```

After information for the last family member has been entered, you see the following:

```
Here is your family data:
Dan was born 10/19/60
Blake was born 1/28/63
Jody was born 6/11/65
```

Congratulate yourself with a treat if you got it all to work.

For detailed information about the program, refer to the following sidebar "Things that make the BDAYS.C program tick."

The global variable `family` is what makes all those functions possible. Because `family` is global, it can be used in both the `getdata` and `print_data` functions.

Because the `date` structure is nested inside the `family` structure, both definitions must be global.

To have a function return a structure variable, it must be declared as that type of structure variable. For example:

```
struct family getdata(int member)
```

This prototype defines the function as one that accepts an integer value as input and returns a structure variable built like the `family` structure as output. That's all there is to returning a structure to a function.

- ✔ The structure variable itself must be declared *and* returned inside the function (`getdata` in BDAYS.C). A standard `return` command is all you need in order to return the structure variable (see the following sidebar, "Things that make the BDAYS.C program tick").

- ✔ A problem obviously exists if you have more than ten people in your family — for example, you're from Montana. But I digress. To write a decent database program, you need more array space. No, declaring a *humongous* array is not the answer. The answer is covered in the next two lessons.

- ✔ Another problem: Wouldn't it be nice to save this stuff to disk? It's really only a few more lines of code. You have to wait until Chapter 12 to figure all that out, though.

- ✔ Don't delete the BDAYS.C source code! You modify it later.

BLOW BY BLOW

Things that make the BDAYS.C program tick

The source code needs two header files: STDIO.H for the standard input and output functions and STDLIB.H for the atoi function. (You read more about standard input and output in Lesson 12-5.)

The structure date and the nested structure family are both declared before the main function so that they can be global. That way, all other functions in the program can use those types of structures.

Notice how the getdata function is prototyped:

```
struct family getdata(int
    member);
```

The function is prototyped as a family structure. That's because a family structure is the type of variable it returns.

The print_data function requires a structure of the family type as input. Inside the function, the structure is referred to using the person variable:

```
void print_data(struct family
    person);
```

Enough with outside the program! Inside the program, a structure array of ten elements is created:

```
struct family myfamily[10];
```

The array is of the family structure type and is given the name myfamily. The value 10 is an arbitrary number here; you can replace it with any old value you like. Because the program doesn't know how many people are in your family, it asks:

```
printf("How many people in your
    family?");
    f = atoi(gets(numb));
```

The gets function reads the keyboard, and then the atoi function converts the input to an integer, which is saved in the f variable. (Remember that C functions work from the inside out.) This info is what the for loop uses to determine how many elements in the array you need to fill up:

```
for(x=0;x<f;x++)
    myfamily[x] = getdata(x);
```

Each element in the array represents information for a family member. To fill in the array, the getdata function is called. That function returns a structure variable, which is saved in the myfamily array. The for loop repeats, letting you fill in one element for every family member.

To display the results, a second for loop is used:

```
for(x=0;x<f;x++)
    print_data(myfamily[x]);
```

The print_data function is sent to each structure in the array (myfamily[x]), which it then displays on-screen.

That's the end of the program; on to the functions:

The getdata function requires an integer as input and returns a structure variable of the family type:

```
struct family getdata(int
    member)
```

The integer variable is referred to as member inside the function. Also inside the function, a structure variable of the family type is created, named new:

```
struct family new;
```

(continued)

(continued)

The `new` structure is used inside the `getdata` function to gather information.

The `member+1` math in the `printf` function is done so that the family members are numbered 1 through 10; otherwise, 0 through 9 would be displayed, which freaks out most normal people:

```
printf("Family member
  %i:\n",member+1);
```

The `getdata` function then proceeds to fill in the structure:

```
printf("Name:");
gets(new.name);
```

For the name, a string is read from the keyboard and stored in the structure's `new.name` variable. You do not have to use `strcpy` for this process because `new.name` is already a string variable and `gets` stores your input there, just as it would in any string variable.

Note how the nested structure variables are used:

```
new.birthday.month = temp;
```

and

```
new.birthday.day = temp;
```

and, finally:

```
new.birthday.year = temp;
```

When the function is done, it returns the `new` structure to the `main` function:

```
return(new);
```

That's all you need to return the structure. For example, if `getdata` were an `int` function, you would merely pass the integer variable back using the `return` command. You need no asterisks or ampersands; don't make your life any more difficult than it already is.

Finally, the `print_data` function merely displays each structure member, which is something you've already been over in this chapter.

Lesson 11-3 Quiz

1. Declaring a global structure enables you to do what?

   A. Place the structure definition out in space, along with the `includes`, `defines`, prototypes, and Mr. Spock.

   B. Have the structure accessible by all the functions in the program.

   C. Use structure variables of that type anywhere in the program.

   D. Live in peace and harmony with mankind.

2. Which of the following functions requires as input a structure of the type `banana`?

   A. `void gorilla(banana)`

   B. `void chiquita(struct banana)`

   C. `void republic(struct banana nabana)`

   D. `void anna(banana montana)`

3. Which of the following functions returns a structure of the type `mold`?

    A. `void jello(struct mold)`

    B. `struct mold *jello(void)`

    C. `struct mold coffee(void)`

    D. `mold cheese(int swiss)`

4. How long did the Hundred Years' War last?

    A. 96 years.

    B. 98 years.

    C. 100 years.

    D. 116 years.

Time to go outside, stare into the distance, and sigh thoughtfully.

Lesson 11-4: Making Sacrifices to Malloc

Mem'ries, like a PC full of RAM
Kil-o-bytes are full of memories
That's the way I am. . . .

Programming would be so much easier if you just knew what users wanted. For example:

```
#include <stdio.h>

void main()
{
  puts("42\n");
}
Or:
#include <stdio.h>

void main()
{
  puts("You left your car keys on your dresser.\n");
}
```

Alas, as a programmer, you must anticipate every possible thing that could happen in your program. One of the hardest things to guess, especially in a program that fiddles with lots of data, is how much stuff a user types: How many records are needed in a database or how big a graphics image must be or how long a word-processing document is.

The solution to the how-much-memory puzzle is to allocate more memory. No, not more memory than you need. Creating a huge array when a user needs only a few elements is wasteful. What you really need is to create storage space your program may need on the fly. Need a 120-element array? Just create it right there in your program. All you need is a special function that can set aside more memory and a pointer.

- ✔ If you successfully completed Chapter 10, the preceding request for a pointer should not depress you.

- ✔ The special function is malloc, which grabs a chunk of memory and sets it aside for your program to use. Malloc is the *m*emory *alloc*ation function, not a pagan god.

- ✔ You need a pointer because pointers hold memory addresses. When malloc allocates a chunk of memory, it needs to tell your program where that memory is. The variable designed to hold such information is, obviously, a pointer. Ta-da!

- ✔ Pointers hold memory addresses (that is, pointers without their asterisks).

- ✔ Your computer probably has 4 to 16 or more megabytes of memory in it. When your program runs, it sets aside storage space for all the variables you've declared. Only if you need more variables do you have to go out and fetch the memory, allocating it to any new variables or arrays you create on the fly. That's all the malloc function does. Please don't think that malloc magically creates new RAM in your computer.

A poor example of not allocating any memory

Every variable in your program has its own little storage space. The first part of Chapter 10 goes over this subject, explaining how variables have a memory location and a size. (The memory location can be found with a pointer variable and the size of the variable with the sizeof keyword.)

Fortunately, the compiler sets aside the storage space for you automatically. The only time you will have trouble is one day when you decide to be clever with pointers and forget to create any variables, such as in the following program.

Type this source code into your editor. Save it to disk as HOWDY.C, which is probably what Kernighan and Ritchie would have called HELLO.C had they lived in Texas and not New Jersey:

Name: HOWDY.C

```
#include <stdio.h>
#include <string.h>

void main()
{
    char *string;

    strcpy(string,"Howdy! Howdy! Hi!");
    printf("%s",string);
}
```

Compile.

What? Were you expecting an error? If you were paying attention, you probably guessed correctly that no memory storage has been allocated in the program. The pointer variable `string` is merely a pointer variable. Nowhere in the program is storage for the string set aside, but that's not cause for alarm to the compiler.

Run. (Be aware, however, that your system may crash.)

```
(null)Null pointer assignment
```

```
Howdy! Howdy! Hi!
Run-time error R6001
- null pointer assignment
```

At least the Microsoft C program runs. Sorta. But it still has that darned `null pointer assignment` error. Truthfully, that error is one of the most frustrating things any C programmer ever encounters. It's a pointer error, and it has to do with memory allocation.

Your problem: No space was set aside for the string. You can do that in two ways. The first is to create a string buffer and use it, such as redefining the `string` variable to an array:

```
char string[80];
```

The second way is to use the malloc function to allocate memory for the string on the fly.

- malloc is introduced in the following section.

- The program compiles and links just fine. You don't get any errors because everything you have done is correct. Of course, the compiler doesn't see the Big Picture. It doesn't know that no space for the string was ever allocated.

- Whenever you see the null pointer error, it means that a string or other variable was accessed through a pointer but that the pointer was never initialized to anything or was improperly initialized.

- To make the program work without redefining the string variable, you have to allocate string storage, like this:

```
char buffer[80];
```

Then you have to set the string pointer equal to the buffer's address:

```
string = buffer;
```

Then the program would work. But that's not the point of this lesson, so don't bother.

Grant me more space, O Malloc!

The malloc function is what gets you out of tight spots when you don't create a large enough array or storage space for your program's needs. Or, to put it another way, malloc is what enables you to define your program's storage needs on the fly instead of having to guess about it beforehand.

What malloc needs to know is how much storage space you require and what type of space is needed. If you need 80 bytes of string storage, for example, you tell malloc to grab 80 bytes of character storage. If everything goes well, malloc coughs up an address, which you then save in a character pointer variable.

If everything doesn't go well (which means that you're out of memory), malloc returns a NULL pointer, which is the same thing as zero. In that case, the memory can't be allocated, and your program should display some "out of memory" error to disappoint the user.

- See the following sidebar "Function malloc" for the full format of the malloc function.

- The NULL pointer is merely a fancy-schmancy way of saying zero — just like FALSE is zero.

Function malloc

The malloc function (pronounced "MAL-lock," for *memory alloc*ation) is used to grab a chunk of memory and assign it to a variable in your program. Here's the format:

pointer = (*type* *)malloc(*size*);

Malloc attempts to set aside a chunk of memory equal to size, which is the number of bytes needed. size can be a constant or the size of a variable or structure determined with the sizeof keyword.

Type is the type of variable you're allocating; char for characters and strings; int for integers; float for floats; and so on. This system ensures that malloc returns the proper type of variable for which you're allocating space.

What malloc returns is the address of the chunk of memory. And what type of variable holds a memory address? Anyone? Yes, it's a pointer variable. The pointer variable (used without its asterisk because it's a memory address) must be of the proper type

for the memory you're allocating: char for string storage, a struct for new structure storage, and so on.

If no memory can be allocated (memory is "full"), malloc returns a NULL pointer value. That's why most malloc functions appear inside or near an if test, which checks for the NULL to see whether memory is available.

You must include the MALLOC.H file for the malloc function to behave itself:

#include <malloc.h>

Also on the #include list is STDLIB.H:

#include <stdlib.h>

Although this header file is not required, every reference I have says to include it anyway for ANSI C compatibility. So I'm including it in all my programs, even though they run just fine without it (unless, of course, some other function requires the STDLIB.H file).

✔ Most malloc functions appear before or *inside* an if statement, which ensures that the memory was allocated. In this book, I put the if statement after the malloc statement:

```
string = (char *)malloc(80);
if(string==NULL)
```

Other books may do the following:

```
if((string = (char *)malloc(80)) == NULL);
```

Although both statements do the same thing, the former is far more readable, in my opinion.

✔ malloc has only a limited amount of memory to give you, which is the "free" memory in your PC. C programmers refer to this memory storage space as "the heap." That's just a name for the chunk of memory in your PC from which malloc doles out memory.

✔ You may encounter a program in another book or reference that uses the ALLOC.H header file to define the `malloc` function. Alas, the Microsoft Visual C++ compiler does not come with the old ALLOC.H header file, so you have to substitute the MALLOC.H header file instead.

✔ Some older compilers may not come with MALLOC.H, in which case you should include the ALLOC.H header file instead. (How would you know? Compile it and see whether it works. If not, use ALLOC.H.)

✔ This book uses both the MALLOC.H and STDLIB.H header files to define the `malloc` function.

Properly allocating space for Howdy, Howdy, Hi

The shocking news is that the HOWDY.C program can really work. You may remember that I scold you in Chapter 10 for thinking that you could wantonly create a pointer without initializing it. With `malloc` in your pocket, though, you can create any old pointer, allocate memory for it, and then use it like a normal variable. The following program shows how it's done to the HOWDY.C program.

Know your ancient pagan gods

Moloch. A real monster, this Ammonite (and Phoenician) god required children as sacrifices. Several of King Solomon's wives worshipped Moloch and eventually converted old King Solomon over to that cult.

Molech. *See* Moloch.

Baal. A Semitic fertility god and also the sun god. Jezebel, the wife of Ahab, who was King of Israel, turned the country away from Yahweh to worship Baal. The prophet Elijah did battle with the priests of Baal, and, lo, they were smitten. Even so, eventually the kingdom of Israel switched to Baal worship, so Yahweh smote them and scattered them over the earth.

Beelzebub. The Lord of the Flies himself, this name is a contraction (or, can you say "concatenation"?) of Baal (*see* Baal) and *zebûl*, which means exalted. In Milton's *Paradise Lost*, Beelzebub was second in command to Satan. In *Bohemian Rhapsody*, Beelzebub has a devil put aside for Freddie Mercury.

Marduk. The chief Babylonian god. He gained prominence as a rival to Yahweh when the Hebrews were held captive in Babylon. He has no counterpart in the C programming language.

Modify the source code for HOWDY.C in your editor, making the changes and additions as noted earlier. Don't forget the extra `include` files! The following sidebar about the HOWDY.C program explains the program's mechanics. Save it to disk using the same name, HOWDY.C:

Name: HOWDY.C

```
#include <stdio.h>
#include <string.h>
#include <malloc.h>
#include <stdlib.h>

void main()
{
    char *string;

    string = (char *)malloc(80);
    if(string==NULL)
        printf("Not enough memory");
    else
    {
        strcpy(string,"Howdy! Howdy! Hi!");
        printf("%s",string);
    }
}
```

Compile and run.

```
Howdy! Howdy! Hi!
```

HOWDY.C has no string storage. None! Not one byte! The storage for the string is created by `malloc`, and the location of that storage space is passed over to the `string` pointer. That pointer variable is then used to reference the string in memory in the `printf` statement.

- ✔ The most common use of `malloc` is in disk access programs. They typically grab up chunks of memory as information is read from disk.

- ✔ You don't have to *define* the NULL value in the program. Because NULL is already defined in the STDIO.H header file, you can use it as a NULL pointer (or the value zero) whenever you like.

- ✔ If you're about my age (mid-30s) and grew up in San Diego, California, you should remember "Howdy! Howdy! Hi!" as the phrase Johnny Downs used during his afternoon kiddie show on Channel 10.

The friendly HOWDY.C program broken up into meaningless tiny pieces

The program requires the STRING.H header file for the strcpy function. For malloc, I have included both the MALLOC.H and STDLIB.H header files:

```
#include <string.h>
#include <malloc.h>
#include <stdlib.h>
```

The pointer variable string is the only variable created in the program:

```
char *string;
```

Creating a pointer does not allocate memory for what the pointer points to. In the preceding example, you're merely telling the compiler that you're planning to use a pointer. This example has no other variables, especially no other string variables, for the pointer to access. Still, it doesn't cause an error (which it may do in other programming languages).

To give the string something to point to, memory is allocated with the malloc function. In this case, the program needs about 80 bytes:

```
string = (char *)malloc(80);
```

malloc is told to set aside 80 bytes of storage. The (char *) is a typecast. It changes the type of memory address returned by malloc to be a character pointer — a string. Although this program compiles and runs properly without that typecast, if you use malloc with other variables at other times, it may not work. To be consistent, you should typecast malloc every time you use it.

Refer to Lesson 5-4 in Volume I of this book for more information about type casting. The type cast for a pointer is merely the variable type followed by a space and an asterisk.

The value malloc returns is stored in the string variable. It either represents the address of the 80-byte block of memory or it's a NULL pointer, with a value of zero. An if statement is required in order to test that condition:

```
if(string==NULL)
    printf("Not enough memory");
```

If the NULL pointer is returned, a Not enough memory error is displayed. Because an if-else structure is used, the program ends right here. Otherwise, you would have to end it with an exit function.

The else part of the statement handles the condition when memory has been allocated successfully:

```
else
{
    strcpy(string,"Howdy! Howdy! Hi!");
    printf("%s",string);
}
```

You must use the strcpy function to move a string constant into a string variable, as just shown. An equal sign just doesn't cut it.

Finally, a printf function displays the string, which is now stored in memory at the location held in the string pointer variable.

Lesson 11-4 Quiz

1. What do you need in order to use the `malloc` function?

   A. The BAAL.H header file.

   B. Blood and fire.

   C. A cowl and an altar.

   D. The MALLOC.H header file, the amount of memory to allocate, and a pointer to hold the address of that memory.

2. The father of the modern computer is John von Neumann. How is his last name pronounced?

   A. von NEW-man.

   B. von NOW-man.

   C. von NOY-man.

   D. von NYOO-man.

3. If `malloc` cannot find any memory, what value does it return?

   A. FALSE.

   B. Zero.

   C. NULL.

   D. –1.

4. Why does `malloc` require a pointer variable for the value it returns?

   A. `malloc` returns a memory address and, like, duh, pointers hold memory addresses.

   B. Because they just couldn't think of a way to make it more difficult.

   C. Pointers are not allocated any memory by the compiler, so you use `malloc` to do it for you.

   D. The value returned is located outside the program, and only pointers can see it.

Bonus question!

Siegfried and Roy. Which is which and does it matter?

Lesson 11-5: Structures and (Gasp!) Pointers

If you don't know how many structures your program needs, you can use `malloc` to allocate space for them on the fly. This process sounds cinchy. Lesson 11-4 shows how cinchy it is to allocate space for a string. Grabbing space for a structure should be just as easy.

Alas, there's one thing you probably didn't think of: `malloc` returns the block of memory as a *pointer*.

Oh! Go look in a mirror! Your hair is standing on end!

Seriously, don't panic. To grab memory space and stick a structure in there, you need a pointer to a structure. It isn't the ordeal you may imagine.

- Before you attempt to work through this lesson, ensure that you totally understand pointers as presented in Chapter 10.

- Pointers to a structure must be declared of that specific structure type. This requirement is nothing new; if you're creating a pointer to examine `char` variables, you declare a `char` pointer. If you have a `family` structure (as shown in an earlier lesson), you declare a `family` pointer for it.

- A `family` pointer. I bet the Republicans would like that.

What you need to create a structure from thin electrons

All of a sudden, like one of those chest pains that you hope is just gas, you decide that your program needs a new structure. With the help of `malloc`, you create it from all that excess RAM lying around inside your PC. Here's what you need to make that happen:

- The size of the structure so that `malloc` can allocate the proper number of bytes

- A pointer variable of that structure type

- A way to access the members of a pointer-structure thing

To get the size of the structure, you can get with the `sizeof` keyword — just as you can grab the size of any variable or array in C. That way, `malloc` doesn't go nuts on you and allocate several gigabytes of storage.

A pointer variable for a structure is no big deal. Structure pointers are declared just like any other type of pointer:

```
struct nilsson *thepoint;
```

Because `thepoint` has an asterisk before its name, it's defined as a pointer and not as a normal structure variable. You use the `thepoint` variable to store the address returned by `malloc`, which tells the world the location of the new structure in memory.

Finally, you have to use the strange pointer structure notation. It looks like this:

```
crew->captain
```

Although that's normally `crew.captain`, when you use a pointer to a structure, the strange `->` thing is used instead. Don't ask me why; I didn't make this stuff up.

- ✔ You don't use the `*` in a pointer structure — you use `->` to refer to the members.

- ✔ You don't need the `&` (ampersand) here because the memory address is returned from the `malloc` function.

- ✔ As usual, you must define the structure before you declare any structure variables, normal or pointer.

- ✔ If you plan to use the structure and its pointers in several functions, declare them as global variables, as explained in Lesson 11-3.

- ✔ The `sizeof` keyword was really designed to get the size of unknown objects, such as structures and arrays. It works hand in hand with `malloc`.

- ✔ If you were superstitious, you could claim that `sizeof` is the name of a pagan minion who served the evil god `malloc`.

Your first strange structure and pointer program

Suppose that you have this *thing* for *Star Trek*. Not the new one with the bald guy mincing about and quoting Shakespeare. I'm talking about the solid, good old TV series. You remember, where Captain Kirk beamed down to the planet, beat up some aliens, and kissed all the green women. Those were the days.

Beam up this secret information about the STDB.C program

The structure is declared inside the `main` function because, after all, that's the only function in the program. If other functions used that structure, it would have to be global.

```
struct st_info *episode;
```

The pointer variable `*episode` is created to point at a structure of type `st_info`, just as any other structure variable would be declared. That asterisk makes it a pointer and not a structure variable. It's a pointer designed to hold the memory address of a structure of the `st_info` type.

For the `malloc` function to allocate space for a new `st_info` structure, it has to know the size of that structure. The `sizeof` command figures that out:

```
episode = (struct
   st_info*)malloc(sizeof(struct
   st_info));
```

In this line, `malloc` allocates just enough memory to accommodate one `st_info` structure. `Malloc` is also typecast to return a pointer (memory location) of the `st_info` type. The address returned is stored in the struct pointer `episode`.

As usual, the pointer is compared with the NULL value to ensure that a true memory address was returned. Otherwise, an error message is displayed and the program quits:

```
if(episode==NULL)
{
    puts("No more memory,
dude!");
    exit(0);
```

```
}
```

After `malloc` has successfully set aside a chunk of memory for use as the structure, you can begin stuffing it with information. Because you're accessing the structure through a pointer variable, the `->` thing must be used rather than the dot. Otherwise, all assignments work the same as before:

```
episode->number = 29;
```

For string constants, you must use the `strcpy` function:

```
strcpy(episode->name,"Operation:
   Annihilate!");
strcpy(episode->description,"The
   one where they beam down to
   the planet.");
```

Finally, the information inside the structure is displayed. Again, this process works just as it does with a regular structure variable, except that the `->` thing is used instead.

One of the final `printf` statements may need some explaining:

```
printf("\"%s\"\n",episode->
   name);
```

Something like this example could seriously drive a beginner nuts, but only if you look at it and think "Picasso" rather than "C language." The formatting string contains four items: `\"` is the escape sequence for a double quote; `%s` is a string placeholder; `\"` is another double quote; and `\n` is a newline. What's displayed is a string in double quotes on a line by itself. Not a difficult concept, but not exactly easy on the eyes.

In your quest to keep track of all your favorite *Star Trek* episodes, you concoct a program in C. The first version of that program may look something like the following program.

Type this code into your editor. Keep in mind that buying a database program would be simpler but that you're here to understand C programming and not to make your life easier. The source code contains some new doodads to type, so you should be careful. Watch out for that annoying `printf` statement toward the end with all the quotes and backslashes. Save the program to disk as STDB.C:

Name: STDB.C

```
#include <stdio.h>
#include <malloc.h>
#include <stdlib.h>
#include <string.h>

void main()
{
    struct st_info {
        int number;
        char name[30];
        char description[128];
        };
    struct st_info *episode;

    puts("My Star Trek Database");

    episode = (struct st_info*)malloc(sizeof(struct
            st_info));

    if(episode==NULL)
    {
        puts("No more memory, dude!");
        exit(0);
    }

/* Fill the structure using pointers */

    episode->number = 29;
    strcpy(episode->name,"Operation: Annihilate!");
    strcpy(episode->description,"The one where they beam
```

(continued)

(continued)

```
            down to the planet.");

/* Display the data */

    printf("Star Trek Episode %i\n",episode->number);
    printf("\"%s\"\n",episode->name);
    printf("Description: %s\n",episode->description);
}
```

Compile and run.

```
My Star Trek Database
Star Trek Episode 29
"Operation: Annihilate!"
Description: The one where they beam down to the planet.
```

Pretty nifty, huh? All that information was stored in space the program allocated on the fly. With proper modifications, other structures and pointers could be created just like that.

Unfortunately, there really isn't any advantage to creating the storage on the fly, at least not in this program. My purpose was to show you *how* it can be done. In real life, this program would work just fine with a regular structure declared as you normally would.

- ✔ A structure you allocate with `malloc` is created no differently from any other structure. The only thing different about the structure is its pointer variable and the way the members inside the structure are accessed.

- ✔ The official name for the `->` thing is "arrow pointer."

- ✔ There were 72 episodes in the original *Star Trek* series. I got my information for the STDB.C program from the Internet, so please don't write me if it's incorrect or if you have some minor quibble. (I did not put this program in this book so that some Trekkie would get his foam-rubber ears all hot and bothered.)

And now, the rest of the story

Using structures and pointers involves more than just allocating space for one structure. Most programs don't need only one new structure. They may need dozens of structures — new ones created all the time. An array isn't the answer, and using `malloc` to allocate individual structures is really only a half-solution.

To make a program allocate as many structures it needs, C language scientists and others in white lab coats devised something called a *linked list*.

Linked lists fall into a category I call Advanced Untouchable C Concepts. Here's a sample structure from a linked list to prove my point:

```
struct st_info {
    int number;
    char name[30];
    char description[128];
    struct st_info *next;
    };
```

The last member of the structure is a pointer — a pointer to the same type of structure being declared. (See? Already I have an annoying topic to discuss!)

Every time a new structure is allocated with malloc, its address is saved in the preceding structure — in the next variable in the st_info structure, for example. That enables you to create new structures and keep track of them without having to create an array or perform some other feat of programming magic.

This concept isn't tough to grasp — it's just complex. The following check marks should help you get some background about the topic, in case you ever encounter it in another C book somewhere.

- A linked list essentially consists of structures that contain pointers.

- Every time you create a new structure with malloc, its memory location is saved in the preceding structure — like clues in a scavenger hunt.

- Special care is taken in a linked-list program to keep track of the first structure in the list. Without knowing where that structure is, you would never be able to find the remaining structures. Why? Because each structure contains the next structure's memory location in its next variable.

- The last structure in the list contains a NULL pointer rather than the address of another structure. This info is just more mental overhead your program must keep track of.

- I'm not chickening out! I'm out of room! If I had a larger book to write, I could put in here the extra two lessons that describe linked lists. Alas, space is just too tight. Rather than let you down, I have placed both lessons on my *C For Dummies* page on the World Wide Web:

```
http://www.wambooli.com/c.for.dummies/
```

✔ You can also find a mirror for that site on the ...*For Dummies* World Wide Web site:

```
http://www.dummies.com
```

✔ In addition to the linked-list lessons, I occasionally upload other lessons about advanced topics, such as direct memory addressing, screen formatting, Windows programming, and some C++ junk. Check either page often if you have Internet access.

Lesson 11-5 Quiz

1. Match the patron saint with the group he protects:

   A. Clare of Assisi   1. Air travelers

   B. Joseph of Cupertino   2. Comedians

   C. Martin de Porres   3. Hair dressers

   D. Vitus   4. Television

2. How does `malloc` know how big of a chunk of memory a structure needs?

   A. `malloc` knows because `malloc` is all-powerful.

   B. `malloc` doesn't know — `malloc` guesses (and is usually correct).

   C. You add up the `int`s, `float`s, and `char` buffers and then use double that amount.

   D. The `sizeof` command gets the figure for you.

3. Which of the following declares a pointer of the `setter` structure type?

   A. `pointer setter;`

   B. `*setter;`

   C. `struct setter *english;`

   D. `struct *setter;`

4. Which geegaw do you use to access a member of a structure through a pointer?

   A. `->`

   B. `**`

   C. `*->`

   D. `*.`

Chapter 11 Final Exam

1. What must be done before you can declare a structure variable?

    A. You must check the sheep entrails for good omens.

    B. You must define a structure.

    C. You must set aside space with `malloc`.

    D. You must find a small box to stand on.

2. What is the most common street name in America?

    A. Park.

    B. Maple.

    C. First.

    D. Main.

3. What is the name of the variable created in this structure?

```
struct building {
  int type;
  char name[30];
  char address[40];
  int safety_record;
} hotel;
```

    A. `type, name, address and safety_record`

    B. `hotel`

    C. `building.hotel`

    D. `building`

4. For the structure in Question 3, how do you display the `type` value?

    A. `printf("Type: %i",building.type);`

    B. `printf("Type: %i",type);`

    C. `printf("Type: %i",hotel->type);`

    D. `printf("Type: %i",hotel.type);`

5. Who discovered the diesel engine?

    A. Henry Ford.

    B. Rudolph Diesel.

    C. Charles D'Easle.

    D. Burt Chrysler.

6. The best way to let a structure be known to every function in your program is to

   A. Make the structure global.

   B. Write that structure in uppercase.

   C. Declare the structure in every function.

   D. Use a `define` directive to declare the structure.

7. Which of the following functions accepts a structure as a variable?

   A. `struct func function(void);`

   B. `void function(struct func);`

   C. `void function(struct func shun);`

   D. `int func(struct a b);`

8. Which of the following functions returns a structure variable?

   A. `struct func function(void);`

   B. `void function(struct func);`

   C. `void function(struct func shun);`

   D. `int func(struct a b);`

9. How long does it take to hard-boil an ostrich egg?

   A. Four hours.

   B. An hour.

   C. About 30 minutes.

   D. Because of the low water content, ostrich eggs cannot be hard-boiled.

10. How can you get more memory for variables in your program?

   A. Declare them as larger variables.

   B. Grab more memory with the `malloc` function.

   C. Use arrays.

   D. Build a huge module rather than those piddly little DOS modules you've been working with.

11. Which of the following `malloc` functions allocates memory for another integer?

   A. `malloc(sizeof(int));`

   B. `malloc(2);`

C. `malloc(int new);`

D. `malloc(sizeof(1 int));`

12. What would be the most expedient way to get off Gilligan's island?

    A. By boat.

    B. By balloon.

    C. By being rescued.

    D. By killing Gilligan.

13. What type of value does `malloc` return if it successfully allocates memory?

    A. A pointer.

    B. A memory address.

    C. Any value other than NULL.

    D. TRUE.

14. Because `malloc` returns a pointer, what type of variable must you declare for use with a `malloc` function?

    A. A pointer.

    B. A structure.

    C. The type of variable for which `malloc` assigns space.

    D. An integer.

15. How do you declare a structure pointer?

    A. The structure variable must be declared as a pointer.

    B. The structure must be defined as a pointer.

    C. All members of the structure must be pointers.

    D. Toss in a few asterisks and — presto!

16. What is the main weirdo thing about referencing a structure pointer variable?

    A. Nothing is weird about it.

    B. You do not use an asterisk in referencing the members.

    C. You do use the `->` thing rather than the period.

    D. Uh, do you mean a pointer inside the structure or a structure created by pointers?

Chapter 12
The Disk Drive Is Your Slave

• •

Lessons in This Chapter

▶ Hello, disk!
▶ Would you like binary or text with that?
▶ Formatted file input and output
▶ Reading and writing file chunks
▶ Just your standard I/O

Programs in This Chapter

CREATE.C	ITLIVES.C	CREATOR.C	VIEW.C
DUMP.C	HISCORE.C	SCORE.C	HISCORES.C
SCORES.C	STOCKS.C	NOIO.C	ROT13.C
WORDS.C			

Vocabulary Introduced in This Chapter

FILE	fopen	fprintf	fclose
fgetc	EOF	fgets	fscanf
fwrite	fread	fputc	fgetchar
fputchar			

• •

Save! Save! Save! It's the mantra of anyone using a computer. You must save your stuff to disk. Save your work. Save your place in that game you shouldn't be playing. Save a note to yourself. Whatever you save, it's kept neat and tidy on disk where you can access it later, print it, copy it, reedit it, delete it, whatever.

Obviously, nothing gets saved to disk unless a program has those necessary save-to-disk functions. C is just chock-full of saving, reading, writing, opening, closing, and other interesting disk functions. They enable your program to become truly useful. Without saving to disk, for example, you would have to reenter all that data in your Dining Out Database every time you wanted to use it. That smells of inefficiency.

This chapter covers the ins and outs (actually, input and output) of disk access. This stuff is kind of cinchy, especially if you have been working with a computer and its hard disk and know how to save stuff to disk. The reason I placed it back here in this book is that disk access in C uses pointers and structures. Now that you know about both of them, this disk stuff should be a snap.

Lesson 12-1: Hello, Disk!

Nestled deep in your PC's lexicon is a batch of jargon associated with saving stuff to disk. The DOS lingo is basic and fairly cryptic: Save and Load. Save means to save something to disk, creating a new file or overwriting an older version. Load means to grab something from disk, transferring it into memory.

In Windows, the lingo is still Save, but the friendlier Open replaces the ghastly Load. It also has a Close command for wrapping up a file when you're done with it.

The C language has various lingo dealing with disk as well. Save isn't used. In C, you open, read, write, and close. The Open command is used to either create a new file or peer into an existing one; reading is done after opening, by *loading* information from disk into memory; you write information from memory to disk; and when you're done with it all, you close.

- ✔ If you can understand the basic Open, Read, Write, and Close commands, you have all of C language disk access down pat.

- ✔ In C, of course, you don't open a file, you `fopen` it.

- ✔ And you don't close a file, you `fclose` it.

- ✔ Yup, the f probably stands for *f*ile, though I wouldn't place a Vegas bet on it.

- ✔ Writing and reading information to and from disk is done by commands you're already familiar with: `printf`, `gets`, `puts`, and the whole assortment of screen and keyboard commands have disk access counterparts: `fprintf`, `fgets`, `fputs`, and so on.

- ✔ Sounds `fcinchy`. Could be `ffun`. Don't be `fridiculous`.

- ✔ No matter what the terms, you should always remember that your computer's *operating system* takes care of the details. In C, you merely have to open, read, write, and then close. The operating system keeps track of the file on disk for you. After all, that's its job.

✔ If you're using DOS, that's your PC's operating system.

✔ If you're using Windows, DOS is your PC's operating system.

✔ If you're not using DOS or Windows, something else is your operating system: UNIX, Linux, the Macintosh system, TRSDOS, CP/M, whatever.

✔ Windows, even Windows 95, uses DOS to access the disk. This statement is true no matter how blue in the face Microsoft gets trying to explain things otherwise.

Writing a small smackerel of something to disk

If you're going to be a mad scientist, you need a lot of money. Better inherit it. That Transylvanian castle on the craggy mountain is spendy real estate. Those electrical devices don't come cheap. Then you have to bribe the gravedigger's union and find decent help. Hunchbacks don't come cheap, you know.

Oh, forget it all! If you're going to create something, do it with the C language and create a small text file on disk. The following program does the job nice and neat, with no ugly suture marks or electrodes sticking out of anyone's neck.

Type the following source code into your editor. You can probably guess how it works, but don't make such a bold move until after you have read the next section. Save this program to disk as CREATE.C:

Name: CREATE.C

```
#include <stdio.h>
#include <stdlib.h>

void main()
{
    FILE *myfile;

    myfile = fopen("alive.txt","w");
    if(!myfile)
    {
        puts("Some kind of file error!");
        exit(0);
    }

    fprintf(myfile,"I created a file! It's alive!");
    fclose(myfile);
}
```

Compile and run!

Nothing happens. Well, nothing you can see (unless you got a disk error). If the program worked properly, it created a new file on disk, ALIVE.TXT. To view that file, use the DOS TYPE command:

```
C:\CSTUFF> type alive.txt
I created a file! It's alive!
```

The TYPE command displays the contents of the ALIVE.TXT file — a file you created all by yourself and without the help of an electrical storm and anyone named Igor.

✔ Normally, I would write a Blow-by-Blow sidebar for this program. Instead, I discuss and document the internal workings in the next section.

✔ The STDLIB.H file is included to make the `exit` command work properly. Normally, for all file access in C, you need only the STDIO.H header file.

✔ If the file ALIVE.TXT already exists on disk, your CREATE.C program overwrites it. Yes, you have ways to prevent that, which you read about in a few pages.

How disk access works in C

When you want to talk to a file on disk, you *open* it. If the file can be opened (or created), the operating system returns a *file handle* to your program — like a claim ticket you get for checking your coat in a fancy restaurant. The handle is how you refer to the file in your program.

In CREATE.C, a file handle variable is declared as follows:

```
FILE *myfile;
```

`FILE` is defined in the STDIO.H header. It's a structure that contains trivial information about the file. What you're doing is creating a pointer to the structure and naming it `myfile`. The program uses this handle to identify a file you open on disk.

The file is opened using the `fopen` function:

```
myfile = fopen("alive.txt","w");
```

`fopen` opens or creates the file `alive.txt`. The `"w"` means that the file is being opened in "write" mode. The file-opening modes are listed in Table 12-1.

Table 12-1	**Access Modes for the** fopen **Function**		
Mode	*Opens a File for*	*File Created?*	*Existing File?*
"r"	Reading only	No	If not found, fopen returns an error
"w"	Writing	Yes	Overwritten
"a"	Appending	Yes	Appended to
"r+"	Reading and writing	No	If not found, fopen returns an error
"w+"	Reading and writing	Yes	Overwritten
"a+"	Reading and appending	Yes	Appended to

Function fopen

The fopen function opens or creates a file on disk. If the file is found or created, fopen returns a file handle through which the rest of your program can access the file. The format is

handle = fopen(*filename*,*mode*);

The fopen function requires two arguments: *filename* and *mode*. Both are strings, and either string constants (enclosed in double quotes) or string variables can be used.

filename is the name of the file you want to open or create. It must be the full filename, including extension. It can also include the drive letter, colon, and pathname. Upper- and lowercase letters make no difference to DOS (or Windows) for a filename, but they are significant in UNIX and other operating systems.

mode is a tiny string that tells fopen how to open the file: for reading, writing, or appending or a mixture of all three. Table 12-1 lists all the various *mode* options. Mostly, fopen creates a new file on disk if one doesn't already exist. For "r" and "r+" modes, *filename* must exist. Also be aware that fopen does destroy files that already exist on disk in certain modes (see the "Existing File?" column in Table 12-1).

If all goes well, fopen returns a FILE handle in the handle variable, which your program can then use to access the file through other file functions.

If a problem occurs, fopen returns a NULL pointer.

You must include the STDIO.H header file in your source code to be able to use the fopen command (if not, you're in ftrouble):

#include <stdio.h>

Structure FILE

FILE is a macro — a define thingy created in the STDIO.H command to help you create a file handle to access files on disk. In a way, FILE is a type of variable used to create file handles. Here's the format:

```
FILE *handle;
```

FILE is followed by a space and then an asterisk and the name of a variable, handle. It's through handle that you access files on disk. Multiple file handles can also be declared:

```
FILE *handle1, *handle2,
   *handle3;
```

The file handles are declared like any variable in C. The same variable-naming restrictions apply, though these variables are never initialized and never declared without their asterisks.

```
#include <stdio.h>
```

You must include the STDIO.H file in your source code or else the compiler does not understand what the heck the FILE thing is all about.

Internally, FILE is a structure that your program and the operating system use to keep track of trivial information about the file on disk and what your program reads and writes.

The fopen function returns a file handle as an address, which is stored in the myfile variable. The first thing you have to do is check for a NULL pointer:

```
if(!myfile)
```

This line could have been written as if(myfile==NULL). Either way, it checks to see whether a NULL pointer was returned by the fopen function. If so, it means that an error occurred in opening the file. Which error? Who knows. A general error message is displayed and the program quits:

```
puts("Some kind of file error!");
exit(0);
```

If the file was successfully opened (or created), a string of text is sent to the file with the fprintf function:

```
fprintf(myfile,"I created a file! It's alive!");
```

The fprintf function works almost like the regular printf function, with two differences. First, the fprintf statement sends its output to an open file on disk, not to the screen. Second, a file handle is required, like myfile in the preceding example. It tells the operating system to which file the information must be sent. (Yes, it's possible to have more than one file open at a time.)

Function fprintf

The fprintf function sends information to a file on disk. The file must already be opened with the fopen command and a file handle variable available. Here's the format for fprintf (type it straight through, no spaces):

```
fprintf(handle,"format_string"
   [,var[...]]);
```

This is essentially the same deal as the printf function, but with a new doohickey in the format: *handle* is a file handle variable returned to your program from an fopen command. It tells the computer in which file to print the information.

Other than the *handle* item, everything else in fprintf works just like the regular printf function. Refer to Lesson 2-1 in Chapter 2 of *C For Dummies,* Volume I, for additional details.

Finally, the program closes the file, telling the operating system to save everything to disk and free up the file handle:

```
fclose(myfile);
```

The fclose function closes the file represented by the myfile variable.

- ✔ The fopen command can either open an existing file on disk or create a file. It all depends on which mode you use in opening the file (see the previous "Function fopen" sidebar).

- ✔ Also see the "Function fprintf" and "Function fclose" sidebars for more information.

- ✔ It's possible to have more than one file open at a time, which is why there's such a thing as a file handle. That handle tells the various disk functions which disk file to access. Also, a handle variable is much easier to deal with than the text name for the file.

- ✔ Even though the file handle is a pointer, you never use it with its asterisk. (Well, I don't know; someone might.) It's always used as a memory address (no asterisk).

- ✔ To write information to a file on disk, you use one of the C language's file output commands: fprintf or fputs, for example. To read information from the file, you use one of C's file input commands: fscanf or fgets, for example.

- ✔ Closing a file is the only way to ensure that the last bit of information is written to the file. Always remember to close your files because it doesn't happen automatically when your program quits.

- ✔ Seventy percent of the dust in your house is shed human skin.

Function `fclose`

The `fclose` function tells the operating system that you're done accessing a file on disk. The operating system closes the file, writing any last remaining bits of information to disk and saving the date and time and other trivia for the DIR command to display. Here be the format:

`fclose(handle);`

handle is a file handle variable returned by the `fopen` command. It tells the operating system exactly which file on disk to close.

The `fclose` function closes only one file at a time. If you have used `fopen` to open a bunch of files, you must use separate `fclose` commands, one for each file you opened.

You must close your files! If you do not, information may not be saved to disk. I know that this may not make sense, but it's true. Just because WordPerfect asks you whether you want to save before you quit doesn't mean that the C language does!

Reading something from disk

Reading a file from disk is just as easy as reading text from the keyboard. You open the file, read the information, and then close the file. The following source code shows you how to deal with all that. It's cinchy.

You can use the CREATE.C source code as a base and modify it to look like the following source code. Save it to disk as ITLIVES.C:

Name: ITLIVES.C

```c
#include <stdio.h>
#include <stdlib.h>

void main()
{
    FILE *myfile;
    char c;

    myfile = fopen("alive.txt","r");
    if(!myfile)
    {
        puts("ALIVE.TXT not found!");
        exit(0);
    }
```

```
    do
    {
        c = fgetc(myfile);
        putchar(c);
    }
    while(c != EOF);

    fclose(myfile);
}
```

Compile and run. You should see

```
I created a file! It's alive!
```

Ta-da!

- ✔ The program opens the file ALIVE.TXT in "r" mode, read-only. If fopen returns an error, it's most likely that ALIVE.TXT doesn't exist. (Use the CREATE.C program to create it!)

- ✔ This program reads in any text file named ALIVE.TXT.

- ✔ The program uses a do-while loop to read and display the characters found in ALIVE.TXT.

- ✔ The fgetc function is defined nearby in a sidebar. It's similar to the getch function, which reads the keyboard.

- ✔ The EOF in while(c != EOF) stands for the *end-of-file* character. Just like a NULL byte in a string in C, an EOF character lives at the end of every text file. The program's do-while loop scans through every character in the program until that EOF is encountered, and then it stops.

- ✔ A better, albeit more cryptic, way to write the loop is

```
while((c=fgetc(myfile)) != EOF)
    putchar(c);
```

This method basically combines the several statements into one. It's harder to read, but it still works.

- ✔ A whole gaggle of functions read and write information to and from disk. Finding the appropriate one for your program is covered in the next lesson.

Function `fgetc`

The `fgetc` function works just like the `getc` or `getch` functions, but it reads characters from an open file and not from the keyboard. The format is shown here:

`c = fgetc(handle);`

`handle` is a file handle returned from an `fopen` command. It indicates from which file the characters are read. The file must somehow be opened for reading.

The character returned is stored in the `char` variable c. If c equals EOF, the end-of-file character, no more information can be read from the file.

Like most of the file-reading and -writing functions in C, the `fgetc` function is defined in the STDIO.H file. Be sure to include it in your source code or else the linker gets all huffy:

`#include <stdio.h>`

Preventing an accidental overwrite

It's very important to decide *how* you want to open a file. Earlier in this chapter, Table 12-1 lists all the various modes: opening a file for reading, writing, or appending and combinations of both. You can choose a mode that requires a file to already exist or one that utterly zaps any file from disk without so much as a whimper.

The CREATE.C program opened the file ALIVE.TXT using "w" mode. From Table 12-1, you can divine that "w" mode opens a new file for writing and also may destroy an existing file named ALIVE.TXT.

To prevent overwriting a file you might want to keep, you can run a test first by attempting to open the file for reading. If the file exists, you can ask the user whether he or she wants to overwrite it. Isn't that common courtesy?

Macro `EOF`

The EOF macro is one of those `define` things, one that lives inside the STDIO.H file. What it represents is the end-of-file character, the last byte in a file on disk.

You typically use the EOF macro inside an `if` comparison or as part of a `while` loop. When the EOF returns from a disk-reading function, it means that no more information is left in the file.

The following source code is for CREATOR.C, a much nicer version of CREATE.C and one that protects against accidentally overwriting a file on disk.

Type the following source code into your editor. Because it's a major modification to the CREATE.C code, you can start with that, if you want. Save the final thing as CREATOR.C:

Name: CREATOR.C

```c
#include <stdio.h>
#include <stdlib.h>
#include <ctype.h>

void main()
{
    FILE *myfile;
    char c;

    myfile = fopen("alive.txt","r");

    if(myfile)      //the file exists
    {
        puts("ALIVE.TXT already exists!");
        printf("Overwrite it? [Y/N]");
        c = toupper(getchar());
        if(c!='Y')
        {
            puts("Okay. Good-bye.");
            fclose(myfile);
            exit(0);
        }
    }

    myfile = fopen("alive.txt","w");
    if(myfile==NULL)
    {
        puts("Some kind of error");
        exit(0);
    }

    fprintf(myfile,"I created a file! It's alive!");

    fclose(myfile);
}
```

Compile! Run!

```
ALIVE.TXT already exists!
Overwrite it? [Y/N]
```

Press **N** and then Enter:

```
Okay. Good-bye.
```

The file was not overwritten. Now run it again:

```
ALIVE.TXT already exists!
Overwrite it? [Y/N]
```

Press **Y** and Enter.

Nothing happens! Actually, the file was re-created. You can run the ITLIVES.C program to check.

- If you don't see the `ALIVE.TXT already exists!` message, the file hasn't been created. Don't worry — CREATOR.C creates it automatically, with no feedback. Run CREATOR.C a second time to prove that it works.

- The program discovers that ALIVE.TXT is already on disk because it attempts to open the file in "r" mode. That way, `fopen` doesn't overwrite the file, but merely returns a file handle. If so, the program asks whether you want to overwrite it. If you don't, the file is closed and an `exit` function quits the thing. Otherwise, the file is closed and re-opened in "w" mode, which overwrites it.

- Notice how the file was opened and closed! This is very important. If you plan to change file modes, you must close the file and then open it again.

- Notice also how the `myfile` variable is used twice. Like any variable, it can assume different values in the program.

- The CTYPE.C header file is included in the CREATOR.C source code so that the `toupper` function will work. See Lesson 9-5 in Chapter 9 for more information.

- If you want to open a file *and* keep any information that's already in the file, use one of the appending file modes from Table 12-1.

BLOW BY BLOW

The kinder, gentler CREATOR.C program

The main purpose of the CREATOR.C program is to ensure that a file is overwritten only if necessary. The first step in preventing that is to ensure that the file is already on disk:

```
myfile = fopen("alive.txt","r");
```

The fopen command in "r" mode returns a file handle if the file exists. If not, it returns a NULL, which means that a disk error has occurred or, more likely, that the file doesn't exist (the second fopen command catches any disk errors):

```
if(myfile)    //the file exists
```

If the file exists, the statements in the if construction are executed. First, users are warned:

```
puts("ALIVE.TXT already
    exists!");
```
```
printf("Overwrite it? [Y/N]");
```

As a former frustrated computer user, you should be gentle with your error messages, as just shown. Granted, that text is rather brief, but it beats the tar out of Error 377 or the sole ? that the old CP/M operating system displayed.

The getchar function reads the keyboard, and then the toupper function converts to uppercase the key that's typed. The key is saved in the c variable:

```
c = toupper(getchar());
```

An if comparison determines whether the Y key was pressed:

```
if(c!='Y')
```

This line reads, "If the character stored in c is not equal to 'Y'." You want to make sure that any other key a user presses doesn't overwrite the file — which is the condition you're trying to avoid here. (Only if a user presses Y is the file overwritten; anything else is a "no!")

If any key other than Y is pressed, the program quits. A bye-bye message is displayed, and, most important, the file is closed before the program exits:

```
puts("Okay. Good-bye.");
```
```
fclose(myfile);
```
```
exit(0);
```

With all that aside, the program can continue. The file is reopened in "w" mode, which overwrites whatever is already there:

```
myfile = fopen("alive.txt","w");
```

Again, a test is made to make sure that no error occurred. If so, an error message is displayed and the program quits:

```
if(myfile==NULL)
{
    puts("Some kind of error");
    exit(0);
}
```

Otherwise, information is written to the file, and then the file is closed, just as in the CREATE.C program.

Lesson 12-1 Quiz

1. What is the densest object in the universe?

    A. The Hope diamond.

    B. Newt Gingrich's brain.

    C. Any fruitcake.

    D. A black hole.

2. Match the C language disk function with what it does:

    A. fopen   1. Opens a file on disk.

    B. fclose   2. Closes a file on disk.

    C. fprintf   3. Prints something to disk.

    D. fgetc   4. Gets a character from disk.

3. What does the fopen command return?

    A. Any improperly addressed correspondence.

    B. A file handle.

    C. A pointer.

    D. A memory location.

4. What does the FILE thing do?

    A. It's like file, only LOUDER.

    B. It creates a pointer you can use as a file handle.

    C. Blesses the function with disk access.

    D. It makes rough edges smoother.

Lesson 12-2: Would You Like Binary or Text with That?

If you have been using computers for some time, you probably have been brainwashed into thinking that dozens of types of files exist. Hoo boy, do they have you fooled!

Only two types of files are in C: text and binary. *Text* files are those you can read. *Binary* is everything else — those weird characters that are meaningful only to the computer.

Your C compiler is probably tuned to open all files in text mode. Even so, you can specify — nay, *demand* — that a file be opened in text mode, if you like. The next section shows you how.

✔ To read binary files (anything that's not text), you have to open the file in *binary* mode. This involves specifying an extra doohickey (the letter *b*) in the `fopen` command. The section "Taking a dump," later in this chapter, shows you how it's done.

✔ Actually, all files are binary. Text files are merely readable.

✔ Binary files contain non-ASCII characters and often raw information used by other programs. For example, the EXE and OBJ files the compiler and linker create are both binary.

✔ I've heard gurus refer to binary files as "raw" and to text files as "cooked." I don't know whether that applies here.

✔ Which reminds me of the tale of the grizzled programmer, eyes frazzled and wandering dazed into a nice steak house. After 48 hours of solid programming, he wasn't fully prepared to interact with a human. When the server asked how he wanted his steak, he said "Cooked!"

Your own TYPE command

Nothing is as easy to program, or as necessary to a programmer, as a utility designed to help you view files, specifically your *code,* on disk — something like the following.

Type the following program into your editor. The only new part in there is the `fgets` statement, which is explained in the following "Function `fgets`" sidebar. Otherwise, it's just a program that reads lines of text from disk. Save it as VIEW.C:

Name: VIEW.C

```
#include <stdio.h>
#include <stdlib.h>

void main(int argc,char *argv[])
{
    FILE *viewfile;
    char buffer[81];     //storage

    if(argc<2)
```

(continued)

(continued)

```
    {
        puts("Missing filename!");
        puts("Here is the format:");
        puts("VIEW filename");
        exit(1);
    }

    viewfile = fopen(argv[1],"r");
    if(!viewfile)
    {
        printf("Error opening \"%s\"\n",argv[1]);
        exit(1);
    }

    while(fgets(buffer,80,viewfile))
        printf("%s",buffer);
}
```

Function fgets

The fgets function is the disk-reading counterpart to the gets function. Unlike gets, with fgets, two additional items are in the parentheses:

```
string =
    fgets(storage,size,handle);
```

storage is a holding bin for the characters fgets reads from disk. It's a char array, an empty string. The size of the holding bin is the size value, which is also what tells fgets how many characters to read from disk. The handle variable is a file handle value returned from an fopen function. It tells fgets which disk file to read. The file must be opened in read mode for this process to work.

The fgets function reads size number of characters from disk, or it stops if it encounters the newline (\n) character or the EOF.

Either way, the characters are saved in the storage buffer, to which fgets appends a NULL character, making it a "real" string in C.

If fgets cannot read a string from disk, it returns a NULL pointer.

The string that fgets reads is stored in the storage variable. Because fgets also returns the string as a pointer (string, in the preceding example), however, you could do something like this:

```
puts(fgets(buffer,80,myfile);
```

The puts function displays the text fgets reads from disk.

fgets is one of the fine family of functions in the STDIO.H header file:

```
#include <stdio.h>
```

Viewing the stuff that makes VIEW.C work

Because the VIEW.C program requires a filename to be typed at the command line, it's declared with the `argc` and `argv` values:

```
void main(int argc,char *argv[])
char buffer[81];
```

The storage buffer for characters read from disk must be *one larger* than the number of characters read. That's because `fgets` tacks on a NULL byte (`\0`) to end the string it reads.

A test is then performed to determine whether the proper number of arguments was typed:

```
if(argc<2)
```

If a filename wasn't typed after `view` at the DOS prompt, the `if` test fails, some error messages are displayed, and the program quits. Otherwise, the program attempts to open the file:

```
viewfile = fopen(argv[1],"r");
```

The filename stored in `argv[1]` is opened in read mode. If it has an error, it's probably that the file doesn't exist. If so, `viewfile` contains a NULL pointer, which is checked in an `if` comparison:

```
if(!viewfile)
```

The test reads, "Not viewfile," which means that if `viewfile` is anything other than the NULL, the test fails. Otherwise, `viewfile` contains a NULL pointer and the program displays an error message and quits.

To display the contents of the file, a `while` loop is used. It takes advantage of the fact that `fgets` returns a string if it successfully reads text from the file. Otherwise, `fgets` returns a NULL, which causes the `while` loop to stop:

```
while(fgets(buffer,80,viewfile))
```

In this example, `fgets` reads 80 characters of text from the file represented by the handle stored in `viewfile`. The 80 characters (or fewer, if a newline is found) are stored as a string in the `buffer` array.

A `printf` function displays the string read from disk:

```
printf("%s",buffer);
```

You could have used a `puts` function here, but `puts` automatically adds a newline (`\n`) at the end of everything it displays. It has the effect of double-spacing the output, which isn't a true representation of how the file looks on disk.

Compile! Run!

```
Missing filename!
Here is the format:
VIEW filename
```

Okay, okay. Type **view view.c** at the DOS prompt to see what happens:

```
C:\CSTUFF> view view.c
```

Just like the TYPE command, VIEW displays the contents of text files.

- ✔ The fgets function requires storage space for the information it reads from disk — just like the gets statement needs an empty string (character array) for stuff you type at the keyboard. The storage for fgets in the VIEW.C program is the buffer variable:

```
char buffer[81];
```

The storage space must be one byte larger than the amount of characters read from disk. That extra byte enables fgets to stick a null byte (\0) on the end of the text, making it an official C string.

- ✔ The fgets function is best suited for reading in chunks of text, just as the gets function is used to read in complete strings. For reading in one character at a time, use the fgetc function, as was done in ITLIVES.C in the preceding lesson.

- ✔ The file you specify is opened in read mode. See the "r" specified in the fopen command? If the file doesn't exist, VIEW.C displays an error. If the file does exist, the contents are read but the file is not written to or erased.

- ✔ The argv[1] thing is a string! Refer to Lesson 10-10 in Chapter 10 for proof.

Taking a dump

Dump is an inelegant term, but one that programmers are stuck with. At its roots, *dump* is a verb that means to transfer information from one place to another, usually without messing with the information along the way. It's information in the raw!

A common PC example of a dump is the *screen dump.* In the old days, you could press the Print Screen key on your keyboard to "dump" the characters on-screen to your printer. (Windows doesn't do that.)

In UNIX, a *core dump* is a copy of important files and whatnot saved to disk whenever some major disaster occurs. The idea is that some guru could examine the raw data and determine what went wrong.

You can dump too! You don't even need a special program; the VIEW.C program you created can do it. Type the following line at the DOS prompt:

```
C:\CSTUFF> view view.obj
```

(Funny characters, funny noises . . . .)

Okay. It can do it, but not well. How about a program designed to display raw data on disk — something like the following.

Crack your knuckles, and open a new sheet in your text editor. Carefully type the following source code. It differs from the VIEW.C program in that the bytes that are read are displayed in hexadecimal, not in ASCII (readable) text. Save the file to disk as DUMP.C:

Name: DUMP.C

```c
#include <stdio.h>
#include <stdlib.h>

void main(int argc,char *argv[])
{
    FILE *dump_me;
    int i;
    int x = 0;

    if(argc<2)
    {
        puts("Format: DUMP filename");
        exit(0);
    }

    dump_me = fopen(argv[1],"rb");
    if(dump_me==NULL)
    {
        printf("Error opening %s\n",argv[1]);
        exit(1);
    }

    while((i=fgetc(dump_me))!= EOF)
    {
        printf("%0.2X ",i);
        x++;
        if(!(x%16)) putchar('\n');
    }
    fclose(dump_me);

    printf("\n%s: size = %u bytes\n",argv[1],x);
}
```

Compile. Fix any errors, which you should be used to by now.

Run it by typing the following command at the DOS prompt:

```
C:\CSTUFF> dump dump.obj
```

You see something like the following:

```
80 08 00 06 64 75 6D 70 2E 63 2B 88 18 00 00 00
14 54 43 38 36 20 42 6F 72 6C 61 6E 64 20 43 2B
2B 20 35 2E 30 F9 88 05 00 00 F9 03 01 76 88 0E
```

And so on, until you finally see

```
4C 55 44 45 5C 73 74 64 6C 69 62 2E 68 00 28 74
20 32 88 04 00 00 E8 01 8B 8A 02 00 00 74
dump.obj: size = 878 bytes
```

What you're looking at is raw data, binary stuff that text-viewing programs such as VIEW.C would utterly choke over. Because you opened the file in binary mode and displayed the information as hexadecimal values rather than as text, the program doesn't choke.

Why hex? Because hex numbers can be displayed using two digits whereas decimal values require one, two, or three. The %0.2X placeholder in the printf function formats each value to be displayed as a two-digit hexadecimal number.

- ✔ The fgetc function can read from both binary and text files.

- ✔ Variable x is used as a counter in the program, ticking off the number of bytes read from disk. That's why it's initialized to zero when it's declared.

- ✔ The printf statement in Line 25 contains a space after the x. Don't forget that space, or else the hexadecimal numbers that are displayed will run into each other.

- ✔ Line 27 keeps the output neatly formatted on-screen:

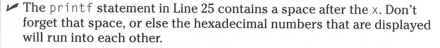

```
if(!(x%16)) putchar('\n');
```

The x%16 thing returns zero whenever the value of x is divisible by 16. Because the ! in the if comparison reverses that, the if condition is true whenever x can be divided by 16. In that case, the putchar function displays a newline character (\n).

- ✔ Refer to Lesson 5-7 in Chapter 5 of *C For Dummies,* Volume I, for more information about the % (modulus) operator.

- ✔ Honestly, unless you're really, *really* nerdy, the hex numbers won't mean anything to you. Then again, binary files aren't designed for human eyeballs.

- ✔ The DUMP.C output is just the kind you can use to scare your nonprogramming friends.

✔ A program called DUMPER.C in Appendix B is an overblown, heavy-duty cousin to DUMP.C. It displays offset values as well as the ASCII values of some of the bytes in a binary file. Check it out to see what can happen when an author gets bored and greedy while working on a program.

✔ I had a boss who used the term "mind dump" for what sensible people would call "brainstorming."

Lesson 12-2 Quiz

1. Two types of files are on your computer:

   A. Binary and text files.

   B. Fat files and skinny files.

   C. Happy files and sad files.

   D. Files that divide everything into two groups and files that don't.

2. Match the file mode with the type of file opened and how it's opened:

   A. "wb"   1. Write binary.

   B. "rb"   2. Read binary.

   C. "wt"   3. Write text.

   D. "rt"   4. Read text.

3. Modify VIEW.C so that it displays the message Press Enter after every 24 lines of text are displayed and then waits for a user to press the Enter key.

4. What is Donald Duck's middle name?

   A. The.

   B. Fauntleroy.

   C. Thaddeus.

   D. He doesn't have a middle name.

Lesson 12-3: Formatted File Input and Output

Not every file you read or write is plain text or nonsensical binary information. Most stuff you save to disk is formatted. How do you format it? Why, with the file version of the printf command: fprintf. I would go so far, in fact, as to say that reading and writing disk information is just the same as reading the keyboard and writing to the screen. It's all I/O as far as the computer sees it.

✔ Saving formatted information to disk is just like displaying it on-screen.

✔ Reading formatted information from disk is just like reading the keyboard.

✔ Strange as it may seem, the PC keyboard and screen are treated as "files" by DOS (and Windows). The screen is the *standard input* device, like a file that can only be read. The keyboard is the *standard output* device, like a file you can only save to.

✔ Lesson 12-5 gets into more of the standard I/O stuff.

The big deal about formatted output

Formatted output to disk is the same as formatted output to the screen; it's just information displayed in a friendly, organized way. For example, you can save a high score to disk as formatted output. Heed the following program.

Let your fingers dance upon the key caps as you type the following source code. Save the turkey to disk as HISCORE.C (it's pronounced "high score," not "his core"):

Name: HISCORE.C

```c
#include <stdio.h>

void main()
{
    FILE *scores;
    int s = 1000;

    scores=fopen("scores.dat","w");
    if(scores==NULL)
    {
        puts("Error creating file");
    }
    else
    {
        fprintf(scores,"%i",s);
        fclose(scores);
        puts("High score saved to disk!");
    }
}
```

Compile and run.

```
High score saved to disk!
```

That's all the visual feedback you get. Otherwise, a file named SCORES.C was created on disk and the value 1000 written to that file. The score is now etched in silicon for all to marvel at and attempt to defeat.

To see the file, use your VIEW.C program created earlier in this chapter:

```
C:\CSTUFF> view scores.dat
1000
```

True to form, fprintf printed the value 1,000 to disk. If you look back at the program, however, you see that 1000 was stored in a *numeric* variable. The fprintf function translated that value into text characters to be stored on disk.

- ✔ The fprintf function works just like printf but sends its output to a file on disk rather than to the screen. In this case, the value 1000 was printed to disk (refer to the "Function fprintf" sidebar in Lesson 12-1).

- ✔ Because the SCORES.DAT file was opened in "w" mode, any existing file by that name is overwritten. That's okay — you want the new high scores to replace the old ones.

- ✔ You can use fprintf to print a variety of information to a disk file in a number of interesting formats. If you plan to read that information back in, however, it's best to write it as a structure and not just printed information. See the next lesson for more information.

Reading formatted information from disk

The string "1000" stored on disk doesn't do much for your program. As discussed way back in Volume I, there's a big difference between "1000" the string and 1000 the number. If you plan to read that value back from disk, you probably will want 1000 the number and not "1000" the string.

Oh, drat! Another puzzle. . . .

Don't worry about translating strings into numbers. And don't even think about using the atoi function to make it happen. All you have to do is properly read the formatted information from disk. It takes cunning, a sense of fair play, and a great deal of cheating because the following program does the job without your having to waste brain molecules.

Type it! Save it to disk as SCORE.C:

Name: SCORE.C

```
#include <stdio.h>

void main()
{
    FILE *scores;
    int s;

    scores=fopen("scores.dat","r");
    if(scores==NULL)
    {
        puts("Error opening file");
    }
    else
    {
        fscanf(scores,"%i",&s);
        fclose(scores);
        printf("The high score is %i\n",s);
    }
}
```

Compile and run:

```
The high score is 1000.
```

No biggie, right? But consider that the value 1000 was stored in disk as a *string*. The fscanf function read it in that way — just as scanf would read keyboard input — but it stored it in the s variable, an integer. That, boys and girls, is how you read and write formatted data to and from disk.

- ✔ I hate the fscanf function. It's finicky and doesn't do what you think it should do. For this simple example, it was fine; for just about everything else you could think of, I recommend writing the information to disk with structures, as covered in the next lesson.

- ✔ Like scanf, the fscanf function requires the & (ampersand) before the variable it files. If you have read Chapter 10, you know that & tells fscanf (and scanf) the memory address of the variable. In SCORE.C, &s means the address of variable s and not the value of variable s.

- ✔ The file SCORES.DAT is opened in "r" read mode. This means that the file must exist on disk, so I'm assuming that you've already run the HISCORE.C program before you run this one.

- ✔ The atoi function converts strings (ASCII) into integer values. You have to wander all the way over to Lesson 3-1 in Chapter 3 of Volume I of this book if you need a review.

Function fscanf

The fscanf function is the disk counterpart to the scanf function. The major difference (as with printf versus fprintf) is that formatted information is read from a disk file opened for reading. The format is very similar:

```
fscanf(handle,"%s",&var);
```

handle is a file handle variable returned from an fopen function. It identifies the file from which scanf reads its formatted information. Otherwise, the function is identical to the one introduced in Lesson 2-2 in Chapter 2 of Volume I of this book. Refer to that lesson for the gory details.

The fscanf function returns the value EOF (as defined in the STDIO.H file) if it encounters the end of file while reading from disk.

Writing an array to disk

Anyone who has ever played a computer game (at least a game worthy of boasting about) knows that there never is only one high score. The following modification to the HISCORE.C program compensates for that situation by writing an entire array of scores to disk.

Start with the source code for HISCORE.C, and modify it to look like the following source code. The HISCORES.C program is essentially the same as the original HISCORE.C, but an array of ten items is written to disk rather than to a single item. Save the new source code to disk as HISCORES.C:

Name: HISCORES.C

```c
#include <stdio.h>

void main()
{
    FILE *scores;
    int s[10] = { 1000, 990, 985, 960,
        955, 950, 945, 945, 945, 930 };
    int x;

    scores=fopen("scores.dat","w");
    if(scores==NULL)
    {
        puts("Error creating file");
    }
    else
    {
```

(continued)

(continued)

```
        for(x=0;x<10;x++)
        {
                fprintf(scores,"%i",s[x]);
        }
        fclose(scores);
        puts("High scores saved to disk!");
    }
}
```

Compile. Run. Although the ten scores are written to disk by the `fprintf` statement, the only feedback you see is the final message:

```
High scores saved to disk!
```

- HISCORES.C uses an initialized array (refer to Chapter 9 for more information about arrays).
- The `for` loop spins 'round ten times, each time sending a different score to disk with the `fprintf` function. All this is basic printing array element stuff, though the elements are printed to disk rather than to the screen.
- Even though a numeric variable is used, `fprintf` writes a number string, not a value, to disk.

Reading an array from disk

Saving the scores to disk is, of course, only half the battle. The other half is reading the scores back in, which is done with a program sort of like the following.

Modify the original SCORE.C source code in your editor to resemble the following source code. Save the file to disk as SCORES.C:

Name: SCORES.C

```
#include <stdio.h>

void main()
{
    FILE *scores;
    int s[10];
    int x;
```

```
scores=fopen("scores.dat","r");
if(scores==NULL)
{
    puts("Error opening file");
}
else
{
    for(x=0;x<10;x++)
    {
        fscanf(scores,"%i",&s[x]);
    }
    fclose(scores);

    puts("High scores:");
    for(x=0;x<10;x++)
    {
        printf("%i\n",s[x]);
    }
}
}
```

Compile.

Run:

```
High scores:
-1
-1
-1
2912
0
12107
2942
2912
0
0
```

Whoa! Somebody's been cheating!

- ✔ The SCORES.C program reads information from disk with `fscanf` just as a similar program would read values from the keyboard with `scanf`.

- ✔ The information read from disk is stored in the s array using a `for` loop. A second `for` loop displays each element in the array.

Welcome to debugging school

Something is obviously amiss with the preceding two programs. You will face situations like this all the time in your C programming career. Consider yourself lucky with disk problems because looking at files on disk is much easier than examining variables in memory. Time to sleuth. . . .

First: No disk errors occurred, so somehow the information was read from disk incorrectly or else it was written to disk incorrectly.

Second: Check the information on disk. It tells you which problem you have, either reading or writing. Use the VIEW.C program you created in the preceding lesson:

```
C:\CSTUFF> view scores.dat
100990985960955950975975975930
```

There's your problem. Obviously, both programs work, but the information on disk — all the high scores — has been pasted together into one, huge number.

`fprintf` has done what you told it to do, but `fscanf` can't read in the numbers. Why? Because what it sees is *one huge number*. It reads it in but interprets the value as garbage. Then, because it can't read in any other values, it displays them as garbage as well:

```
-1
-1
-1
2912
0
12107
2942
2912
0
0
```

Like `scanf`, `fscanf` requires a *separator* between each item it reads. This separator can be a space, a tab, or (most commonly) a newline (\n) between each of the high-score values saved to disk. Though the problem is with `scanf` reading the values, the solution is to fix the way the values are written to disk. (Get used to this type of illogic because the C language is riddled with it.)

Whip out the source code to HISCORES.C in your editor and change the `fprintf` statement to read:

```
fprintf(scores,"%i\n",s[x]);
```

Just stick a newline character, \n, after the %i so that each score is written on a "line" by itself in the file. That's it.

Save the HISCORES.C source code to disk. Recompile and run to rewrite the SCORES.DAT file with the proper information:

```
High scores saved to disk
```

Now ensure that the SCORES.DAT file contains the proper information:

```
C:\CSTUFF> view scores.dat
1000
990
985
960
955
950
945
945
945
930
```

Looks good. Now run the SCORES.C program to confirm that it worked:

```
High scores:
1000
990
985
960
955
950
945
945
945
930
```

✔ I always suspect the scanf function whenever I encounter an input problem. If you remember that fscanf works as long as each element saved to disk has a separator (like the newline), you'll be okay. Otherwise, I recommend that you write and read structures to and from disk, which is covered in the very next lesson.

✔ The scores are stored on disk, each one on its own line (ending with \n). Because of this arrangement, you could use any string-reading disk function, such as fgets, to read the file. Unfortunately, because fgets (like gets) reads in strings, you would have to convert the strings to integers before they were stored in the array. Aw, never mind. . . .

Lesson 12-3 Quiz

1. If variable earth contains the value 42, how does that value look when saved to disk by an fprintf function?

   A. It looks like 42.

   B. It looks like "42" but without the quotes.

   C. Like this: @#%$ (sort of).

   D. The value is stored, followed by the EOF byte.

2. Which of these does not belong?

   A. Pooh-bah.

   B. Head honcho.

   C. Queso Grande.

   D. Sensei.

3. For fscanf to read information from disk properly, what must you do to the data as it's written?

   A. Each data tidbit must be written with the fprintf function.

   B. Each data tidbit must be enclosed in double quotes.

   C. Each data tidbit must be separated from the rest, most likely with a newline (\n).

   D. I don't know about you, but "data tidbit" sounds like the name of some new cheese-flavored snack cracker.

4. Anything you can print on-screen or read from the keyboard can be written to or read from a file on disk.

   A. True.

   B. False.

   C. Is this a true-false question?

   D. My mouth is still watering for a "data tidbit."

Snack time!

Lesson 12-4: Reading and Writing File Chunks

Formatted input and output are okay for some stuff. Most of the time, however, you probably will write complex information to disk, such as a list of high scores along with the winners' names. Although you could use fprintf for that task, whenever you're working with two different types of variables as a unit, you should be using a structure.

Writing and reading structures to and from disk makes your program truly database-like. You write a chunk of information to disk and then read it back — just like any other file-reading and -writing program, although when you work with structures to and from disk, the files tend to get a little long.

✔ C has no function for writing a structure to disk. The fwrite command, however, writes a chunk of memory to disk. To save a structure, you use fwrite, which is covered in this lesson.

✔ The fwrite's companion function is fread, which you can use to read a chunk of information from a disk file.

✔ Make sure that you're familiar with the sizeof command before you sit down and get dirty with this lesson (refer to Lesson 10-1 in Chapter 10).

✔ Also make sure that you know what the malloc function does (refer to Lesson 11-4 in Chapter 11).

✔ This lesson finally gets into appending information to a file, which I haven't yet discussed.

✔ Pray that you never meet someone who really sounds like Barney the Dinosaur.

The basic skeleton for your structure-to-disk program

If you're going to write more than one structure to disk, you need some type of complex program to create, write, and then read the structures — a sort of minidatabase nightmare project!

The following is the beginning of a program that creates and writes structures to disk and then reads them back in. This segment is merely the basic skeleton for the program, which consists of a switch-case structure that acts as a menu. You fill in the meat later, but first make sure that this part works properly.

Type this monster into your editor, saving it to disk as STOCKS.C:

Name: STOCKS.C

```c
#include <stdio.h>
#include <stdlib.h>
#include <conio.h>
#include <ctype.h>

#define FALSE 0
#define TRUE !FALSE

struck stock_data
   char name[30];
   float buy_price;
   float current_price;
   ;

void write_info(void);
void read_info(void);

void main()
{
   char c;
   int done=FALSE;

   while(!done)
   {
      puts("\nStock Portfolio Thing\n");
      puts("A - Add new stock\n");
      puts("L - List stocks\n");
      puts("Q - Quit\n");
      printf("Your choice:");

      c = getch();
      c = toupper(c);

      switch(c)
      {
         case('A'):
            puts("Add new stock\n");
            write_info();
            break;
         case('L'):
            puts("List stocks");
            read_info();
```

```
            break;
        case('Q'):
            puts("Quit\n");
            done = TRUE;
            break;
        default:
            puts("?");
            break;
        }
    }
}

void write_info(void)
{
}

void read_info(void)
{
}
```

Compile. Fix any missing curly bracket, parenthesis, or semicolon errors. Remember that case statements end with a colon and not a semicolon.

Run:

```
Stock Portfolio Thing

A - Add new stock

L - List stocks

Q - Quit

Your choice:
```

Make sure that it all works. Press **A**. Press **L**. Press the **K** or Escape key to see whether unwanted input is handled properly. Then press **Q** to quit.

The following check marks chew slowly over the STOCKS.C program as it sits thus far. All the stuff in this program, however, should have been known to you by the time you reached the end of *C For Dummies*, Volume I.

✔ The CONIO.H header file is required for the getch function to work.

✔ The CTYPE.H header file is required for the toupper function (refer to Lesson 9-5 in Chapter 9).

- ✔ The structure stock_data is declared as a global structure, which makes it available to all functions in the program.

- ✔ The `while-not-done` type of loop was covered in Lesson 7-3 in Chapter 7 of Volume I of this book.

- ✔ Refer to Lesson 7-5 in Volume I for more information about the `switch-case` thing.

- ✔ The `write_info` and `read_info` functions are called "dummy" functions. (Oh, ha-ha.) They contain no instructions but are still considered functions by the compiler.

- ✔ No disk access is in the program so far. That's because the file you open, read, and write to only needs to be opened with the `write_info` and `read_info` functions. The file doesn't have to stay open the whole time the program runs.

Writing a structure to disk

Because C has no `fwritestructure` function, you have to settle for one of the other disk-writing functions. The best one you have is `fwrite`, which writes a chunk of memory to disk. The helpful "Function `fwrite`" sidebar is nearby. If you just stumbled across the `fwrite` function, you might not assume that it could write a structure. It can. All you have to know is the structure's starting address in memory and its size. These are cinchy things to figure out.

You can find the starting address of any variable in memory by pasting the & (ampersand) before its variable name — just as you would do if you were assigning a pointer to that variable (refer to Lesson 10-2 in Chapter 10).

The size of a structure variable can be found by using the `sizeof` command, which you work with in Lesson 11-5 in Chapter 11. However, that lesson used the size of the structure definition to help create a structure variable with `malloc`. For example:

```
sizeof(struct st_info)
```

This statement returns the size of the structure `st_info`. If you've already declared a structure variable of that type, however (`episode`, for example), you can get the size of the structure with the following statement:

```
sizeof(episode)
```

As long as the structure variable exists, you can get its size without the `struct` keyword in the `sizeof` command.

Function `fwrite`

The `fwrite` function writes one or more "chunks" of memory to disk. Though you can write almost any type of buffer to disk, `fwrite` is most handy when it writes a structure to disk. Here's the format:

```
c =
    fwrite(&buffer,size,items,handle);
```

buffer is the name of the variable you want to write to disk, such as a `char` buffer (string) or the name of a structure variable. (It's a pointer to the chunk of memory you want to write to disk.)

size is the size of the buffer in bytes (or characters). It can be a constant value or the size of a variable or structure as returned by the `sizeof` command.

items refers to the number of items (from memory location *buffer* and of the size *size*) you want to write. This value is usually one.

handle refers to the file handle returned from a file opened for writing or appending.

The `fwrite` function returns a value, `c`, which is equal to the value of *size* (typically, one), indicating the number of chunks written to disk. If a disk error occurred, `fwrite` returns zero or some value less than the value of *size*.

If you were going to write this structure to disk, you would use an `fwrite` command, like this:

```
fwrite(&episode,sizeof(episode),1,myfile);
```

The structure variable `episode` is written to disk; its size is determined by the `sizeof` command; only one chunk is written to disk; and the file that's written to is represented by the file handle variable `myfile`.

- ✔ Oh, you probably can write many interesting chunk-size things to disk with `fwrite`. I use it mostly to write structures, as just shown.

- ✔ The ampersand before the structure variable name gives the `fwrite` function the address of that variable in memory — not the variable's value.

- ✔ There's no need to specify the `struct` keyword for the `fwrite` function — or for the `sizeof` command. After you create the structure variable, the compiler knows to which structure definition it belongs.

Creating the `write_info` function

The object of the `write_info` function is to create a structure of the `stock_data` type, fill in the structure, and then write it to disk. The only truly new thing here is the `fwrite` function. Otherwise, it should all be familiar territory.

Add the following code to your source code file for STOCKS.C. If you need to know the details, refer to the following STOCKS.C program sidebar. Save STOCKS.C back to disk when you're done:

```
void write_info(void)
{
    FILE *stocks;
    struct stock_data stock;
    char input[12];

    printf("Enter stock name:");
    gets(stock.name);
    printf("How much did you pay for it? $");
    stock.buy_price = (float)atof(gets(input));
    stock.current_price = stock.buy_price/11;

    stocks = fopen("stock.dat","a");
    if(stocks==NULL)
    {
        puts("Error opening file");
        exit(1);
    }

    fwrite(&stock,sizeof(stock),1,stocks);

    fclose(stocks);
    puts("Stock added.");
}
```

Compile and run.

Press **A** when you see the program's menu.

```
Your choice:Add new stock

Enter stock name:
```

Type **Blorfus Industries** and press Enter.

```
How much did you pay for it?
```

Type **153.89** and press Enter.

```
Stock added.
```

You return to the main menu. Press **Q** to quit.

Now you can look at the data structure as it sits in the disk file. First, use the VIEW.C program to see it:

```
C:\CSTUFF> view stocks.dat
Blorfus Industries//_A
```

Ugh. That's because, unlike `fprintf`, the `fwrite` function actually writes binary data to disk — just the way the information is stored in memory in the `stocks` structure. This capability makes reading the information from disk easier, but it makes looking at it on disk painful.

Better write the rest of the program to see what the data really looks like.

- ✔ You can use your DUMP.C program to see the raw bytes stored on disk. Of course, that still doesn't mean anything to you.

- ✔ You can see one big difference between the way VIEW.C and DUMP.C display information: What DUMP.C displays is *longer.* That's because the information is read in *binary* mode; the file was opened with "rb" and not just "r." Because VIEW.C uses text mode, it stops reading information when it thinks that the last bit of text is read. DUMP.C waits until the last true byte of the file (the EOF) is encountered.

- ✔ Append mode ("a") always writes information to the end of a file. If the file doesn't exist, it's created.

- ✔ If you want to add another stock, rerun the program and use the A command again.

- ✔ You cannot, unfortunately, delete a stock you added or even edit a stock's information. That would make the program overly complex at this point — something I'm sure that both of us would rather not get into now.

Adding the `read_info` function

Because you can't readily get at the information in any other way, you should finish the STOCKS.C program by completing the `read_info` function. Only by using that function and `fread` can you get your data back into the computer.

Load the STOCKS.C source code back into your editor. Complete the `read_info` function as written in the following example. (Later in this section, the "`read_info` function" sidebar explains this function in detail.)

The only new piece is the fread function, which isn't utterly new if you know about fwrite (see the nearby "Function fread" sidebar). Save the file back to disk:

```
void read_info(void)
{
    FILE *stocks;
    struct stock_data stock;
    int x;

    stocks = fopen("stock.dat","r");
    if(stocks==NULL)
    {
        puts("No data in file");
        return;
    }

    while(TRUE)
    {
        x = fread(&stock,sizeof(stock),1,stocks);

        if(x==0) break;

        printf("\nStock name: %s\n",stock.name);
        printf("Purchased for: $%.2f\n",stock.buy_price);
        printf("Current price: $%.2f\n",stock.current_price);
    }

    fclose(stocks);
}
```

Compile and run.

Press **L** on the menu to list the stocks you've saved to disk. You may see something like the following:

```
Stock name: Blorfus Industries
Purchased for: $153.89
Current price: $13.99

Stock name: Toxic Waster, Inc.
Purchased for: $100
Current price: $9.09
```

Then you see the main menu again. The read_info function properly read the values from disk. Press **Q** to quit the STOCKS.C program.

✔ The "current price" of the stock is merely the purchase price divided by 11 — which was saved to disk by the write_data function. I do this in honor of all the stocks I've purchased, which typically go down in price.

✔ See the box on the next page for a description of what happens inside the read_info function.

✔ The "Function fread" sidebar describes how the fread function works. It's essentially doing the opposite of fwrite: reading a chunk of memory from disk and storing it in RAM.

Tossing a chunk-o-structure to disk in the STOCKS.C program

The write_info function is self-contained. It creates its own structure variable, opens a file, writes the variable to disk, and then closes the file. It was done this way so that the rest of the program doesn't have to keep track of global variables or whether a file has already been opened.

The file handle variable stocks is declared first, along with a structure variable stock of the stock_data type and an input buffer named input:

```
FILE *stocks;
struct stock_data stock;
char input[12];
```

Next, the function fills in the stock structure:

```
printf("Enter stock name:");
gets(stock.name);
printf("How much did you pay for it? $");
```

The atof function converts text input into a floating-point number. Because atof returns a double, however, the (float) typecast is added to properly store the value in the float variable stock.buy_price:

```
stock.buy_price =
   (float)atof(gets(input));
```

```
stock.current_price =
   stock.buy_price/11;
```

Because the program doesn't have the brains to look up the current stock price (which is especially hard for companies you make up), the current price of the stock is calculated by dividing the stock purchase price by 11. Sometimes this happens in real life. (If you want to get clever, multiply the stock by a random number.)

Next, the function opens the file STOCK.DAT in *append* mode:

```
stocks = fopen("stock.dat","a");
```

In this mode, the file STOCK.DAT is created if it doesn't exist; otherwise, the file is opened for writing with any new information written to the *end* of the file. (Table 12-1 has more information about file-opening modes.)

The fwrite function then sends the structure to disk:

```
fwrite(&stock,sizeof(stock),1,stocks);
```

The address and size of the stock structure variable is used, along with 1 (for one chunk to disk) and the file handle variable name, stocks. Then the file is closed and the string "Stock added." displayed.

Family secrets behind the `read_info` function

Like the `write_info` function, `read_info` keeps all its information local: The `stock` structure variable is declared inside the function, and the STOCK.DAT file is opened, read, and closed inside the function. No leftovers remain for the rest of the program to worry about or fuss with:

```
stocks = fopen("stock.dat","r");
```

The STOCK.DAT file is opened for reading. If the file doesn't exist, the `stocks` variable contains a NULL pointer. You could display an error message, but, most likely, it may simply mean that someone is running the program for the first time and hasn't yet saved anything to disk:

```
puts("No data in file");
```

The message "No data in file" is much friendlier than having a "Disk error" message and then quitting the program. In this example, a single `return` statement is used to bail out of the function and go back to `main`, where the menu is redisplayed:

```
return;
```

To read the structures from disk, a `while` loop is used:

```
while(TRUE)
```

In this example, you find an `endless while` loop. It may make sense to simply run the `while` loop based on the value `fread` returns. After all, `fread` returns zero if no more items remain to be read from disk. Unfortunately, the way the loop is set up, when that happens, the last structure read from disk is redisplayed. To prevent that, the `while` loop repeats forever, and a `break` statement is used to stop the loop.

The `fread` function reads in a chunk of disk the size of a `stock` structure and saves it in the `stock` structure:

```
x =
    fread(&stock,sizeof(stock),1,stocks);
```

Like the `write_data` function, the structure is created locally, inside the function. Multiple structures (or an array) are not created; doing so is not necessary because you can reuse the same structure over and over to read multiple values from disk. This process works just like reusing the same input buffer for keyboard input.

If the value returned from `fread` is zero, the `break` cancels the endless `while` loop:

```
if(x==0) break;
```

Otherwise, the information read from disk is displayed:

```
printf("\nStock name:
    %s\n",stock.name);
printf("Purchased for
    $%.2f\n",stock.buy_price);
printf("Current price:
    $%.2f\n",stock.current_price);
```

After the loop stops, an `fclose` statement closes the file and control returns to the `main` function, where the menu is displayed again.

Function fread

The fread function ("file read," not "freed") reads a chunk of information from disk. It's essentially the reverse of the fwrite function. The formats are the same, in fact, and the statements will probably look the same in your source code, except for the fread/fwrite names. Here's the format:

```
c =
    fread(&buffer,size,items,handle);
```

buffer is the name of the variable to which you store information read from disk. It can be a character buffer or a structure variable.

size is the size of the chunk fread reads from disk. If you're loading a structure, the sizeof command can be used to determine how big the structure is.

items refers to the number of items read from disk. This value is usually one.

The handle variable represents a file you have opened for reading.

The fread function returns a value equal to the number of chunks read from disk (the value of size, which is typically one). If a disk error occurred or the EOF was encountered, fread returns zero.

The final STOCKS.C program

Here's the final result of your labor. The STOCKS.C program should look like this in your editor:

```
#include <stdio.h>
#include <stdlib.h>
#include <conio.h>
#include <ctype.h>

#define FALSE 0
#define TRUE !FALSE

struct stock_data {
    char name[30];
    float buy_price;
    float current_price;
    };

void write_info(void);
void read_info(void);
```

(continued)

(continued)

```c
void main()
{
   char c;
   int done=FALSE;

   while(!done)
   {
      puts("\nStock Portfolio Thing\n");
      puts("A - Add new stock\n");
      puts("L - List stocks\n");
      puts("Q - Quit\n");
      printf("Your choice:");

      c = getch();
      c = toupper(c);

      switch(c)
      {
         case('A'):
            puts("Add new stock\n");
            write_info();
            break;
         case('L'):
            puts("List stocks");
            read_info();
            break;
         case('Q'):
            puts("Quit\n");
            done = TRUE;
            break;
         default:
            puts("?");
            break;
      }
   }
}

void write_info(void)
{
   FILE *stocks;
   struct stock_data stock;
   char input[12];
```

```
   printf("Enter stock name:");
   gets(stock.name);
   printf("How much did you pay for it? $");
   stock.buy_price = (float)atof(gets(input));
   stock.current_price = stock.buy_price/11;

   stocks = fopen("stock.dat","a");
   if(stocks==NULL)
   {
      puts("Error opening file");
      exit(1);
   }

   fwrite(&stock,sizeof(stock),1,stocks);

   fclose(stocks);
   puts("Stock added.");
}

void read_info(void)
{
   FILE *stocks;
   struct stock_data stock;
   int x;

   stocks = fopen("stock.dat","r");
   if(stocks==NULL)
   {
      puts("No data in file");
      return;
   }

   while(TRUE)
   {
      x = fread(&stock,sizeof(stock),1,stocks);

      if(x==0) break;

      printf("\nStock name: %s\n",stock.name);
      printf("Purchased for $%.2f\n",stock.buy_price);
      printf("Current price: $%.2f\n",stock.current_price);
   }

   fclose(stocks);
}
```

You don't have to stop here. You can keep modifying the program, if you like. Add functions to search through the records on disk or sort the stocks by name or price. This is how most crazy programs start and how most programmers come to realize that 4 o'clock comes twice a day!

Lesson 12-4 Quiz

1. Which function is used to write structures to disk?

   A. `fread`

   B. `fwrite`

   C. `fstruct`

   D. There is no function to write structures.

2. Which function can be used to read a structure from disk?

   A. `fread`

   B. `freed`

   C. `fried`

   D. There is no function to read a structure from disk either.

3. Which of the following American authors is the most-published?

   A. Edgar Allan Poe.

   B. Mark Twain.

   C. Dr. Seuss.

   D. Stephen King.

4. What's wrong with the following `fwrite` statement?

   ```
   fwrite(struct cheddar,sizeof(struct
          cheddar),1,diskfile);
   ```

   A. Nothing, assuming that everything was set up properly (variables declared and the file opened).

   B. There should be an ampersand before the first `struct cheddar`.

   C. Nothing will be written to disk.

   D. Something else, but I can't quite put my finger on it.

Lesson 12-5: Just Your Standard I/O

I/O is input and output, the reason your computer lives. Without either input or output, your PC becomes useless. For example, goldfish barely have any I/O, which makes them about the most useless pet.

Okay, okay: Goldfish may still be pretty to look at. I suppose that they fall under the Entertainment category of pet-keeping. Even so, a C program can also look pretty and still, having no I/O, be next to useless.

> ✔ Goldfish lovers and fans: Please don't write me letters about how your goldfish is fully I/O capable or enhanced. I needed an example. If you can suggest another type of pet, feel free.

> ✔ You have never, in your short C programming career, written a program without any I/O. Even this book's silliest program had some I or some O in it.

> ✔ Some programs that don't display information or take input from the keyboard still do I/O. Although the tiny program that runs your PC's clock may not display text or read the keyboard, it communicates with the PC's ticker. That's low-level I/O, but it's still I/O.

A programming language without any I/O

C is a programming language without any I/O. It has none. Not one command in C is geared toward doing any I or any O. You may balk at this statement, but consider the following program.

Type this program into your editor. The absent #include <stdio.h> statement is intentional and is explained a little later in this chapter. (You don't need it for this program.) Just type what you see here. Save it to disk as NOIO.C:

Name: NOIO.C

```
void main()
{
    int x;

    x=255;

    while(x)
    {
        x--;
    }
}
```

Compile and run. Here's what you see on your screen:

Yup. Nothing. The reason is that the program — and it is a program because it does something — has no I/O. There is no input. There is no output. And there's no STDIO.H file.

The mysteries of Studio H

You're probably so used to typing #include <stdio.h> at the beginning of any source code you write that you don't even bother with what it means. There's no reason to, until you discover that the C language has no input or output commands.

Like me, you probably pronounce it "studio H." Of course, you and I are both wrong. It's the *standard I/O* file. Studio H is most likely some high-tech beauty salon in Manhattan.

Whenever you read the keyboard, write to the screen, or access the disk, you're using a *function,* which is defined in the STDIO.H file. That's why it's included all the time: You need the functions defined inside STDIO.H for your program to communicate with you.

✔ STDIO.H is the *standard input/output header* file. It contains all the basic functions you use for input and output: printf, gets, fopen, getchar, and so on. That's why it has been included in all your programs — without STDIO.H, your programs would have no I/O and no way to communicate with you.

✔ The C language contains only 33 keywords or commands. Anything else you use is either a function contained in one of the header files or a function you write on your own.

✔ See Table 1-1 for the complete list of C language keywords.

✔ On the PC, the CONIO.H header file contains additional I/O functions, those written specifically for the PC's keyboard and screen.

Give me that old, standard I/O

Standard I/O is more than just a C language header file. It's the way your computer communicates with you. The STDIO.H file in C is just a set of routines, customized for your computer, that handle all the standard I/O tasks.

Your PC has two primary standard I/O devices:

> ✔ The keyboard is the standard input device, nicknamed stdin for *st*andar*d in*put.
>
> ✔ The screen is the standard output device, nicknamed stdout for *st*andar*d out*put.

The utterly oddball thing about the stdin and stdout devices is that DOS treats them just like a file on disk. You can, if you like, "open the screen" for output or "open the keyboard" for input.

Granted, opening the screen as a file sounds kind of dumb. It would be silly to use fopen and then fprintf and fclose when a puts or printf function does the job in only one step. Not only that, because DOS keeps the stdin and stdout devices open all the time, some C language functions were designed specifically to read and write from stdin and stdout.

Now the question begs: Why the heck bother?

That's a tough one. The point to the rest of this chapter is using the stdio and stdout "files" as a means to modify DOS output. You can write programs called *filters* that modify standard input and output, which would be really keen had Microsoft not gone out of its way to kill off DOS. . . .

> ✔ The next section introduces you to your first filter program.
>
> ✔ The official DOS name for the keyboard, or stdin, device is the "console," or CON.
>
> ✔ The official DOS name for the screen, or stdout, device, is also the "console," or CON.
>
> ✔ CON is considered one device by DOS: The input comes from the keyboard, and the output goes to the screen.
>
> ✔ Both stdin and stdout are defined in the STDIO.H files as "handles" for disk functions writing to the screen and reading from the keyboard. More about this subject in a few pages.
>
> ✔ The stdin and stdout devices are automatically opened by DOS for use as input and output, just like files on disk. Like Denny's, they never close.
>
> ✔ Don't you find it odd that "never close" and "always open" mean the same thing?
>
> ✔ If you've ever used the DOS COPY CON command to create a file, you've used the standard input device to write text directly to a file: "Copy a file from the console device to another spot on disk." This is an old computer concept that Chairman Bill & Co. borrowed from UNIX for use in MS-DOS.

✔ DOS has three other standard I/O devices under it: `stderr` is the error-output device, usually the screen; `stdaux` is the first serial port in your PC; and `stdprn` is the standard printer device.

✔ Don't be lulled into believing that writing a modem program is as easy as opening the `stdaux` device. Alas, its purpose as the serial port "file" is more trivial than useful. All the major communications programs access the PC's serial port hardware directly. When it comes down to bits and bytes, the `stdaux` device is just too darned slow.

✔ The reason that C has no I/O functions is actually one of its charms. By customizing a STDIO.H file for your computer, you can compile source code written for other computers and have it all work. Other languages must be custom-tuned to each computer they work on.

Filters and > and < and even | again

The following program is a *rot13* filter. It takes text and rotates it 13 places, encrypting it rather simply. Passing text through the filter a second time decrypts it (refer to Lesson 9-5 in Chapter 9).

This program uses `stdin` to read information from the standard input device (the keyboard). The `rot13` function from the old SCRAMBLE.C program then modifies that information, rotating the alphabetic characters 13 places. The results are then sent to the standard output device, `stdout`, using the `fputc` function.

Save the source code to disk as ROT13.C:

Name: ROT13.C

```
#include <stdio.h>
#include <ctype.h>

void main()
{
    char ch;

    do
    {
        ch = fgetc(stdin);
        if(isalpha(ch))
        {
```

```
            if(toupper(ch)>='A' && toupper(ch)<='M')
                    ch+=13;
            else
                    ch-=13;
        }
        fputc(ch,stdout);
    }
    while(ch!=EOF);
}
```

Compile. Fix any errors and recompile if necessary.

Before you run the program, know that it's a filter. It accepts standard input from the keyboard, or it can accept redirected input from a file or some other device on the PC.

Start with standard input. Run the program:

```
C:\CSTUFF> rot13
_
```

The cursor sits and waits. No, nothing is wrong. You must supply standard input by typing at the keyboard. Type something like this:

```
A pig fell in the mud.
```

Press the Enter key:

```
N cvt sryy va gur zhq.
```

End input by pressing Ctrl+Z and then Enter:

```
^Z
```

Ctrl-Z is the end-of-file character (EOF) for DOS text files. The ROT13.C filter program, just read from standard input, modified the input and sent it to standard output. Pressing Ctrl+Z told the program that input was over.

Function `fputc`

The `fputc` function is used to write a single character to a file opened for writing. It's the disk equivalent of the `putchar` function. Here's the format:

x = fputc(*c*,*handle*)

c is a character, either a single character variable or a character constant enclosed in single quotes.

handle is the name of a file handle variable returned from an `fopen` function. Or, in the case of standard I/O, it can be the name of the standard output file, `stdout`, which is the same as the PC's screen.

If `fputc` is successful, it returns the character it wrote to disk in variable x. Otherwise, it returns the EOF value.

A better example is to filter a file. Use your text editor to create the following:

```
There were these two nuns walking in the park. One of the
         nuns said to the other one, "I believe I have a
         pebble in my shoe." So they stopped and sat on a
         park bench, while the one nun removed her shoe,
         plucked out the pebble, and then put her shoe
         back on. The nuns then got up and continued
         walking through the park and enjoying the day.
```

Save the file to disk as SAMPLE.TXT.

Now use the ROT13.C filter and redirected input at the DOS prompt to process the file:

```
C:\CSTUFF> ROT13 < SAMPLE.TXT
```

Press Enter, and you see the rotated copy of the text:

```
Gurer jrer gurfr gjb ahaf jnyxvat va gur cnex. Bar bs gur
         ahaf fnvq gb gur bgure bar, "V oryvrir V unir n
         crooyr va zl fubr." Fb gurl fgbccrq naq fng ba n
         cnex orapu, juvyr gur bar aha erzbirq ure fubr,
         cyhpxrq bhg gur crooyr, naq gura chg ure fubr
         onpx ba. Gur ahaf gura tbg hc naq pbagvahrq
         jnyxvat guebhtu gur cnex naq rawblvat gur qnl.
```

Looks Dutch, but it's simply rotated English. You could save this example to a file and run it through the ROT13.C filter again, and the text would translate back to the original.

You can also rotate the output of a DOS command. Try this:

```
C:\CSTUFF> DIR | ROT13
```

That's the DIR command, a pipe (or vertical bar) character, and then the ROT13 filter. Press the Enter key, and you see a rotated directory listing. Notice how only the filenames and other text characters are rotated? Thanks to the isalpha function in the program, only text characters are affected by the filter.

- ✔ DOS comes with three filter programs: MORE pauses the display after each screenful of text; SORT sorts lines of text; and FIND locates lines of text in a file.

- ✔ The ‹ symbol is used at the DOS prompt to redirect input from a file into a filter program (or any program that accepts standard input).

- ✔ The | symbol is the pipe, not an I or a 1. (Look for it on the same key as the backslash character on your keyboard). The | "pipes" the output of a DOS command (standard output) through a filter.

- ✔ No, *DOS For Dummies* does not cover these jewels, although *MORE DOS For Dummies* does. (This stuff is considered an advanced topic.)

- ✔ The ROT13.C program uses two disk functions to read and write from the standard input and output devices: fgetc and fputc. Normally, you would have to open a file before you use these functions, but because stdin and stdout are already opened by DOS, the fopen and fclose functions are unnecessary.

- ✔ The format for fgetc is in Lesson 12-1 (see the previous "Function fputc" sidebar).

- ✔ I know that some of my "fans" would assume that the nun story would be in poor taste. I'm happy to prove them wrong!

- ✔ The stdin and stdout devices are defined in the STDIO.H header file. This is how they can be used in the ROT13.C source code without having to be defined first or created with the fopen function: they're already defined in STDIO.H and opened by DOS.

Dedicated standard input functions

You should grow to expect this: C has functions designed to read stdin and write to stdout automatically. Though the ROT13.C program works, you could write it more efficiently by replacing the following line:

```
ch = fgetc(stdin);
```

with this one:

```
ch = fgetchar();
```

The `fgetchar` function is used to read a character from the `stdin` device. There's no need to specify the `stdin` name and definitely no need to `fopen` the `stdin` file.

Likewise, the following line:

```
fputc(ch,stdout);
```

can be more logically replaced with this shortcut:

```
fputchar(ch);
```

Again, it's easier. The `fputchar` function automatically writes a character to the `stdout` device.

Make the preceding changes to the ROT13.C program. Save and recompile. The results are the same, but you've used more appropriate C language functions.

✔ The `fgetchar` function always reads a character from the `stdin` device, the keyboard. There's no need to open any file or use the `stdin` variable.

✔ The `fputchar` function always writes a character to the `stdout` device, the screen. You don't have to open a file or ever specify `stdout`.

A final filter example

You can use the basic outline of the ROT13.C program to create any filter you want. It's just too bad that no one uses DOS anymore, or else you could probably make a tidy sum spinning out useful filters and selling them to everyone.

As an example of how you might not make money, the following program takes standard input and removes all the spaces and tabs, leaving all the words on a line by themselves. I can't imagine right off how that would be useful, but it does show you how simple it is to convert the basic ROT13.C program into any other type of filter.

Type the following source code into your editor. Save it to disk as WORDS.C:

Name: WORDS.C

```
#include <stdio.h>
#include <ctype.h>

void main()
{
    char ch;

    do
    {
        ch = fgetchar();
        if(isspace(ch))
        {
            while(isspace(ch))
            {
                ch = fgetchar();
            }
            fputchar('\n');
        }
        fputchar(ch);
    }
    while(ch!=EOF);
}
```

Compile! Now you can run it at the DOS prompt, but it's much more effective to run it with some redirected input. Type the following command:

```
C:\CSTUFF> words < sample.txt
```

This command feeds the text from the SAMPLE.TXT file into the WORDS filter as standard input. Press the Enter key, and you see every word from the file displayed on a line by itself.

To modify output from a DOS command, try this example:

```
C:\CSTUFF> dir | words
```

Each word in the DIR command's output is displayed on a line by itself, making all that information virtually useless.

Up the stream without a paddle

One final disk thing: *streams*. You hear this word over and over again with disk access in C. Your C library reference may even refer to some function as "reading a data stream." Sounds very Montana, but it has nothing to do with wearing funny pants and catching trout.

A stream (specifically, "buffered stream I/O") simply refers to the way information is read from disk. The stream itself is just the long strand of bytes written to a file, one after another, like those candy bead necklaces five-year-olds love to eat.

You can view a data stream (the raw bytes on disk) by using the DUMP.C program you created earlier in this chapter. "Stream I/O" routines in C deal with accessing a file or reading or writing the bytes stored in the file. This stuff is nothing big.

The "buffered" part of the "buffered stream I/O" refers to the fact that the function does not read the bytes one at a time. Instead, it reads a large chunk of the file and stores that chunk in memory — in a buffer. When you fopen a file, it reads, for example, 8K of information into a buffer in memory. (DOS does this, actually.)

When you access the file using some odd C function (a "stream I/O" function), it then reads or writes its information to the buffer and not directly to disk. This method is more efficient than reading or writing only one byte at a time to a file. (And it explains why you may sometimes write a bit, byte, or pebble to a file and not see your PC's hard drive light flicker.)

Though buffered stream I/O is efficient, the drawback is that the buffer isn't written to disk until it gets full or the file is closed. The moral here is that you should always properly close a file before your program quits. If you don't, the last bit of information written to disk may not officially be on disk.

Other functions exist in C to do "unbuffered I/O" to disk. You may encounter them in a reference or your C language library. Use them only when normal I/O doesn't work; those low-level routines can wreak havoc on a disk if they're used with wanton abandon.

- ✔ The WORDS.C program uses the fgetchar function to read standard input; the fputchar function sends the character to standard output.

- ✔ The isspace function is one of those CTYPE.H functions introduced in Lesson 9-5 in Chapter 9. It returns TRUE if the character examined is a tab, space, or Enter character (ASCII codes x09, x20, and x0D, respectively).

- ✔ Those characters (tab, space, and Enter) are referred to as *white space* characters in the C language lexicon (refer to Lesson 4-4 in Chapter 4 of *C For Dummies,* Volume I).

- ✔ The while loop is used to help the program skip over two or more white-space characters in a row. It continues reading characters until a nonwhite-space character is found. Notice that an fputchar function then displays the newline character (\n) and the following fputchar function (outside the while loop) displays the character in ch. This way, no nonwhite-space characters are lost in the while loop.

✔ On the whole, it's a rather short and simple program that does something nonprogrammers would consider quite complex.

✔ You could modify the WORDS.C program to count the words in addition to displaying them each on a line. Just declare a counter variable x initialized to zero. Increment the counter every time the statement fputchar('\n') is executed. Then display the summary at the end of the file.

Or you could prefix each word with its count number. An fprintf statement like the following would do the trick:

```
fprintf(stdout,"%i: ",x);
```

Remember that fprintf requires a file handle. Here, the stdout handle is used, which is defined in the STDIO.H header file to be the standard output device (the screen).

Lesson 12-5 Quiz

1. True or false: The C language has no I/O functions.

2. The standard input and output devices are

   A. The CON.

   B. The CON sonar.

   C. The CON sonar, aye.

   D. The stdin and stdout devices, which, on a PC, are the keyboard and the screen.

3. The stdin and stdout keywords are defined in STDIO.H. What are they used for?

   A. Standard input and output.

   B. The keyboard and screen.

   C. File handles.

   D. Love handles.

4. Match the actor with his real name:

   A. Cary Grant   1. Archibald Leach

   B. Danny Thomas   2. Joe Yule, Jr.

   C. Mickey Rooney   3. Muzyad Yakhoob

   D. Rock Hudson   4. Roy Scherer, Jr.

5. True or false: You never have to open or close the stdin or stdout files.

Bonus question

How do you most often mistype the #include <stdio.h> thing at the beginning of your source code?

A. #include ,stdio.h.

B. #include <Stdio.H>

C. #include <studio.h>

D. #inclued <stdiou.H>

Chapter 12 Final Exam

1. Which of these does not belong?

A. Kevin Bacon.

B. Sir Francis Bacon.

C. Roger Bacon.

D. Farmer John Bacon.

2. Which of the following file-opening modes creates a file and potentially deletes a file already on disk?

A. "w"

B. "w+"

C. "zappit"

D. "get nasty"

E. "kaboom!"

F. "fffzzzzt..."

3. What's to prevent a file-reading function, such as fgetc, from just merrily reading along way past the end of the file?

A. The flarge_dog function that lurks at the back of each file.

B. The fgetc function returns an error if you attempt to read beyond the end of the file.

C. The fgetc function returns the EOF character as the last character in the file.

D. The fgetc function repeats the previous character read.

4. How does your program know which file you're reading or writing information from or to?

   A. The filename is implied in each function.

   B. All the file commands after an `fopen` function relate to the file just opened.

   C. All C file functions require a file handle variable, which tells them which file they're working with.

   D. It just knows.

5. Which of the following is *not* the name of someone in the Bible?

   A. Alacahazaradashar.

   B. Mahershalalhashbaz.

   C. Tilgarthpilneser.

   D. Zaphnathpaaneah.

6. Whenever you open a file, you should always do what when you're done with it?

   A. Wipe its little chin.

   B. Burp it.

   C. `fclose` it.

   D. Say thank you and go on with your day.

7. True or false: If you open a file in "r" mode, it won't be overwritten.

8. Define binary data:

   A. Data from the planet Binar.

   B. Data composed of ones and zeroes.

   C. Anything but text.

   D. Actually, anything is binary data.

9. When does the `fgets` function know when to stop reading characters from disk?

   A. When it encounters a newline (\n).

   B. When it encounters the EOF.

   C. When it reads the maximum number of characters you specify.

   D. All of the above.

10. What must you do to ensure that fscanf reads data from disk properly?

    A. Enclose it in double-dog parentheses.

    B. Specify the proper formatting string for fscanf.

    C. Separate each data tidbit with a separator, like a newline (\n).

    D. Just use another function.

11. To send formatted information to disk, you can use which function?

    A. fprintf

    B. fputs

    C. fwrite

    D. fformat

12. True or false: You can use the fwrite and fread functions to write and read just about anything to a disk file.

13. True or false: Information written to disk with fwrite must be read back using a similar fread function.

14. Why do you need the STDIO.H file at the beginning of your source code?

    A. It's a C language tradition dating back to the 13th century.

    B. To provide input and output functions, the standard ones.

    C. So that the *tres chic* guys and gals at Studio H in Manhattan will give us programmers a deep discount on our flat-tops.

    D. To provide amusement for the compiler.

15. A filter is a type of program that does what?

    A. Accepts standard input, modifies it, and produces standard output.

    B. It's a type of program that filters, like that spongy thing you never change in your goldfish tank.

    C. Removes grit and excess shed human skin.

    D. False!

16. What was Elvis' favorite amusement park ride?

    A. Bumper cars.

    B. Roller coaster.

    C. Tilt-a-whirl.

    D. None (any ride tended to make Elvis sick).

Chapter 13
The Missing Chapter

- -

Lessons in This Chapter

▶ Defensive driving

▶ How to play craps

▶ Basic banking

▶ Why you shouldn't hit your sister

Programs in This Chapter

BABYLON5.C   NIGHTLINE.C   SIMPSONS.C

SNL.C   COPS.C   OPRAH.C

Vocabulary Introduced in This Chapter

oviposit   enervate   xyster

cupidity   sobriquet   donjon

- -

All kidding aside, this book just got too fat, and I had to pull out Chapter 13. It's basically a catch-up chapter that covers how C references the date and time, describes some interesting time functions, and discusses some miscellaneous stuff on binary math and whatnot — all in all, rather forgettable, skippable stuff anyway.

The remnants of Chapter 13 will eventually find their way online, at this book's unofficial Web page. Visit it at

```
http://www.wambooli.com/c.for.dummies/
```

Until then, give yourself a much needed break. The next and final chapter wraps up your beginning C language experience.

"I made him spend two-and-a-half hours doing C programming."

Chapter 14
Building Big Programs

· ·

Lessons in This Chapter

▶ Making programs with multiple modules

▶ Bigger and better things

▶ More multiple-module madness!

▶ You and your programs

Programs in This Chapter

SORT-IT.C	SORTFN.C	MODULE.C	NODULE.C
MADLIB2.C	A.C	Q.C	CLS.C
NUTS.CPP			

Vocabulary Introduced in This Chapter

`extern`

· ·

*T*he largest program I have on my hard disk weighs in at 5,529,360 bytes. The smallest program I have measures a paltry 27 bytes. The larger program is obviously more versatile than my little program, but do you think that the big one was written using one source code document, like my little program?

You can bet a pot of Pooh's hunny that a 5,400K program would have a source code file much larger than 5,400K. If you could stick this type of document into a text editor, it would drive you, well, *insane* to make even the tiniest update. No, a better solution for creating a large program probably exists. The solution is program *modules*.

This chapter wraps up Volume II of *C For Dummies* with a discussion of program modules, which is the best way you can go about building huge programs in C. I've also added miscellaneous lessons in this chapter that tell you how to complete your C training, enabling you to graduate to full Jedi codester and face Darth Vader and the evil Emperor. . . . Oh, wait. Different story. I'm sorry.

Lesson 14-1: Making Programs with Multiple Modules

This multiple-module stuff is about two things: building bigger programs and reusing common chunks of code. These concepts are similar because most of your big programs will reuse the same chunks of code from previous big programs you've created. It's like cannibalism (minus the guilt).

To build a big program, you need more source code. Unless you've just coded all the text to *War and Peace,* that code obviously will consist of lots of functions. You could stuff it all into a single file, but that would be horrid. Tolstoy didn't write *War and Peace* all on one sheet of paper, after all. If he had owned a word processor, he probably would have spun off each chapter as a document unto itself. The same thing should happen with your larger programs.

When you create something big, you probably will stuff various functions into their own source code files. Then you will compile each of them individually and link the whole lot of them together into one, huge, final program.

Figure 14-1 illustrates the compiling and linking multiple-modules concept. Each source code file is a *module.* It's compiled into an object code file. Then the object code files are each linked together to form the final program file.

✔ Most programming is done with several source code modules compiled and then linked into one program. The single source code/object code/program files you've been working on throughout this book are an exception.

✔ *Module* is the name given to each source code file.

✔ An *object code file* is the thing that's created when you compile your source code. On the PC, object code files end with the OBJ filename extension. (Review Lesson 1-2 in *C For Dummies,* Volume I, if you have forgotten any of this stuff.)

✔ The *linker* is the program that links various object code files into a final program. After some 1,000 pages of using the linker, you can finally warm up with a happy glow, knowing why it's called a linker and not a "build program thing."

✔ Another nice thing about multiple modules is that you can reuse ones that contain common routines, as explained in Lesson 14-2, later in this chapter.

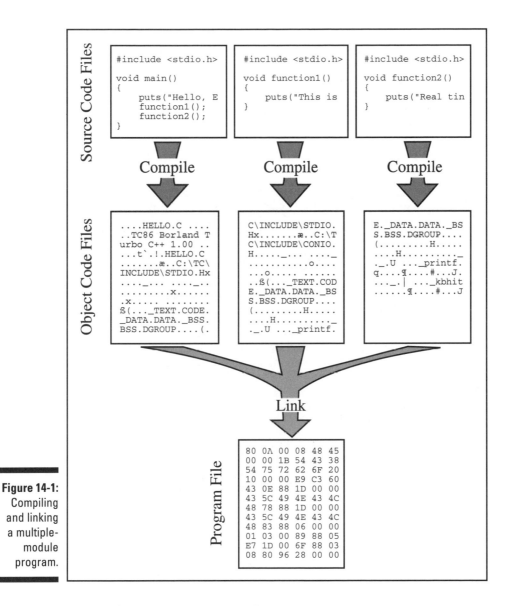

Figure 14-1:
Compiling and linking a multiple-module program.

Banishment to the DOS prompt!

You probably have in your integrated programming environment some command that lets you create a single large program using several source code files. This process is probably called building a "project" or some such nonsense. It's all nice and cozy and easy to understand and all that. Unfortunately, because Borland and Microsoft both change their integrated environments too often, I can't precisely document that here.

It is with a profound sense of cheerfulness that I now banish you and your programming skills to the DOS prompt. In fact, this chapter *requires* that you build and compile your program at the DOS prompt. It's just easier to show you how things work if you compile your programs at the DOS prompt. If you've been basking in the warmth of your cozy integrated environment, *leave!* Prepare to dip into the cold, unforgiving DOS command-line environment for the duration.

- Heck, primitive C programmers worked with stone tools at a command prompt. You can live with it too!

- Most of the legion of grizzled C programming veterans cut their teeth at command prompts on various computers hither, thither, and yon.

- Honestly, my main reason for doing it this way is that the integrated environments are wildly different. At the command line, both Borland and Microsoft C behave similarly.

- Make sure that the `-c` option is not specified in your TURBOC.CFG file. You want the `bcc` command to both compile *and* link for the programs in this chapter.

- You must run the MSVCVARS program before you can successfully compile and link programs at the DOS prompt. The MSVCVARS program was created when you installed Microsoft C on your hard drive.

Playing Moses

To have fun with multiple modules, you need a program file created from several source code files. The quickest way to cook up one of those now is to take a program you've already created and, like Moses and the Red Sea, split it in two. You then link the separate pieces together to create one program again.

Summon the SORTME.C program. Load that program into your editor and break out your virtual reality scissors. You're going to split that source code into two separate files. The first one is named SORT-IT.C, and the second one is named SORTFN.C.

(Because you're at the DOS prompt, I'm assuming that you have a DOS text editor to work these programs. If not, you can use Windows Notepad to edit the files and switch back and forth between the Notepad window and the DOS prompt.)

Use your editor to copy the following code from the SORTME.C file and paste it into a new editor window. Save the file to disk, and name it SORT-IT.C:

Name: SORT-IT.C

```c
#include <stdio.h>

#define SIZE 6        //size of the array

void sort(int *array,int size);

void main()
{
    int lotto[] = { 10, 48, 1, 37, 6, 24 };
    int i;

    printf("Here is the array unsorted:\n");

    for(i=0;i<SIZE;i++)
        printf("%i\t",lotto[i]);

    printf("\nAnd here is the sorted array:\n");

    sort(lotto,SIZE);

    for(i=0;i<SIZE;i++)
        printf("%i\t",lotto[i]);
}
```

Go back to the original SORTME.C file and copy the following code, which is just the sort function, from that file and paste it into a new, blank sheet in your editor. Save the new file to disk as SORTFN.C:

Name: SORTFN.C

```c
void sort(int *array,int size)
{
    int a,b,temp;

    for(a=0;a<size-1;a++)
        for(b=a+1;b<size;b++)
            if(array[a] > array[b])
            {
                temp=array[b];
                array[b] = array[a];
                array[a] = temp;
            }
}
```

Now you should have two new files on disk: SORT-IT.C and SORTFN.C. Both were pulled from the original SORTME.C file; SORT-IT.C contains the main function and I/O functions, and the SORTFN.C file contains only the sort function. Better link the files together before Pharaoh's army comes and slaughters everyone, even the oxen.

Compile and link both files. Type the proper command for your compiler:

For Borland compilers:

```
bcc sort-it.c sortfn.c
```

Type **bcc**, a space, and then the names of the two files separated by a space. Then press the Enter key.

For Microsoft compilers:

```
cl sort-it.c sortfn.c
```

Type the **cl** command, a space, and then the names of the two files to compile and link, separated by a space. Then press Enter.

For a generic compiler:

Refer to your manual for specific compiling and linking commands. In some cases, you may have two sets of commands, such as cc and then link. Generally, you compile the modules one at a time and then use the link command to chain them all together.

Fix any errors! You see the errors listed after the module name, something like this:

```
Error sort-it.c 17: Statement missing ; in function main
```

or this:

```
sort-it.c(17): error C2146: syntax error: missing ';' be-
          fore identifier 'printf'
```

The message tells you in which module the error occurs and the line number on which the compiler thinks the error is located (17, in the example). Fix and recompile using the same command.

The end result is a program file named after the module containing the main function. Run the program:

```
Here is the array unsorted:
10   48   1    37   6    24
```

```
And here is the sorted array:
1      6     10    24    37    48
```

> ✔ The compiler creates OBJ (object) files from each source code file. The compiler doesn't glue them together, however — that's the job of the linker.

> ✔ The linker gets its name, in fact, from its capability to link together various OBJ files.

> ✔ The program's size is not affected by linking multiple modules, so don't believe that you must keep all your code in one source code file to make the resulting program smaller. It just doesn't work that way.

> ✔ Here's a trivial bit for you: Moses had a stammer.

Accessing variables in other modules

The key to sharing variables between modules is to make them global. A multiple-module program is, after all, just like a program with one huge source file. The way you share variables between functions in a huge source file is to make them global.

Create the following source code in your editor. The code has four global variables of four common types. Save it to disk as MODULE.C:

Name: MODULE.C

```c
#include <stdio.h>
#include <string.h>

char buffer[30];
char chair;
int ent;
float rootbeer;

void main()
{
    printf("Noms de famille:");
    gets(buffer);
    chair = buffer[0];
    ent = strlen(buffer);
    rootbeer = 100/ent;
    showme();
    puts("And you're done");
}
```

There's no point in compiling and linking right now. You're still one module short of a complete program. To finish the job, you have to create the module containing the `showme` function, the NODULE.C module.

Start with a clean, new sheet in your editor, and create the following source code. Save the code to disk as NODULE.C:

Name: NODULE.C

```
#include <stdio.h>

extern char buffer[30];
extern char chair;
extern int ent;
extern float rootbeer;

void showme(void)
{
    puts("\nHere is your data:");
    printf("Name: %s\n",buffer);
    printf("Character: %c\n",chair);
    printf("Name length: %i\n",ent);
    printf("Name percentage: %.2f\n",rootbeer);
}
```

This module uses the global variables defined in the MODULE.C module. It accesses them with the `extern` keyword. That's what lets the compiler know that the global variables are defined in another module. (See the nearby "Keyword `extern`" sidebar for more information about the `extern` keyword.)

Compile! Link! Create! Here are the commands:

For Borland compilers:

```
bcc module.c nodule.c
```

Follow the `bcc` command with the name of each module. Make sure that there's a space between the filenames. Press the Enter key.

For Microsoft compilers:

```
cl module.c nodule.c
```

After the `cl` command, type a space and then the two filenames separated by a space. Press Enter.

For generic compilers:

Refer to your program manual for the compiling and linking instructions.

If you discover any errors, fix them. (A misspelled word, such as `shomwe` rather than `showme`, can result in a linker error.)

Run the program!

```
Noms de famille:
```

Type your last name, and then press the Enter key:

```
Here is your data:
Name: Wambooli
Character: W
Name length: 8
Name percentage: 12.00
And you're done
```

The variables were declared as global in MODULE.C. They were accessed and displayed in NODULE.C. The final line, `And you're done`, was displayed after control returned to MODULE.C.

Keyword `extern`

The `extern` keyword assures the compiler that a global variable has been defined and exists in another program module. It then informs the linker to go out to that module and find the variable at link time. Here's the format:

`extern` *type name;*

The external variable essentially is declared just like any other global variable except that the word *extern* precedes it. `Type` is a variable type, and `name` is the name of the variable — just like declaring any variable in C.

For this process to work, the variable *name* you identify as external must be declared in another program module. Furthermore, it must be declared as a global variable. (Variables inside functions cannot be referenced outside the function.)

✔ The `extern` keyword is what makes sharing variables between modules possible (refer to the preceding "Keyword `extern`" sidebar).

✔ You don't have to identify *all* the global variables in every module of your program. You have to declare a global variable as an `extern` in only those modules that use that variable.

✔ You can declare a global variable in *any* module in a multiple-module program. They don't all have to be in the `main` function, though it's nice to keep them all in one spot.

✔ You may see a "no prototype" warning error when you compile and link the programs. To avoid seeing that error, prototype the `showme` function in the MODULE.C source code as follows:

```
void showme(void);
```

✔ The `Noms de famille` prompt means to enter your last name. It's some foreign-language thing.

✔ Doesn't "one module short of a complete program" sound like a put-down along the lines of "one beer shy of a six-pack" or "a card short of a full deck"?

Lesson 14-1 Quiz

1. What is perhaps the worst jelly bean flavor in the universe?

   A. Chocolate.

   B. Coconut.

   C. Licorice.

   D. Jalapeño.

2. How do you create a multiple-module program?

   A. Just split up your source code into separate files.

   B. Link the various object (OBJ) files.

   C. Hire 64 programmers to work on it, and promise them stock options.

   D. With the `extern` keyword.

3. How do you pass a variable to a function in another module?

   A. Declare the variable global.

   B. Declare the variable global, and flag it as an `extern` in the module.

    C. You don't have to do anything because passing the variable is unaffected by which module the function is in.

    D. Use the `long` keyword — or the `hail Mary` keyword.

4. What type of program lends itself to multiple modules?

    A. A huge program.

    B. A banking program.

    C. A program that lends without collateral but at an exorbitantly high interest rate.

    D. Any program, actually.

Bonus joke in German

Was sind die drei Lagen auf der Bratsche?

Erste Lage, Notlage, und Niederlage.

Lesson 14-2: Bigger and Better Things

Time to play Let's Pretend.

Let's pretend that you're a high-paid programmer working for Mollosoft (a small company in Issaquah, Washington) and you have to come up with this huge Madlib program. Recalling your early days in Volume I of this book, you look up the MADLIB1.C program in Lesson 2-3.

Alas, that old Madlib program is too simple (and considering what Mollosoft is paying you, that's probably not what they want). Compared to your brilliant, sunlike knowledge of C today, that program is but a flickering candle, a flitting fly on the face of . . . .

Enough already!

Start with a place for your work

When you work with multiple modules, it helps to keep them all in one place. That calls for a subdirectory.

Use the `mkdir` command to create a new subdirectory in your CSTUFF directory on disk. Name the new directory MADLIB2:

```
C:\CSTUFF> MKDIR MADLIB2
```

Change to the new directory with the cd command:

```
C:\CSTUFF> CD MADLIB2

C:\CSTUFF\MADLIB2>
```

Now you're ready to crack your knuckles and start coding.

Building the main module

The program you're about to create has three modules. The first module contains the main function. Here 'tis:

Name: MADLIB2.C

```
char *noun;
char *adj1;
char *adj2;
char *smell;
char *friend;
char *verb;
char *day;
char *occupation;

void main()
{
    get_questions();
    print_answers();
}
```

Type this source code into your editor. Eight pointers are defined as global variables, and then the main function calls two functions. Save it to disk as MADLIB2.C.

You don't have to compile yet, so just move on to the next module.

> ✔ The program doesn't need the STDIO.H header file because it contains no I/O: just some global variable definitions.
> ✔ The pointer variables declared in this module are made global. Every other function in every other module can have access to them.

And now, the guts (Part 1)

To link together several modules in a program, you need — what? Anyone? Anyone?

Yes, you need *other modules*. Start with the first one shown here, which isn't as horrid as it looks.

Type this source code into your editor. Because it's basically eight sets of similar while and if loops, you can copy and paste to create them all. The following Blow-by-Blow sidebar tells you what's going on. This module essentially asks questions — hence the name you should use to save it to disk: Q.C:

Name: Q.C

```
#include <stdio.h>
#include <stdlib.h>
#include <string.h>
#include <malloc.h>

#define TRUE 1

extern char *noun;
extern char *adj1;
extern char *adj2;
extern char *smell;
extern char *friend;
extern char *verb;
extern char *day;
extern char *occupation;

void get_questions()
{
    char buffer[64];
    int len;

/* Get the NOUN */

    while(TRUE)
    {
        printf("Enter a noun:");
        gets(buffer);
        len = strlen(buffer);
        if(len) break;
    }
    noun = (char *)malloc(len+1);
    if(noun==NULL)
    {
```

(continued)

(continued)

```
            puts("\nMemory error");
            exit(1);
    }
    strcpy(noun,buffer);

/* Get ADJ1 */

    while(TRUE)
    {
        printf("Enter an adjective:");
        gets(buffer);
        len = strlen(buffer);
        if(len) break;
    }
    adj1 = (char *)malloc(len+1);
    if(adj1==NULL)
    {
        puts("\nMemory error");
        exit(1);
    }
    strcpy(adj1,buffer);

/* Get the ADJ2 */

    while(TRUE)
    {
        printf("Enter another adjective:");
        gets(buffer);
        len = strlen(buffer);
        if(len) break;
    }
    adj2 = (char *)malloc(len+1);
    if(adj2==NULL)
    {
        puts("\nMemory error");
        exit(1);
    }
    strcpy(adj2,buffer);

/* Get the SMELL */

    while(TRUE)
    {
```

```
            printf("Enter a smell:");
            gets(buffer);
            len = strlen(buffer);
            if(len) break;
        }
        smell = (char *)malloc(len+1);
        if(smell==NULL)
        {
            puts("\nMemory error");
            exit(1);
        }
        strcpy(smell,buffer);

/* Get the FRIEND */

        while(TRUE)
        {
            printf("Enter a friend's name:");
            gets(buffer);
            len = strlen(buffer);
            if(len) break;
        }
        friend = (char *)malloc(len+1);
        if(friend==NULL)
        {
            puts("\nMemory error");
            exit(1);
        }
        strcpy(friend,buffer);

/* Get the VERB */

        while(TRUE)
        {
            printf("Enter a verb:");
            gets(buffer);
            len = strlen(buffer);
            if(len) break;
        }
        verb = (char *)malloc(len+1);
        if(verb==NULL)
        {
            puts("\nMemory error");
```

(continued)

(continued)

```
            exit(1);
        }
    strcpy(verb,buffer);

/* Get the DAY */

    while(TRUE)
    {
        printf("Enter a day of the week:");
        gets(buffer);
        len = strlen(buffer);
        if(len) break;
    }
    day = (char *)malloc(len+1);
    if(day==NULL)
    {
        puts("\nMemory error");
        exit(1);
    }
    strcpy(day,buffer);

/* Get the OCCUPATION */

    while(TRUE)
    {
        printf("Enter an occupation:");
        gets(buffer);
        len = strlen(buffer);
        if(len) break;
    }
    occupation = (char *)malloc(len+1);
    if(occupation==NULL)
    {
        puts("\nMemory error");
        exit(1);
    }
    strcpy(occupation,buffer);
}
```

BLOW BY BLOW

The same routines over and over inside the Q.C source code

The Q.C source code isn't a bear to type; it's a copy-and-paste job. You can probably write it in a more elegant way, but it would make the program more complex and harder to describe. It's best to start out with the Big Note Easy Reading method, which is a technique I stole from the Liberace Big Note piano books.

The program's first significant moment comes when all the global variables declared in the MADLIB2.C module are referenced in this module:

```
extern char *noun;
extern char *adj1;
extern char *adj2;
extern char *smell;
extern char *friend;
extern char *verb;
extern char *day;
extern char *occupation;
```

The extern keyword tells the compiler that these variables exist elsewhere in the program, in another module. Extern is followed by the proper variable declaration. The compiler doesn't allocate storage space for the variables; it merely knows that they exist externally to this module.

The program then asks eight questions and fills in each string variable with the eight text answers. An endless while loop is used to ensure that users type a response to each question:

```
while(TRUE)
```

The question is asked, and an answer is stored in the buffer:

```
printf("Enter a noun:");
```

```
gets(buffer);
```

A strlen function then checks to see whether the buffer contains a string or whether the user typed nothing:

```
len = strlen(buffer);
```

If the user didn't type anything, the value of len is zero and the loop continues to repeat endlessly. Otherwise, len is non-zero (TRUE), so a break statement leaves the loop:

```
if(len) break;
```

The second part allocates space for the string. Remember that only pointers were declared in the MADLIB2.C. A malloc function is used to allocate space for the string:

```
noun = (char *)malloc(len+1);
```

The amount of space needed is calculated as the length of the string plus one character for the NULL byte. The space is then allocated to the proper variable (noun, in the preceding line).

A test is then made to ensure that memory was allocated; if not, the program quits:

```
if(noun==NULL)
{
    puts("\nMemory error");
    exit(1);
}
```

Otherwise, a strcpy function is used to copy the string input from the buffer to the newly allocated space assigned to the external pointer variable:

```
strcpy(noun,buffer);
```

These steps are repeated for each of the eight string variables declared in the program.

More guts (Part II)

The final module of the MADLIB2.C program displays the answers you enter inside a funny story — which is the essence of a Madlib.

Type the following source code into your editor. Name the file A.C, for *a*nswers:

Name: A.C

```c
#include <stdio.h>

extern char *noun;
extern char *adj1;
extern char *adj2;
extern char *smell;
extern char *friend;
extern char *verb;
extern char *day;
extern char *occupation;

void print_answers()
{
    printf("Yesterday I saw the ugliest %s I'd\n",noun);
    printf("ever seen. It was %s, %s and it\n",adj1,adj2);
    printf("smelled like %s. So I told %s\n",smell,friend);
    printf("to %s to it. But %s refused\n",verb,friend);
    printf("since it was %s and %s\n",day,friend);
    printf("is a %s.\n",occupation);
}
```

Compile and link everything. Refer to the following instructions for your compiler:

To link the modules in Borland C, use the bcc command followed by each module name:

```
bcc madlib2.c a.c q.c
```

Put a space between each module name. Do not use commas or plus signs to connect the files.

In Microsoft C, follow the cl command with each module name:

```
cl madlib2.c a.c q.c
```

You will probably never compile-only a program, but here are the instructions in case you do

Most of the time in your multiple-module career, you compile and link all at one time. For a brief moment, however, you may want to compile a module without linking it to anything. For example, you may want the compiler just to reassure you that there are no errors. If so, you have to do a compile-only operation.

To compile any source code file without linking, you use the compile-only switch. For Borland C, it's the `-c` option after `bcc` on the command line:

```
bcc -c module.c
```

In this example, the source code file MODULE.C is compiled *but not linked*. Any compiler errors are displayed as usual.

In Microsoft C, you use the `/C` option after the `cl` command to compile-only:

```
cl /c module.c
```

In this line, the compiler creates an object file for MODULE.C, but it does not link the file.

Separate each filename with a space.

Refer to your C compiler's manual for linking instructions.

If you see any errors, fix them. Then recompile using the same command.

The result is a program called MADLIB2.C, which you can run right now. Follow the instructions on-screen and enter all the responses requested. For example:

```
Enter a noun:car
Enter an adjective:big
Enter another adjective:ugly
Enter a smell:toast
Enter a friend's name:Tom
Enter a verb:run
Enter a day of the week:Monday
Enter an occupation:banker
```

Press Enter to see the story:

```
Yesterday I saw the ugliest car I'd
ever seen. It was big, ugly and it
smelled like toast. So I told Tom
```

(continued)

(continued)

```
to run to it. But Tom refused
since it was Monday and Tom
is a banker.
```

If you don't think that this is the most hilarious Madlib ever concocted, make up your own, better one. It should be a cinch to do if you use MADLIB2.C as a base.

Lesson 14-2 Quiz

1. If you're going to be working on a big project, it's always best to

   A. Put everything in its own directory.

   B. Get a *humongous* advance.

   C. Work for a company that has generous stock options.

   D. Overbid.

2. True or false: It is not necessary to compile each module after you create it.

3. Which country has the most universities?

   A. China.

   B. India.

   C. Russia.

   D. United States.

4. How would a module use the following external variable?

   ```
   extern char *pointer;
   ```

   A. `puts(extern *pointer);`

   B. `puts(*pointer);`

   C. `puts(extern pointer);`

   D. `puts(pointer);`

Lesson 14-3: More Multiple-Module Madness!

The purpose of multiple modules is not to make your source code files smaller. Although that helps, the real advantage is that you can create common routines in C and easily reuse them by linking in the new module or OBJ file. This is how some programmers can slap together decent-looking stuff in no time: They simply borrow bits and pieces of programs they've completed in the past.

 ✔ There's no use in reinventing the wheel every time you start a new project.

 ✔ As you continue to program, you gather various functions and modules that handle routine tasks. You can reuse them on new projects to your heart's content.

 ✔ Take advantage of your compiler's software library. It has dozens and dozens of routines for doing both simple and complex things, from manipulating the screen to moving blocks of memory to drawing graphics and bleating out sounds.

Bringing in other modules

Don't you prefer DOS programs and utilities that clear the screen before they do their stuff? Me too. Like me, you probably have this type of routine just lying around on your hard disk, probably left over from Lesson 5-6 in Volume I of this book.

Make sure that you're in the MADLIB2 directory you created in the preceding lesson.

Copy the ZAPSCRN2.C file from your CSTUFF directory into MADLIB2.C, and rename the file CLS.C. Here's the DOS command you need:

```
C:\CSTUFF\MADLIB2> COPY ..\ZAPSCRN2.C CLS.C
```

(This command works only if you're in the MADLIB2.C directory and have the old ZAPSCRN2.C program in the CSTUFF directory.)

The CLS.C program (formerly ZAPSCRN2.C) isn't ready to be linked into anything in its present state. You must first edit the file to remove its main function and then recompile and link before it becomes useful:

Name: CLS.C

```c
#include <stdio.h>
#include <dos.h>

#define VIDEO 0x10      //Video interrupt
#define COLS 80         //Screen width
#define ROWS 25         //Screen rows

void cls(void);
void locate(int row,int col);

void cls(void)
{
  union REGS regs;

  regs.h.ah=0x06;       //call function 6, scroll window
  regs.h.al=0x00;       //clear screen
  regs.h.bh=0x07;       //make screen "blank" color
  regs.h.ch=0x00;       //upper left row
  regs.h.cl=0x00;       //upper left column
  regs.h.dh=ROWS-1;     //lower right row
  regs.h.dl=COLS-1;     //lower right column
  int86(VIDEO,&regs,&regs);

  locate(0,0);          //"home" the cursor
}

/* LOCATE Function
  Move the cursor to position row,col, where row ranges
  from 0 to 79 and col from 0 to 24. Upper left corner =
  0,0; lower right corner = 79,24
*/

void locate(int row,int col)
{
  union REGS regs;

  regs.h.ah=0x02;       //video function 2, move cursor
  regs.h.bh=0x00;       //video screen (always 0)
  regs.h.dh=col;        //cursor's column position
  regs.h.dl=row;        //cursor's row position
  int86(VIDEO,&regs,&regs);
}
```

Edit the CLS.C source code so that it resembles the preceding source code. (If you're new to this book, just type the preceding source code.) You're essentially removing the main function from the program and leaving cls and locate, which are two handy functions any program can use. Remember to save when you're done editing.

To make the cls function useful to the MADLIB2.C program, you must call it and link it in. Modify the main function in MADLIB2.C to read

```
void main()
{
  cls();
  get_questions();
  cls();
  print_answers();
}
```

Save the MADLIB2.C file back to disk.

Compile and link. Remember that you're adding the new CLS.C module to the rest. Here are the compiling commands:

```
bcc madlib2.c a.c q.c cls.c
```

```
cl madlib2.c a.c q.c cls.c
```

Fix any errors.

Run!

The output is unchanged, but the cleared screen really makes it more enjoyable.

Time to go nuts! You can get really excessive with modifications to a program after you start linking in alien modules. For example, you can now use the locate function to display text in a specific row and column on-screen. Getting fancy is no longer a problem!

- ✔ Not to burst any bubbles or anything, but the cls and locate functions are really nothing special. Most compilers include similar functions in the CONIO.H, GRAPH.H, or DOS.H header files.

- ✔ The cls equivalent command for Borland C is clrscr. It clears the screen and homes the cursor (just like cls). You must include the CONIO.H header file for the clrscr function to work.

✔ The equivalent `locate` command in Borland C is `gotoxy`. Although it works like `locate`, the row and column values are reversed. As with `clsscr`, you must include the CONIO.H header file.

✔ I pronounce `gotoxy` as "go to ecks why," not "go-TOX-ee," like a detergent.

✔ In Microsoft C, the `_clearscreen` function is used to clear the screen and home the cursor, like `cls`. You must include the GRAPH.H header file for it to work.

✔ The `settextposition` function in Microsoft C is the equivalent to this book's `locate` command (with `row` and `column` values in that order). You must include the GRAPH.H header to make the compiler happy.

Many modules for you!

I've written many communications programs, but have written the core routines only once. For each new program, I bring in the core file, which I call CMCORE.C (for communications core), and just write new routines. There's no need to stew over reinventing the wheel every time.

As with the CLS.C module, you can create other modules by using the bits and pieces of programs introduced to you in this book. For example, the following is a RANDOM.C module, which you can link into those programs that require a random number:

Name: RANDOM.C

```
/*
 * Random-number routines: rnd and seedrnd
 */

#include <stdlib.h>
#include <time.h>        //for the seedrnd() function

int rnd(int range);
void seedrnd(void);

/* Generate a random value */

int rnd(int range)
{
  int r;

  r=rand()%range;        //spit up random num.
  return(r);
```

```
}

/* Seed the randomizer */

void seedrnd(void)
{
  srand((unsigned)time(NULL));
}
```

Here's a module containing the input function introduced in Lessons 9-2 and 9-3 in Chapter 9:

Name: INPUT.C

```
#include <stdio.h>
#include <conio.h>

#define CR 0x0d        //carriage return
#define LF 0x0a        //line feed
#define BACKSPACE 0x08
#define NULL 0         //empty character
#define TRUE 1
#define FALSE 0

void input(char *string, int length);

void input(char *string, int length)
{
    int done = FALSE;
    int index = 0;
    char ch;

    string[0] = NULL;    //init the buffer

    do
    {
        ch = getch();

/* Check to see if the buffer is full */

        if (index == length)
        {
            switch(ch)
```

(continued)

(continued)

```
            {
                case CR:
                    break;
                default:
                    ch = NULL;
                    break;
            }
        }

/* Process the keyboard input */

        switch(ch)
        {
            case CR:            //Enter key
                putchar(ch);
                putchar(LF);
                string[index] = NULL;
                done = TRUE;
                break;
            case BACKSPACE:
                if(index==0)
                {
                    break;
                }
                else
                {
                    putchar(ch);
                    putchar(' ');
                    putchar(ch);
                    index--;
                    break;
                }
            case NULL:
                break;
            default:            //display & sto
                putchar(ch);
                string[index] = ch;
                index++;
                break;
        }
    }
    while(!done);
}
```

The following module contains printing functions that are introduced in Chapter 8:

Name: PRINT.C

```c
/*
 * Printing routines
 */

#include <dos.h>

#define PRINTER 0x17        //BIOS printer port
#define LPT1 0x00           //LPT1, your first printer
#define EJECT 0x0c          //Eject page printer command

void prnstring(char *string);
void eject(void);
void prnchar(char c);

void prnstring(char *string)
{
  while(*string)      //while there's a character to print
      prnchar(*string++);   //print it and increment
}

void eject(void)
{
  prnchar(EJECT);
}

void prnchar(char c)
{
  union REGS regs;

  regs.h.ah=0x00;           //print character function
  regs.h.al=c;              //character to print
  regs.x.dx=LPT1;           //printer port to print to
  int86(PRINTER,&regs,&regs);
}
```

✔ There's no need to type these functions. Merely edit the original source files from which they came and save the file to disk under a new name.

✔ To use any of these functions in your programs, simply call them and link in the proper source code module.

✔ Don't forget to call the seedrnd function before using the rnd function in a program. This step ensures that the number is randomized based on the time of day. Also remember that rnd returns a number in the range of zero to the value you indicate.

Lesson 14-3 Quiz

1. Which of the following is a real-life, honest-to-goodness Elvis activity?

    A. Shooting flash bulbs floating in a swimming pool.

    B. Putting on gloves and a football helmet to launch fireworks at his friends.

    C. Shooting TV sets at home and on the road.

    D. Buying people Cadillacs.

2. You can pull in any old function to become a module in your program. Just remember to

    A. Remove any main function from the program, leaving only the function you want to use.

    B. Recompile the source code.

    C. Link the source code into your new program.

    D. All of the above.

3. True or false: Your compiler library contains routines similar to cls, locate, and random.

4. Coffee is a

    A. Seed.

    B. Fruit.

    C. Bean.

    D. Legume.

Lesson 14-4: You and Your Programs

If you've made it this far, congratulations!

I bailed out of my first C programming book after Chapter 2. The next C programming book got me to Chapter 2 and a little way into Chapter 3. I was able to get up to Chapter 6 in the last C tutorial book I bought, and then I read Chapter 9 on disk access and haven't opened that book since.

Basic C programmer knowledge tidbits

Programmers have a lingo all their own. Most of these folks have been programming for years, weaned on ancient VAX or UNIX systems in college. That experience gives them an insight that can't be taught but that can be mimicked.

For starters, I recommend picking up *The New Hacker's Dictionary,* edited by Eric Raymond (The MIT Press, ISBN 0-262-68069-6). You may not get every tidbit in the book, but it helps you to understand a programmer's mindset.

In addition to the book, take into consideration these suggestions:

✔ Be able to quote spontaneously from *Monty Python and the Holy Grail.*

✔ Use foo as a sample variable or filename (from *foobar,* for Fouled Up Beyond All Recognition).

✔ Always call storage space a "buffer."

✔ Revere *Star Trek* (the original '60s TV show).

✔ Lose your hygiene skills (unless you want to keep your wife or girlfriend — or both!).

✔ Keep in mind that old food is still good. Pizzas are better the next morning. Doughnuts don't gain true favor with a programmer until you can audibly rap them on a tabletop.

✔ Discover 2:00 a.m.

You can always ignore these suggestions and start a trend of your own. Remember that I slipped into the programmer community quite easily, and — like you — I am self-taught.

What I'm trying to say is thanks for reading this book and for getting this far. I hope that it has been a fun journey for you, and I also hope that you have had some sleep and exercise during the past few days.

A few, lingering thoughts are always waiting for you as you finish a massive two-volume tome like *C For Dummies* or any other programming book. This lesson gives you a summary of those thoughts to help you make the transition from budding learner to blossoming codester.

Debugging

Every programming project has warnings, errors, and bugs in it. Of the three, bugs are the most evil. They aren't typos. They aren't a user's fault. They're misjudgments in program logic, things you didn't think of, and misplaced or unfinished thoughts. They'll drive you bonkers.

In C, you see the warnings and errors when you compile and link. These problems are easy to fix because most compilers give you a clue about which line contains the offensive statement. Newer environments even highlight a missing semicolon, parenthesis, or curly bracket. Fixing it is a snap.

Linker errors mean missing header files, or missing OBJ files, if you're making a multiple-module project. Again, this error is easy to fix.

Bugs are just frustrating. The program runs, but not *right*. Here are some hints for tracking down bugs:

Make liberal use of random printf **statements.** At various spots where your program goes astray, stick in a printf statement to display the variable's values. Use the exact variable format you're using in the program:

```
printf("\n***%i***\n",*var++);
```

In this example, the value of variable *var++ is displayed. It may look something like this:

```
***245***
```

That number would appear when your program runs, giving you an idea of whether the variable contains the program value. If not, then you know where to adjust the program.

Repeating the same printf statement before and after a function also tells you what's going on.

Mind your parentheses. Especially in a complex if comparison, make sure that you have the proper number of parentheses and the right items between them. The compiler doesn't tell you when you have a goofy if comparison:

```
if(toupper(cheddar[i]=='H'))
```

In this example, the first right parenthesis should appear after the cheddar[i] variable, not after the 'H'. The if comparison still works and probably would be TRUE all the time, but it's not what you intended.

Also check while loop conditions for this same type of error.

Remember the break **in a** switch-case **structure.** Your program continues to flow through every case item in a switch-case structure until a break is encountered. For example:

```
switch(ch)
{
   case 'A':
   case 'E':
   case 'I':
   case 'O':
   case 'U':
        puts("It's a vowel");
   case 'B':
// and so on....
   case 'Z':
        puts("It's a voiced consonant");
   default:
        puts("It's an unvoiced consonant");
}
```

If ch is a vowel, the following is displayed:

```
It's a vowel
It's a voiced consonant
It's an unvoiced consonant
```

Granted, this error would be easier to see than some program in which math was done for various case statements. In some cases, such as A-E-I-O-U in this example, you want execution to flow through the case statements. Even so, don't forget the breaks where you need them.

Don't mess up a for loop. Here's something the compiler never catches:

```
for(x=0;x=5;x++);
```

If you have ever been poisoned by the BASIC language, you may forget that the second item in a C language for loop is a condition, not a comparison. In the preceding example, it doesn't read, "Keep looping while the value of x is equal to 5." It reads, "Keep looping while TRUE because x equals 5 now." Remember that x=5 is an assignment, not a comparison. Assignments usually evaluate as TRUE in an if or while condition.

The second item in a for loop is usually a comparison, such as in an if statement, but typically with a less-than or greater-than operator.

While you're on the subject of loops:

Beware of endless loops! They can creep up on you. Many programs need some type of endless loop but then rely on some type of machine inside the loop to break out. There's nothing wrong with this technique, but make sure that the method for breaking the loop works!

Honestly, sometimes I think that endless loops are the only reason programmers insist on using computers with a manual Reset button.

- ✔ Debugging isn't limited to this handful of tips. Just about anything you do in C can cause an error if it's done incorrectly.

- ✔ Many integrated environments come with debugging tools and tracers. I've never used them. If you do, remember that the tracing information adds bulk to your program size. Be sure to turn off the tracing options when you finally compile your program for real.

- ✔ You end up hunting bugs more than you actually code. One programmer I know said that "coding" should really be called "bugging."

- ✔ Another programmer maxim: The last 10 percent of a project takes 90 percent of the time to complete.

Programs to help you

A smattering of traditional C language helper programs and utilities are available. Some of these programs may have come with your compiler (though they tend to be command-line programs). You may be able to download others from the Internet or some online service. They aren't necessary, but they can help!

Grep. Grep is actually a UNIX command, though versions of it exist for DOS too. Grep is a tool that scans one or more files for specific bits of text and displays the results. If you want to find all the references to the blech function in your code, for example, you could use something like

```
grep -i "blech" *.c
```

This command searches for the text blech in all source code files (*.c). The -i tells grep to ignore upper- and lowercase differences.

Yeah, they could have thought of a better name for it. Grep stands for Global Replace Expression Print — not very mnemonic, but that reflects its UNIX background.

Lib (Librarian). A librarian command can be used to organize a group of modules into one handy unit for linking. Rather than always have to remember which module contains the cls function and which contains rnd, you merely link in a common library file that contains them both.

Borland C++ still comes with the old Tlib command, used to create library files. I've never used the command, though it seems like a handy thing to have for real-life programmers.

Lint. Lint is a compiler warning and error-checking program. It scans your source code and looks for things that may go wrong: missing semicolons, nonportable pointers, and missing pairs of parentheses or curly brackets.

Most of today's compilers and linkers generate warnings and errors similar to the old lint program. Inside your integrated environment, you can set the degree of various items for which the compiler flags as an error or warning. In the old days, running your source code through lint before compiling saved you from some nasty (and hard-to-find) errors.

Make. Make is yet another utility that today's compilers render obsolete. In the olden days, you would use the make command to build or rebuild source code and object files into a program; make, not cl or bcc, was the command you typed to compile and link.

What make did was to compare the dates and times of your source code, object, and program files. If one file was newer than another, it was recompiled and linked to create a new program. After fussing with your source code, you simply typed make and the make program did the rest for you.

Borland C++ still comes with the make utility. Because it's based on the traditional UNIX make utility, the Borland make has a rather crude and cryptic syntax. Because the bcc command now takes care of pretty much the same things as make does, however, there's no point in going into it here.

Microsoft C++ has a make utility called nmake. I'm not familiar with it at all because I stole my copy of Microsoft C++ and don't have the manual. (That's not true: I have the manual — I just haven't played with nmake enough to say anything substantial about it.)

Touch. This fun but strange program stamps every file in the current directory (or only those files you specify) with the current date and time. Your operating system normally puts the date and time on a file when you save it to disk. Touch changes that.

If you want to update the MADLIB2.C file with the current date and time, for example, you type

```
touch madlib2.c
```

This line doesn't change the source code file; only the file's date and time are reset. This process is how big companies such as Microsoft and Borland are able to ship you files and programs that all have the same date and time; they merely touch the whole lot of them before the product ships.

New versions of old junk

I had a boss once whose favorite end-of-project saying was, "Shoot the engineer." Such a drastic step is often necessary because engineers (of which "computer programmer" is a type) love to tinker and tinker until it's "just so." And then they tinker some more. Toward the end of a project, we would walk around the offices with riot guns and blow away all the engineers. Boy, how the nighttime clean-up crew hated us. . . .

Seriously, "Shoot the engineer" doesn't mean killing anyone. It means prying away their keyboard and source code from them to finish a project. (To some engineers, this is akin to death. Many Academy Awards could be given out around the last day of a project.)

No programming project is ever "done." Eventually, you want to add something new or change the way something looks, and it's never really basic stuff that changes. It's something called *creeping elegance,* which is the desire to tinker with something in a manner that impresses only yourself.

Of course, no project has to be over. When you're done with one version, you just create another. You have Version 1.0, then 1.1, then 2.0, and maybe Version 3.0. Or you can be like Microsoft with Word and Excel and skip up to Version 6.0 or whatever version number your competition is up to.

After your users tire of version numbers (meaning that they will no longer pay for an upgrade), you have to think of new product *names.* After all, no newbies care whether they have Hello 3.4 or Hello 4.0. Your next step: Hello II.

You can continue with version numbers for the II edition of your product, or you can go down the wordy route to produce naming: Follow Hello II with Hello Plus and then Hello Plus Gold. Lure advanced users into purchasing Hello Pro. Then get real trendy and go for a year: Hello 2000.

- ✔ The word is out: Most people, even first-time shoppers, avoid Version 1.0 of any program. Solution: Don't call it that!

- ✔ Keep in mind that year-names date a product. I blanched when Microsoft announced that the new version of Windows would be Windows 95. It's now 1997 as I write this chapter, which makes the "new" Windows seem as though it's two years old. And we all know how two-year-olds can be.

- ✔ Forget about naming things "2000." That year will come and go. How about Hello Millennium?

Where to go from here?

Go out and program! Code, code, code! You can do it. There are only a few topics this book did not discuss. These topics are discussed on this book's unofficial Web site and, if there's enough interest, in a potential Volume III of this book (but don't hold your breath for it).

Here are the additional topics that would be fun to explore, had I the room in this book:

- ✔ Programming Windows
- ✔ Graphics programming
- ✔ Sound programming
- ✔ Online communications programming

There are other, nerdier topics, plus some specific stuff that goes into more depth than this book or Volume I ever got into. In all honesty, learning C is an ongoing trek. Just as I said in Volume I, no programmer is fool enough to say, "I know *everything* about C that there is to know!" Good programmers learn new tricks all the time.

- ✔ If you want a Volume III of this book, write to Brand Manager, Dummies Press, 7260 Shadeland Station, Indianapolis, IN 46256.
- ✔ If you want to visit the unofficial Web page, point your Web browser to http://www.wambooli.com/c.for.dummies/.

The odd end-note

Of course, if you *really* want to end this book on an odd note, try the following program. Type the source code into your editor. Save it to disk as NUTS.CPP (you must use the CPP ending on the file when you save):

Name: NUTS.CPP

```
#include <iostream.h>

void main()
{
    cout << "I think I'm going to go nuts.\n";
}
```

Heh, heh.

Compile and link. (The same commands you've been using to compile and link should work for this program, though you have to be sure to specify the CPP extension rather than just C.)

Run:

```
I think I'm going to go nuts.
```

No, you're not going nuts. You just wrote, compiled, and ran your very first C++ program. Now, there's a whole can of worms I *really* don't have the pages for!

- ✔ There's an off-chance that you may have a very old compiler that doesn't understand C++. Most of the new stuff does, but if you're running, for example, an ancient Turbo C compiler or some type of generic compiler, it may not get the program at all.

- ✔ The IOSTREAM.H header file is to C++ what STDIO.H is to C. It contains basic I/O functions and definitions.

- ✔ The cout in the program is a name representing standard output — the stdout device. (Technically, it's the "output stream." Uh-huh.)

- ✔ The << thing is the *insertion operator*. It sends the string to the standard output device, cout. Hey! No printf!

- ✔ My opinion? Forget C++! For all its fancy object-oriented hogwash, the honest truth is that most of C++ programming is pure, basic C programming. There's no situation, in fact, in which you cannot do something in C that someone else is doing in C++. Take the NUTS.CPP program as an example: How many ways could you write something that does the same thing using plain C? See what I mean?

- ✔ Another bit o' trivia: Back before C++ came out, there was serious debate over whether to call the next version of the C language D or P. I don't know where the P came from or what it means. Must be some kind of inside joke.

Lesson 14-4 Quiz

1. What is a bug?

   A. Any type of insect, including arachnids and worms and viruses, even.

   B. Something nasty that creeps into your program, typically an error in logic and not anything the compiler or linker catches.

C. Something a user does to foul up input.

D. A listening device.

2. What did the `lint` program do?

A. Cleansed one's belly button.

B. A humorous prank, it caused this thin layer of dust to cling to the outer surface of your CRT.

C. Cleaned up your source code.

D. Flagged potential errors and goofs in your source code.

3. Pretty much anyone can tell you that the first name of Lewis (of the famed Lewis and Clark team) was Meriwether. What was Clark's first name?

A. Bob.

B. Bill.

C. Joe.

D. Spunky.

4. The middle item in a `for` loop is a

A. Condition.

B. Comparison.

C. Assignment.

D. Preposition.

Chapter 14 Final Exam

1. What is a *module?*

    A. A Horta egg.

    B. A source code file that's one of many source code files.

    C. No, it's the object code file, not the source code file.

    D. "Module" is how Tolstoy refers to various chapters in *War and Peace.*

2. It's called a linker because

    A. Ed Linker wrote the first one.

    B. The programmer was a big Lincoln Logs fan.

    C. It rhymes with stinker.

    D. It links together various object code modules.

    E. *What's* called a linker?

3. To share a variable between two or more modules, you

    A. Declare the variable as an `extern`.

    B. Declare the variable as a global.

    C. Declare the variable as a global `extern`.

    D. Declare the variable in both modules.

4. What was the original name of Bill Gates' company before it became Microsoft?

    A. Microcomputer Software.

    B. Micro Corps.

    C. Traf-o-Data.

    D. Gates & Allen Software.

5. Just to be fair, who or what is Borland named after?

    A. The legendary prospector Frank Borland.

    B. Borland, California.

    C. Phillipe Borlande, the company's founder.

    D. A character in a science fiction novel.

6. True or false: The first module in a multi-module program must be called `main`.

7. Name the only sport in which the winning team moves backward.

8. Art Linkletter.

   A. Who?

   B. Art would use the `link` command to create LETTER.EXE.

   C. *Kids Say the Darndest Things.*

   D. "I heartily endorse this game."

9. Which is the longest type of snake?

   A. Anaconda.

   B. Royal python.

   C. Indian python.

   D. Monty python.

10. It's obvious that the author has run out of legitimate questions for this final exam.

    A. True.

    B. False.

    C. Unfortunately, because I promised that every final exam in this book would contain 16 questions, I must live up to it.

    D. And just why are there questions anyway when the answers are in the back of the book?

11. What happens if you forget to link in a module?

    A. The linker produces an error.

    B. The compiler produces an error.

    C. No error appears, though the program won't run right.

    D. None of the above.

12. Which two countries have participated in every modern Olympics since 1896? (Pick two.)

    A. Australia.   E. Canada.

    B. France.   F. Germany.

    C. Great Britain.   G. Greece.

    D. Turkey.   H. United States.

13. True or false: You must recompile all modules when you add a new module to a program.

14. True or false: There's no need to declare a header file such as STDIO.H for all your modules if you plan to link them together.

15. What mystical power did Elvis claim to have?

   A. He could move clouds.

   B. He could communicate with animals.

   C. He could sense colors by touch.

   D. He could leave his body during sleep.

16. True or false: You are now done learning the C language.

Go ahead — collapse!

Appendix A
Answers to Exercises

• •

*H*ere are the answers for the various quizzes and exams at the end of each lesson and chapter in this book. Since the passage of Goals 2000 in the United States, I subscribe to the notion that *everyone is a winner;* therefore, no matter what, you passed every single quiz or exam in this book. Give yourself a star. If you ever plan to be anything in this world, however, you must know the correct answer from an incorrect one. Grade yourself as follows:

- For every wrong answer, subtract one from your score.
- For every correct answer, add one to your score.
- The person with the highest score gets the highest-paying job.
- The person with the next-highest score gets to work for Microsoft, which doesn't pay well but has excellent benefits.
- The person with the lowest score gets to program for an unappreciative volunteer organization.

Lesson 8-1 Quiz Answers

1. It's an endless `for` loop, so give yourself a brown M&M if you answered either A or B.

2. B.

3. B.

4. A.

5. C. Traditionally, you get a gift on only the 1st, 5th, 10th, 15th, 20th, 25th, 50th, and 60th anniversaries. Nontraditionally, leather is given for the third year.

Lesson 8-2 Quiz Answers

1. C.
2. C.
3. B.
4. A.

Lesson 8-3 Quiz Answers

1. D.
2. C.
3. The code can be rewritten using any endless loop structure:

```
while(1)
    printf("Hello Moon!\n");
```

or

```
for(;;)
    printf("Hello Moon!\n");
```

4. I think the sign means that the road needs fixing.

Lesson 8-4 Quiz Answers

1. D.
2. B.
3. D.
4. D.

Lesson 8-5 Quiz Answers

1. C. Answer B is incorrect because } characters appear all over a program, but only the final one in the main function ends the program.
2. D. It returns whatever value ZERO represents.
3. C.
4. A.

Chapter 8 Final Exam Answers

1. A. The `kbhit` function returns TRUE if any keys have been pressed and are waiting to be read from the keyboard buffer.

2. A. It's not a problem that `kbhit` doesn't read the characters, but those characters must be dealt with later in the program.

3. D. Although the toaster helps, it's the dextrose in the bread that turns it brown.

4. D.

5. E. There's no symbol for the square root in C?

6. C. Variable `a` is incremented to 11 and then its value given to variable `x`.

7. D. It's the fortress effect; you cannot surround a variable with incrementation operators — or any operator — like that.

8. B. California was most likely named by the Spanish conquistadors from the novel *Las Serged de Esplandian*. It was a utopia.

9. D.

10. B.

11. False. Real pirates spent the booty or gambled with it right away.

12. A. Windows reads the code as an `ERRORLEVEL` but doesn't do anything with the value.

13. C. Big Ben is the name of the bell in the famous tower.

Bonus Answer:

All the titles are books published in 1995. I did not make up any of them.

Lesson 9-1 Quiz Answers

1. D. The first element in an array is always element zero, `[0]`.

2. A.

3. E. All the items are true: Patrice was the smartest girl in high school, and her scores were intimidating.

4. A, B, and C declare floating-point arrays with three elements. The final declaration has room for only two elements.

5. B; the big blue ox was named Babe.

Lesson 9-2 Quiz Answers

1. B.

2. D. There are 17 characters in the string. The array must be 18 characters long, however, to count for the NULL byte. The compiler would figure that out for you automatically (answer A), but the strlen function would return 17 because it doesn't count the NULL byte.

3. A, B, and possibly D. A.) The string is most definitely altered. B.) The string would now read I want a fur boat. C.) This one is untrue because it's the 14th element being altered when you count element zero (whine[13] is the 14th element). D.) Because the question asks what would happen *after* the following statement, this answer is also correct.

4. C.

Lesson 9-3 Quiz Answers

1. B. The Enter key generates code 0x0d. It doesn't move the cursor unless you write the code to do that. Also, not every keyboard makes a clicking noise.

2. D.

3. C.

4. Probably C with some of D mixed in.

Bonus answer: Escape from your program

Whip out the source code for INPUT4.C and put it in your editor. You're about to make several changes that incorporate an Escape key to cancel input.

First, you have to change the prototype of the input function. It now returns a TRUE/FALSE integer value, so change Line 14 of your source code to read

```
int input(char *string);
```

Likewise, change the function declaration at Line 25:

```
int input(char *string)
```

In the input function, add the following variable declaration, just below the int done = FALSE:

```
int cancel = FALSE;
```

In the first switch-case structure, add the following line before the case CR:

```
case ESC:
```

This way, both the ESC and CR keystrokes are accepted by the program when the buffer is full.

In the second switch-case structure, add the following code to handle the Escape key (just before the case CR: series of statements):

```
case ESC:
  done = TRUE;
  cancel = TRUE;
  break;
```

Finally, after the final while(!done); statement, add the following line:

```
return(cancel);
```

That takes care of the input function. Now change the main function in the program to deal with it. The input function now returns a value of FALSE if something was typed or TRUE if the Escape cancel key was pressed. An if-not-else structure fixes things:

```
if(!input(string))
  printf("Darn glad to meet you, %s!\n",string);
else
  printf("\n*** Canceled");
```

Save the source code to disk as INPUT5.C. Compile and run.

Test the program a few times, and check the bounds, backspace, and finally the Escape key to cancel.

Lesson 9-4 Quiz Answers

1. C. You can't sort without making a comparison.

2. C.

3. D. This one is primarily true with bubble sorts, which are slow. Other types of sorts go faster, though the larger the array, the longer it takes.

4. A. The other items all can be found in various children's videos.

Lesson 9-5 Quiz Answers

1. A.

2. C. The toupper function converts lowercase letters to uppercase; isupper returns TRUE if a character is uppercase.

Questions 3, 4, and 5 refer to this snippet of code:

```
if(toupper(c) == 'Y')
```

3. False. The toupper function converts the contents of variable c to uppercase for the comparison. The variable's contents are not changed. You need something like the following to do that:

```
c = toupper(c);
```

4. True.

5. Probably true.

Lesson 9-6 Quiz Answers

1. C. The strcpy function is the only way to copy a string in C — unless you write your own function, of course.

2. C. The analemma is used mostly on sundials to account for variations in the sun's height in the sky throughout the year.

3. B.

4. C. The strcmp returns zero when it has a match. Zero just happens to be interpreted as a logical FALSE by if, while, and other C language functions.

Bonus Answer:

B. Marconi invented radio.

Lesson 9-7 Quiz Answers

1. B. You need more than one item to concatenate them.

2. B. Because the `strupr` function happens last (functions work from the inside out), the `noodle` string is all uppercase in the end.

3. A.

4. The little blue people of Saturday morning cartoon fame could answer A, B, and C. I prefer answer D.

Lesson 9-8 Quiz Answers

1. B.

2. A. Remember that because all arrays have zero as their first element, the second item in the second row would be `theatre[1][1];`.

3. D.

4. A.

5. A.

6. C. Cornbury (Edward Hyde) was rocking on his porch, wearing a woman's dress and knitting a doily, when his colonists first paid a visit. It was later discovered that he came to America to avoid creditors back home in England. His most lasting contribution to New York was giving his name to a chunk of land along the Hudson River. Today, it's still called Hyde Park.

Chapter 9 Final Exam Answers

1. A. Zero is the first element in every array.

2. C. That person may be the other things, but most people in line at an all-you-can-eat restaurant are hungry.

3. A.

4. D. `fish[2]` is the third element in the array.

5. A.

6. C.

7. A.

8. A.

9. A. It may take longer for a big database to print, but sorting was the answer I was looking for.

10. A.

11. C.

12. None. Carbon dioxide is not poison; carbon monoxide is.

13. D. Strings can be copied only by using the proper function.

14. A, though because FALSE is also zero, you could have answered C.

15. C. It's short for *taxi*meter *cab*riolet.

16. C.

17. D.

18. B.

19. A.

20. B. `array[2]` is the third string in a two-dimensional array.

21. C. "There is a fifth dimension beyond that which is known to man. . . ."

Lesson 10-1 Quiz Answers

1. A, though some compilers may produce a warning error, in which case answer B is also correct.

2. B.

3. C. A variable in memory actually has four descriptions: size, location, name, and type. So far, you know only size and location.

4. F. "Ping-pong" is the *sound* the ball makes.

5. A.

Lesson 10-2 Quiz Answers

1. D. Yes, it's all of the above — and more to come.

2. Both A and B will work; A uses two statements, and B declares everything on the same line.

3. A.

4. A-1, B-2, C-3, D-4.

5. B. Most people assume that Columbus had trouble funding his voyage because people in the late 1400s thought that the world was flat. Not so! They knew that the world was round but felt that Columbus was taking the wrong, *long* way to the Orient, when eastern passages had already been proven. (Ironically, they were right, but Columbus discovered the Americas, which made up for it.)

Lesson 10-3 Quiz Answers

1. C. The pointer and the variable to which it's assigned must be of the same type.

2. C.

3. B. You need an ampersand before an array element. You do not need the ampersand before the array name.

4. C.

Lesson 10-4 Quiz Answers

1. B.

2. C.

3. D. November 23 is actually Kinro-Kansha-No-Hi, the Labor Thanksgiving Day.

4. A and B are probably wrong, though A is most definitely wrong: You should never initialize a pointer with a constant value.

5. A. Beware pointers and * multiplication!

Lesson 10-5 Quiz Answers

1. A.

2. D.

3. B.

4. D. Always use the table.

5. D.

Lesson 10-6 Quiz Answers

1. A-1, B-2, C-3, D-4.

2. C.

3. They all have. Jing Abalos appeared in *Batman Fights Dracula* (1967), which was a foreign film, but my database doesn't say which country; Robert Lowery was in *Batman and Robin* (1949), which was an old serial; Lewis Wilson was the caped crusader in *Batman* (1943), another serial; and Kevin Conroy plays the voice of Batman in *Batman: The Animated Series,* which was originally released as a feature, *The Adventures of Batman and Robin* (1992).

4. C. You still have to declare the array using array notation. Otherwise, after it's properly initialized, a pointer can do anything you can do with array notation, and better.

Lesson 10-7 Quiz Questions

1. Why does `while(*s)` work when s has been initialized to point to a string?

2. If your library reference defines a function as requiring `char *string` as input, what type of input does it *really* want?

3. What's wrong with the following?:

```
int *array[3] = { 1, 2, 3 };
```

4. Name the only X-rated film ever to win an Academy Award (though the film was later rerated R).

Lesson 10-8 Quiz Answers

1. D. It was *Fatal Bond* in which she appeared, not *Fatal Blood* (sounds like a Linda Blair flick).

2. B. The `socks` function requires a `float` as input — not a pointer, so you need `socks(*smell);`.

3. A. Just pass the pointer's address.

4. D. Beware of pointers and multiplication! The value of the `*stinky` variable is multiplied by 100. That value is available to the `main` function because `stinky` is a pointer.

Lesson 10-9 Quiz Answers

1. C. Quonset Hut is a trademark for the cheesy-looking corrugated-metal ugly things the military is fond of.

2. B.

3. C.

4. A.

5. C; the function declares the array as a pointer.

6. B.

   Bonus question: A.

Chapter 10 Final Exam Answers

1. C.

2. C. The `sizeof` keyword always gives you the proper answer, though Table 3-3 lists the size for all PCs.

3. A. Although everything about pointers tends to annoy most programmers, the truth is that the dual nature of pointers drives everyone batty.

4. C. Before a pointer can be used, it must be *initialized*. This is the biggest bonehead mistake most programmers make.

5. B.

6. E. Unknown. On his deathbed, Dr. Einstein said something in German to his nurse. Because the nurse did not speak German, however, no one will ever know what Einstein's last words were.

7. C.

8. B.

9. C.

10. A.

11. C. Always use the table.

12. A-3, B-2, C-A, D-4, E-5, F-7, G-6, and H-8. (I'll bet that you thought I'd do another one-to-one, straight-across answer, huh? The Ms are the hardest codes to remember.)

13. C.

14. A.

15. B.

16. B, though the pointer could also be an integer array.

17. C.

18. A.

19. A, a floating-point pointer.

20. D. It really prevents a function from discarding its variables and their values after the function is done with its func.

Lesson 11-1 Quiz Answers

1. B. They may not be "jolly" variables, but they're variables.

2. A.

3. D, believe it or not. Aeolus is the god of the winds, Chloris is the goddess of flowers, and Nike is the god of victory (not the god of footwear).

4. C. If you use the putchar function (answer B), you would not have to enclose the variable name in single quotes.

Lesson 11-2 Quiz Answers

1. D, though you have to use strcpy only when you're copying string constants into a structure.

2. C. And I need not mention that initializing an array of structures is tedious and something you probably won't want to do more than once.

3. A. You can copy array elements just as you can copy any two variables in C. You cannot, however, copy the entire array with an equal sign.

4. A-4; B-3; C-1; D-2. There may be some debate about the water goblet and the red wine glass. Generally speaking, your water goblet is larger.

Lesson 11-3 Quiz Answers

1. C.

2. C. You must declare a structure variable (nabana) as well as define the structure type in the function.

3. C. B also returns a structure of the type mold, but it returns a pointer to the structure, which isn't really what the question asked for.

4. D. The Hundred Years' War lasted for 116 years.

Lesson 11-4 Quiz Answers

1. D.
2. C.
3. C, though because the value is zero, answers A and B are also correct (though improper).
4. A.

Lesson 11-5 Quiz Answers

1. A-4; B-1; C-3; D-2.
2. D.
3. C.
4. A.

Chapter 11 Final Exam Answers

1. B.
2. A.
3. B.
4. D.
5. Rudolph Diesel invented the diesel (compression) engine in 1892.
6. A.
7. C. Remember that you must define both the structure and a variable inside the function.
8. A.
9. A.
10. B.
11. A.
12. It has been theorized that *Gilligan's Island* is a metaphor for our lives. We all have our personal Skippers, Howells, and Gingers. Only by conquering our inner Gilligan, however, are we able to escape the traps of our lives. It makes sense: Whenever the castaways came close to being rescued, Gilligan fouled it up. If only Gilligan had had an "accident," I'm certain that they would have gotten off the island and freed up the airwaves for more decent TV, like *Gunsmoke*.

13. B. `malloc` does not return a pointer; rather, a pointer is the type of variable that holds the value (memory address) that `malloc` returns.

14. C. (Sorry about the strange wording of this question.)

15. A.

16. C.

Lesson 12-1 Quiz Answers

1. D.

2. A-1; B-2; C-3; D-4.

3. C. `fopen` returns a pointer to a file handle. If you want the file handle itself, you use the `fileno` function, though this is something you rarely need to know.

4. B. The FILE macro lets you create a pointer to a structure that holds a file handle.

Lesson 12-2 Quiz Answers

1. A, though everything is really a binary file. Text is meaningful only to us humans.

2. A-1; B-2; C-3; D-4.

3. What you come up with could look like this:

```
#include <stdio.h>
#include <stdlib.h>
#include <conio.h>
void main(int argc,char *argv[])
{
    FILE *viewfile;
    char buffer[81];     //storage
    int x = 0;
    char c;
    if(argc<2)
    {
        puts("Missing filename!");
        puts("Here is the format:");
```

```
        puts("VIEW filename");
        exit(1);
    }
viewfile = fopen(argv[1],"r");
if(!viewfile)
{
    printf("Error opening \"%s\"\n",argv[1]);
    exit(1);
}
while(fgets(buffer,80,viewfile))
{
    printf("%s",buffer);
    x++;
    if(!(x%24))
    {
        printf("Press Enter:");
        while(!kbhit())
            ;
        c = getch();
        if(c=='\x1b') exit(0);
        putchar('\n');
    }
}
}
```

4. Believe it or not, Donald Duck's middle name is still Fauntleroy.

Lesson 12-3 Quiz Answers

1. B.

2. C. The other terms are all derived from Japanese.

3. C.

4. A.

Lesson 12-4 Quiz Answers

1. D. There really isn't a structure-writing function per se. You can, however, sue the `fwrite` function to write the block of memory the function occupies to disk.

2. A. Trick question: The `fread` function can be used to read a structure from disk, but it is not a specific structure-reading function.

3. B. Mark Twain is, in fact, the only American author in the top ten list of most-published authors worldwide.

4. C. The first item in the `fwrite` function should be the name of a variable or a memory location (the starting point of a chunk to be written to disk). When you put `struct cheddar` there, you're only defining a structure, which isn't a variable, so nothing would be written to disk. Your compiler should alert you to this error as some type of bad or missing parameter.

Lesson 12-5 Quiz Answers

1. True. The I/O functions live in STDIO.H and other header files.

2. D, but also A on a PC, which calls the keyboard and screen the CON device.

3. A.

4. A-1; B-3; C-2; D-4.

5. True; the files are always open.

Chapter 12 Final Exam Answers

1. D.

2. A and B.

3. C.

4. C.

5. A. I made that one up. The others are really in there: Mahershalalhashbaz was Isaiah's son; Tilgarthpilneser was the king of Assyria; and Zaphnathpaaneah was the name given to Joseph by Pharaoh.

6. C.

7. True.

8. C, but also D.

9. D.

10. C.

11. A.

12. True. Even so, you should open a file in binary mode if you plan to write or read binary data.

13. False. Not necessarily true, but true for structures. For example, you could write text information to disk with `fwrite`, in which case just about any text-reading disk function can read it back.

14. B. Remember that C has no I/O functions of its own.

15. A.

16. A. Elvis loved them bumper cars!

Chapter 13 Quiz Answers

There was no quiz for Chapter 13. No final exam either.

Lesson 14-1 Quiz Answers

1. A. I don't know about you, but nothing is more disappointing to me than biting into a chocolate jelly bean — especially in the dark in a movie theater.

2. B.

3. C. Passing a variable to a function is not affected by placing that function in another module.

4. A.

Lesson 14-2 Quiz Answers

1. A.

2. True; although you can compile after writing the source code, you don't have to because both Borland and Microsoft C++ compile and link at the same time.

3. B. India has more than twice as many universities as the United States, with 7,513 as of 1990.

4. D.

Lesson 14-3 Quiz Answers

1. All of them.

2. D.

3. True.

4. C. Coffee is a bean, though it's surrounded by a fruity pulp.

Lesson 14-4 Quiz Answers

1. B.

2. D. Lint didn't fix anything; it only pointed out potential problems.

3. B. It was William, but Bill is close enough.

4. A.

Chapter 14 Final Exam Answers

1. B.

2. D.

3. B. The variable is shared by declaring it as a global. To access it from another module, you use the extern keyword.

4. C. Bill Gates' company originally produced devices that monitored traffic; hence, Traf-o-Data.

5. A.

6. False.

7. The only sport in which the winning team moves backward is tug-o-war.

8. Art Linkletter wrote a book and hosted a TV show called *Kids Say the Darndest Things*. He is also quoted on the box of the old Life game as saying, "I heartily endorse this game."

9. B. The Royal python can grow to be as much as 35 feet (10.7 meters) long.

10. A. Very true.

11. A. The linker catches all missing module (and missing header file) errors.

12. A and G; Australia and Greece.

13. False. You need only compile the new module and then link all the modules together.

14. False. Because you never know which other modules will be linked, you should always reference all header files required in any given module.

15. A. Believe it or not, Elvis actually claimed that he could make clouds move. Of course, you can too . . . if you look long enough!

16. False. Most definitely false. Yes, false.

Appendix B

Program Samples and Stuff

•••

*T*his appendix has some bonus programs you can type to help you practice some of the keen things you have read about in this book. When you type these programs, you do not have to type all the comments; they are there to explain what's going on — they're not anything you need to waste valuable typing molecules on.

The Scrolling Marquee

The MARQUEE.C program uses a pointer to creep through a string and display the results on-screen as a scrolling marquee. It's a variation of the final rendition of the STRING.C program from Lesson 10-7.

Name: MARQUEE.C

```c
/* Scrolling marquee program */
/* Uses cls() from Lesson 5-6 */
/* Uses locate() from Lesson 5-6 */
/* Uses input() from Lesson 9-3 */

#include <stdio.h>
#include <stdlib.h>
#include <string.h>
#include <conio.h>
#include <dos.h>
#include <alloc.h>

#define CR 0x0d        //carriage return
#define ESC 0x1b       //Escape key
#define TAB 0x09
#define LF 0x0a        //line feed
#define BACKSPACE 0x08
#define NULL 0         //empty character
```

(continued)

(continued)

```c
#define TRUE 1
#define FALSE 0
#define LENGTH 80      //size of the string
#define COLS 80        //screen width
#define VIDEO 0x10     //video interrupt
#define ROWS 25        //screen rows
#define DELAY 250      //millisecond delay
#define MROW 12        //the row on which text is displayed

void input(char *string, int length);
void cls(void);
void locate(int row,int col);

void main()
{
    char buffer[81];     //space character padding
    char text[LENGTH];   //input string
    char *marquee;       //the marquee
    char *sto;
    int m_size;
    long x;

/* Initialize the buffer full of spaces */

    for(x=0;x<80;x++)
        buffer[x] = ' ';      //spaces

    buffer[80] = '\0';        //NULL at the end

/* Get input */

    cls();
    puts("Enter a phrase to be scrolled 'cross the
            screen.");
    input(text,LENGTH);

/* Allocate the marquee */

    m_size = 80 + 80 + strlen(text) + 1;
    if((marquee = (char *)malloc(m_size)) == NULL)
```

```
        {
            puts("Out of memory");
            exit(1);
        }

/* Create the marquee */

    strcpy(marquee,buffer);
    strcat(marquee,text);
    strcat(marquee,buffer);

/* display the marquee and scroll */

    sto = marquee;

    for(;;)
    {
        marquee = sto;

        while(*(marquee+80))
        {
            locate(0,MROW);
            for(x=0;x<79;x++)
                putchar(*(marquee+x));
            if(kbhit())
            {
                getch();    //read key
                exit(0);    //exit on key
            }
            delay(DELAY);   //pause one second
            marquee++;
        }

    }
}

void input(char *string, int length)
{
    int done = FALSE;
    int index = 0;
    char ch;
```

(continued)

(continued)

```
      string[0] = NULL;    //init the buffer

   do
   {
       ch = getch();

/* Check to see whether the buffer is full */

       if (index == length)
       {
           switch(ch)
           {
               case CR:
                   break;
               default:
                   ch = NULL;
                   break;
           }
       }

/* Process the keyboard input */

       switch(ch)
       {
           case CR:                  //Enter key
               putchar(ch);
               putchar(LF);
               string[index] = NULL;
               done = TRUE;
               break;
           case BACKSPACE:
               if(index==0)
               {
                   break;
               }
               else
               {
                   putchar(ch);
                   putchar(' ');
                   putchar(ch);
                   index--;
                   break;
```

```c
                    }
            case NULL:
                break;
            default:                    //display & sto
                putchar(ch);
                string[index] = ch;
                index++;
                break;
        }
    }
    while(!done);
}

void cls(void)
{
  union REGS regs;

  regs.h.ah=0x06;          //call function 6, scroll window
  regs.h.al=0x00;          //clear screen
  regs.h.bh=0x07;          //make screen "blank" color
  regs.h.ch=0x00;          //upper left row
  regs.h.cl=0x00;          //upper left column
  regs.h.dh=ROWS-1;        //lower right row
  regs.h.dl=COLS-1;        //lower right column
  int86(VIDEO,&regs,&regs);

  locate(0,0);             //"home" the cursor
}

/*
 row ranges from 0 to 79
 col from 0 to 24
*/

void locate(int row,int col)
{
  union REGS regs;

  regs.h.ah=0x02;          //video function 2, move cursor
  regs.h.bh=0x00;          //video screen (always 0)
  regs.h.dh=col;           //cursor's column position
  regs.h.dl=row;           //cursor's row position
  int86(VIDEO,&regs,&regs);
}
```

A Card-Shuffling Routine

This card-shuffling routine randomizes 52 elements (cards) in an array and assigns them suit and face values. It's the start of your first card game!

The SHUFFLE.C program uses the same logic as LOTTO.C in this book; a control array is filled with zeros, and then ones are used to tell the program which cards have been drawn.

Here's the secret: The card drawn (and the lotto ball in the LOTTO.C program) is the array *element* number. The element itself is either FALSE (zero or not drawn) or TRUE (one or drawn). That's how the program keeps track of which card you've drawn. The element number is then used to determine which card it is.

Suppose that the rnd function produces the value 15. If array element 15 contains one, then that card has been drawn and the program loops to grab another random number. If array element 15 contains zero, however, that card has not been drawn. The program uses the value of the element to prevent the same card from being drawn twice. The element number, on the other hand, is used to determine which card you've drawn.

Because this is a wacky, almost advanced, concept, I thought that it could use some extra explanation here on the sidelines.

Name: SHUFFLE.C

```c
/*
 * Card-shuffling program
 * By Dan Gookin
 */

#include <stdio.h>
#include <stdlib.h>
#include <time.h>

#define DECK 52           //Cards in a deck
#define HEARTS 0x03       //Heart character
#define DIAMONDS 0x04     //Diamond character
#define CLUBS 0x05        //Clubs character
#define SPADES 0x06       //Spade character

int draw_card(void);
void shuffle(void);
int rnd(int range);
void seedrnd(void);
```

```
/*
 * The cards array is stuck out here in no-man's
 * land to make it available to both the shuffle
 * and draw_card functions
 */

    int cards[DECK];    //Deck of Cards

void main()
{
    int x=DECK;
    int card;
    char c,s;

    puts("Card shuffling demonstration program");

    shuffle();

/*
 * Sift through the entire deck, decrementing
 * variable x from 52 down to 0.
 *
 * Start by drawing the card, one for each loop.
 *
 * The card%13 math converts the random number from
 * 1 to 52 into chunks of 0 to 12 -- like the cards
 * in a suit. The +1 makes the numbers 1 through 13.
 *
 * The switch-case structure weeds out the ace, ten,
 * jack, queen, and king, setting their characters
 * in the c variable.
 *
 * The (card%13)+'1' sets the remaining characters
 * equal to 2 through 9; adding them to the character
 * '1', which, according to the ASCII table from
 * Volume I, works out just fine.
 */

    while(x--)
    {
        card = draw_card();
        switch((card % 13) + 1)
        {
```

(continued)

(continued)

```
            case(1):
                c = 'A';
                break;
            case(10):
                c = 'T';
                break;
            case(11):
                c = 'J';
                break;
            case(12):
                c = 'Q';
                break;
            case(13):
                c = 'K';
                break;
            default:
                c = (card%13)+'1';
        }

/*
 * A complex if-else structure handles the suits,
 * dividing the values into four chunks. This sets
 * the s char variable equal to the characters for
 * hearts, diamonds, etc.
 *
 * The final printf displays the values
 */

        if(card>=0 && card<=13)
            s = HEARTS;
        else if(card>=14 && card<=26)
            s = DIAMONDS;
        else if(card>=27 && card<=40)
            s = CLUBS;
        else
            s = SPADES;

        printf("%c%c\t",c,s);

/*
```

```
 * This little gem is for formatting only. You divide
 * x (the loop counter) by four -- X MOD 4. When the
 * result is zero, a newline is printed. The ! (not)
 * reverses the results of the MOD; otherwise, the
 * newline would print three times in a row.
 */

        if(!(x%4))
            putchar('\n');
    }
}


/*
 * The draw_card routine returns a random number
 * from 1 to 52 for each card in the deck.
 * It never returns the same card twice as long
 * as you call the shuffle routine -- just like
 * in real life!
 */

int draw_card(void)
{
    int card;

    do
    {
        card=rnd(DECK); //draw card
    }
    while(cards[card]); //is card drawn?

    cards[card]=1;      //mark it as drawn

    return(card+1);     //make it 1 to 52
}

/*
 * The shuffle routine does two things:
 * It initializes the randomizer and
 * initializes the cards[] array.
 */
```

(continued)

(continued)

```
void shuffle(void)
{
    int x;

    seedrnd();

    for(x=0;x<DECK;x++)
        cards[x] = 0;
}

/* Generate a random value */

int rnd(int range)
{
  int r;

  r=rand()%range;              //spit up random number
  return(r);
}

/* Seed the randomizer */

void seedrnd(void)
{
  srand((unsigned)time(NULL));
}
```

The Program Dumper

You're introduced to DUMP.C in Lesson 12-2. Here is its bigger brother, which displays fully formatted output plus a pause after each screen of text. (This program wasn't in the original plans for Appendix B — I just went nuts with the DUMP.C program and finally realized that what I coded was too complex for Chapter 12.)

Name: DUMPER.C

```
/*
 * Dumper, by Dan Gookin
 * Displays the contents of a file
 * in hexadecimal and ASCII
 */
```

```c
#include <stdio.h>
#include <stdlib.h>
#include <conio.h>
#include <ctype.h>
#include <string.h>

void main(int argc,char *argv[])
{
    FILE *dump_me;                  //File handle storage
    int i,t,x,b;
    char c;
    char buffer[16];

/* Check to see whether a filename was typed */

    if(argc<2)
    {
        puts("Format: DUMPER filename");
        exit(0);
    }

/* Open the file and make sure that it's okay */

    dump_me = fopen(argv[1],"rb");
    if(dump_me==NULL)
    {
        printf("Error opening %s\n",argv[1]);
        exit(1);
    }

/*
 * The file is open. It's displayed in uppercase
 * using the STRUPR function.
 * Read each byte in the file and display it
 * using the format:
 *
 * OFFSET - 16 HEX bytes - 16 ASCII chars
 *
 * Each row contains 16 hex bytes and 16 ASCII.
 * Variable X is the file length counter.
 * Variable B counts to 16 for each row.
 */
```

(continued)

(continued)

```
    x = b = 0;

    printf("%s:\n",strupr(argv[1]));

    printf("%0.4X: ",x);          //starting offset = 0
/*
 * The while loop continues until the EOF is encountered.
 * The character read is stored in integer variable I.
 */

    while((i=fgetc(dump_me))!= EOF)
    {
        printf("%0.2X ",i);  //show char as 2-digit HEX
        x++;                 //increment file size count
        buffer[b] = i;       //store char in buffer
        b++;                 //increment buffer count
/*
 * X MOD 16 returns ZERO every time X is divisible by 16,
 * so you can use if(!(x%16)) to determine whenever 16
 * characters have been read from the file.
 */

        if(!(x%16))
        {
            printf("  ");        //two spaces
/*
 * The following displays the ASCII values of the
 * characters read and stored in the BUFFER. The
 * ISCNTRL function determines whether the character
 * is a control character. If so, a dot is displayed.
 * Otherwise, the character is displayed.
 */

            for(t=0;t<16;t++)
            {
                if(iscntrl(buffer[t]))
                    putchar('.');
                else
```

```
                    putchar(buffer[t]);
            }

/*
 * After the ASCII display, a new line is shown, starting
 * with the offset. Then B is reinitialized back to zero.
 */

        printf("\n%0.4X: ",x);
        b = 0;
    }

/* 384 is 24 rows of 16 items -- a screen. After each
 * screen, a "Press Enter" message is displayed. The
 * same MOD logic is used in this IF comparison.
 * The \R in the PRINTF statement allows the "Press
 * Enter" message to overwrite the initial offset
 * value that would otherwise appear there.
 * The KBHIT function sits and waits for any character
 * to be pressed. However, if the ESC key (code '\x1b')
 * is pressed, the program quits. Otherwise, the offset
 * value is reprinted and the program continues with
 * the next 16 characters.
 */

    if(!(x%384))
    {
        printf("\rPress Enter:");
        while(!kbhit())
            ;
        c = getch();
        if(c=='\x1b') exit(0);
        printf("\n%0.4X: ",x);
    }
    }
    fclose(dump_me); //ALWAYS CLOSE YOUR FILES!

/*
 * Display summary information
 * STRUPR converts the filename to ALL CAPS
 */

    printf("\n%s: size = %u bytes\n",strupr(argv[1]),x);
}
```

Making Sweet Music

Your PC can't sing. That doesn't mean that it lacks musical capabilities — it just has to be taught. You see, although every PC has a speaker, the PC's BIOS lacks any routines to play notes or make gurgles. This was a horrid oversight on the part of IBM because making a PC sing is really no big thing. (*A-ratta-tat-tat!*)

Music can be created on your PC by sending a rapid series of ticks to the speaker. One tick pushes the speaker cone out, and the second pushes it back in. Varying the rate, or *frequency,* of these ticks creates audible sound. Because all musical notes have a specific frequency, juggling the PC's speaker at that frequency creates the proper pitch.

The pitches for common musical notes are listed in Table B-1. For example, the A note warbles at a frequency of 440 hertz. Middle C runs at 523 hertz. To play that note, you manipulate the PC's speaker at a rate of 523 times per second. At least that's how it was explained to me.

Table B-1		Musical Notes and Their Frequencies					
Note	*Frequency*	*Note*	*Frequency*	*Note*	*Frequency*	*Note*	*Frequency*
C	131	A#	233	G#	415	F#	740
C#	139	B	247	A	440	G	784
D	147	C	262	A#	466	G#	831
D#	156	C#	277	B	494	A	880
E	165	D	294	C	523	A#	932
F	175	D#	311	C#	554	B	988
F#	185	E	330	D	587	C	1047
G	196	F	349	D#	622	C#	1110
G#	208	F#	370	E	659	D	1175
A	220	G	392	F	698	D#	1247
						E	1319

Playing a song on your computer involves translating the notes from sheet music or some other source into frequencies and then sending those values to a function that ticks the speaker.

Borland C has a built-in function, sound, that ticks the speaker. Because Microsoft C lacks a specific function, you must use special microprocessor port commands (outp and inp) to manipulate the speaker directly. For this reason, separate programs must be compiled for either Borland or Microsoft C, as flagged in the following program.

Name: AMERICA.C

```
/*
 * Music-playing routine
 * Borland compilers only!
 */

#include <dos.h>

void playsound(int note,int duration);

void main()
{

/*
 * The song being played, "America the Beautiful,"
 * is stored as a series of frequencies and durations
 * in a two-dimensional array.
 *
 * The song[][2] declaration defines the array as a
 * set of pairs; the compiler figures the size of the
 * thing.
 *
 * The first item, song[x][0], is the note's frequency.
 * The second item, song[x][1], is the duration in
 * milliseconds. I've used 125 as an eighth note; 250
 * for a quarter note; 375 for a dotted-quarter note;
 * and 750 for a dotted half note; a whole note would
 * have been 1000, or one second.
 *
 * A null byte ends the song.
 */

    int song[][2] = {
        392,250, 392,375, 330,125, 330,250,
        392,250, 392,375, 294,125, 294,250,
        330,250, 349,250, 392,250, 440,250,
        494,250, 392,750, 392,250, 392,375,
        330,125, 330,250, 392,250, 392,375,
        294,125, 294,250, 587,250, 554,250,
        587,250, 659,250, 440,250, 587,750,
        392,250, 659,375, 659,125, 587,250,
```

(continued)

(continued)

```
          523,250, 523,375, 494,125, 494,250,
          523,250, 587,250, 494,250, 440,250,
          392,250, 523,750, 523,250, 523,375,
          440,125, 440,250, 523,250, 523,375,
          392,125, 392,250, 392,250, 440,250,
          523,250, 392,250, 587,250, 523,750,
          0, 0
      };
      int x = 0;

/*
 * The while loop continues to fetch new items
 * from the song[][] array until zero is read.
 * Variable X keeps track of the elements.
 *
 * A delay of 1/10 second is made after each note
 * is played by the playsound() function. Otherwise,
 * the notes would all run together and sound gross.
 * (Comment it out to hear what I mean.)
 */

      while(song[x++][0])
      {
          playsound(song[x][0],song[x][1]);
          delay(100);
      }
}

/*
 * The playsound function uses the Borland C
 * sound and delay functions to play a sound on
 * the PC's speaker. sound() accepts a frequency
 * value, and delay() accepts a millisecond value.
 *
 * The nosound() function turns off the PC's speaker.
 */

void playsound(int note,int duration)
{
    sound(note);
    delay(duration);
    nosound();
}
```

Name: AMERICA.C

```c
/*
 * Music-playing routine
 * Microsoft compilers only!
 */

#include <time.h>
#include <conio.h>

void playsound(int note,int duration);
void delay(int duration);

void main()
{

/*
 * Refer to the notes in the Borland example
 * for an explanation of how this array works
 * and for other comments about the main()
 * function.
 */

    int song[][2] = {
        392,250, 392,375, 330,125, 330,250,
        392,250, 392,375, 294,125, 294,250,
        330,250, 349,250, 392,250, 440,250,
        494,250, 392,750, 392,250, 392,375,
        330,125, 330,250, 392,250, 392,375,
        294,125, 294,250, 587,250, 554,250,
        587,250, 659,250, 440,250, 587,750,
        392,250, 659,375, 659,125, 587,250,
        523,250, 523,375, 494,125, 494,250,
        523,250, 587,250, 494,250, 440,250,
        392,250, 523,750, 523,250, 523,375,
        440,125, 440,250, 523,250, 523,375,
        392,125, 392,250, 392,250, 440,250,
        523,250, 392,250, 587,250, 523,750,
        0, 0
    };
    int x = 0;
```

(continued)

(continued)

```c
        while(song[x++][0])
        {
            playsound(song[x][0],song[x][1]);
            delay(100);
        }
}


/*
 * The playsound function manipulates the PC's
 * speaker by using a bunch of routines not
 * explained in this book. (Nifty!) Honestly,
 * this is a well-used routine for the PC;
 * most programmers just "steal" this code
 * without bothering to know what it does.
 * (I used a routine like this for years,
 * and it can also be found in your HELP
 * file in the BEEP.C program example.)
 */

void playsound(int note,int duration)
{
    int status;

    if(!note) return;

    note = (unsigned)(1193280L / note);

    _outp(0x43,0xb6);                 //prep the port
    _outp(0x42,(char)note);           //tell it which
    _outp(0x42,(char)(note >> 8));    //note to play
    status = inp( 0x61 );             //save the status
    _outp(0x61, status | 0x03);       //play the note

    delay( (clock_t)duration );       //delay

    _outp( 0x61, status );            //turn the speaker off

}

/*
```

```
* The delay function uses the Microsoft C clock()
* function, which keeps track, in milliseconds,
* of how long a program has been running.
*
* clock_t is a variable type representing how
* long a program has run. (It's like a long int.)
*
* The delay function calculates how long to wait
* by adding the duration to the current time. Until
* that time passes, a while loop sits and spins.
*/

void delay(int duration)
{
    clock_t done;

    done = duration + clock();
    while( done > clock() )
        ;
}
```

The DOS Pig Latin Filter

Here's your multiple module test, in the following two source code listings.
You should compile them both and then link them to form the pig latin filter,
PL. Refer to Lesson 12-5 in Chapter 12 for more information about DOS
filters, though I'm sure that you can find lots of uses for the `iglatinpay`
function in your programs!

(Refer to Chapter 14 for more information about linking multiple modules.)

Name: PL.C

```
/*
 * DOS Pig Latin Filter
 * Refer to Lesson 12-5 for more information about
 * filters. This program uses the standard type of
 * filter, as introduced for the ROT13.C program.
 */

#include <stdio.h>
#include <ctype.h>
```

(continued)

(continued)

```
void iglatinpay(char *english);

void main()
{
    char word[32];      //input storage
    char *w;            //pointer to the word buffer
    char ch;
    int count;

/*
 * This is a standard construction for filters:
 * fgetchar reads STDIN, and fputchar writes STDOUT.
 *
 * Along the way, the isalpha() function is used to
 * find the beginning of a word. If so, a while loop
 * is set up to read that word and store it in the
 * word[] buffer. The word is only read at this
 * point, not displayed.
 *
 * When the end of the word is found, it is capped
 * with a NULL byte and sent to the iglatinpay()
 * function to be turned into pig latin. That word
 * is then send to STDOUT.
 */

    do
    {
        ch = fgetchar();
        if(isalpha(ch))            //a word starts
        {
            count=0;
            while(isalpha(ch))     //read the word
            {
                word[count] = ch; //store it
                count++;
                ch = fgetchar();  //keep reading
            }
            word[count] = '\0';    //cap with a NULL
            iglatinpay(word);      //process the word
```

```
/* This routine displays the word stored in word[] */

        w = word;
        while(*w)
        {
            fputchar(*w);        //use STDOUT
            w++;
        }

/* Finally, original non-alpha character is displayed */

        fputchar(ch);
        }
        else                     //the else part
        {                        //handles non-alpha
            fputchar(ch);        //I/O
        }
    }
    while(ch!=EOF);
}
```

Name: PIGLATIN.C

```
/*
 * The Actual Pig Latin Word-Making Function
 *
 * This function takes a word (all letters terminated
 * with a NULL) and converts it into pig latin by
 * following some made-up rules. The word is stored
 * in the piglatin[] buffer. Various string routines
 * copy and concatenate parts of the reconstructed
 * word into that buffer. The original starting letter
 * is also saved in a buffer, append[], because only
 * strings can be concatenated to each other, not
 * single chars.
 *
 * A pointer variable saves the original address of
 * the word being translated, so the word is sent and
 * returned as the same variable. This saves going
 * through the pains of returning a string from a
 * function.
 */
```

(continued)

(continued)

```c
#include <stdio.h>
#include <ctype.h>
#include <string.h>

void iglatinpay(char *english)
{
    char piglatin[32];        //temporary word sto.
    char *e;
    char append[] = "h";      //first letter sto.
    char ch;

/*
 * Start by saving the starting address of the word
 * being sent to this function. The E pointer
 * variable will remember that for you.
 */

    e = english;

/*
 * All pig latin is written in lowercase with initial
 * caps. (At least that's the easy way to handle
 * things here.)
 */

    strlwr(english);          //make it all lowercase

/*
 * RULES FOR TRANSLATING ENGLISH INTO PIG LATIN
 * As told to a switch-case loop
 *
 * First rule: Words starting with a vowel
 * are merely given the AY ending.
 *
 * Note how strcpy() is used first and then strcat()
 * is used to continue building the pig latin word.
 *
 * Also: See how the case statements "fall through,"
 * enabling several of them to catch common
 * situations.
 */
```

```
    ch = *english;          //save the first character
    switch(ch)
    {
        case 'a':
        case 'e':
        case 'i':
        case 'o':
        case 'u':
            strcpy(piglatin,english);
            strcat(piglatin,"ay");
            break;

/*
 * Second rule: Words starting with SH, CH,
 * TH, PH, RH, WH, and QU have both letters
 * moved to the end before adding AY.
 */

                    //continuing switch-case
        case 'c':
        case 'p':
        case 'r':
        case 's':
        case 't':
        case 'w':
            if(english[1]=='h')
            {
                english+=2; //point at third char
                            //after ?H sound
                strcpy(piglatin,english);
                            //add the starting letter
                append[0] = ch;
                strcat(piglatin,append);
                            //and then the 'H' and AY
                strcat(piglatin,"hay");
                break;
            }
        case 'q':
            if(english[1]=='u')
            {
                english+=2;
                strcpy(piglatin,english);
                append[0] = ch;
```

(continued)

(continued)

```
                        strcat(piglatin,append);
                        strcat(piglatin,"uay");
                        break;
            }

/*
 * Standard rule: Move the first letter to the
 * end of the word and add AY.
 */
                        //continuing switch-case
        default:
            english++;
            strcpy(piglatin,english);
            append[0] = ch;
            strcat(piglatin,append);
            strcat(piglatin,"ay");
            break;
    }

/*
 * To "return" the word to the calling function,
 * you simply copy the word you constructed (which
 * is in the piglatin[] buffer) to the location of
 * the word being translated, which was saved in
 * the E pointer.
 */

    strcpy(e,piglatin);

/*
 * Finally, make the initial cap of each word.
 */

    *e = toupper(*e);
}
```

Index

······································

Notes

Notes

7/29/96

The Internet For Macs® For Dummies® 2nd Edition	by Charles Seiter	ISBN: 1-56884-371-2	$19.99 USA/$26.99 Canada
The Internet For Macs® For Dummies® Starter Kit	by Charles Seiter	ISBN: 1-56884-244-9	$29.99 USA/$39.99 Canada
The Internet For Macs® For Dummies® Starter Kit Bestseller Edition	by Charles Seiter	ISBN: 1-56884-245-7	$39.99 USA/$54.99 Canada
The Internet For Windows® For Dummies® Starter Kit	by John R. Levine & Margaret Levine Young	ISBN: 1-56884-237-6	$34.99 USA/$44.99 Canada
The Internet For Windows® For Dummies® Starter Kit, Bestseller Edition	by John R. Levine & Margaret Levine Young	ISBN: 1-56884-246-5	$39.99 USA/$54.99 Canada

MACINTOSH

Mac® Programming For Dummies®	by Dan Parks Sydow	ISBN: 1-56884-173-6	$19.95 USA/$26.95 Canada
Macintosh® System 7.5 For Dummies®	by Bob LeVitus	ISBN: 1-56884-197-3	$19.95 USA/$26.95 Canada
MORE Macs® For Dummies®	by David Pogue	ISBN: 1-56884-087-X	$19.95 USA/$26.95 Canada
PageMaker 5 For Macs® For Dummies®	by Galen Gruman & Deke McClelland	ISBN: 1-56884-178-7	$19.95 USA/$26.95 Canada
QuarkXPress 3.3 For Dummies®	by Galen Gruman & Barbara Assadi	ISBN: 1-56884-217-1	$19.95 USA/$26.99 Canada
Upgrading and Fixing Macs® For Dummies®	by Kearney Rietmann & Frank Higgins	ISBN: 1-56884-189-2	$19.95 USA/$26.95 Canada

MULTIMEDIA

Multimedia & CD-ROMs For Dummies® 2nd Edition	by Andy Rathbone	ISBN: 1-56884-907-9	$19.99 USA/$26.99 Canada
Multimedia & CD-ROMs For Dummies® Interactive Multimedia Value Pack, 2nd Edition	by Andy Rathbone	ISBN: 1-56884-909-5	$29.99 USA/$39.99 Canada

OPERATING SYSTEMS:

DOS

MORE DOS For Dummies®	by Dan Gookin	ISBN: 1-56884-046-2	$19.95 USA/$26.95 Canada
OS/2® Warp For Dummies® 2nd Edition	by Andy Rathbone	ISBN: 1-56884-205-8	$19.99 USA/$26.99 Canada

UNIX

MORE UNIX® For Dummies®	by John R. Levine & Margaret Levine Young	ISBN: 1-56884-361-5	$19.99 USA/$26.99 Canada
UNIX® For Dummies®	by John R. Levine & Margaret Levine Young	ISBN: 1-878058-58-4	$19.95 USA/$26.95 Canada

WINDOWS

MORE Windows® For Dummies® 2nd Edition	by Andy Rathbone	ISBN: 1-56884-048-9	$19.95 USA/$26.95 Canada
Windows® 95 For Dummies®	by Andy Rathbone	ISBN: 1-56884-240-6	$19.99 USA/$26.99 Canada

PCS/HARDWARE

Illustrated Computer Dictionary For Dummies® 2nd Edition	by Dan Gookin & Wallace Wang	ISBN: 1-56884-218-X	$12.95 USA/$16.95 Canada
Upgrading and Fixing PCs For Dummies® 2nd Edition	by Andy Rathbone	ISBN: 1-56884-903-6	$19.99 USA/$26.99 Canada

PRESENTATION/AUTOCAD

AutoCAD For Dummies®	by Bud Smith	ISBN: 1-56884-191-4	$19.95 USA/$26.95 Canada
PowerPoint 4 For Windows® For Dummies®	by Doug Lowe	ISBN: 1-56884-161-2	$16.99 USA/$22.99 Canada

PROGRAMMING

Borland C++ For Dummies®	by Michael Hyman	ISBN: 1-56884-162-0	$19.95 USA/$26.95 Canada
C For Dummies® Volume 1	by Dan Gookin	ISBN: 1-878058-78-9	$19.95 USA/$26.95 Canada
C++ For Dummies®	by Stephen R. Davis	ISBN: 1-56884-163-9	$19.95 USA/$26.95 Canada
Delphi Programming For Dummies®	by Neil Rubenking	ISBN: 1-56884-200-7	$19.99 USA/$26.99 Canada
Mac® Programming For Dummies®	by Dan Parks Sydow	ISBN: 1-56884-173-6	$19.95 USA/$26.95 Canada
PowerBuilder 4 Programming For Dummies®	by Ted Coombs & Jason Coombs	ISBN: 1-56884-325-9	$19.99 USA/$26.99 Canada
QBasic Programming For Dummies®	by Douglas Hergert	ISBN: 1-56884-093-4	$19.95 USA/$26.95 Canada
Visual Basic 3 For Dummies®	by Wallace Wang	ISBN: 1-56884-076-4	$19.95 USA/$26.95 Canada
Visual Basic "X" For Dummies®	by Wallace Wang	ISBN: 1-56884-230-9	$19.99 USA/$26.99 Canada
Visual C++ 2 For Dummies®	by Michael Hyman & Bob Arnson	ISBN: 1-56884-328-3	$19.99 USA/$26.99 Canada
Windows® 95 Programming For Dummies®	by S. Randy Davis	ISBN: 1-56884-327-5	$19.99 USA/$26.99 Canada

SPREADSHEET

1-2-3 For Dummies®	by Greg Harvey	ISBN: 1-878058-60-6	$16.95 USA/$22.95 Canada
1-2-3 For Windows® 5 For Dummies® 2nd Edition	by John Walkenbach	ISBN: 1-56884-216-3	$16.95 USA/$22.95 Canada
Excel 5 For Macs® For Dummies®	by Greg Harvey	ISBN: 1-56884-186-8	$19.95 USA/$26.95 Canada
Excel For Dummies® 2nd Edition	by Greg Harvey	ISBN: 1-56884-050-0	$16.95 USA/$22.95 Canada
MORE 1-2-3 For DOS For Dummies®	by John Weingarten	ISBN: 1-56884-224-4	$19.99 USA/$26.99 Canada
MORE Excel 5 For Windows® For Dummies®	by Greg Harvey	ISBN: 1-56884-207-4	$19.95 USA/$26.95 Canada
Quattro Pro 6 For Windows® For Dummies®	by John Walkenbach	ISBN: 1-56884-174-4	$19.95 USA/$26.95 Canada
Quattro Pro For DOS For Dummies®	by John Walkenbach	ISBN: 1-56884-023-3	$16.95 USA/$22.95 Canada

UTILITIES

Norton Utilities 8 For Dummies®	by Beth Slick	ISBN: 1-56884-166-3	$19.95 USA/$26.95 Canada

VCRS/CAMCORDERS

VCRs & Camcorders For Dummies™	by Gordon McComb & Andy Rathbone	ISBN: 1-56884-229-5	$14.99 USA/$20.99 Canada

WORD PROCESSING

Ami Pro For Dummies®	by Jim Meade	ISBN: 1-56884-049-7	$19.95 USA/$26.95 Canada
MORE Word For Windows® 6 For Dummies®	by Doug Lowe	ISBN: 1-56884-165-5	$19.95 USA/$26.95 Canada
MORE WordPerfect® 6 For Windows® For Dummies®	by Margaret Levine Young & David C. Kay	ISBN: 1-56884-206-6	$19.95 USA/$26.95 Canada
MORE WordPerfect® 6 For DOS For Dummies®	by Wallace Wang, edited by Dan Gookin	ISBN: 1-56884-047-0	$19.95 USA/$26.95 Canada
Word 6 For Macs® For Dummies®	by Dan Gookin	ISBN: 1-56884-190-6	$19.95 USA/$26.95 Canada
Word For Windows® 6 For Dummies®	by Dan Gookin	ISBN: 1-56884-075-6	$16.95 USA/$22.95 Canada
Word For Windows® For Dummies®	by Dan Gookin & Ray Werner	ISBN: 1-878058-86-X	$16.95 USA/$22.95 Canada
WordPerfect® 6 For DOS For Dummies®	by Dan Gookin	ISBN: 1-878058-77-0	$16.95 USA/$22.95 Canada
WordPerfect® 6.1 For Windows® For Dummies® 2nd Edition	by Margaret Levine Young & David Kay	ISBN: 1-56884-243-0	$16.95 USA/$22.95 Canada
WordPerfect® For Dummies®	by Dan Gookin	ISBN: 1-878058-52-5	$16.95 USA/$22.95 Canada

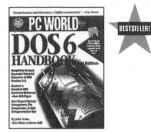

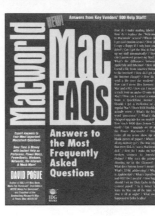

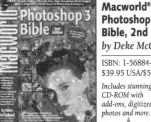

IBM PRESS

இப் புத்தகங்கள் மிகவும் நல்லவை
(way cool)

OS/2® Warp Internet Connection: Your Key to Cruising the Internet and the World Wide Web

by Deborah Morrison

OS/2 users can get warped on the Internet using the OS/2 Warp tips, techniques, and helpful directories found in *OS/2 Warp Internet Connection*. This reference covers OS/2 Warp Internet basics, such as e-mail use and how to access other computers, plus much more! The Internet gets more complex every day, but for OS/2 Warp users it just got a whole lot easier! Your value-packed disk includes 10 of the best internet utilities to help you explore the Net and save money while you're on-line!

EXPERT AUTHOR PROFILE
Deborah Morrison (Raleigh, NC) is an award-winning IBM writer who specializes in TCP/IP and the Internet. She is currently the editor-in-chief of IBM's *TCP/IP Connection* quarterly magazine.

7/29/96

ISBN: 1-56884-465-4
$24.99 USA/$34.99 Canada
Includes one 3.5" disk

Available: Now

Official Guide to Using OS/2® Warp

by Karla Stagray & Linda S. Rogers

IDG Books and IBM have come together to produce the most comprehensive user's guide to OS/2 Warp available today. From installation to using OS/2 Warp's BonusPak programs, this book delivers valuable help to the reader who needs
to get up and running fast. Loaded with working examples, easy tips, and operating system concepts, *Official Guide to Using OS/2 Warp* is the only official user's guide authorized by IBM.

EXPERT AUTHOR PROFILE
Karla Stagray and Linda Rogers (Boca Raton, FL) both have a unique understanding of computer software and hardware. As award-winning IBM writers, Stagray and Rogers have received Society of Technical Communicators awards for various endeavors.

ISBN: 1-56884-466-2
$29.99 USA/$39.99 Canada

Available: Now

OS/2® Warp Uncensored

by Peter G. Magid & Ira H. Schneider

Exploit the power of OS/2 Warp and learn the secrets of object technology for the Workplace Shell. This all new book/CD-ROM bundle, for power users and intermediate users alike, provides the real inside story—not just the "what," but the "how" and "why" — from the folks who designed and developed the Workplace Shell. Packed with tips and techniques for using IBM's REXX programming language, and the bonus CD includes new bitmaps, icons, mouse pointers, REXX scripts, and an Object Tool!

EXPERT AUTHOR PROFILE
Peter G. Magid (Boca Raton, FL) is the User Interface Design Lead for the Workplace Shell and has over 12 years of programming experience at IBM. He is a graduate of Tulane University, and holds a B.S. in Computer Science.

Ira H. Schneider (Boca Raton, FL) has focused on enhancements to the Workplace Shell and has over 25 years of experience with IBM. He has held numerous lead programming positions within IBM and graduated from Northeastern University with a B.S. in Electrical Engineering.

ISBN: 1-56884-474-3
$39.99 USA/$54.99 Canada
Includes one CD-ROM

Available: Now

OS/2® Warp FAQs™

by Mike Kaply & Timothy F. Sipples

At last, the ultimate answer book for every OS/2 Warp user. Direct from IBM's Service Hotline, *OS/2 Warp FAQs* is a comprehensive question-and-answer guide that helps you optimize your system and save time by putting the answers to all your questions right at your fingertips. CD includes FAQs from the book in an easy-to-search format, plus hard-to-find device drivers for connecting to peripherals, such as printers.

EXPERT AUTHOR PROFILE
Mike Kaply (Boca Raton, FL) is currently on the OS/2 Help Manager Development Team at IBM in Boca Raton, Florida. He holds a B.S. degree in Mathematics and Computer Science from Southern Methodist University.

Timothy F. Sipples (Chicago, IL) is an OS/2 Warp specialist from IBM. He has written for *OS/2 Magazine* and was named "Team OS/2er of the Year" by *OS/2 Professional*.

ISBN: 1-56884-472-7
$29.99 USA/$42.99 Canada
Includes one CD-ROM

Available: Now

OS/2® Warp and PowerPC: Operating in the New Frontier

by Ken Christopher, Scott Winters & Mary Pollack Wright

The software makers at IBM unwrap the IBM and OS/2 mystique to share insights and strategies that will take business computing into the 21st century. Readers get a long, hard look at the next generation of OS/2 Warp for PowerPC.

EXPERT AUTHOR PROFILE
Ken Christopher (Boca Raton, FL) is Program Director of Development for OS/2 for Power PC. He has been a key player in the development on OS/2 Warp.

Scott Winters (Boca Raton, FL) is lead architect of OS/2 for the PowerPC. He has been instrumental in the development on OS/2 Warp on the PowerPC platform.

Mary Pollack Wright (Boca Raton, FL) is currently the technical editor for the OS/2 Technical Library. She has been part of the OS/2 team since 1985. Her technical articles on OS/2 have been published in the *OS/2 Developer* magazine and *OS/2 Notebooks*.

ISBN: 1-56884-458-1
$29.99 USA/$39.99 Canada

Available: Now

IBM and OS/2 are registered trademarks of IBM. ----FAQs and the IDG Books Worldwide logos are trademarks under exclusive license to IDG Books Worldwide, Inc., from International Data Group, Inc.

For scholastic requests & educational orders please call Educational Sales at 1. 800. 434. 2086

FOR MORE INFO OR TO ORDER, PLEASE CALL ▶ 800. 762. 2974

For volume discounts & special orders please call Corporate Sales, at 415. 655. 3000

7/29/96

Order Center: **(800) 762-2974** *(8 a.m.–6 p.m., EST, weekdays)*

Quantity	ISBN	Title	Price	Total

Shipping & Handling Charges

	Description	First book	Each additional book	Total
Domestic	Normal	$4.50	$1.50	$
	Two Day Air	$8.50	$2.50	$
	Overnight	$18.00	$3.00	$
International	Surface	$8.00	$8.00	$
	Airmail	$16.00	$16.00	$
	DHL Air	$17.00	$17.00	$

*For large quantities call for shipping & handling charges.
**Prices are subject to change without notice.

Ship to:

Name _____

Company _____

Address _____

City/State/Zip _____

Daytime Phone _____

Payment: ☐ Check to IDG Books Worldwide (US Funds Only)

☐ VISA   ☐ MasterCard   ☐ American Express

Card # _____ Expires _____

Signature _____

Subtotal _____

CA residents add applicable sales tax _____

IN, MA, and MD residents add 5% sales tax _____

IL residents add 6.25% sales tax _____

RI residents add 7% sales tax _____

TX residents add 8.25% sales tax _____

Shipping _____

Total _____

Please send this order form to:

IDG Books Worldwide, Inc.
Attn: Order Entry Dept.
7260 Shadeland Station, Suite 100
Indianapolis, IN 46256

*Allow up to 3 weeks for delivery.
Thank you!*